Lieutenant General Sir Samuel Auchmuty 1756–1822

Lieutenant General Sir Samuel Auchmuty 1756–1822

The Military Life of an American Loyalist and Imperial General

John D Grainger

Pen & Sword
MILITARY

First published in Great Britain in 2018
by Pen & Sword Military
An imprint of Pen & Sword Books Limited
47 Church Street
Barnsley
South Yorkshire
S70 2AS

ISBN 978 1 52673 092 3

A CIP catalogue record for this book is
available from the British Library

Typeset in Ehrhardt
by Mac Style

Printed and bound in the UK
by TJ International Ltd, Padstow, Cornwall

Pen & Sword Books Limited incorporates the imprints of Atlas,
Archaeology, Aviation, Discovery, Family History, Fiction, History,
Maritime, Military, Military Classics, Politics, Select, Transport,
True Crime, Air World, Frontline Publishing, Leo Cooper,
Remember When, Seaforth Publishing, The Praetorian Press,
Wharncliffe Local History, Wharncliffe Transport,
Wharncliffe True Crime and White Owl.

For a complete list of Pen & Sword titles please contact
PEN & SWORD BOOKS LIMITED
47 Church Street, Barnsley, South Yorkshire, S70 2AS, England
E-mail: enquiries@pen-and-sword.co.uk
Website: www. pen-and-sword.co.uk

Contents

Maps vi
Introduction xiii

Chapter 1 An Episcopalian Family 1

Chapter 2 The Family Scattered 22

Chapter 3 India, 1783–97 38

Chapter 4 Egypt, 1799–1803 66

Chapter 5 United Kingdom, 1803–6 98

Chapter 6 South America, 1806–8 120

Chapter 7 India, 1810–11 157

Chapter 8 Java, 1811 180

Chapter 9 The East Indies after Auchmuty 215

Chapter 10 India, 1811–13 233

Chapter 11 Britain and Ireland, 1813–22 246

Notes 253
Bibliography 273
Index 281

Maps

1. Chart – The Scattered Family vii
2. India viii
3. Egypt ix
4. Kent x
5. River Plate xi
6. Java xii

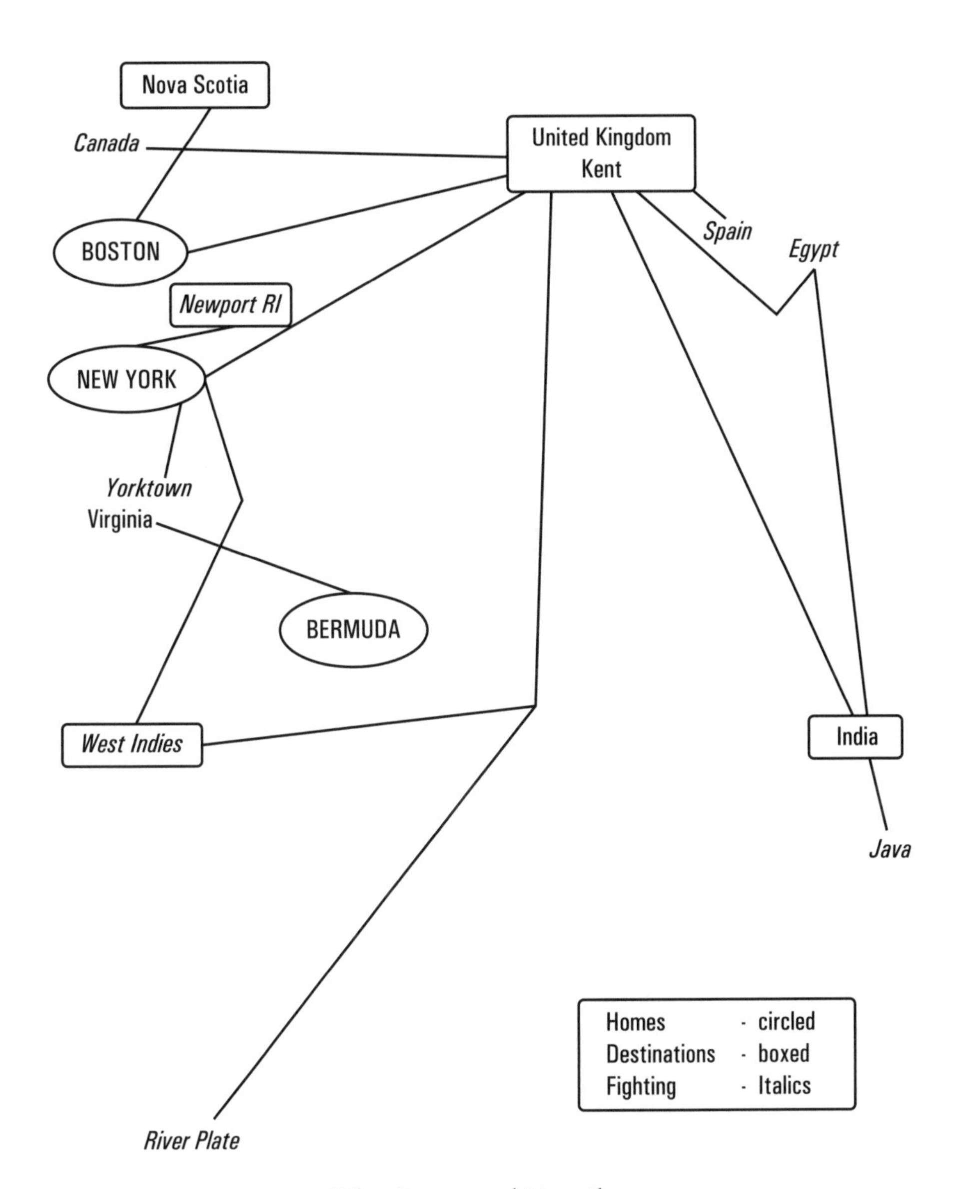

The Scattered Family.

Rampur
Delhi
OUDH
Kanpur
Benares
Calcutta
Bombay
Hyderabad
INDIA
c1798
Mysore
Madras
BRITISH RULED

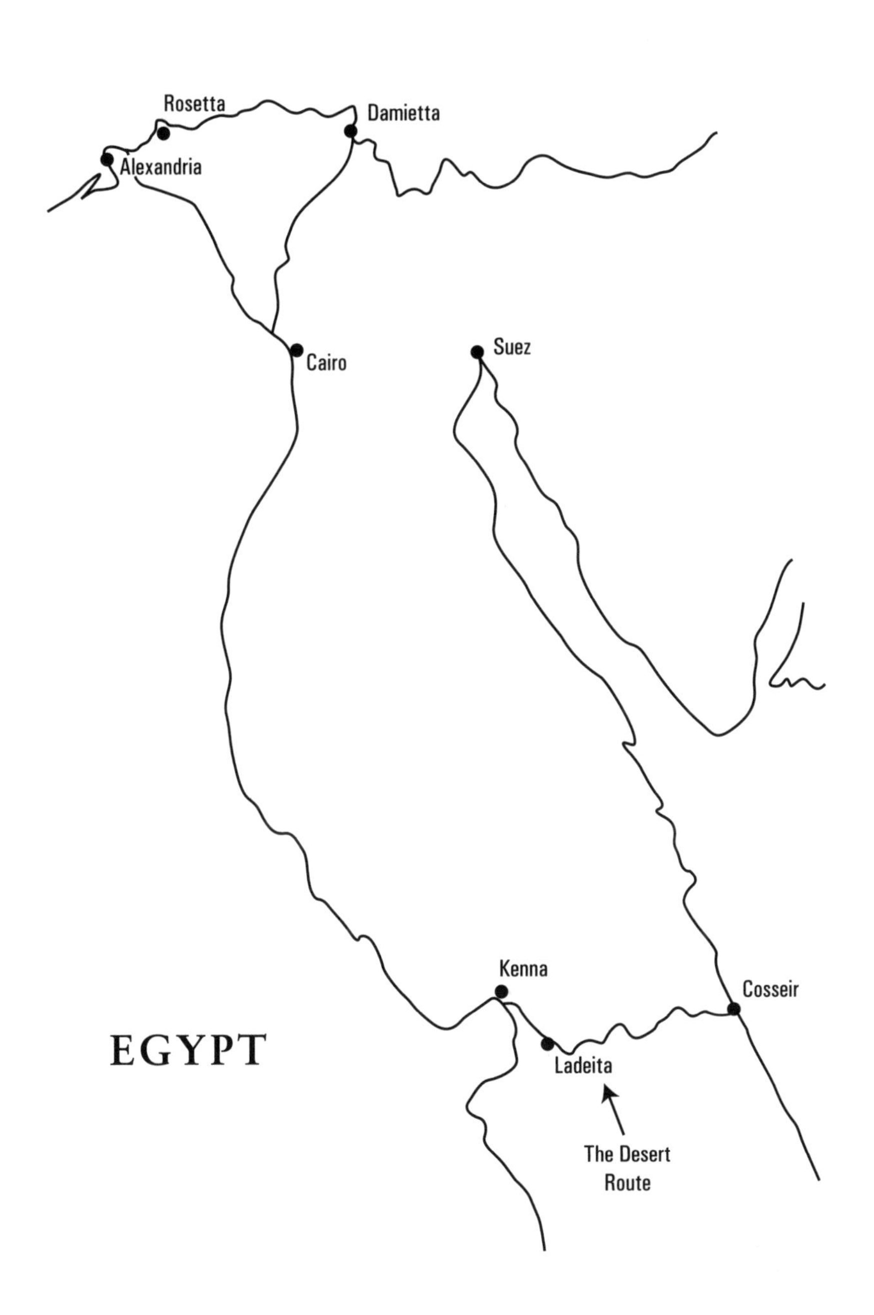
Rosetta
Damietta
Alexandria
Cairo
Suez
Kenna
Cosseir
Ladeita
The Desert
Route
EGYPT

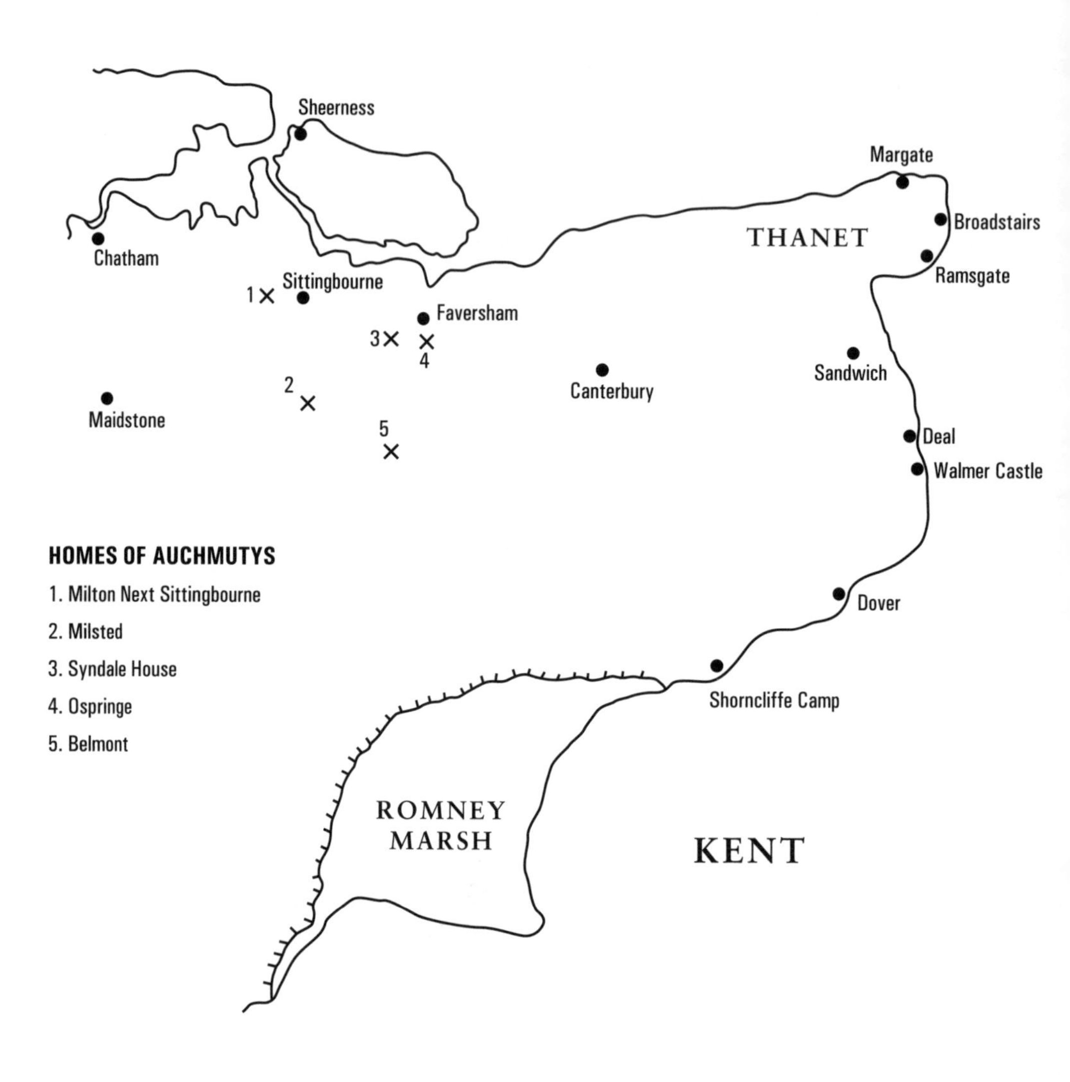
Sheerness
Margate
Broadstairs
THANET
Ramsgate
Chatham
Sittingbourne
1
Faversham
3
4
Sandwich
Canterbury
2
Maidstone
5
Deal
Walmer Castle
HOMES OF AUCHMUTYS
1. Milton Next Sittingbourne
2. Milsted
3. Syndale House
4. Ospringe
5. Belmont
Dover
Shorncliffe Camp
ROMNEY
MARSH
KENT

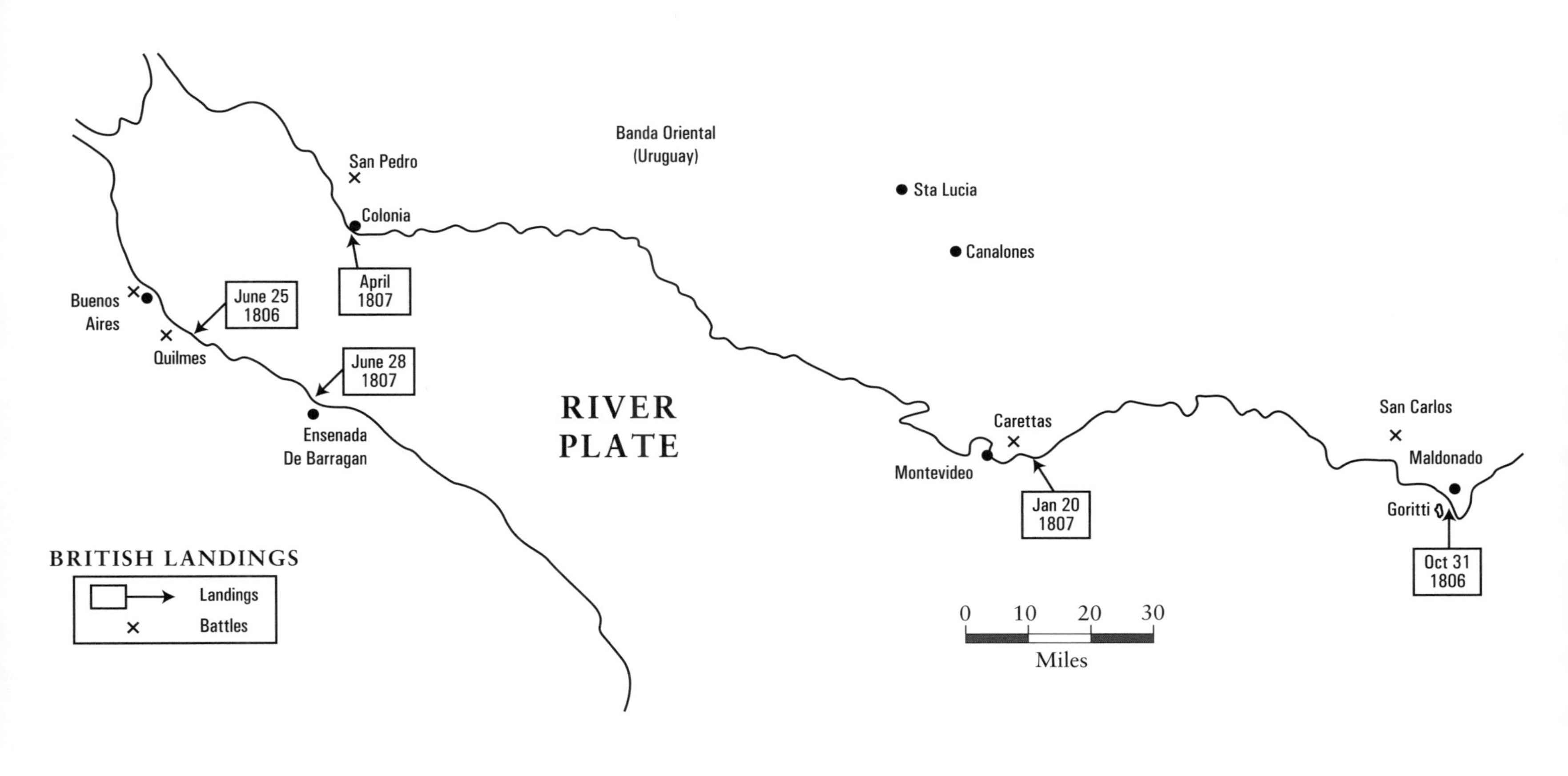
Banda Oriental
(Uruguay)
San Pedro
Colonia
Sta Lucia
Canalones
Buenos
Aires
June 25
1806
April
1807
Quilmes
June 28
1807
Ensenada
De Barragan
RIVER
PLATE
Carettas
Montevideo
Jan 20
1807
San Carlos
Maldonado
Goritti
Oct 31
1806
BRITISH LANDINGS
Landings
Battles
0
10
20
30
Miles

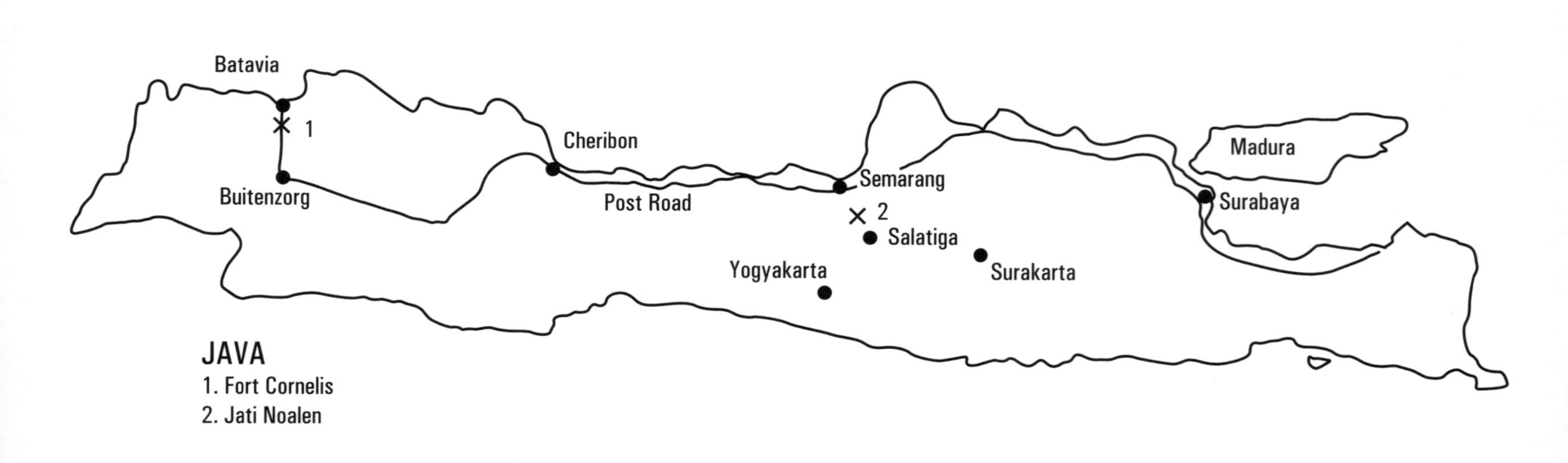
Batavia
1
Buitenzorg
Cheribon
Post Road
Semarang
2
Salatiga
Yogyakarta
Surakarta
Madura
Surabaya
JAVA
1. Fort Cornelis
2. Jati Noalen

Introduction

Some years ago I wrote an entry for the *New Oxford Dictionary of National Biography* on General Sir Samuel Auchmuty. I had first encountered him when researching events in the River Plate in 1806–8 for a volume of documents for the Navy Records Society. He piqued my interest because of his wide-ranging career as a soldier, and his connection with many of the imperial issues of his time. I have expanded on the Society's volume with a wider account of events at the time in the South Atlantic.[1]

Auchmuty was involved in events in the American colonies in the War of Independence, in India during the decisive expansion of British power from a few coastal forts and the revenues of Bengal to the domination of the whole country, and in several of the military events in Egypt, Kent, and Java during the Revolutionary and Napoleonic wars. And yet he scarcely rates more than a mention in any of the books describing these events and times. In each case he appears to be overshadowed by another – by Cornwallis in India, by Baird in Egypt, by Whitelocke in South America, by Minto and Raffles in Java – and yet he was the efficient agent of action in many of these cases, notably in South America and Java. He rose to be the Military Secretary to the Commander-in-Chief in his first time in India, he was the Adjutant General in Egypt, he was the one successful and victorious commander in the River Plate expedition, he was the Commander-in-Chief at Madras, and the conqueror of Java. In too many of these he has been written out of the account. In each case someone else either took the blame or the credit.

Deeper investigation into his life and career also reveals that he had extensive connections with other families in the new United States and in Britain, and in the latter case many of them were military and naval families and deeply involved in the history of the British Empire. His family connections therefore became another aspect of his life which merited investigation.

Then there is the general trajectory of his life and career, from the British defeat in North America and the loss of the major section of the British Empire, to the acquisition of the next empire in Asia soon after; and to the curious set of imperial policies between 1793 and 1815 by which large parts of the world were conquered – in India, in Indonesia, Egypt, Buenos Aires, West Indian islands, the Cape of Good Hope and other places – in many of which Auchmuty was involved, only to see them in many cases returned to the original colonisers or simply abandoned at the end of the French wars. Such a career is certainly of interest as a link between the two empires and general British imperial policy.

Not only that but his origins in New York and his actions in 1776–7 marked him as an active Loyalist, though he appears scarcely at all in the accounts of those people. Further, he rose to the rank of General in the British Army, and so was the most successful of all the Loyalists; and yet his life and achievements are ignored; histories of the Loyalists are generally more inclined to dwell on the unpleasant experiences of the Loyalists in their home colonies and their difficulties after their expulsion than on one of them who adapted well to his new life and made a success of it.[2]

One obvious reason for the general lack of interest in the man and his career – apart from his apparent secondary role in many of the events – is that he did not leave a set of papers which could be edited by a sympathetic relative or found after his death and deposited in a library for consultation by interested historians. And yet there remain plenty of letters to him and by him, though to be sure they are mainly official rather than personal. He was by no means an outstanding, boisterous, or notorious character, though he does seem to have evoked strong feelings of like and loyalty among his friends and relations, and among his soldiers. He was a Loyalist, and given his work, he may be defined above all as an Imperial Loyalist.

Auchmuty's life thus has a particular interest in itself, one which is worth resurrecting from the apparent concerted efforts of contemporaries and succeeding historians to conceal it. This is a man who won battles for the empire to which he was conspicuously loyal, only to see his victories thrown away. The plan of the following work, therefore, consists of two parallels: in the first the man's career is examined, what he did and where he went; in the second a wider view is taken, in which an examination is undertaken of the effects of his career and achievements. So, to take one example, his military activities in South America, where he conquered Montevideo but was then superseded by an incompetent commander-in-chief, was one of the major factors in bringing about the independence of Spanish America from its home government. So we have the irony of a man whose life seems to have been predicated on imperial loyalty apparently promoting the break-up of another empire. There is a third parallel in all this and that is to include the activities and achievements of other members of his family and his connections, many of whom were also Loyalists.

Weaving all these elements into a single narrative has not been easy, but its complications and ramifications seem to be a part of the less than straightforward history of Auchmuty's times. His life was an illustration of those times.

Chapter 1

An Episcopalian Family

Samuel Auchmuty, later general, was born in New York City in 1756. The family was of some prominence in the British American colonies at the time and in the revolution twenty years later it espoused, generally, the Loyalist persuasion, and so was eventually persecuted, imprisoned, impoverished, and scattered by its political (and religious) enemies.

Samuel's family's origin was ultimately in Scotland, in Fife, where there is a small village called Auchmuty still, and where his ancestors had, with their apparently characteristic familial decision, taken the Royalist side in the Scottish Revolution of 1637–50, and during the English occupation of Scotland in the 1650s. The key to these disastrous decisions, a century apart, was their adhesion to the local version, in Scotland and America, of the Anglican Church, referred to in both countries as Episcopalian. This appears to be a major factor in the careers of the later generations of the family.

The consistent choice of losing sides in these civil conflicts was counterbalanced by a fecundity of childbearing and a willingness from the early days to colonise newly acquired parts of the British Empire. The name Auchmuty derives from the place in Fife, the county north of the Firth of Forth, where even in the seventeenth century three different Auchmuty families can be discerned, based at Balmerino and Drumeldrie – the most important branch – and at Newburn in the south of the 'kingdom' (of Fife), and some other places. The families were of some local prominence, one man was a member of the Scottish Parliament for St Andrews in 1583, another fought and died at Flodden Field in 1513; another, a burgess of Edinburgh, married a daughter of Lord Balcarres (a Fifeshire lord) in 1591. On the whole they may be classed as minor gentry, to use a rather later description. A Robert Auchmuty, who held multiple ecclesiastical posts in and about Stirling, officiated at the baptism of James VI in 1566;[1] that is, he was a Catholic amid the more widespread Protestantism of his country, and clearly a Royalist too.

The name, if not the particular families, has been traced back to the thirteenth century, and the various holders of the name are said to have repeatedly held 'high office'. This seems something of an unlikely conclusion, and is attributable to the fact that only family members have studied the records, and have viewed these through rose-tinted glasses. Given that the name only very rarely occurs in historical records, if the word 'high' is deleted it would be acceptable as a description of their position. They were thus of minor importance nationally, though locally prominent, but they were also linked with more important families, and did their share of working and dying for the Scottish kings.[2]

The Episcopalianism of the family emerges in the seventeenth century. The main branch of the family, centred at Halhall and Newburn in Fife, was connected with several other local gentry and lordly families in and about Fife. Three sons of Sir David Auchmuty of Halhall, who died in 1650, were closely involved with Charles I; two of the sons were knighted, James in 1633, and David in 1651 by King Charles II during his brief and troubled reign in Scotland; a third son, Alexander, was a Servitor of King Charles I.[3]

The Scottish branch of the family faded away in the eighteenth century, with only three members known, two of them in military contexts. Similarly the Drumeldrie branch died out during the next century; the Balmerino lands of that branch were sold in 1644. The Scottish Revolution, like all such events, was hard on opponents, and tended to impoverish them. A Margaret 'Auchmoutie' was condemned and executed as a witch at Saltpreston in 1661.[4] (The spelling of the surname is a variable in all sources.) Also the production of large families died out as the restrictive Scottish laws on inheritance took a grip; families limited themselves in size to one or two children to preserve their inheritance; in a time of poor hygiene and epidemic diseases this was almost a guarantee of family extinction in no more than the medium term.

Just as members of the family took their small parts in the wars and revolutions of sixteenth- and seventeenth-century Scotland, so other branches became established in less unwelcoming lands overseas. Arthur Auchmuty, of which Scottish branch is not known, was present in 1641 at the Battle of Castle Forbes in County Longford in Ireland. He had settled in that area as one of the Scottish Protestant invaders of Ireland in the plantations organised in the first half of the century. Longford had been shired in 1598 – that is, organised as an English-type county, with a local government system controlled by the 'settlers'. But it was not 'settled' by Protestant English and Scottish landowners until the 1620s, which is possibly when Arthur Auchmuty arrived. Other Auchmutys, Alexander and John, were granted land in neighbouring Cavan, the county to the north of Longford, by the organising 'planters', but they soon sold off their allocation. What their connection was with the neighbouring Longford Auchmutys is not known, but proximity would suggest they were at least related.[5]

The Irish rising of 1641 blotted out many of the new settlers, but the survivors recovered their lands after the Cromwellian conquest in the 1650s. Arthur's eldest son John inherited these lands, and a second son, another Arthur, moved to Dublin. John, born in 1649 when his father was 50 years old, did not inherit until the end of the century, for old Arthur lived to be 99, a major achievement in such a violent century. He was the second son: old Arthur had four sons and four daughters. John is described as a 'captain': he fought in Wolseley's Horse in the Williamite conquest in 1689–91; to describe his military career as 'distinguished' is a large exaggeration; in the most detailed account of the war he is mentioned exactly twice.[6]

Captain John had another large family, six sons and four daughters. He was also MP for County Longford in 1695 and 1703 in the Dublin Parliament. He married Isabella, the daughter of the Revd James Stirling of Temple Michael, also in County Longford, and they had sons. (The contrast in fecundity with the struggling Scottish families is much to be noted.) His eldest son, James, born in 1681, attended Trinity College in Dublin, and became Dean of Armagh, one of the senior posts in the Anglican Church in Ireland – which is now called the Church of Ireland.[7]

The second son of Captain John, Robert, was born in 1687. He moved first to London where he lived for several years and then emigrated to North America. The intellectual and religious baggage he took with him was therefore of a particular sort. His elder brother (James) and his grandfather (James Stirling) were both ministers of the Anglican Church in Ireland, and Robert maintained that religious orientation. His genealogical background for two centuries – whichever branch of the Scottish family the Irish branch came from – was landowning gentry, not quite aristocratic, though they might have thought they were; certainly they were well connected and well above any peasantry; nor was the family in any way middle class or commercial. Moving into the Church, and later into the law, was a typical move for such families at this time. The inheritance of Captain John also included male inclinations towards the military.

The Irish branch of the family continued the tradition of quiet prosperity. Always based at Newtown (or Newtown Forbes) in the north of County Longford, but never of any great distinction or wealth, it was one of those families which provided a mainstay of the Irish Protestant Ascendancy, the British (rather than Irish) and Anglican landowners who lived off the rents provided with continuing if increasing reluctance by their Irish tenants. The sons of the family were regularly educated at Trinity College, Dublin, in every generation, and a partial genealogy can even be constructed from these records.[8] The family clearly flourished throughout the eighteenth century, just as did the American branch (until the revolution there, at least).[9]

Robert lived, was educated, and married for the first time in London, and three of his nephews, John, Samuel, and Arthur, are attested, and the first and third attended Trinity College in Dublin in what had become the family tradition. Samuel's son, also Samuel, was born in 1739, and he had three sons of his own, Samuel, Thomas, and Benjamin, who were all at Trinity between 1768 and 1780. Newtown is regularly listed as their home, but only one of the parents is identified further. This was Arthur, the father of Arthur Gates Auchmuty, who attended Trinity in 1728, at the age of 17. The father is described as '*colonus*', that is, a farmer, or more likely a landowner. He was probably the youngest son of Captain John, who had died only two years before. None of the other fathers are identified further – they were thus also landowners and gentlemen, no doubt. One of Robert's brothers, Forbes, none of whose descendants are known, lived on until 1788, dying at the age of 96. From this family came an 'Auchmutty' who served with the East India Company in Ireland at the end of the eighteenth century, and three sons of his who followed him in that work.[10]

Robert Auchmuty became a lawyer. After education at Trinity he was admitted to the Middle Temple in London in 1705 and to the Bar in 1711.[11] He married a lady whose Christian name was Elizabeth; she was the daughter of Henry and Mary Clare. Henry was a Citizen of London and in the Merchant Taylors' Guild. The date of the marriage is not known, but it had taken place by June 1707, according to a release and indenture of fine for a house and land in London. The fine was £400, so Robert was possessed of some wealth, though this was probably paid by his father-in-law.[12] (This may well mark the moment of the marriage, of course; Robert was 20 at the time.) The only other record of the marriage is a sermon preached to commemorate Elizabeth's death. The sermon was on 24 April 1715, so she had died some days before then; it was published at the request of her relatives – presumably the Clares and Robert – but it says absolutely nothing about her personally.[13] It appears from the ages of Robert's children that she had given birth to a daughter, Henrietta, who was married in Boston, Massachusetts, before 1731 (when she had a child) and she was therefore born some time before 1715. It is perhaps no coincidence that Robert left for America soon after; these various items about her suggest strongly that Robert was grief-stricken by his wife's death.

Robert moved to Massachusetts next year, probably in the suite of the new governor, Samuel Shute, who took office in that year. Robert may not have made much of a mark in legal circles in London, but in Boston he became outstanding. Presumably the education and training at the Middle Temple was more than sufficient to outshine the local Massachusetts lawyers; he is also said to have been eloquent and witty; legal anecdotes about him continued to be related long after his death. Success was sufficient to persuade him to settle in Massachusetts, and to stay there after Shute's time as governor ended. He clearly established himself as a prominent member of the Massachusetts legal and political community.

He married again in his new home, to Mary Julianna Treillhard, and had more children, two daughters and three sons.[14] His career prospered so that he was appointed judge of the Vice-Admiralty Court in Boston, which took cases in Massachusetts (which then included Maine), Rhode Island, and New Hampshire. This was not a notable nor a popular position in the local power hierarchy, but it was a lucrative one. He was already living in 'a handsome house' in Essex Street in Boston by 1738 when the family moved to an estate in Roxbury, outside the city. He was a vestryman of King's Chapel from 1723 at least. The family's acquisitiveness for land, and its Episcopalianism, obviously continued.[15]

Robert was also, necessarily, a political animal. He was deeply involved in the plotting which brought about the fall of Governor Belcher in 1740 and his replacement by William Shirley in 1741. Shirley was, like Robert, a lawyer with Inner Temple training, and they were colleagues in the Admiralty Court; they were clearly able to work together. It seems probable that they had known each other in London: they both moved out of Boston to live in Roxbury.[16] Robert developed views on the need to extend British control into French Canada, writing a brief pamphlet in 1744, while in London – the original manuscript is in the British Library – entitled *The Importance of Cape Breton to the British Nation,* at a time when the French fortress at Louisbourg was seen as a threat.[17] This helped promote the idea of a British expedition against the fortress which Shirley launched next year; the place was captured, but all this was not enough to persuade the government in London to hold on to it at the peace treaty in 1748.[18]

Robert had wider connections and interests than simply being one of Shirley's earlier followers, and so he survived Shirley's later enmity, and his governorship. He was sent to represent Massachusetts in a dispute with New Hampshire over their mutual boundary, which was being sorted out by a group of royal commissioners in London in 1742–4, and later in another dispute, this time with Rhode Island. It was while he was in London that he wrote and published the pamphlet on Cape Breton.

He died in 1750, at the good age of 63, leaving a reputation for capability, even wit, in the law, and having survived the intricacies and personal enmities of politics in Boston more or less unscathed. With his legal earnings and his Roxbury estate, he had become a wealthy man – he had contributed £200 to the building of the King's Chapel in 1747. He left a considerable legacy not only in property, but of children, and of legal pupils as well: he was notable as a teacher and trainer of the next generation of lawyers.[19] These last two categories, children and pupils, intermingled.

Robert and Mary Julianna's two daughters were called Henrietta and Isabella, and the three sons were Samuel, Robert, and James. The names are all, except one, clearly part of the family inheritance. Isabella was the name of Robert's mother, the wife of Captain John; Robert was, of course, the father's own name; James was the name of Robert's elder brother, the Dean of Armagh. These are all family names, such as would be expected in any family. The names of the two eldest children, Henrietta and Samuel, are not attested anywhere in the family before. Henrietta had been born while Robert was still in England, to his first wife, for Henrietta's own children were born in 1731 and 1732, so she was born before 1715, when her mother died, and so perhaps about 1710 or so. She was no doubt named for her grandfather, Henry Clare. The next child, Samuel, was born in 1721, so his last marriage, to Mary Julianna, had taken place at the latest by 1720. We must assume that he travelled to America with his first daughter. Samuel's name is the exception in not being named for an earlier family member; but he was born in 1721, and was no doubt named for Robert's mentor, Governor Samuel Shute, who may well have been the boy's godfather. It is worth noting that the name was quickly adopted into the Irish branch of the family, indicating that, as other evidence suggests, the two branches continued to keep in touch.

Robert's pupils turned out to be a notable group. Apart from his own sons, we know of three of these pupils: William Bollan, John Overing, and Benjamin Pratt (or Prat). William Bollan, whom Robert must have tutored in the 1740s, was married to Governor Shirley's daughter Frances, and spent much of his time in London as the agent of Massachusetts colony; when he returned to Boston, having finally been prised out of agency, he became involved in arguments with various other local figures. He was considered a good lawyer, but was clearly more ambitious than his abilities perhaps warranted.[20] John Overing was another man considered to be a good lawyer. He became the husband of Henrietta, Robert's eldest child, and their two children, Henry John and Mary Julianna Overing, were born in 1731 and 1732 respectively. Overing became Attorney General for Massachusetts for a time; he died in 1748.[21]

Benjamin Pratt is the most interesting of the three pupils. He was the son of a farmer who was part owner of an iron works at Cohasset, Massachusetts, but, after an accident at the age of 18 which left him with only one leg and in constant pain, he moved to Boston to study. After a long period of Harvard education, helped by sympathetic tutors who provided supportive scholarships, he graduated, and then studied law with, among others, Robert Auchmuty. He was physically unpleasant to look at, it seems, being small and on crutches, which at the time was considered more a personal failing than a disability, and he was socially inept, but he was a very clever and eloquent lawyer. As a result he built up a good practice and became relatively wealthy. In private he is said to have been 'amiable', and it is this perhaps, as well as his obvious intelligence (and eventual wealth), which attracted Robert Auchmuty's second daughter, Isabella. They married in 1749.[22]

With the death in 1750 of Robert Auchmuty, the sources for the family's activities tend to dry up for a decade. The children of his second wife were now in their twenties, and were making their way in the world by learning their work and careers. Internal politics in Massachusetts was relatively quiet, particularly during the Seven Years War of 1756–63 (also known as the French and Indian War), after the second removal of Governor Shirley. Matters became more heated after that time, especially in Boston, and several of Robert's children became politically involved.

Robert Auchmuty's career and position had placed his family in a situation which meant they were inevitably involved in public affairs. Indeed, no one with ability and a modicum of wealth could fail to be involved in political matters in the second half of the eighteenth century in North America. Lawyers had a certain advantage in that they were trained in public speaking and were supposed to be able to marshal a convincing argument; they were thus all too often looked to in political crises for leadership, which, given their legal situation, they were rarely able to provide. Despite his connection with Governor Shirley, Robert had largely avoided such involvement, except in diplomatic matters – as in the boundary disputes – which required clear thinking and argument, rebuttal, and advocacy. He had undoubtedly, however, fully identified himself with Massachusetts, as his advocacy of the province in its disputes with its neighbours, and his pamphlet on holding Cape Breton (seized by an expedition out of Massachusetts) demonstrates. But the following generation was to be unable to restrict itself to such subjects and attitudes.

When he died Robert's children seemed to be provided for. His daughters were married. Henrietta Overing was now a widow, but she had a son who would soon be able to support her, while her husband had been a successful lawyer and would have left her well provided for. Isabella had married Benjamin Pratt the year before her father's death; his success indicates moderate wealth also. Two of Robert's three sons were also married. Samuel, the eldest, had married a widow, Mary Nicholls, whose first husband, Captain Henry Tucker, had recently died; they married in 1749, the same year as Isabella and Pratt; Samuel thereby acquired a stepdaughter, Frances Tucker, who was 5 years old at the time of the marriage. Their first child, Robert, was born in 1750, and six more children were born in the next twelve years. They youngest of Robert's sons, James Smith Auchmuty, was either already married or soon would be, for he had a son adult enough to go to war in the 1770s. He inherited 'a fortune' from his grandfather James Smith. The middle son, another Robert, did not marry until the 1760s.[23]

This next decade and more was the time when British North America finally trampled over its French and Spanish competitors and enemies in the Seven Years War, 1756–63.[24] Of the Auchmuty family only Benjamin Pratt was at all seriously involved in public affairs during that time. The sons of Robert were all adult by the 1750s, though none seems to have taken part in the fighting in the Seven Years War. Benjamin Pratt emerged in the 1750s as one of the most able lawyers in Boston, and by 1757 he was able to buy an estate at Milton, one of the richer suburbs of the city. He became active on various public committees of the city, and was elected Moderator of the Town Meeting in 1757, and a member of the colony's House of Representatives in that year and the two following. He became a supporter of Governor Pownall, and was involved in negotiations with other colonies about the conduct of the Seven Years War, and with the problem of caring for the Acadians, expelled from their Nova Scotia homeland.

His association with Pownall (governor 1757–60) provides an early instance of the heating up of Massachusetts politics which was eventually to grow into the fire of revolution. When Pownall's term of office finally ended (in 1760, the year when the threat of French domination finally came to an end with the conquest of Montreal and thus all Canada) it was proposed that he should return to England in the 'province ship'. This was a vessel which was paid for by the colony, particularly by the merchants of Boston, which was intended to be a guard for the port and its shipping against enemies. The intention seems to have been to refit the ship in England during the winter, and that on its return to Boston in the spring it would bring out the 'reimbursement money' paid by the mother country to the colony. The ship would be away from Boston for the winter, when it was usually kept inside the harbour anyway. At least this was the story later produced by the friends of Pownall.

The proposal, apparently sensible, was seized on by the local enemies of Pownall's advisors, among the latter of whom was Benjamin Pratt. 'In the midst of war', it was pointed out, the city was to be deprived of its maritime protection, and all for the convenience of the retiring governor; it was an obvious case, his opponents claimed, of 'extravagance'. A mob was conjured, and the governor went home in a private vessel. And while the population was thus greatly heated, the election for new representatives was held – by sheer coincidence, of course – and Pratt, associated with the former governor, failed to be returned.[25]

As one door shuts, another opens. Pratt was still a wealthy man and a lawyer in demand. A new job proposal arrived, that he become Chief Justice and Counsellor for New York. Again, however, he found himself in the middle of a local political dispute. His appointment was to be 'during good behaviour', which unexceptionable phrase concealed the fact that it was the New York colonial Assembly which would judge his 'behaviour'. That is, he was to be subject to the political authority of the Assembly and the governor, and not appointed 'during His Majesty's pleasure', which was the term usually used, and which was an effective shield against local pressure – which pressure was clearly intended to be applied by the new terms of his appointment.

Pratt took the point. He had been apprised of the conditions by his brother-in-law, Samuel Auchmuty, who was by then well established in New York. Pratt had been informed of the appointment, but was not sent a copy of the commission. He wrote to another of Samuel's brothers-in-law, the lieutenant governor, Cadwallader Colden, enquiring as to the precise terms. No doubt Pratt had been at once suspicious when the commission did not arrive, and Auchmuty's information confirmed his doubts. He wrote to Colden in precise terms: he was, he said, 'liable to be broke by the Governor if he don't please him, and to be Starved by the Assembly if he don't please them'. This was from a man reputedly verbose in court; no one need say that a lawyer cannot be both precise and succint.

On being reassured by Colden, and receiving a commission which stated that he was to be appointed 'during Our pleasure', Pratt took the position in New York, but he found no other judges willing to operate (they were unwilling to be appointed during the royal pleasure), and that the Assembly refused him a salary because of those words in his commission. On the other hand, his accuracy and speed in court was widely admired. But he disliked his situation, not surprisingly, and in the summer of 1762, after being in post for just four months, he took leave of absence to return to his home at Milton, where his family had remained, with the clear implication that he might not return. This left New York without a single working judge, possibly for a long time still to come. However, during his leave of absence

Colden found a way to pay him a salary of £550 sterling, and he returned to work in New York in September.

In the midst of all this Pratt wrote to the Lords of Trade in London – the department which attempted to administer colonial policy – pointing out the wider significance of the situation he was in. Unless judges were independent of local pressures, unless they were appointed, that is, 'during His Majesty's pleasure', and paid for their work independently of the local financial system, other judges would need to be appointed – for New York's jails were full of accused people awaiting trial – and those judges would respond to local pressures by rendering decisions which would progressively separate the colony from Britain; they would not enforce the imperial laws of trade, which were locally unpopular, and the royal lands would be lost by encroachments which would be validated by the judges' partial decisions. That the point was taken, though it was probably redundant for him to have to make it, is shown by the rapid and relieved approval of the Privy Council in London when Colden came up with a scheme to pay Pratt's salary out of a fund of royal moneys not subject to the Assembly's control.[26]

Pratt had only a few months longer to live after this triumph, dying after an operation to amputate his remaining leg, in January 1763. His career links the pre-revolutionary period to the approaching political storm. Twice he had found himself trapped in the political space between increasingly assertive authorities: the royal government on the one side, personified in the colonies by the governors, and at a greater distance by the Lords of Trade and ultimately the king, and on the other the local political activists in and out of the Assembly, who made their names and local reputations by defying, usually at a safe distance and behind a rioting mob, that royal and imperial authority. The control of the law courts was clearly seen as a priority among the activists; Pratt's rejection of that clearly marked him as a popular enemy, and the controversy was one of the elements tending towards political revolution.

One of the factors which had operated in Massachusetts' society, and possibly in New York as well, to produce unpopularity for Pratt, was Pratt's attendance at the King's Chapel in Boston, the centre for Anglican worship in the city. The Auchmutys were also attenders – the late Robert had contributed £200 to its construction – and both Pratt and his father-in-law were, or had been, vestrymen there. But Boston and Massachusetts were self-consciously

Puritan, and, although a certain tolerance had developed, as one would expect in a mercantile city, it was always possible to use an Anglican's church membership against him. In New York, of course, one of the dominant religious sects was that of the Dutch Calvinists, though, again, the commercial city required tolerance to be practised, for the sake of moneymaking.

Being Anglicans, of course, predisposed Pratt and the Auchmutys towards an acceptance of the authority of the head of their Church, the king (and therefore his government). The Puritan churches and sects and chapels, on the other hand, encouraged an antipathy towards royal authority because it was manifested in part by discrimination against Puritans and other Dissenters (and, of course, also Catholics).[27] This religious divide was one of the many fissures in colonial society; another was a class division between, crudely, rich and poor, the middle class of merchants and lawyers in between. So the fact that Robert Auchmuty and Benjamin Pratt were wealthy and Anglican and took up posts in the royal government were all items to set them against the local Puritans and political mobs who were, to put it no stronger for the moment, impatient with the exercise of royal power and authority in the colonies.

Pratt's brothers-in-law, Robert and Samuel Auchmuty, became much more deeply involved in public affairs in the decade after his death, and, like him, their political stance was in part the result of their Anglicanism, which led to Loyalism later during the revolution. Samuel Auchmuty had at first begun to head in the direction of a career in either law or the civil service. He had accompanied his father to London during his mission concerned with the Rhode Island boundary dispute in 1742–4, and returned to Boston with an appointment as Admiralty Registrar, but then his father came to his disagreement with Governor Shirley, and the Admiralty Board was constrained to cancel the appointment. (Shirley was related to the Duke of Newcastle, Secretary of State in London.) While they were in Britain father and son had evidently renewed contact with Robert's family in Ireland, and Dean James Auchmuty at Armagh had suggested that Samuel enter the Church. By 1747, with a Master of Arts from Harvard, he was able to go back to England for ordination by the Bishop of London, there being no bishop in the American colonies.

He taught for a decade in the Negro School in New York, the clientele and curriculum of which he greatly extended. He married the widow Mary

Nicholls Tucker, and took charge of St George's Chapel in Beekman Street in the city in 1752. He was certainly a success at the school, but his class snobbery got in the way of his ecclesiastical work. This attitude may have been innate in him, but it was surely encouraged by his marriage (though there is no suggestion that others in the family held such views). His wife Mary Nicholls Tucker was the widow of Captain Thomas Tucker, who was a member of a family long settled and prominent in Bermuda, and a ship's captain. She was also the sister-in-law of Alexander Colden, brother of Cadwallader, the lieutenant governor who had supported Benjamin Pratt. This social position was, of course, also a political one.

When the long-lived incumbent of the Trinity Church in New York, Dr Henry Barclay, died in 1764, Samuel was immediately chosen to replace him, and it was Cadwallader Colden who, as the lieutenant governor, inducted him into the position.[28] The absence of a bishop made it necessary for governors and lieutenant governors to undertake these tasks. There will be further consideration of this man after examining the career of his brother.

The Revd Samuel's younger brothers, Robert and James, stayed in Boston. The youngest, James Smith Auchmuty, is scarcely known. He did marry, and inherited a local fortune from his godfather, James Smith. His son was old enough to die in battle in the West Indies during the War for Independence, so James was already married by the time old Robert died. The younger Robert was admitted to Harvard in 1746 (though he did not matriculate), but nothing is known of him from then until 1761, when he is recorded as building a house on a part of his father's estate in Roxbury which he had inherited. This suggests that he had already become fairly wealthy, presumably by his inheritance. Next year, 1762, he became a barrister, and as the son of old Robert, we may assume that he had been his father's pupil. But since the elder man died in 1750 we are in the dark as to young Robert's activities in the 1750s, though it may be assumed that he had been an active and successful lawyer.

He was, however, certainly regarded as one of the most prominent lawyers in Massachusetts by the 1760s, in the same league as his brother-in-law Benjamin Pratt, and as his younger contemporaries John Adams and James Otis. Like all his family, he inclined to the Crown's side in the various disputes between Britain and its colonies, and, partly as a result of these opinions, he gained several lucrative royal posts. His appointment in 1762 as a Advocate General in the Court of Admiralty led on to his appointment as judge in the Vice-Admiralty Court four years later. This had been the position held by his father from 1733 until 1741. There was a clear continuity here, for when Robert senior went off to London in 1742 his deputy Charles Russell became the judge, and Robert junior had been Russell's own deputy for some years until he was appointed to the higher position.

This was a senior position in the royal administration and as such had been an automatic target for those who were determined to work for separation from Britain, or who resented what was seen as the gradual extension of royal power. Once the position was firmly established, however, such opposition subsided; it was clearly necessary to have such a court, and the alternative to one based at Boston was one based in London or Halifax or New York. However, since the post carried a salary of £600 a year, this was another point of attack, and it was certainly larger than, for instance, what Pratt received as Chief Justice in New York.[29] The salary was awarded 'through the corruption of the times', according to a Boston news journal.[30]

The Vice-Admiralty Court adjudicated in matters of prize and customs charges, and in the enforcement of the Acts of Parliament regulating trade. Given that the British Parliament was keen to enclose the whole empire within a mercantilist ring-fence, and the colonists were anxious to sell their goods in the best market, whether in or out of the empire, and to import their requirements cheaply, understanding that they could only benefit by competition, conflict over the issue of these Navigation Acts was inevitable, and for the present these conflicts were fought out mainly in the law courts.

Auchmuty was therefore a busy man, more than covering his own salary in condemnations or fines, which went to the Crown. One notable case was brought by the customs authorities against the merchant John Hancock (later famous for his dominating signature on the Declaration of Independence). He was condemned to lose his ship, provocatively called *Liberty*, and his counsel John Adams successfully opened up the issue of 'liberty', as though Hancock had not been attempting to import goods without paying duty (and so gaining an unfair advantage by being able to undersell his Bostonian competitors). Adams' demand, in fact, was for a trial before a jury rather than a judge alone; he knew that a Bostonian jury would be composed of men who were as opposed to the customs duties as Hancock, and as active smugglers as he was. Obviously, given this challenge, Auchmuty had to proceed carefully, and the case took a long time; in the end, Adams' arguments – though perhaps not his call for liberty – and the possibility of mob violence, persuaded the prosecuting counsel to drop the case.

The manifest fairness of the judge in conducting the case defused much of the political criticism of him, at least for a while, and at the same time it enhanced Auchmuty's legal reputation. Politically he was, of course, identified as a supporter of the British cause, his post, his salary, his religion, his upbringing, and his inheritance all compelling him in that direction. Yet he and the radicals could still work together. In 1770 he, John Adams, and Josiah Quincy were the defence team for Captain Thomas Preston, who was accused of ordering the firing by British soldiers which produced the Boston 'massacre'. The three successfully secured Preston's acquittal, but Auchmuty refused to act for the private soldiers, who were also accused.[31]

By now Auchmuty was married, to Deborah Cradock of Boston. Like his father he lived in Roxbury, and was a close associate of Governor Francis Bernard (governor 1760–70), and was regarded as a member of the 'cabinet council' which met at times in Auchmuty's own house. He was a friend of Thomas Hutchinson, who was another adviser to Bernard, and was his successor as governor (in 1771–4). Auchmuty was identified as one of a dozen or so men who comprised the 'government group' and were caricatured in a pamphlet of 1769. The group included Andrew Oliver the Lieutenant Governor, and Jonathan Sewall, as well as Auchmuty. Corruption, 'dissimulation and hypocrisy' were charged on these men, all accusations which were notably vague and absent of content. But the production of the pamphlet marked an increasing savagery in the political disputation.[32]

In his professional capacity at the Admiralty Court Auchmuty was one of the commissioners named to investigate the case of the destruction of the revenue schooner *Gaspee*, burned by a group of Rhode Islanders who resented the law-enforcing activities of the captain and crew. There were five commissioners, and Auchmuty served along with the Rhode Island Governor, the chief justices of New York, New Jersey, and Massachusetts – this last being David Oliver, brother of Andrew Oliver. The commander of the *Gaspee*, obeying the instructions of the London government, had been doing his best to enforce the customs regulations; evidently he was being too successful, and the Rhode Island smugglers – effectively the whole of the mercantile community of the colony, backed and protected by the colony's government – reacted by destroying the ship.[33] In Boston itself, the destruction of the tea which was imported by the East India Company in 1773 was another incident of the same sort. Again the proximate cause was an attempt by customs officials, under the orders of the governor, to enforce the regulations.

Next year (1774) Auchmuty's friend and colleague Governor Thomas Hutchinson was, in effect, deposed and replaced by General Thomas Gage, who arrived with much greater powers than Hutchinson ever had.[34] He steadily increased the pressure on the 'Patriots', as the proponents of separation were becoming called. There can have been little point in continuing the Vice-Admiralty Court hearings in the circumstances. One of his letters to London complaining of local disloyalty had been obtained by Benjamin Franklin and was published after being shown around widely in Massachusetts, along with other letters from various friends of Hutchinson. These letters had effectively destroyed Hutchinson's local authority, as well as that of his lieutenant governor Oliver (another of the authors); anyone else involved was inevitably affected as well.[35] By October 1774 Auchmuty had given up. He requested leave of absence from his post, accepting that he would have to forgo his salary. His intention was to go to England 'for a visit'.[36] The military occupation of Boston by General Gage came soon after his request for leave, and overtook his intention; he was thus unable to leave the city.

In New York, Robert's brother Samuel had become well known as the assertive rector of the Trinity Church, at the corner of Broadway and Wall Street. Trinity was the pre-eminent Anglican church of New York both in prestige and in the building itself. It was, when Samuel took charge, about seventy years old, built in the English style, with a steeple 175ft in height, which made it the tallest structure in the city at the time, and as such it can be seen as a mark of the confident assertiveness of the Anglican Church. It was the church attended by every governor and lieutenant governor, and by much of the wealthy set in the city. They could thus be harangued in sermons by the eloquent rector.

Samuel's opinions were also expressed freely in his private correspondence. He referred to the Dutch – Calvinists, mostly – in his parish as 'loggerheads', and contested the attempts of the Presbyterians to obtain a charter of incorporation for a church of their own in the city. During the Stamp Act crisis in 1765 he called non-Anglicans 'rebels' and 'Republicans', and yet when the Act was repealed he congratulated a group in a meeting in his house, though he did so in the context of 'non-resistance', which was the chosen contemporary Anglican method of persuading authority to change its mind.[37]

At the same time, he was active in both education and charity work. He had helped to found King's College, and served as its governor – it is now Columbia University; he worked for the establishment of a charity to support the widows and children of Anglican clergy, and more widely to extend charity to the needy, including a group of destitute Scottish emigrants who arrived in 1774; he actively promoted his Anglican beliefs, preaching the virtues of obedience to authority and non-resistance. In many ways he was a model Anglican minister. He reported regularly to the diocese of London, of which the colonial churches were technically a part, on the affairs of the church in New York.[38]

He was also ambitious. He campaigned repeatedly for the establishment of an American Anglican episcopate, and in 1770 presided over a convention of Anglican clergy which accepted that this was needed. By calling such a convention, which included clergy from Connecticut and New Jersey, as well as from New York, he was, of course, following the trend of the times – as in the Stamp Act Congress – which was to work towards the closer linking of the colonies one with another. But his advocacy of an American episcopate produced a local backlash, not only from the Dissenters, who feared the persecuting authority wielded by bishops; he was also accused of wishing to be the first of the bishops. This was, in fact, probably an accurate supposition. He is described by the historian of these events as 'militant'.[39]

At the same time it should have been clear – and it surely was in Canterbury and in London – that to establish any American episcopate would be in effect to bring forward the growing separatism of the colonies from Britain. The only way in which the new Anglican ministers could be ordained was to travel to England for examination and undergo the ceremony at the hands of a bishop there. This was therefore both a symbolic linkage and a political one – the English church could be certain of the political opinions of the new priests as well as their theological fitness. Samuel Auchmuty had, of course, done this himself in the 1740s. The very fact that he advocated an American episcopate and was rumoured to seek the post for himself was probably one of the factors which counted against it.

Auchmuty was by no means alone in all this: the question had been under virtually constant discussion since Queen Anne's time, with plans which emanated from England or the colonies regularly failing for one reason or another. The issue was as much political as religious or administrative – the establishment of new bishoprics was a task for Parliament, not just for the Anglican Church – and in the 1760s the instability of British governments prevented discussion; then from 1770 the Prime Minister Lord North calmed matters in Parliament, but was unwilling to take decisions which would stir up even more of the instability that already existed in the colonies. The turbulence caused by the 'Patriots', whether this was part of their intention or not, was in effect one of the major factors which prevented the establishment of an American episcopate.[40]

Samuel Auchmuty also had a growing family. Six of his children survived childhood, three daughters, Mary Julianna, Margaret, and Isabella, then three sons, Robert Nicholls, Richard Harrison, and Samuel; then a final daughter, Jane. He also had a stepdaughter, Frances Tucker, who married in 1764. Her husband was Captain John Montresor, a Royal Engineer who had made a name for himself as an engineer and surveyor during the French and Indian (or 'Seven Years') War, and in the following Pontiac's War in the western territories. He was employed in America from 1766 doing surveys in several colonies, producing well-regarded maps of New York, Boston, and New Providence in the Bahamas, and in planning fortifications on the Delaware River in Pennsylvania and at Crown Point on the route towards Canada.[41] In the process he became wealthy, a matter which would return to trouble him and his family later.

Montresor and Frances were married in 1764 and spent a couple of years in England before Montresor returned to New York. His family were originally Huguenot refugees who fled French persecution instituted after the Revocation of the Edict of Nantes in 1685, and his father and grandfather had both served in the British Army as artillerists and engineers. He and his father had accompanied Braddock on his ill-fated march towards Fort Duquesne in 1755, and he presumably knew George Washington. In 1772 Montresor bought an island in the East River of New York which became known as Montesor's Island (it is now Randall's Island), at the junction of the

Harlem River, Long Island Sound, and the East River. He and his growing family (six children who survived, four who did not) lived there between his periods of detached duty. He eventually settled at Belmont House in Kent.

The significance of the story of this marriage is that it widened still further the Auchmuty family's imperial connections, one of the themes of this book. Frances' mother Mary Nicholls was, of course, the widow of the Bermudan Captain Tucker, but now her husband John Montresor was active in many of the American colonies from Canada to the Bahamas. The eldest daughter of Samuel and Mary, Mary Julianna, also married a Royal Engineer, Frederick George Mulcaster, when he was a lieutenant. This was a species of royal connection, since the bridegroom's father had been of the household of the Prince of Wales, the father of King George III. His home was at Bishopsthorpe, in Kent, while the American Auchmutys retained their connection with the family in Ireland.

Then in 1772 the second daughter of Samuel and Mary, Isabella, married William Burton, who was also from Kent, also in the British Army, and presumably she went across the Atlantic with him. They lived in Boston and had property there, at the time of the rising disturbances, and their connection with Robert Auchmuty was well known. This part of the family is little-known, but it is said that Burton was an officer in the army; if he was in Boston in these years he was part of the occupation force. The repeated Kentish connections became even more important later.[42]

As with his brother, the Revd Samuel Auchmuty's position in New York as an avowed, 'militant', supporter of the royal government became steadily less comfortable as the crisis of authority in the city and elsewhere deepened. He had been less than discreet in his correspondence with his son-in-law Montresor (who was in Boston as part of the army of occupation), denouncing the New Yorkers generally and the city officials particularly. The Continental Congress was meeting, and he described it as having 'rebellious followers' – not altogether inaccurately, of course, as it turned out, and he could have also pointed to its rebellious members. As also happened with his brother Robert in Boston, one of his letters was acquired by the Patriots; Montresor was already by then unreachable by mail in blockaded Boston, so any letters were liable to be intercepted. It was regarded as so incendiary that it was immediately published.[43]

The Revd Samuel Auchmuty was now denounced in turn with the usual lack of restraint displayed by colonial editors and pamphleteers, whose specialties lay in ignoring context and distortion by omission. There is no doubt, however, that Auchmuty's political opinions were already well known, and the Trinity Church was the meeting point of the wealthy and the Anglican establishment in the city. This group was probably no more than a tenth of the population of the city, but they had the air, or the pretensions, of a ruling oligarchy. One result of the publication of his letter was a marked falling off of attendance at his church, either because his presence was toxic or his opinions were unwelcome. He also burnt what letters he held, or announced that he would cease writing more – perhaps both of these.

New York was by no means as revolutionary a city as Boston, and the proportion of Loyalists in the population has been put as high as half the population, but it was just as liable to riot and dispute as other American cities, in part due to the class divisions of the society, which were aggravated by the political disputes.[44] Auchmuty, in fact, had been largely ignored by the disputants until the letter affair, possibly as a result of his espousal of the 'non-resisting' position of the Church, which, of course, led his political opponents to discount him. His influence was actually minimal, largely confined as it was to his own congregation, which anyway largely agreed with him. He was so obvious a Tory that any of his pronouncements in politics would be automatically discounted in advance by his opponents, and by those who were sufficiently thoughtful. At the same time, he was undoubtedly respected for the consistency of his views, and for the work he had done in charities and in building up his parish. Had the decision ever been taken by the Anglican Church to establish a colonial episcopate he would surely have been one of the prime candidates for the first 'native' appointment – but the Anglican Church was hardly at its most imaginative or vigorous at the time.

Wherever the attitudes and beliefs of members of the Auchmuty family can be traced or discovered, they always centred on membership of the Anglican Church, in Scotland, in Ireland, and in the American colonies, at least from the time of the Scottish Revolution in the 1560s. This guaranteed a certain modicum of success for many years, when their government was of the same persuasion, but one of its effects was to drive out those who were part of the defeated party when a political revolution occurred. With at least one Catholic priest in the family earlier who had been prominent enough to officiate at the baptism of the son of Mary, Queen of Scots, the family was perhaps then already a target. Abandoning Catholicism for Episcopalianism, the active family members moved to Ireland, while their Scottish roots withered. In Ireland they moved into the typical middle-class occupations of the seventeenth and eighteenth centuries: landowning, the Church, the law, the army. And to make one's future in the law, London was the main resort, and membership of the Anglican Church a necessity.

Hence Robert Auchmuty's move to London, and hence also his later move, possibly impelled by the death of his first wife, and possibly by his connection with the new governor, to Boston. There his descendants two generations later found themselves again, as in Scotland, on the losing end of a revolution. (In Ireland the same thing eventually happened, but only in the twentieth century.) In the colonies the men of the family took to the same occupations as in Ireland (and perhaps in Scotland), in the Church and the law and the army. Their relative prominence in Boston and New York made them minor targets of the revolutionary mobs, and the convulsions which gripped those colonies from 1773 onwards once again sent the family into a new exile. In this movement Samuel Auchmuty junior, the subject of this book, was directly caught up.

Chapter 2

The Family Scattered

The American Revolution broke up communities and families, and the fate of the Auchmuty family was typical of the destruction it caused. Within a few years several of its members were dead as a direct or indirect result of political events, and others, including my main subject, the younger Samuel Auchmuty, were scattered far afield, well away from their original homes.

The breaking began, suitably enough, at the original epicentre of the revolution, at Boston. Robert Auchmuty had tried to get leave from his post as judge of the Admiralty Court as early as 1774, but it appears he was not able to leave the city for the next two years. (The same happened to his colleague Governor Thomas Hutchinson.) So not only did he live through the military occupation of the city by the British Army, but through the subsequent siege by the American forces in 1775–6 as well. His home at Roxbury was taken over by the military during the siege, and then it was eventually confiscated and condemned to be sold by the Massachusetts government in 1779.

Robert got away from the city before July 1776, and went, it appears, first to Halifax, Nova Scotia, as did many Bostonian refugees. He then sailed for New York, no doubt to join the members of his family there, sailing in a Bermudan ship which was taking military stores to the city. It was intercepted by a cruiser out of New York in July 1776, though what happened then is not known – we have only a report of the interception.[1] In the end he reached England, and settled in London, spending much of the rest of his life (he died in 1788) working on claiming compensation for his losses (from the British government), and assisting other American refugees to do the same.[2]

If Robert was going to New York he was presumably going to join his brother the Revd Samuel. Of his other siblings it is probable that the eldest (step-)sister Henrietta (Overing) lived at Newport, Rhode Island; her son Henry John died there in 1782, and her daughter at Boston in 1811. Henry

John had four children who were even further scattered: two remained at Newport, one died at Bermuda, another at Tobago. Newport, as a major New England port, was very likely to be a place from which men would sail to islands in the West Indies; it was also a major naval base during the revolutionary war; by living there during the war it is clear that the Overing branch of the Auchmuty family favoured the rebel cause.[3] Isabella, the widow of Benjamin Pratt, may also have stayed in Boston; her children seem to have stayed in the city; only one of them married and had children.[4] The dates of the deaths of both of these ladies are not known, but they could well have survived until the War of Independence (which some of them may well have called the American Rebellion) was over.

The last child of Robert, James Smith Auchmuty, was captured and held a prisoner, a fact recorded in July 1776 in a letter from General Charles Scott to the Provincial Congress.[5] His wife and child were also held. He had appealed to John Jay for help and financial assistance, complaining that where others had been helped he had not 'received a shilling'. He had another son who was old enough to be killed in a British Army campaign in the West Indies. James Smith Auchmuty gave his parole to stay at Danbury in Connecticut until he was exchanged, and then like many other Massachusetts Loyalists he went to Halifax, Nova Scotia. Unlike most – and unlike his father – he stayed there and practised law, becoming, like his father, a judge, and ascending to be a judge on the provincial Supreme Court.[6] The Burtons, William and Isabella (Samuel's third daughter), also appear to have left Boston with the evacuation and to have moved to Nova Scotia, though this was only temporary; they soon moved on to England and settled in Kent.

Already, therefore, within a year of the beginning of the fighting, the Boston branch of the family had been scattered to Halifax, to the West Indies, to New York and on to England, while some of the family stayed on in Boston or at Newport, Rhode Island. It must be assumed that the women did not have any strong feelings in politics, unlike the men, or that they approved of the revolutionaries' actions, or, more likely, that they were disregarded by all sides and their opinions ignored; there was a degree of chivalry displayed on both sides in allowing women and children to take refuge, or to join their husbands who were enemies. Either way the Boston branch of the family was thoroughly broken up, though not wholly extinguished.

The movement from Boston to Halifax, though intended presumably to be merely temporary, was the beginning of the Anglicisation of Canada. Many of the exiles moved on to England, like Robert Auchmuty and the Burtons, but many also stayed in Nova Scotia, converting it from the Scottish and French land into an English one; and, of course, still others moved to other parts of Canada, so that within a few years Upper Canada became Ontario and a completely English-speaking country. Nova Scotia was also the initial destination of the escaped slaves who had taken the British side on promise of freedom and were evacuated in the last years of the war; most were eventually moved on to Sierra Leone, but some remained in Nova Scotia or moved to Canada.[7]

It is worth noting here that another branch of the wider family took part in the revolution on the revolutionary side. Arthur Gates Auchmuty was probably a grandson of Captain John of Longford, Ireland, and a nephew of James Auchmuty, who was Dean of Armagh. He emigrated from Ireland in the 1760s, already over 50 years of age, and had settled at first in Lancaster County, Pennsylvania. He was a Dublin alumnus, as were so many of the family in Ireland, born at the family home at Newtown, County Longford. He became an Indian trader in Pennsylvania, and moved on regularly to settle at new places as the Indian-occupied territory retreated in the face of the expansion of white settlement, eventually locating in Northumberland County. He must have been married before emigrating since he had a son, Samuel, who was old enough to serve in the American Army during the War of Independence, supposedly from the time of Valley Forge to the end of the war, though this is only a claim by the family.[8]

This is clearly a further example of the choices made by other Auchmutys. It is not known if Arthur Gates in Pennsylvania and Samuel in New York were in contact with each other, or with the other American branches of the family, when the war began. One hint of such a contact, however, is that Arthur Gates was buried in the Trinity churchyard at Newport, Rhode Island.[9] This was the church attended by the Overings, who lived in the town, and by the eldest son of the Revd Samuel, Robert Nicholls Auchmuty. Robert Nicholls lived until 1813, so if Arthur Gates came to Rhode Island, it was probably as an old man as he had been born in 1711 or 1714. Samuel the American soldier, his son, on the other hand, is buried at Millerstown, Pennsylvania; Samuel's son, who became a doctor, was born in 1785. This should be a good indication that Arthur Gates took the revolutionary side in the war, but that he also remained true to his family's religious history as an Episcopalian.

Here therefore is another break in the family. Robert Nicholls Auchmuty, the eldest son of the Revd Samuel Auchmuty, served as a volunteer with the British forces, but settled at Newport, Rhode Island, after the Revolutionary War, and married his cousin Henrietta Overing. He was, like his father-in-law, a member of the Trinity Church at Newport where Arthur Gates Auchmuty was buried. How diligent Robert Nicholls' service with the British Army had been is not known; all the family record claims is that 'he fought valiantly for his sovereign', which is so unspecific as to be suspicious, and has all the marks of a family oral tradition.[10] It may seem that Robert Nicholls and Arthur Gates were essentially neutrals, no doubt torn between loyalty to their Church and to the family and to their country, but perhaps too old to consider serving in any army. Robert Nicholls, however, was employed by the British government at the end of the war to investigate and assess claims of refugees as a Commissioner of Claims; this would suggest a loyalty to Britain.

The New York branch of the family, however, had a worse time than any of the other scattered branches. The Revd Samuel was a prominent Loyalist even before such a term was applied to anyone, as the Minister of the Trinity Church. In the city he was so prominent that he was therefore a prime target for intimidation by the 'patriot' mob. In 1776, as fighting at Boston became steadily more serious, the city of New York was taken over and fortified by the rebels. This was done in an amateurish way, largely with barricades on the streets, though it showed that the revolutionaries were in earnest.[11] One of the leaders of the project was Colonel Alexander Turnbull, who claimed to be the rightful Lord Stirling (and was known as such to Americans – though how this was squared with the general republicanism is not clear); he had adopted the American side in the dispute. He was evidently concerned to drive out his local political opponents from the city, and the Revd Samuel was one of them.

Stirling sent a message, by one of Samuel's sons, that if he read the prayers for the king in Trinity Church on the next Sunday, probably – this was sometime before June 1776 – he would be attacked. The son (we do not know which one it was, but it was probably not the elder, Robert

Nicholls) did not deliver the message to his father, since he knew it would simply anger him.[12] He and some of his classmates from the King's College armed themselves and attended the church service as a bodyguard for the Revd Samuel. Stirling gathered a group of soldiers – he was in effect the commander of the city militia forces – and as soon as Auchmuty began the prayer he marched into the church, with a fifer playing 'Yankee Doodle', and out again. Though Samuel is said to have not faltered in reciting the prayer, as soon as the service was over, he locked up the church and left New York with his family for New Jersey. Stirling's tactic of musical, marching intimidation – terrorism by music – had clearly worked.[13]

The city was clearly a dangerous place for Loyalists, but they were still numerous. The absence from New York of the Governor, William Tryon, who was in England between April 1774 and June 1775 due to his ill-health, left the Lieutenant Governor Cadwallader Colden in charge, but his irascibility was unhelpful. Tryon returned in July 1775 to resume his duties, and just missed the arrival of George Washington, recently appointed Commander-in-Chief of the Continental (that is, the rebel) Army. The citizens of New York turned out for both men impartially during their successive parades through the streets on the same day.

Tryon worked hard and ingeniously to organise and encourage the city's Loyalists, but was compelled to live on a ship in the harbour for safety, and then to move it outside as the city came under increasingly determined rebel control.[14] It was during Tryon's absence that the pressure on the Revd Samuel at Trinity became finally unbearable and he left.

The Revd Samuel was thus out of the city when the British forces under General William Howe landed on Long Island and defeated the American forces. ('Lord Stirling' was captured in the first fighting.)[15] When Howe had retaken the whole city, the Revd Samuel decided to return. The Americans refused to give him a pass through their lines, and so he instead went 'on foot, through circuitous paths' and reached the city independently.[16] He arrived at about the time of the 'Great Fire', which burned down a quarter of the city – including his house and his church.[17]

He had left his wife and daughters in New Jersey, though his wife at least was given a pass, supposedly signed by George Washington himself, to return to New York.[18] After all, once Samuel was in the city, there was no point in keeping the wife out of it – and, as at Boston and Newport, it is probable that women's opinions were disregarded, which at least tended to protect them. Exactly which of their daughters had been with him in exile in Brunswick in New Jersey is not obvious. The youngest, Jane, may be assumed to be one of them, since she was only 14 years old at the time. The two older daughters were both married by now, and to men whose homes were in England, or who had been driven out from Boston. His stepdaughter Frances Tucker Montresor was probably in America, for her husband the Royal Engineer Captain John Montresor is known to have been active in the fighting in both Boston and New York in 1776; it is unlikely that they were still living on Montresor's Island during the rebel seizure of power in the city, and the captain at least had been in Boston during the siege.

The Revd Samuel died in March 1777, no doubt of shock and exhaustion, aggravated by the loss of his church and his home; he was thus clearly an early casualty of the war, even if he did not actually fight.[19] It is apparent from the comments about his wife and daughters as temporarily separated from him that his sons were not with him. The eldest, Robert Nicholls, is said, rather vaguely, as noted above, to have joined a volunteer company in support of the British Army, though neither dates nor units are listed, and this did not prevent him from settling in Rhode Island after (or during) the war. The second son Richard Harrison Auchmuty, on the other hand, is listed as a hospital mate of the Royal Hospital in New York in a bureaucratic document of 1779, though he is elevated to the status of a 'surgeon' in the family history.[20] Since this exaggeration clearly did take place, it is reasonable to assume that Robert Nicholls' service in the volunteers may have been elongated, or even invented by family memory, perhaps by confusion with the other brothers. There were certainly a considerable number of these volunteer units formed from Loyalist New Yorkers, all with elaborate names.[21] On the other hand, it is certainly curious that nothing specific is stated for him.

The third son, Samuel (the subject of this book), took a more determined military path, joining an American Loyalist unit as a volunteer.[22] With it he landed on Long Island during Howe's invasion, and took part with it in the battles of Brooklyn and White Plains in 1776, all of which suggest that he joined before the landing took place, when the British forces were camped on Staten Island for some time.

There were lessons in these fights for a young officer. General Howe was a clever tactician, and was able to move his forces back and forth both to confuse and surprise his inexperienced enemy. Washington, however, skilfully withdrew his army from Long Island onto Manhattan Island after the initial defeat. The British followed, in a somewhat leisurely manner, and secured all the city of New York during September and October 1776; at that time Washington pulled out of the city and marched away southwards. During that time the 'Great Fire' burned a large part of the city, including the house and church of the Revd Samuel, and therefore that of his wife and children.[23]

While fighting in the city, of course, the young Auchmuty would have been able to provide good information to his senior officers about the layout of the city, and quite possibly about many of its inhabitants, though the city was hardly unknown to the British Army, and once the city had been taken it seems unlikely that there were many active rebels left. For the young Samuel Auchmuty the destruction of his home was followed a few months later by the death of his father. His mother and sisters at some point moved to England, though perhaps not for a couple of years – their home was in New York and it was firmly under British control. One brother was working in the hospital in New York, and later joined Lord Cornwallis's southern expedition; the other was perhaps in another volunteer unit. There had become progressively less to hold Samuel to New York.

It would seem that the boy (he was only 18 at the time he joined the forces) took to the military life from the start. He was made an ensign in the 45th Regiment of Foot in January 1777, an indication of an intention to become a professional soldier, and not remain just as a volunteer.[24] It would also imply that he had acquitted himself creditably as a private soldier-volunteer.

One of the advantages he had in his military career was his education; he had attended King's College in New York for three years, in effect receiving as close to a university education as was possible in North America at the time, and all his written records exhibit a clear and organised mind. This brought him early military advancement: he was promoted to lieutenant in at some point in 1777.[25] Next year several groups of men of the regiment, together presumably with officers, were transferred into American units, leaving open officers' positions. Samuel's promotion was thus quite likely to be due to the fact that that he apparently did not volunteer to shift into one of these American units. Instead he chose to join the rump, or cadre, of the regiment which was withdrawn to England. (There is no doubt that it was his choice: in such circumstances an American as an officer in a British regiment would certainly be able to choose whether to fight on against his neighbours.) Most of the officers will have transferred to the American units, hoping to gain promotion in the fighting, and those who returned (or went) to Britain were also presumably promoted. The remains of the regiment, only 100-men strong, and including Lieutenant Samuel Auchmuty, landed at Chatham later in 1778.[26]

The New York Auchmutys were therefore, within a year, as scattered by the Revolutionary War as the Bostonian branch. The father was dead, the mother probably remained in New York for a time, seeing it was her home and was under firm British control. Two of their daughters were married, as was her daughter Frances Tucker, and all of them had homes in Kent – the Montresors at Belmont near Faversham, Mary Juliana Mulcaster and her husband at Bishopthorpe, uncle Robert as well, and the Burtons also. One assumes that Samuel will have visited them soon after he landed at Chatham. The youngest daughter Jane was still in America. Of the three sons, all were in some way or other now attached to the British Army, one as a hospital mate in New York, one as a (probably brief and) temporary volunteer, the third as an officer in a regular regiment.

Before following Samuel's career in the British Army, it would be well to tidy up the fortunes of the rest of the family in this period. The youngest daughter, Jane, appears briefly in Philadelphia after that city was taken by General Howe in 1777; her appearance is fleeting, to be sure, but perhaps memorable. The army officers put on an elaborate fete to mark the departure of General Howe back to Britain in June 1778. They called it the 'Meschianza', and it included a mock tournament in which each of the participants fought a joust or two on behalf of a lady. In the list of men involved the first name is that of Colonel Lord Cathcart of the 17th Dragoons, and 'Miss Auchmuty' is his lady.[27] Cathcart was in America with his wife, and his son also took part in the parade though without a lady. Since her sisters were married and away by this time this 'Miss Auchmuty' can only be Jane. She was thus in Philadelphia in 1777–8. She was still only 16, so it seems probable that her mother was also there. However, the army withdrew from the city later in the year, and she and her mother, if she was there, presumably left as well. Eventually she married the Revd Richard Tylden of Milsted near Sittingbourne in Kent as his second wife; their first child was born in 1789, so some years will have passed between her leaving Philadelphia and her marriage.[28] It does not seem that her husband was ever in America, so it may be assumed that she was given refuge, with her mother, in Kent, where her relations were no doubt keen to see her married. Her mother died in 1797 and was buried at Milsted church, so the two women stayed together all through from the death of the Revd Samuel in 1777.[29]

Her brother-in-law, Captain John Montresor, was also in Philadelphia at the time of the occupation; one may well assume that his wife was there with him, though many officers had left their wives in New York (or in England). He was put in charge of constructing the defences of the city, and later was in control of the operations against Fort Mifflin, which blocked British access to the city by the river. (Ironically this fort had been planned and constructed by him in the years before the war began.[30]) All these places were evacuated along with Philadelphia when the British forces left the city later in 1778. Montresor then had the dubious pleasure of destroying the fortifications and works he had designed and built. General Howe resigned his command in May; Montresor could not get along with his successor, General Sir Henry Clinton, and also resigned, then returned to Britain when he purchased a house in London and the estate of Belmont in Kent (not far from the home of Jane's future husband).

Jane's brother Richard Harrison Auchmuty, the hospital orderly, campaigned with Cornwallis in 1780, aiming to retake the Carolinas and Georgia. He was with the army at Yorktown during the siege and was marched away as a prisoner of war when Cornwallis surrendered. There is no doubt that he and Cornwallis were acquainted, though exact evidence is not forthcoming. But Cornwallis was a conscientious commander, and Richard was a nurse ('hospital mate'), and will have been busy during the siege in caring for the numerous sick and wounded. Cornwallis undoubtedly visited the sick and wounded – it was part of the commander's duties – where he will have met Richard. Richard was imprisoned in one of the prisoner-of-war camps at Winchester, Virginia, or at Frederick, Maryland or in Lancaster County, Pennsylvania; he and many of his fellow prisoners died of neglect and starvation – the American treatment of prisoners-of-war was as bad as that of Americans by the British.[31] (If he was at Lancaster it was ironic, for this was the same area where his distant cousin Arthur Gates Auchmuty had first settled several decades before.) Meanwhile, Arthur

Gates's son Samuel was serving in the American Army opposing Cornwallis (and Richard) at Yorktown.

Also serving in the American Army at Yorktown was Henry St George Tucker, as a militia lieutenant colonel, and he wrote one of the clearest accounts of the action.[32] He is a more distant Auchmuty connection, through the Revd Samuel's wife Mary Nicholls Tucker, whose first husband, Thomas Tucker, was a Bermudan sea captain. Like Henry St George, he was a member of the Tucker family which was prominent, if not dominant, in the affairs of Bermuda for over a century.[33] This was another family deeply riven by the American rebellion. The current patriarch was Colonel Henry Tucker, who was Bermuda's agent in London. He had two daughters and four sons. One son, Henry, married the daughter of Governor Bruere of Bermuda and became part of the Bermuda administration, eventually becoming President of the island Council; therefore, a Loyalist. Thomas Tucker had died in 1744 more than five years before his widow had remarried to the Revd Samuel Auchmuty in New York, and his daughter was 5 years old at the time. This would mean that, assuming that their marriage had lasted some years, he himself had been born in the first decade or so of the eighteenth century. (He was probably the son of Henry Tucker (1683–1734) whose wife was called Frances, and who thus brought that name into the family.) He was therefore a member of the second (or third) generation of Tuckers in Bermuda, though it has not been possible to discern precisely his parentage; he had presumably moved away from the island in his capacity as a captain (in the army, it seems) and had, also presumably, settled in New York on or before his marriage.

One of the daughters of Colonel Henry, who was the son of the Henry who died in 1734, was another Frances, and had married a cousin (yet another Henry). He was deeply implicated in a plot to steal the island's supply of gunpowder for the use of the American Army besieging Boston. His brother Henry St George Tucker had moved to Virginia, where he attended the William and Mary College (because it was cheaper than the alternatives), and he had been the instigator of this gunpowder plot. Apparently espousing the rebellion from the beginning, unlike the other members of the family who stayed in Bermuda, he no doubt knew that there was a considerable supply of gunpowder on the island and passed this information on to the Virginia commanders. In accomplishing the theft he was clearly much assisted by the fact that his family was so prominent on the island. It also set the pattern of relations between Bermuda's merchants and the revolution: remaining 'loyal', the merchants also remained more than willing to trade with the rebels. Some were caught, most made profits.[34]

A third brother, Nathaniel Tucker, moved to England, and may therefore have been a Loyalist, though he is said to have written bad poetry in support of the rebels; evidently, however, he wished to stay well clear of the fighting.[35] The fourth brother, Thomas, took the American side, having moved to South Carolina to practise medicine in 1770. He was unsuccessful as a doctor, but became an effective politician, despite (or perhaps because of) a propensity to challenge his opponents to duels. He was elected to the United States' House of Representatives after the war, and was made United States Treasurer by President Jefferson in 1801, holding that position until the advent of Andrew Jackson, another noted dueller, in 1828. His tenure as Treasurer is a record.[36]

Henry St George Tucker became a noted lawyer in Virginia, and his son followed in his footsteps. The sons of Henry, the Loyalist, also prospered, one becoming President of the East India Company, and another a Royal Navy Admiral.[37] How far the Tuckers and the Auchmutys kept in touch is not clear. The connection, after all, was somewhat tenuous. And yet as branches and members in both families rose to prominence it seems quite probable that even if contact had not been maintained, the knowledge of their relationship was acquired. That the Bermuda/Virginia Tucker family was connected with the Auchmutys in Kent is strongly indicated by the recurrence of the Christian names typical of the Tuckers – Thomas, Henry, St George – in the English branch of the Auchmutys.

Robert Nicholls Auchmuty may or may not have been at some time a militia volunteer on the Loyalist side early in the fighting, but he was certainly one of the commissioners of claims acting for the British government in investigating the claims of exiled Loyalists to compensation. His uncle Robert, the former Admiralty judge in Boston, was also active in campaigning in England for compensation for his and others' losses. Possibly the family connection assisted the nephew in gaining his position in Newport. It is curious that he should then have settled back comfortably into Rhode Island life and married there. For some time after the war there continued to be much ill feeling in the newly independent states against the

Loyalists and against Britain, and Robert Nicholls had been both a Loyalist and an employee of the enemy government, and apparently for a time a soldier. He was related also to two men, Robert and the Revd Samuel, who had been reasonably prominent opponents of independence. It would appear that either anti-British feeling in Rhode Island was not particularly strong, or Robert Nicholls was thoroughly conciliatory, and perhaps espoused the rebel cause in public.

Samuel Auchmuty spent the five years of the Revolutionary War with the 45th Foot as a lieutenant, stationed at Chatham for a time. The regiment was, of course, in an emptied-out condition, in which it was intended to attract new recruits. The men who had returned to Britain were the cadre, the officers and non-commissioned officers were to recruit and organise and train their new rank-and-file. Auchmuty was appointed adjutant of the regiment; again this was no doubt a tribute to his education and obvious organisational talents.

The recruitment of a new regiment would take time, but may well have been encouraged by the threat of invasion during 1779, when a Franco-Spanish fleet dominated the western entrance to the English Channel for a month and more. A new Militia Act was passed that year aiming to double the strength of the militia within the country, and at the same time there were offers by various wealthy and titled men to form their own units – sixteen new foot regiments and a regiment of dragoons (the 22nd Light Dragoons) were formed at this time. There was also a strong move to encourage recruiting into established units such as the 45th. In Norfolk the local gentry even asked the War Office to send recruiting parties into the county, not a gesture designed to enhance their popularity. At Nottingham the local idea was to adopt a particular regiment and so encourage local recruitment into it, partly by encouraging local loyalty. A committee was formed of the usual prominent men of the county and this contacted the Secretary at War in London, asking for a regiment to be nominated to which they would so direct their attention. The 45th was nominated, and in August 1779 the various parties of the regiment moved to the city and set about recruiting.[38]

This was in fact the beginning of the territorial regimental system which has theoretically operated in Britain for much of the time since – even the modern shrunken regiments have territorial names. It was also a new stage in the progressive reform and reorganisation of the British Army, an effort which had continued at intervals and fits and starts throughout the eighteenth century. Such measures had regulated the system of promotion by purchase (and the price to be paid), the pay and perquisites of the officers, the stationing of regiments, and the tactics to be employed in battle, among other things.[39] The localisation of the regiments to counties was another stage in that reform, for it seemed that the army would improve if its units acquired a strong loyalty to home localities, mainly the shires, a loyalty which was often much stronger than any theoretical British patriotism. The Nottingham initiative was in effect the beginning of the formal county structure of the army.

Conditions for adopting the name of '1st Nottinghamshire Regiment' were attached to the permission to recruit. The new name could not be used until at least 300 recruits had been raised in the county at the county's expense. To make this achievement more likely to be reached the county committee added 6 guineas to the usual bounty given to recruits. Oxfordshire had also added 6 guineas to the bounty for local recruits, but had spread the recruits so raised through ten different regiments. Nottingham's initiative clearly worked, and the new name was soon officially acquired.[40]

(The county system of regiments was maintained through to the new organisation imposed on the army after the Second World War. It was not, despite the names adopted by the regiments, anywhere near as rigid as it might seem, and one might find men from all over England in any particular county regiment. On the other hand, this organisation was also the basis for the massive recruitment which took place in the early years of the First World War, which produced battalions recruited from towns or workplaces – the Glasgow Tramways, the Grimsby Pals, and so on. In many ways this was a good solution, certainly to recruitment, and the familiarity and camaraderie of men who knew each other is always extremely useful in maintaining unit morale. But in the conditions of warfare in the First World War it could produce local disasters when such battalions charged over open ground against well-dug-in machine guns, and next day the local paper came out with black borders and printed long lists of the dead.[41] This was not of course what was intended by the county system, but the county system certainly produced it.)

Even before the naming of the regiment, the 45th – the numbering of regiments had been one of the fairly recent reforms, adopted in place of using the colonels' names – had apparently succeeded in recruiting its numbers fairly well. The commanding officer, Lieutenant Colonel William Gardiner, had indented to the War Office in July 1779 for 710 stands of arms, which were presumably to be available when the recruits were taken up. A month later Major Henry Knight reported his arrival at Nottingham with three companies of the regiment, and shortly afterwards Captain H.A. Powlett reported that he had brought up the 'additional companies'. It was intended, he said, to send out recruiting parties throughout the country. Samuel Auchmuty will have been in charge of such parties periodically, as were the other regimental lieutenants; in the process he will have seen a good deal of England.[42]

The regiment as a whole, however, did not remain in the county. In 1780 a monthly return (the only one surviving from this period of its history) shows that the regiment was in camp at Warley, west of Birmingham.[43] No doubt the recruiting parties were still operating in Nottinghamshire, but the regiment was clearly needed elsewhere. In 1782 it was in Kent and Sussex, and by that time the recruiting parties had succeeded in filling the regiment's requirements.[44] The method of locating regiments in a geographical area was thus seen to be successful, and it was forthwith applied to all the other regiments of the army.

Lieutenant Samuel Auchmuty is recorded in that monthly return as one of ten lieutenants in the regiment. By that time those officers included, besides the lieutenants, six captains and eight ensigns, together with Lieutenant Colonel Gardiner and Major Knight. (The colonel of the regiment from 1768 to 1785 was Lieutenant General William Haviland.) The arrival of peace in 1783 – though it had been clearly signalled since the defeat at Yorktown two years earlier – was a clear sign that further personal advancement in the army in Britain was highly unlikely for the foreseeable future, for the only way for promotion in peacetime was by purchase, and it is clear that Auchmuty could not afford that route, or by the deaths of more senior officers, and this latter route was much less likely in peacetime. That Auchmuty was in England between 1778 and 1783 is one explanation why he was still a lieutenant, apart from his youth, of course. And in fact the next ten years was one of the most debilitating and dispiriting periods in the history of the British Army, when the memory of the American defeat sapped the morale of officers and men, and financial retrenchment imposed by the government reduced recruiting to minimum numbers. For officers hoping for promotion the way was blocked by a superfluity of officers in the lists above them. There were just two ways forward: to purchase an advance by buying out another officer willing to sell, or India. For Samuel Auchmuty, living on his officer's pay, the first was out of the question. So, perforce, India became his choice.

Also stationed in the south-east of England not far from the Nottinghamshires, was the 52nd Foot, which was under orders for India by early 1783. This was another regiment which had served in America in the early years of the war, and had, like the 45th, seen its soldiers drafted away to make up the numbers in other regiments, while its officers had been returned to Britain at much the same time as those of the 45th, in order to recruit their numbers up to strength; it had been assigned as the Oxfordshire Regiment in the renaming and localising reform the year before which the 45th had begun. Now about 1,000 strong in the rank-and-file, it was beginning to embark for India.[45] No doubt, with such similar histories, the two regiments became acquainted, and in July 1783 Samuel Auchmuty exchanged posts with a lieutenant in that regiment who was unwilling to go East. The exchange was officially recorded on 21 July, though at least part of the 52nd had already sailed for India in March.[46] India was to be the home of Samuel Auchmuty for the next fourteen years, and the making of him as a soldier.

He left just as trouble was building for his Montresor relations. His brother-in-law John Montresor had returned to Britain, at much the same time as Samuel, after his disagreement with Sir Henry Clinton. Then he bought a house in Portland Place in London, and his country house, Belmont near Faversham in Kent. This display of wealth did not initially alert anyone to a problem, but in 1783, as the American war wound down, it became clear that there had been extensive corruption in the army which had served across the Atlantic. Montresor had had the use of large funds for his department. He was required to submit a statement of his accounts, and was then judged to have claimed £50,000 in expenses to which he was not entitled.[47] It may have been a more political discovery, following on from the defeat. It was normal for men in charge of money and supplies to profit from their position, even to the extent of becoming wealthy. Montresor may well have been accused because the government was feeling the financial pinch, and was looking for someone to blame.

The dispute over this continued for the rest of Montresor's life and after – he died in 1799 still owing large amounts to the government – though he was still able to put his sons through military school in France while the argument went on. At the same time, of course, Samuel's uncle Robert was disputing with the same government Audit Office over the extent of compensation due to him and his fellow exiles for their losses. Acquiring such compensation had been part of the peace terms, but with the new United States impoverished as a result of the fighting, and the individual states unwilling to consider compensation, it proved impossible to recover any money from there. It may well be that Samuel's move to India, besides being a matter of ambition, was also a way of evading involvement in these unpleasant disagreements – and, of course, service with the East India Company's forces was a well understood way to wealth at Indian expense. A man could find his career seriously blighted by association with relatives who were in bad odour with the government.

Chapter 3

India, 1783–97

The 52nd (Oxfordshire) Regiment of Foot arrived in India late in 1783, and immediately suffered a disaster when the transport *Kingston* blew up off Madras; many of the 200 men, women, and children on board were killed. Lieutenant Auchmuty, as the regiment's adjutant, was no doubt involved in the aftermath and the subsequent inquiry. The regiment was stationed thereafter in the Coromandel region, on the south-east coast of India, not far from Madras. It arrived, in fact, just in time to take part in the closing stages of the Second Mysore War, which had begun in 1780.

The Mysore War was one of the main reasons for sending more British forces to India in the 1780s. It was part of a long-running, but intermittent, conflict with the Raja Haidar Ali of Mysore, who had developed Mysore into a vigorous kingdom which came to dominate southern India, and which had grown in power since the former Hindu dynasty had been pushed aside by Haidar Ali, who had been the previous sultan's commander-in-chief. He had succeeded in annexing or dominating several of the neighbouring minor states, and in building a formidable military power. Mysore's strength had by the late 1770s developed into a clear challenge to the East India Company.

Until 1707 most of India had been controlled by the Mughal emperors fairly efficiently, if with a good deal of indiscriminate brutality, but in 1707 the long-reigning Shahanshah Aurangzeb died, and for the next twelve years there were constant disputes over the succession, during which there were no less than eleven emperors.[1] Immediately the dispute began the empire's cohesion suffered, and it was quickly revealed that many of the preceding local dynasties supposedly conquered and suppressed by the Mughals had survived and were now capable of reasserting their independence; in addition various officials of the empire tore off sections of the empire and also made themselves independent sovereigns, though often retaining the Mughal title of Nawab (governor). The result was widespread political turbulence and frequent warfare. And in the process the English East India Company expanded its territory at everybody's expense. India therefore by the 1780s, when Auchmuty and the 52nd arrived, was a complex of independent states of which the Company was one of the more powerful, controlling some substantial areas, such as Bengal and the Sarkars, or in other areas single cities, such as Madras or Bombay. For the next two decades it was not at all clear which, if any, of the competing states would prevail, or if the country would remain divided, and just who would survive. The possibility existed of a single conqueror emerging. Mysore was one of these resurfacing survivors, and one of the most aggressive empire builders, though the Marathas had secured the greatest extent of territory.

The Company therefore was one of the contenders for power and territory, and was by no means the most likely to prevail or conquer. The largest territorial state was that of the Marathas, but it was very loosely built. Under the command of recent governors, notably Robert Clive and Warren Hastings, the Company had secured fairly extensive territories and revenues, but its personnel were less than loyal to it, and were primarily interested in looting the country for their personal benefit – they were therefore quite typical of officials in other Indian states in their ambition. And by the 1770s the Company was undergoing an internal crisis of its own. The problems of government and loyalty which the North American war had revealed, and the difficulties of keeping control of events at a distance, which that crisis had shown, were so large and difficult for the British government in London, and were replicated in the case of India. The distance from Britain – a six-month voyage each way, as the 52nd Foot had just experienced – and the intermediation of the Company's own authority between the British government and the Company's 'servants' in India made control exceedingly difficult. Further, the general unwillingness of the Company's military commanders to obey any instructions which conflicted with their own more personal aims emphasised the same difficulties of exercising control over India from Britain as had just led to the loss of the North American colonies. In Britain, also, there was the added complication that the government and servants of the East India Company were widely perceived as wholly corrupt, and that the Company's acquisition of an army and an empire was a perversion of its original purpose. The danger of a British collapse in India was thought to be as great as it had proved to be in America; as if that was not enough, it was also feared that the Company was exercising too much power in Britain, where a number of its wealthy ex-servants bought seats in Parliament.[2]

The Second Mysore War was one of the triggers of concern in Britain. The war was being fought as the 52nd Foot sailed south through the Atlantic and then east across the Indian Ocean. It had begun in 1780, and two serious defeats had been suffered by the Company's army, in 1780 and 1782; these were part of the reason the regiment was being sent to India. The Mysore kingdom had expanded and so was in contact with other major successor states in the region. The Nizam of Hyderabad controlled a large territory to the north, the kingdom of the Carnatic under the Nawab of Arcot lay to the east (and had been brought largely under the Company's suzerainty in the 1750s); to the north-west was the extensive Maratha kingdom, rather dispersed, but with the Maratha chief, the Peshwa, ruling from Poona, not far from Mysore's border. A series of precariously independent cities and states survived along the Malabar (west) coast, including Portuguese Goa and the Company's port of Bombay. Behind all of these lay two regions under Company control, the Presidencies of Madras and Bombay, both small in area, but supposedly potent in military power.

In this Second War (the first had been a brief affair in the 1760s) Haidar Ali had gathered together an alliance of those southern Indian powers at the beginning, but the diplomacy of the Governor-General Warren Hastings had successfully detached the Nizam, and the Peshwa was unenthusiastic; the military ability of Major General Sir Eyre Coote eventually brought about the defeat of the Mysorean armies by 1783. (There was also a maritime war against a French squadron until the news arrived of the Peace of Paris in 1783.) By the time the 52nd Foot arrived, late in that year, the fighting had been largely superseded by diplomatic negotiations for peace. No doubt the arrival of British reinforcements had some considerable influence on the conclusion of those negotiations. Haidar Ali's son Tipu – Haidar Ali had died in 1782 – was equally as fierce and capable an enemy as his father, if rather more erratic.

One of the more significant events of the war was the arrival of unanticipated British reinforcements. This was a force which had been intended to capture the Dutch colony of the Cape of Good Hope, but the overall naval commander, Commodore George Johnstone, had been dilatory and careless, so that the French had been able to reinforce the Cape garrison before the British expeditionary force arrived. Johnstone wanted to use his force to attack the Spaniards at the River Plate, but the army commander, Major General Sir William Medows, interpreted his instructions differently, and insisted that he must sail on to India, where he knew there was fighting. The troops he brought were useful, but he himself was unwilling to become involved with the poisonous relations between the various Company officials, and refused the overall command which was offered to him.[3]

It was in part the troops brought by Medows which permitted Coote to win his battles, but the event also has a relevance for Auchmuty. Medows, like so many British officers of the time, had fought in North America, specifically at New York in 1776, where Auchmuty joined the army as a volunteer; Medows was wounded at the Battle of Brandywine, and returned to Britain to recuperate; they thus shared these experiences. Also relevant is Medows' reaction to being offered the overall command. It was unusual, to say the least, for a general to refuse such an appointment; it was in part a revulsion at the condition of the Company's administration, but it was also just as much a personal reluctance to take the responsibility. Auchmuty no doubt met Medows, who returned to India as a governor of Bombay in 1788; they may even have met in America.

The 52nd was thus not directly involved in the Mysore War, having arrived too late to participate, but it was used in the aftermath in taking a fort on Mount Dilly at Cannanore on the Malabar coast, where a local dispute arising from the greater war had led to the capture and imprisonment of some of the Company's soldiers; they had been shipwrecked and then seized, and imprisoned by the lady Raja Junumabe Adi Raja Bibi II. The regiment was cantoned more permanently for the next years on the eastern side of southern India, in the neighbourhood of Madras.[4]

Meanwhile Parliament had followed the conclusion of peace with Britain's European enemies in 1783 with a new India Act.[5] The Company's conduct had been a political matter in Britain for three decades, ever since the conquest of Bengal and the sudden enrichment of the Company and its servants, and the British government was slowly expanding its distant control over the Company's Indian activities. Now a new overseeing system was installed in London by the consent of Parliament. The new Board of Control was formed half of the Company's Directors and half of unpaid Privy Councillors appointed by the British government. The catch, from the Company's point of view, was that the President of the Board of Control, who was a member of the government in London, had the casting vote if there was a disagreement between these two bodies; he also had the greater political weight as a member of the Cabinet.[6] So all that remained was for a sufficiently forceful and cunning politician to be made President of the Board of Control. William Pitt, the Prime Minister who devised the new system, had just the man, Henry Dundas, one of the master politicians of the time, the controller of the electoral system in Scotland, and an enthusiast for empire. His influence and ability in effect made him the Minister for the Company, and hence for the Indian territories, in the Cabinet.[7]

This new system soon made itself felt in India.[8] The Governor-General was appointed by the Directors, but they required the consent of the Board of Control – that is, the British government – and the Governor-General's own council was reduced to just three members, one of whom was the Commander-in-Chief. This scheme was also applied in the Bombay and Madras Presidencies, each of which had a Governor and Council, and a local Commander-in-Chief as one of its three members. These two lesser Presidencies were also now made specifically subordinate to the Governor-General's council in Calcutta. This seemed to leave the Company running affairs from London, as before, but on a tighter rein, and it also gave the British government new supervisory, even controlling, powers, but it also put the Governor-General, who from now on was usually a British government appointee, in overall control in India from Calcutta; the Governors in Bombay and Madras also became London appointees.[9]

Just as it was the person of the President of the Board of Control in London which was crucial to the British government's direction of Indian matters, so the person of the Governor-General in Calcutta was crucial to establishing control over the affairs of the Company in India itself, and in the direction of the Company's political powers in India. The first task, as seen from London, was to clean up the system in India, which had become a process for enriching individual officials and officers, to the cost of the Indian peasantry and princes, and of the Company. Since one of the major sources of this corruption had been the wars conducted by the Company, the Governor-General was expressly forbidden to indulge in any aggression, though in the competitive world of Indian states this would hardly prevent wars, and anyway was largely disregarded by all the Governors-General;

they could also claim an emergency and the inability to receive advice and instruction from Britain. In times of war the allowances, '*batta*', paid to officers doubled, and sometimes quadrupled; the example of the 'nabobs' who had started out as clerks, and who returned from India enriched to the point where they could buy country houses and seats in Parliament, and of military officers, such as Auchmuty's brother-in-law Captain Montresor, who had enriched themselves from public funds during the American War, were notorious contemporary examples.

The first Governor-General to be appointed under the new system was Lord Cornwallis, and since he was simultaneously Commander-in-Chief it was presumed that no 'accidental' wars would take place. He had been courted for the position by every British administration between 1782 and 1786 but, like other candidates, he had insisted that the 'no war' aspect be modified by legislation which in effect indemnified him in advance from any blame for indulging in any fighting. He also, as did other candidates, required that he be appointed as both Governor-General and Commander-in-Chief, which would in effect put the civil administration above the military. As a distinguished soldier, of course, his credentials as Commander-in-Chief were very strong.[10] The negotiations which were undertaken to persuade him to take up the office left India out on a limb for several years, which did not help, though it did enable the Second Mysore War to be concluded well before Cornwallis arrived.

Lieutenant Auchmuty spent those years with the 52nd Regiment in and about Madras. He was involved, as most officers were, with the many problems of the military in India, though he seems always to have restrained any feelings of the superiority of the military over the civilian arm of the state. It is possible that he was influenced in this by repugnance at the conditions of his homeland, where groups of officers of the victorious army of the rebels, some of them grouped into the Cincinnati Society, were implying that they should have a major role in affairs merely because they were officers, and there were rebellions against the government of the rebel state taking place – the Whiskey Rebellion, for example. But Auchmuty had by now spent several years in Britain, and he was in a king's regiment, not one of those raised by the Company, and the ethos of the royal army was very different from that of the Company. The subordination of the military to civilian authority was already deeply ingrained in the British Army, where the officers had enlisted mainly for reasons other than their pay; he could see the difference with the Company's men, who were all mercenaries. It was an issue which he would have to face later in his career, but it would seem that his opinion had been formed very early on. It seems that he had remained in contact with members of his family who were still in the new United States and this will therefore have made him aware of the troubles of the new republic.[11]

Of the three Indian Presidencies, Madras was, in fact, the least savoury – or rather perhaps, the most unsavoury of them. It had been swamped from the beginning of its existence in bribery, extortion, and the avid acquisition of wealth by any and all officers; the servants of the Company had their hooks into the Nawabs of Arcot – Wala Jah Muhammad Ali until 1795, then his son Umdut al-Umara and they were milking them of their and the kingdom's wealth with greedy enthusiasm.

The new Madras Governor, Lord Macartney, was the first non-Company appointee to such a position, and took office in 1781. He spent much of his time in office arguing with, or quarrelling with, or in dispute with, several other high officials, in particular General Sir Eyre Coote, his Commander-in-Chief, and the Governor-General Warren Hastings, whose overthrow and later impeachment by Parliament was in part the result of revelations by Macartney of the treatment of the Nawab, though in this Macartney had been as culpable as anyone. When he returned to London Macartney recommended several of the changes which were incorporated in the new India Act. A good deal of his trouble was probably his own fault – he fought duels both in India and in London. He was one of the men who was in consideration to be Hastings' successor as Governor-General, and in fact had been appointed to that position when he resigned his post at Madras and set off for England. As a result he refused the post, which went to Cornwallis.[12]

While at Madras he was involved in a bitter dispute with the other generals who operated as Madras Commanders-in-Chief, not only Coote. The result was that Macartney dismissed Major-General James Stuart as Commander-in-Chief (Coote's successor) for disobedience, thus making a strong stand on the question of the superiority of civil authority, even if the dispute was as much personal as institutional. But when he tried to appoint Major-General Sir John Burgoyne as Commander-in-Chief in his place, Burgoyne insisted that he was still under Stuart's authority. Macartney put Stuart under arrest to prevent him issuing any orders, and when Burgoyne countermanded some of Macartney's own orders he was also put under arrest and subjected to a court martial.[13] It was an early object lesson for Auchmuty of the lack of discipline of the Company's officers, and that they invariably put their own personal, or collective, interests before anything else; their loyalty to the Company was easily trumped by their own concerns.

No one could thus claim that matters in Madras did not require reform. Burgoyne was court-martialled, but, given who his judges were, was inevitably acquitted. Lieutenant Auchmuty was one of the officers who took part, though we only know of this because his claim for personal expenses (200 pagodas) took so long to be paid that he had to petition Governor-General Cornwallis for payment.[14] The result of the petition is not known; nor is it known if the earlier personal relations of the Viceroy with the Auchmuty family had an effect on his appointment.

Madras was then clearly the Presidency most in need of serious attention by a broom-wielding Governor-General like Cornwallis, but Bombay and Bengal also required his attention. The Bombay Presidency, for example, was so deeply in debt it could no longer seek loans and had had to ask that its forces not be employed in the conflict with Tipu of Mysore. Tipu, in turn, had clearly sensed Bombay's weakness, and had imposed an embargo on the export of spices from Malabar, which was the principal source of Bombay's income.[15] He had begun to develop a major naval base at Mangalore, from which he would be able to interrupt Bombay's sea routes, and communicate with possible allies – he attempted to contact the Ottoman Empire in 1796.[16] Part of Cornwallis' brief was to wield the broom to clean out the corruption, a process which would necessarily remove the corrupt British officers, but it would also in the process set the Company administration on a much firmer foundation. For unless this was done, and was seen clearly in London to have been done, even if this was not so obvious to those enjoying their perquisites and bribes in India, the whole Company system would collapse.

Cornwallis certainly clamped down on costs, and dismissed all, or at least many of, those tainted by the old corrupt system. He also installed a new system of appointments which had the effect of excluding almost all Indians from the administration, since the ultimate control exercised by the Governor-General was dismissal and sending dismissed officials 'home'.[17] The old prohibition on officials indulging in private trade was to be rigorously enforced, and to compensate for the losses this would entail the official salaries being necessarily increased – for the main reason for the private trading was that the pay the Company provided was inadequate. Cornwallis also attended to the separation of the commercial and political affairs of the Company, to devising a permanent system of land taxation (which turned the tax collectors, the zamindars, into landlords, though not intentionally), and finally, despite the prohibitions included in the India Act, and in Cornwallis' own instructions, he was compelled to go to war.[18]

Lieutenant Auchmuty and the 52nd were in the Madras area from 1784 onwards, and in that time Auchmuty, as well as participating in General Burgoyne's court martial in 1785, operated as the regiment's adjutant, in effect its administrator, no doubt in part as a result of his superior education – he must have been one of the few officers of his rank with what amounted to a university education.[19] In November 1788 he was promoted to captain in the 75th Foot. This was one of four new regiments which had been raised in Britain for Indian service, as a means of boosting the royal army's presence there, without reducing the army in Britain.[20] Its commander, Colonel Robert Abercromby, had raised it and had then brought it out to India. He was, by no coincidence, both a Scot and a relative of the politician Henry Dundas, who was notorious for promoting his fellow countrymen.

The regiment was clearly in need of experienced officers – probably some of the original officers died as soon as the regiment arrived in India, but as a new unit it will in any case have been short of officers experienced in Indian conditions. Its private soldiers were also no doubt short not only of experience of any sort or army capability at soldiering. So a man who had been adjutant of a regiment in India for several years was clearly a prize to be captured.

Auchmuty also acted as Abercromby's Brigade Major at Bombay – Abercromby had come out in advance of the regiment.[21] Promotion to captain and so to the command of a company in the 75th had clearly been sufficient to persuade Auchmuty to move; the appointment as Brigade Major, essentially another administrative position, was no doubt in part a result of the efficiency he had displayed as regimental adjutant. (His promotion to captain was not a matter of purchase, but, like his move to the 52nd in 1783, the opportune choice of a man alert to the chances of advancement without it.) It is also possible that he and Abercromby had been acquainted in North America, and a distant Scottishness may have influenced Abercromby as well. (Abercromby, like Medows, had been in the fighting at New York and Brandywine, and then on until Yorktown, where Auchmuty's brother had been a medical attendant.) Abercromby was soon made Major General and was appointed as Lieutenant Governor and Commander-in-Chief of the Bombay Presidency in 1790. Auchmuty continued as a member of his staff, and both men therefore took part in the Third Mysore War which began in that year.[22]

One of the triggers for the outbreak of this war was the posting of two battalions of the Company's troops into Hyderabad, where they replaced some of the Nizam's own forces. Tipu correctly saw this as a threat, since the Nizam's purpose was to recover Balaghat, a territory which Mysore had acquired from him, and which he now wanted the Company to help him recover. There was a treaty between the Company and the Nizam mandating this, but to do so would, of course, provoke Tipu to war. Cornwallis was trapped in a dilemma, and inevitably chose to support the Nizam, who was the less threatening of the two 'country powers', and fairly closely under the Company's influence.

Tipu was therefore clearly under notice. His territories were, it seemed, threatened by British power emanating from Madras to the east, out of Bombay to the north, and now from Hyderabad to the north-east: that is, the kingdom was in the process of being encircled. The presence of the Company's battalions in the Nizam's territory was also a demonstration that the Nizam was a military ally of the Company, as was, of course, the Nawab of Arcot in Coromandel; the territories of both of these rulers bordered on Mysore. Tipu in turn was encroaching on the territories of the small states and cities between his western boundary along the Western Ghats and the Malabar coast – where his embargo on exports to Bombay was in part designed to establish his clear domination over the kingdom of Cochin, the several Dutch posts on the coast, the French port at Mahe, and the British port at Tellicherry. He had already been warned by the President of Madras, General Sir Archibald Campbell, that any attack on the kingdom of Travancore, the last independent state along that coast, would be regarded by the Company as a declaration of war. Both Mysore and Travancore had been actively fortifying their joint frontier, and Travancore had developed a 40-mile line of bastions linked by a deep ditch and a rampart along its northern boundary, connecting the coast and the mountains of the Ghats.[23]

The problem therefore was not that Cornwallis was prohibited from declaring war, but that both the Company and he were manoeuvring for advantage, collecting allies, arming, and moving troops. This sort of activity would almost invariably result in conflict, and who began the fighting was essentially irrelevant.

Beyond that general situation, Tipu, believing himself both surrounded and threatened, and Cornwallis, who was clearly intent on containing him, if not necessarily going to war, were in fact largely in the hands of subordinates who were barely under either man's control. In 1789 Tipu faced a rebellion among his recently acquired subjects in Cochin and Malabar in the coastal territory north of Travancore, and having suppressed the rebellion he prepared to follow the fleeing refugees into both Cochin, which was one of his own vassal states, and into Travancore, which was not. He was warned again from Madras not to attack Travancore, but he chose to ignore the warning, in part because he realised that the new Governor at Madras, John Hollond, was not serious in his threats. Campbell had gone home. However, Cornwallis was certainly serious about constraining Tipu's adventures, and had prepared for a war which he realised, as soon as the Company's battalions had been handed over to the Nizam, was probably inevitable.[24]

Tipu, of course, had a good deal of justification for his actions, given that his enemies had been given refuge in Travancore by the Maharaja Kartika Tirunal Rama Varna, who had ruled since 1758, had built the fortified lines, and surely knew exactly what he was doing in the crisis. It is fairly clear also that Cornwallis was keen for a war – he had been discussing the possibility since he arrived.[25] However, he was to some extent limited by his instructions, as well as foxed for a time by the complexity of the treaties he had inherited. But he had also inherited a very unstable situation in southern India which could probably only be resolved by a war. It was therefore necessary for him to be able to justify the war by pointing to Tipu's aggressions. The failure of Hollond at Madras to make it as clear as Campbell to Tipu that his attack on Travancore would provoke a war, meant that Tipu went ahead and actually launched an attack, calling Hollond's bluff; his problem then was that he was defeated by the Maharaja of Travancore at the fortified lines.

Hollond then began negotiations, to Cornwallis' annoyance, but was replaced and ejected by the arrival of the new governor at Madras, none other than General William Medows.[26] Medows' arrival assuaged Cornwallis' annoyance, and it signalled clearly to Tipu that a new war with the Company was approaching. Medows' installation as Governor at Madras, together with that of Abercromby at Bombay – both of them military men and both in 1790 (Medows had been Abercromby's predecessor at Bombay) – gave Cornwallis much greater control over policy, and over the British territories in southern India, and over the military in the area, than any previous Governor-General had had. On the other hand, Cornwallis took a clear-eyed view of these two soldiers, understanding that they were capable men when in direct command of troops, but that both required superior direction.[27]

Medows, formerly of Bombay and now Madras, and so fully familiar with the conditions, produced a plan against Mysore which involved simultaneous invasions from three directions: he would march the Madras Army to the Coimbatore area, south of Mysore, gather up supplies there, and then attack Mysore from the south, through the mountains along its southern border. Abercromby would move south from Bombay along the Malabar coast and penetrate through the Western Ghats into Mysorean territory. A force sent by Cornwallis from the Bengal Army would take station inland from Madras, and then attack Mysore from the east. Cornwallis was not happy with a plan demanding so much distant coordination, but let it go ahead. Leading a great, slow, lumbering army, Medows collected his forces at Trichinopoly and then marched towards Coimbatore, capturing a set of poorly defended forts on the way. Coimbatore was taken late in July 1790 and from there several detachments captured the nearby forts; Auchmuty's former unit, the 52nd Foot, was in action at Dindigul and Palghat. Medows, in attacking these places, had therefore already caused one division of his forces, and now he had detachments spread out from Coimbatore into several garrisons during the monsoon, and set them to attacking the lesser places under Tipu's control. In effect he had come to a halt. He was no nearer Seringapatam at Coimbatore than he had been at Madras or Trichinopoly.

Tipu had used the time while Medows was advancing along his southern border to raid directly eastwards into the Carnatic, hoping to draw Medows back eastwards; now he came south through the passes, drove the British garrison from the first fort he came to, captured its guns and supplies, and then set about raiding and harassing Medows' communications. Meanwhile the detachment of the Bengal Army which had been sent to assist him, commanded by Colonel Maxwell, had advanced due west from Madras. Deterred by an unsuccessful but fierce Mysorean attack Maxwell changed his route southwards and brought his force to join Medows, who was vainly lumberingly following Tipu's agile cavalry. Tipu again raided into the Carnatic, reaching as far as the French post at Pondicherry on the coast.[28]

Cornwallis secured the active cooperation of the Nizam and of the Maratha Peshwa at Poona, so that, with Abercromby from Bombay, three allied invasions came down on Mysore from the north. A large Maratha Army with a small British force attached, moving slowly, set a siege to the weak fort at Dharwar, just inside Tipu's northern boundary, and lingered on there for over six months before capturing it; the conquest of this region was the Marathas' aim in the war – it had been theirs earlier. The second invasion came south along the Malabar coast from Bombay, along the narrow coastal plain. It was commanded by General Abercromby, no doubt with Brigade Major Auchmuty in attendance. This was a successful move, partly because this was in part the region which had rebelled against Tipu at the start of the war; by December one part of this force had taken Calicut, and another, under Abercromby himself, defeated a Mysorean force at Cannanore.[29] The point about this campaign is, of course, that, along with Travancore, it meant that Tipu's sea communications were severed – and that included cutting off the revenues from the port duties and intercepting any overseas sources of supplies. He had already attempted to interest the French at Pondicherry in his cause during his raid into the Carnatic but without obvious success.[30] Even unofficial contacts were also now impossible.[31] The third invasion was by the Nizam's forces, but, like the Marathas at Dharwar, they moved unenthusiastically and made only a very limited advance, moving from Hyderabad. Both the Nizam and the Marathas had strictly limited and precise war aims in terms of territory, and were sensibly quite unwilling to become too involved in fighting Tipu's more efficient forces while the British were still unsuccessful in their own main attack.

Cornwallis came south and took over the command, much to Medows' relief. The new plan was to disregard the indirect approach which Medows had used, and to march directly for Seringapatam from the east, even though the route lay through well-populated and well-fortified territory.

There followed a classic display of misdirection by Cornwallis as he feinted here and there until Tipu had no idea where the Madras Army was, or where it was going; eventually Cornwallis shifted to a northerly route which was wholly unexpected, but which permitted him to join up with the allied forces of the Nizam, and with some of the Mahrattas, both coming from the north. Meanwhile Abercromby from the west coast began advancing eastwards, bringing some more of the Marathas along with him. The plan was that the two main forces would join at Seringapatam and lay siege to the city. Cornwallis besieged Bangalore, one of Tipu's main cities, and took it after six weeks, having beaten off several relieving attacks. This victory convinced his northern allies that a British conquest was now quite likely and they began to join in more numerously and more reliably, though the Nizam's forces were regarded as a liability, given their predilection for looting and ravaging, thereby destroying possible supplies and alienating the population.

A slow, deliberate advance brought Cornwallis' forces to Seringapatam, but by the time he arrived, he was hampered by a severe shortage of supplies, which Abercromby's contingent were supposed to relieve. Abercromby, with Auchmuty, was actually quite close, but Tipu had successfully intercepted his messengers, so that Cornwallis, believing that no assistance was available, broke up the siege and retreated; three days later the Mahrattas and Abercromby joined him, but it was now too late. As Cornwallis and Abercromby retreated, respectively eastwards and westwards, Tipu turned south to retake Coimbatore, though this took him until November.[32]

In preparation for a renewed attack on Seringapatam, Cornwallis cleared and widened his route of approach from Madras by capturing the forts and towns between Bangalore and his target; a major and more reliable supply system could then be set up, and a detailed investigation, by means of spies, brought him a greater and more accurate knowledge of Tipu's forces. The final advance began late in January 1792, with Cornwallis marching from Bangalore, and Abercromby coming over the Western Ghats again from Malabar.

Auchmuty was with Abercromby's force, and on the way he wrote to a friend, Captain John A. Byron, who had been invalided home. Byron had been awarded prize money from the capture of Cannanore and Auchmuty sent on the order for payment with his letter. He commented that their second expedition was better supplied and equipped than the first, and he expected to be soon at Seringapatam – Cornwallis, he had heard, was besieging Savandroog, a powerful hillfort halfway between Bangalore and Seringapatam. He complained, as soldiers normally do, about a lack of cooperation by the fleet, including a comment that the Commodore had sent the *Thames* to England without telling the army; this meant that his letter was later than he had intended.[33]

This is the first, and almost the only, personal letter by Auchmuty which survives, though some others are known in extracts – most of his letters we have are official. A further point of interest is that this Captain Byron was in fact the father of the poet Lord Byron, and was known not only as a Royal Navy officer but as 'Mad Jack', and was notorious for marrying rich aristocratic women and dissipating their fortunes.[34] The £41 being sent on to him as prize money would probably not have lasted him for very long, and in fact he was already dead by the time Auchmuty was writing his letter. Auchmuty's letter, written in his neat and legible hand, with correct spelling and grammar and punctuation (making him most unusual among officers either naval or military at that time) shows no indication of any criticism of Byron's lifestyle – perhaps Auchmuty knew nothing of him except by his earlier contact in India – but he was clearly friendly and recalled pleasant times in India earlier.

The two armies invading Mysore from east and west successfully joined forces to form the siege of Seringapatam in mid-February, though the shorter march of Abercromby's army, from the Malabar coast, had been the more difficult, and thus had taken longer; within less than two weeks Tipu began negotiations for peace.[35] (Cornwallis and Abercromby thus renewed an acquaintance which had last existed at the Battle of Yorktown; no doubt Abercromby would have introduced Brigade Major Auchmuty to the Commander-in-Chief, though they had probably been acquainted already during the court martial of General Burgoyne. He may well have recalled that unusual name as that of the hospital mate at Yorktown.[36])

Each of the allies took a slice of Mysore in the peace terms to which Tipu had to submit, but from his point of view the most serious element was the fact that the Company acquired territory on several sides of his kingdom, including Malabar, and the suzerainty over Coorg, which gave the British access to the best pass between the coast and Tipu's remaining territories; the other annexations were the Dindigul region, on Mysore's southern boundary, and the Baramahal area to the east, all territories designed to make Mysore more accessible to British power. But Tipu was able to retain Bangalore on the west coast, and there he soon began to develop a major naval force. Since he had felt surrounded earlier, this was now not just a matter of allies of the Company surrounding him – Marathas, Arcot, Travancore, the Nizam – but now he was enclosed by the lands of the British East India Company itself. His room for manoeuvre was decisively reduced.

This was the moment at which Lord Cornwallis gave up his position as Governor-General and Commander-in-Chief. He sailed for Britain early in 1793. His successors separated his two posts. Sir John Shore, a Company man who had retired to England and was now persuaded to return, became Governor-General; Sir Robert Abercromby transferred from Bombay to become the Commander-in-Chief of India. Auchmuty went with him to Calcutta, acting at first as his Deputy Adjutant General, in effect as his chief of staff and secretary.

When he arrived in Britain, Cornwallis was asked to devise a scheme for the reform of the Indian Army, which was recognised to have substantial problems; it was hoped that a process of reorganisation and reform would solve them. His recommendation was that all the British officers and men in the Company army should be regarded as king's soldiers, and paid and treated and disciplined accordingly – they would thus also be on the same ladder for promotion, an improvement above all for many Company officers who failed to get any real promotion while senior officers tended to stay in theoretically active commands until a great age. The Indian part of the army would then be regarded as a separate force. This was roughly accepted by Dundas and the British government, but it created a large problem for Shore and Abercromby.[37]

In Calcutta Captain Auchmuty was Deputy Adjutant General of the Bengal Army, and was promoted steadily over the next years until he became Lieutenant Colonel and his deputy status as Adjutant General became permanent.[38] On leaving Bombay and the 75th, he sold his captaincy to his colleague in the regiment, Lieutenant Lachlan Macquarie. During the next several years we have a number of letters sent by Captain, later Major, Macquarie (who nearly two decades later became a notable governor of New South Wales – to be succeeded by Colonel Richard Bourke who had been at Montevideo; see Chapter 6). Macquarie's letters claim friendship, but are overwhelmingly devoted to soliciting promotion or a better situation for himself. The two men had clearly become acquainted at Bombay, after their early meeting as Macquarie's ship arrived – 'Major Auchmuty came on board'. Auchmuty's move to Calcutta and his close situation beside the Commander-in-Chief clearly made him a suitable target for importunity. Unfortunately we do not have Auchmuty's replies.[39] No doubt he also received numerous similar letters from other officers, acquaintances, or strangers.

The move to Calcutta brought Abercromby (and Auchmuty) into the midst of the slowly evolving crisis of army reform which followed Cornwallis's recommendations, and which occupied much of Abercromby's time as Commander-in-Chief. Abercromby was also ill, an infection he had acquired which eventually made him blind. The new Governor-General was sympathetic, but could do little until clarity was available from London, which took two years to emerge. Cornwallis' predilection for reform in India had been clear all along – he had made serious progress in taxation, land reform, and the law as well as subduing corruption.[40] Since the army had scarcely been touched during that time it was not difficult to suspect that an army reform package would soon appear, and soon rumours spread among the officers that Cornwallis on his way to England was devising a reform of the army in India; the officers in India heard rumours, then reported them to their agents in London, who worked to discover – and to thwart – the changes.[41] In London it cannot have been a secret that Cornwallis, whether or not he worked on the reform on board ship, had been asked by Dundas to present his suggestions to the Board of Control. A committee of Indian officers in England formed itself to find out what was going on, to lobby about it, and to keep their colleagues in India informed.

Shore and Abercromby took up their offices in the wake of Cornwallis' earlier reforms, which themselves were scarcely yet fully accepted or implemented and worked out. And at once an imperial crisis also developed to add to the internal one brewing in the army. The British territories in Bengal and northern India had fuzzy boundaries. To the west was the kingdom of Oudh, one of the territories detached into independence by a former Mughal official, ruled at the time by the Nawab Asaf-ud-Daulah. It occupied a strategic territory between the British territories in Bengal and the lands outside easy British reach (at least so far) further to the west. The

Nawab had been assisted in the 1770s to expand his territory eastwards at the expense of the Rohillas, who occupied a stretch of territory north-west of Delhi.

The Rohillas were by origin Afghan and Turkish raiders who had arrived partly as allies of the Mughal Emperor in the early 1700s, and partly in the wake of a series of invasions from Persia and Afghanistan in the 1760s. They had not given up their undisciplined and violent ways since then. The Company had helped to push Oudh's boundary eastwards at their expense, and this provided some protection for Oudh, and reduced the Rohillas' capacity for unpleasant raids eastwards, though those raids which did take place had been deflected, and were now directed elsewhere. In 1788 they had occupied the imperial capital of Delhi and looted the city; in the process they had seized the person of the Mughal Emperor Shah Alam II and blinded him. They were raiders, not conquerors, and were detested by all their neighbours. On the other hand, their activities were useful for the British who could cynically stand as protectors of their victims, such as Oudh, while not doing anything actively to discourage the Rohillas – a process of blackmail at one remove.[42]

The First Rohilla War in 1774 had had more repercussions than just giving assistance to Oudh and expanding the Nawab's territories. In Oudh the Nawab was compelled to accept, and pay for, a Subsidiary Force of the Company's troops, at a cost which progressively crippled the fortunes of the kingdom. In Britain the war was seized on by the opponents of both the East India Company and the government of Lord North, who cast the Rohillas in the improbable role of innocent victims. Relations with them had thus seared the administration of Warren Hastings, and further relations with them were therefore something to avoid if possible. Nevertheless the Rohilla territory had been substantially reduced, to Oudh's benefit, and a new Nawab had been installed at the main Rohilla centre, Rampur; he was, in effect, as much a British client as the Nawab of Oudh.[43]

But in 1793 the Nawab Faizullah Khan of Rampur died. He was initially succeeded by his son Muhammad Ali Khan, who had quickly made himself unpopular, and was soon deposed and exiled by his younger brother, Ghulam Mohammed Khan Bahadur. Muhammad Ali, not surprisingly, was soon murdered; but then Ghulam Muhammad turned out to be as cruel and unpopular as his dead brother.

None of this seems to have taken place with any reference to outsiders, but since it was British guns which had put Faizullah Khan on the Rampur throne in the first place, they could claim the power to accept or reject his successor. Whether they had accepted Muhammad Ali as Nawab is not clear – he could have been accepted without argument as the heir by primogeniture, so there may have been no discussion – but it is certain that Ghulam Muhammad could not be accepted by the Company unless he made some very swift diplomatic contact with Calcutta, along with gestures of submission and presents to the Governor-General.

Meanwhile news arrived of the outbreak of yet another French war in Europe. India had been one of France's targets in earlier wars, and it was certain that this policy would revive in the new war. A ready-made ally existed for France in the form of Tipu of Mysore, and in 1794 the issue of the Rohillas at Rampur had thus sunk to the status of a minor nuisance, though it was one which, for strategic reasons, needed to be eliminated, one way or another, and quickly. Any enemy of the Company was a possible ally for any interested and ambitious outsider, Indian or European. Abercromby took a section of the Bengal Army west and met the army of Ghulam Muhammad in battle. The Rohilla Army was reinforced by a large number of volunteers from among the Mahrattas, which brought it to 25,000 men. This is, of course, an estimate by their enemies, and likely to be exaggerated, nevertheless it was a formidable foe, and severely outnumbered Abercromby's own forces. Nevertheless, the battle at Bitaura in October was reckoned to be a British victory, if somewhat costly – 700 men were killed, so it was claimed (by those who opposed the army reforms about to be implemented by Abercromby and Shore). The actual casualties were, in fact, 295 killed and 237 wounded. The victory was sufficient to dislodge Ghulam Muhammad, who was replaced by his nephew Abdul Ali Khan Bahadur, a child, with another uncle as regent. They all remained in the British suzerainty, for which, of course, they paid.[44]

The campaign was by no means easy, though relatively straightforward. The main problem was moving the unwieldy Company army into Rohilkhand, though once it was there the enemy cooperated in his defeat by his essentially undisciplined means of fighting – basically gathering together in a crowd and charging. No doubt this was a fearful thing to encounter (very similar to the Highland Dash which had succeeded against English armies until the Battle of Culloden), but properly disciplined and controlled troops could always defeat such tactics by disciplined fire. Auchmuty was present all through the march and was present at the battle, meanwhile writing regular reports back to Calcutta as to the expeditionary force's progress. He was responsible also for the detail of the march, ensuring supplies and perhaps for some of the diplomacy involved.

Under normal circumstances this would be an unexceptionable matter. The several British armies in India were regularly involved in minor wars, though this was perhaps a somewhat larger matter than most. In the south of India, for example, there were numerous forts and castles where a local chieftain might chance his arm by raiding his neighbours, or venturing at defying the Company in the hope that a minor raid might be ignored if the Company was busy elsewhere. Each siege or assault which then needed to be mounted in reply was difficult and involved casualties; further the Company's forces were always liable to a minor defeat, being subject all too often to the incompetence and/or arrogance of the commanding officers. On a somewhat larger scale the Rampur war was very like that, though it was conducted with some care and brought to victory. But, of course, the situation in Bengal and the north was not normal at the time. The (exaggerated) casualty cost of the battle at Bitaura became a stick with which to beat the Company government, wielded by the disaffected officers who feared the onset of reforms.[45]

Criticism of the conduct of the battle, of course, emanated largely from those who wished to denigrate the Commander-in-Chief and the Governor-General; at Bombay Captain Macquarie, who knew Abercromby, and had been recruited into the army in his regiment, and claimed to be a friend of Auchmuty's, took a different view of the matter. On 1 March 1795 he wrote to Major Auchmuty, congratulating him on his promotion and reciting his usual complaint of money problems and disappointed positions, but he also included:

> My warmest and most sincere congratulations on your safe return to Calcutta, after your late brilliant and successful campaign against the Marathas and the intrepid Rohillas. The happy and glorious termination of that war reflects the highest honours on the conductors of it, and it proves incontestably the superiority of the British arms and discipline when comparatively speaking a handful of men conquer and subdue

> a host of daring, brave, and determined enemy. I for one rejoice on it sincerely.[46]

Macquarie probably did not know any of the details, but his perception of the victory was completely different from Abercromby's critics – but then, of course, he was also being unpleasantly obsequious in the hope of gaining Abercromby's favour. At least his comments indicate that there was a very different point of view about the victory than that which was put about by the critics, and which has often got into the histories – if it is mentioned at all.

The essential problem of the control of the army was that the Company was a commercial enterprise first and a government second, and that the army was a mere appendage to these functions. Many realised this, but no one seemed to be able to tackle it. Cornwallis had made some progress in separating the two roles, but the only solution, which did not come for another sixty years, was to abolish the Company itself. Meanwhile the Company, still to a degree a commercial entity, had to pay for its army out of its commercial gains, and had to pay the British government for the use of elements of the king's army, and was always vulnerable to its own 'servants', especially those with guns. Mutiny had become an automatic reaction for many soldiers, European or Indian, when faced by a change in their situation which they did not like. The soldiers in the Company's army, officers and men, European and Indian, were mercenaries and every mutiny was in fact a sort of strike, but when the strikers were armed the stakes were much higher than usual, and the Company tended to scent 'mutiny' whenever any sort of discontent among the soldiers developed, even if to an objective view, no mutiny had occurred or was intended. That is, the appellation of 'mutiny' was used to rally anti-'mutineer' outrage, supposedly to put the discontented in the wrong. The over-use of the term 'terrorist' in the twenty-first century is similar. Later in his career, Auchmuty would have to tackle the aftermath of another mutiny.

When Cornwallis left India at the end of 1793 it was recognised that he was both weary of the job he had been doing, but also that he was dissatisfied with the results of his reforms, and that the one institution he had hardly tackled in those reforms was the army, partly because he had had to use it in the Mysore War, and one does not begin disruptive reforms in the midst of a difficult war. As a result rumours of what reforms he might be contemplating spread through the Bengal Army. In London Dundas received Cornwallis' plan, but was unable to do anything about implementing it for some time. But to everyone involved it was obvious that two issues were inevitably going to have to be tackled: one was the separation between the Company's army and the royal army, and the other was the overall costs of the military. Dealing with these matters would affect in particular the European officers.

The army, though largely recruited in India from Indians (though there were also European battalions), was officered by Europeans. In effect these men were mercenaries who were largely, but not exclusively, recruited in Britain; they were paid and organised on a separate scale and system from the royal forces which had been sent to India by the British government at various points when there were military crises, but which were hired by, and paid by, the Company. As a result there were the inevitable issues of pay differentials, seniority, command, and social snobbery involved. (The Company officers were largely from middle-class backgrounds; officers in the king's regiments tended towards the aristocratic.) From the Company's point of view – which was, of course, heavily commercial – the cost of the military was one of its major issues, which is to say that reducing that cost was one of the main concerns it attempted to deal with. From the point of view of the officers, reducing the military costs would hurt them in their pockets and their purses. And this clearly meant that the allowances and expenses paid to officers and soldiers on various scales (*batta*) would be affected – that is, reduced.

During 1794, in the first year of Abercromby's command-in-chief in Calcutta and Shore's first year as Governor-General, the Company's Directors in London became aware of a circular letter moving within the officers' circles, which amounted to a statement of the officers' grievances in advance of any reform plan, and knew that there was a continuing discussion over what reforms were likely and what the results would be, and that the opinion among these men was strongly negative towards any reform at all. However, it was clear to both Abercromby and Shore that this was not something which was accepted by all the officers of the army, though it was particularly being pushed by those based in the garrisons at Kanpur (Cawnpore) and Fatehgarh, both of which were stations which were deemed to be so close to potential or actual hostilities that the officers' allowances were on the double-*batta* scale. These were thus the men who would be most likely to suffer financially from any reforms. Hence their opposition to change.

Neither Abercromby nor Shore were seriously concerned at the documents which surfaced and which they saw, and indeed Shore himself sent off to London his own scheme for military reform as early as January 1794, soon after his arrival – he was an old India-hand, and could be reckoned an expert on the subject. But in London it was Cornwallis' scheme which became the subject for the discussion, and so many people were involved – the Directors, the Board of Control, Dundas and Pitt and Cornwallis – that the process took a long time, and rumours, distorting and exaggerating what was being said, as such rumours always do, reached India to alarm further those who had been alarmed already.[47]

Macquarie's letters to Auchmuty, though fairly well spread, give a sense of both Auchmuty's progress through the ranks, and some understanding of the issues involved from the point of view of a relatively junior officer.[48] In the letter of 1 March 1795 already quoted he congratulates Auchmuty on his substantive promotion to major. He notes that the last letter he had received came from Benares (and so was sent during the Rohilla campaign), and that Auchmuty (and so also no doubt Abercromby) was now back at Calcutta. His comments on the result of the Rohilla War tend to fit well with the political results for Rampur, which settled to a relatively stable existence as a political entity, a small duchy, in effect, which lasted into the third quarter of the twentieth century. And when Macquarie comments that 'a handful of men could conquer and subdue a host of daring, brave, and determined enemy', he makes the crucial point which provided the motor for British rule. Lord Cornwallis had made the same point to the Duke of York in 1796: 'a brigade of our sepoys can easily make anybody Emperor of Hindustan'.[49]

Macquarie comments also on the 'expected new military arrangements'. His viewpoint is very much that of every other officer in that he looks to whatever emerges to 'securing me my present appointment, or some one equivalent' – that is, a purely personal one. In a sense he was probably detached from the issues to some extent because he was a king's officer; it was the Company officers who were agitated. A month later he reverts to the subject, noting that 'the new expected regulations' are rumoured to be on their way. In another month – it was May 1795 by now – Macquarie is addressing Auchmuty as Adjutant General, which is a move along from his 'acting' position earlier. He is still hoping that Abercromby might find a position for him, but the issue of the 'new regulations' has dropped away for the moment.

He was then unable to write further for another six months, having become involved in the siege of Cochin. He returned again in December to Bombay, whence he reported rumours that Abercromby would return to Britain soon. He was now addressing Auchmuty as lieutenant colonel, and suggested himself for the position of Deputy Adjutant General if Auchmuty was 'going home' with Abercromby. Another hiatus in the letters followed as Macquarie became involved in the conquest of the Dutch island of Ceylon in 1796 and had a short appointment as governor of Point de Galle in the south of the island. He wrote next from Malacca in Malaya in June 1796 (also recently taken from the Dutch), where he had stopped on a voyage to Macau in an attempt to improve his wife's health, which had deteriorated seriously when he had had to leave her at Bombay during his campaigns. This personal preoccupation had apparently driven out any thoughts of a new position – while on leave and in China he would hardly expect one – but he also missed the next, and for the time being the decisive, stage in the problem of the 'new regulations'. And when he and his wife reached Macau, she died of the consumption she had been suffering from, and this drove Macquarie into a depression which lasted for the next two years. (Auchmuty did not forget him.)

The crisis in the north had in fact arrived and passed during December 1795 and January 1796, while Macquarie was away from India. During 1795 the preliminary notions produced by Cornwallis had been sent out to Governor-General Shore by Dundas, and had been published by Abercromby.[50] This effort at consultation failed. The idea was to calm the fears of the officers, but the result was to increase them, and Shore reported this reaction within a few days.[51] The officers who feared the changes began to firm up their organisation and their opposition. They were already represented in London by an Indian Committee, and now committees, particularly of junior officers, were formed in many of the garrisons. They sent out envoys to persuade officers in the Bombay and Madras armies to join in. The Governors of both these Presidencies were able to keep control without too much difficulty, in part because of the smaller forces involved (and the proximity of Tipu

Sultan, whose power was growing again). In Bengal, however, Abercromby and Sir John Shore found that the sheer size of their area, and the numbers of troops in garrisons, militated against ease of control. (The victory over the Rohillas had also reduced external opposition, thus leaving the way clear for the officers to turn their negative attentions to relations with Calcutta.)

It was only at Christmas time in 1795 that Shore received clear information that a widespread plot was in preparation. The main instigators were Colonel William Popham, the commander at Fatehgarh, Colonel Horton Brisco, commander at Kanpur (who had been involved in an earlier mutiny against Robert Clive in 1767), and Colonel John Forbes, commander at Dinapore – all of which garrisons faced Oudh. Shore in Calcutta reacted with decision, sending to Lord Hobart, the Governor at Madras, for reinforcements, and to the Governor at the Cape of Good Hope (also recently captured from the Dutch) for the loan of a regiment; he even contacted the European mercenary Benoit de Brogne, who commanded among the Marathas, for assistance – he promised the use of a unit of Maratha cavalry, and de Brogne also sold to the East India Company a mercenary regiment which was his bodyguard – 'a body of 600 Persian troopers, superbly armed, mounted, and equipped, with a hundred camel men on hybrid animals, and a small battery of light guns'.[52] As he passed through Oudh the Nawab had tried to persuade him to stay in his service, but de Brogne was going home; two years later, the next Viceroy, Lord Mornington, handed the regiment over to Oudh, no doubt as an economy measure.[53] With this regiment Shore could reinforce his garrison at Calcutta; the Royal Navy was asked to stand by to transport soldiers of the Madras Army to Calcutta.[54]

In fact the activation of all these measures turned out not to be necessary in the end. There was a threat of trouble at Calcutta itself, but it rapidly became clear that the artillery officers would have nothing to do with it, and this blocked any move by the infantry, which had been half-hearted anyway. But Shore took his time and moved with care. He sent out the precautionary requests for assistance, and enlisted de Brogne's regiment, but it was three weeks between his learning of the plot and then his move decisively to block it. And when he did so he struck at its centre. In those weeks messages of loyalty came in from several garrisons and from most of the senior officers. Most of those in the affected garrisons were hostile to the moves of the plotters, and this blocked many serious moves by the more junior officers.

Hence the importance of the garrisons at Dinapore, Kanpur and Fatehgarh, where the commanders took the lead. But at Kanpur news of the reaction elsewhere sowed sufficient doubts in the minds of the plotters in the infantry that their timetable was delayed for long enough for second thoughts to set in. The garrison at Fatehgarh, on the other hand, was led towards the plot by Colonel Popham, and only two out of its fifty officers refused to support him. But once again the artillery was unwilling to join in, and the delay which resulted from this brought home to the more junior officers that what they were in fact intending to do was to carry out a *coup d'état*. This short period for deliberation also revealed their lack of wider support. Their ardour was thus cooled, though it did not deflect them from their overall aim with regard to whatever the new regulations prescribed for them.

Abercromby, once Calcutta was judged to be safe, set out, on Shore's instructions, to visit the disaffected garrisons, travelling secretly and with only a small escort, though it is likely that he took some of his staff with him, which would include Lieutenant Colonel Samuel Auchmuty. His visit to Kanpur brought a declaration of loyalty by the officers, culminating in a ball and dinner in celebration, but also a statement by Abercromby himself which in effect assured those involved in the plot that all would be forgiven. It was in part the news that Kanpur was reverting to loyalty that finally finished off the threat from Fatehgarh; once more 'no reprisals' was promised.[55]

The scale of Shore's precautions, in particular his appeal to the Mahrattas for assistance, is an indication of the magnitude of the threat this conspiracy was thought to have posed. There was sufficient discontent among the officers that if, say, Abercromby had refused to wipe the slate clean, with his declaration of 'no reprisals', it is quite possible that a mutiny would have developed after all. (On the other hand, if there is anything guaranteed to encourage a repetition of such agitation, it is that the leaders and participants should all 'get away with it'.) Discontents in other garrisons than Kanpur and Fatehgarh were sufficiently strong that if fighting began it could well have spread. Shore was by no means certain that he could rely on any forces outside Calcutta closer than Madras, and not necessarily even there. A recent mutiny by an Indian regiment when it had been ordered to march out of the Bengal Presidency into Madras had left several other Indian regiments disturbed.[56] Fighting between the European troops with or without Indian soldiers' support, would have been far too tempting for the numerous enemies of the Company to ignore – and that list included every other state in India. (This was an issue Auchmuty had to confront fifteen years later.) It seems to have been this resolution which finally undermined the resolve of the near mutinous officers and soldiers at Fatehgarh and persuaded them to stand down when their isolation became clear.

The new regulations, when they finally arrived later in 1796 did not solve the problem either. Sir John Shore and Abercromby evaded imposing them in the form they were received, and substituted measures which were less offensive to the officers in India. This watered down Cornwallis' original intentions considerably.[57] By doing so, of course, and by the deliberate 'act of oblivion' enacted by the Company in respect of the record of the mutinous soldiers, the whole issue of the mutiny, or potential mutiny, was brushed aside, and is frequently therefore ignored in later histories.[58]

The Company was, of course, trapped. Reprisals would have either compelled the guilty men to reactivate their mutinous intentions, thus producing a civil war between the Europeans in the British territories, or, had the purge been successful, the Company would have been left with a very much weaker armed force, together with a reputation which would have discouraged any future officer recruits. The fighting between Company forces would have left the way open for Indian enemies to invade, and for the king's regiments to intervene. Either way the Company would have been finished. The result might well have been the complete destruction of the British dominion in India amid widespread violence, destruction, and death, and to ensure its survival a huge increase in the royal army in India, shipped from Britain in a time of war with France, would have been required. It was to avoid this that the Company, Shore, and Abercromby stifled or softened the reforms; in London and in India the possible consequences of greater rigour were surely appreciated.

General Robert Abercromby saw out one more year in Calcutta and returned to Britain in 1797. Lieutenant Colonel Auchmuty returned with him, his final post having detached him from regimental service. He had been in India for fourteen years, during which time he had risen from lieutenant to lieutenant colonel, and he had made a powerful mark as a military administrator as Adjutant General, and had also succeeded in becoming rich, from prize money (he will have received several hundreds of pounds from the Mysore loot and still more from Rampur, in addition to the sale of at least two of his regimental offices). The first and last of these achievements were ambitions common to every officer who went out to India. The second was what ensured that he subsequently rose well above the level of lieutenant colonel. He had also learned of the basic instability of the British position in India, and of the stroppiness of the British officers, who affected a loyalty which was so fragile that they could break out into a mutiny at the mere hint of a threat to their privileges. The basic incompetence of the Company in its role as a government and as a military power was also clear, and was accompanied by a constant confusion between its commercial and governmental roles.

On a personal level he had made useful contacts with several more important men. Some of them were evidently also friends. Byron, of course, was already dead, but Macquarie was rising; Cornwallis may or may not have been useful – Auchmuty is not mentioned in his collected correspondence – but he may have been able to make oral recommendations. Abercromby was clearly a friend, and proved to be useful later. And it is clear that the word had got back to the War Office in London and the Commander-in-Chief in Britain, the Duke of York, that Auchmuty was sensible and efficient. This was the true achievement of his years in India.

Chapter 4

Egypt, 1799–1803

Lieutenant Colonel Auchmuty returned to Britain by sea from Calcutta with Lieutenant General Abercromby, travelling in convoy in one of the East India Company's ships. Sailing with the north-east monsoon, the fleet would have left India in mid-October 1797, reaching the English Channel, after a halt at St Helena to await an escort, in February or March next year.[1] Either in the same ship or in another in the same fleet was Major General Sir David Baird, released from years of captivity in Seringapatam at the end of the last Mysore War. The fleet halted at the Cape to resupply with water and wood, and where fresh provisions were rather more plentiful than at St Helena, the usual rendezvous. The Cape had been recently captured by Lord Keith's expedition in 1796; Baird stopped off at the invitation of the Governor to help train the troops of the garrison there – he was a notorious drill-and-salute martinet.

On arriving in Britain, probably sailing all the way into the Thames estuary to disembark at the Company's East India Dock in the heart of London, Auchmuty would have reported to the War Office and to the Duke of York, the army's Commander-in-Chief. He was entitled to leave, but where he spent it is unknown. His family and relatives who were in England were largely settled in various parts of Kent, and it may be that he would have aimed to stay with each of them in turn. His mother had died the year before, in 1797, having lived with her youngest daughter Jane and her husband, the Revd Richard Tylden, in the village of Milsted near Sittingbourne. Mrs Auchmuty was buried in the local church there by her son-in-law, who was also the local vicar; Auchmuty's uncle, Robert Auchmuty, the lawyer from Boston, had died in 1788.[2]

Possibly at some point Samuel went to Scotland, either with, or to visit, Sir Robert Abercromby whose sight was failing – he was effectively blind by 1803. Auchmuty by this time, as a result of his years in India and the prize money from the wars there, would have been able to afford a house of his own, but we do not know when, or if, he bought one. He was still only a lieutenant colonel, the French War was still on, and he was certainly seeking military employment; it may not have been seen as a prudent move to invest in property when he might well be sent overseas again, or to a distant part of Britain, at any time.

It was necessary that Auchmuty should keep in touch with the War Office if he was to be offered some military employment, making regular visits to remind the officials there of his existence and availability. For this he would need to stay most of his time in or near London – hence the suggestion that he spent much of his time in Kent with members of his family. As it happened, it was really only in the Indian theatre that a land war was still being conducted for the moment, but during 1798, not long after Auchmuty reached England, the French opened up a new theatre of war in the Mediterranean.

The Royal Navy, having lost control of all the possible bases east of Gibraltar to French conquests and influence, evacuated its ships from the Mediterranean in 1797. In the absence of Admirals Jervis and Nelson and their fleets, command of the Mediterranean fell automatically to the French, and so General Bonaparte with a fleet of 400 transports carrying 30,000 soldiers and escorted by a dozen line-of-battle ships, had a clear run to sail eastwards. The fleet left Toulon on 19 May, conquered Malta from the Knights of St John of the Hospital on the way, and then landed in Egypt; Aboukir was taken on 2 July, and the army marched inland to fight the army of the Mamelukes, who ruled Egypt. But the British fleet returned to the Mediterranean, and Nelson, after sailing back-and-forth in search of the French fleet, finally discovered it at anchor in Aboukir Bay, near Alexandria, a month after the French landing. The French ships were largely destroyed in the battle which followed (the 'Battle of the Nile' to the British), but by then the French Army was onshore and had been victorious over the local army of the Mameluke rulers.

Bonaparte sent out subsidiary expeditions to secure control of the local territories, one of them south along the Nile into Upper Egypt in search of the defeated Mamelukes, and later a second under his own command into Palestine, where a combination of Turkish forces, local Arab and Palestinian forces, British sailors under Captain Sir Sidney Smith and Ahmad Pasha al-Jazzar and the fortifications of his city of Acre, and the bubonic plague stopped him, amid a series of battles.[3]

All this took place while Auchmuty and Abercromby and company were sailing home and Auchmuty was resting from his labours, during late 1797 and into 1798 – the Battle of the Nile was on 1 August 1798. It was (and is) by no means clear what Bonaparte's eventual intentions were, perhaps not even to him, but the British had to assume that their position in India was at least on his agenda. From Egypt it would certainly be possible to make contact with the disaffected Indian states, of which Tipu's Mysore was the most likely target. Tipu had sent envoys to France even before the revolution, and the French privateer *La Resolu* had been hovering close to his coast during his war with the Company in 1790–2. (The fight with *La Resolu* had taken place close to the coast where Auchmuty had been in service, and he had commented on it in his letter to Captain Byron.) There were plenty of ships plying between India and Arabia, above all carrying the pilgrim traffic to and from Mecca, and the port for Mecca, Jeddah, was only a relatively short distance from Egypt, while the Sharif of Mecca was always anxious about a possible Mameluke invasion. There was already a group of Frenchmen with Tipu, refugees from fighting at Mauritius, who had formed themselves into a Jacobin club, with Tipu's acquiescence. Tipu had already sent envoys to the Republican regime in Paris, complete with a suggested plan of campaign which would, he thought, rid India of the Company within a year. He also suggested an alliance with Zaman Shah, the Amir of Afghanistan, who was in the habit of making annual looting raids into the Punjab. He suggested that an army of 10,000 French soldiers would be sufficient, given the general animosity towards the Company among the Indian rulers, and he would contribute three times that number when they arrived.[4] Bonaparte had more than three times Tipu's suggested French military contribution under his own command in Egypt, and most of them had little to do once the country had been occupied. There may be no clarity about Bonaparte's precise intentions, but he was sufficient of a strategist to understand that eliminating British rule from India (and replacing it with French rule, whatever Tipu assumed) would provide major political, military, and naval advantages from the French point of view. But first he needed ships in the Red Sea.[5]

The British reaction to the French success in Egypt, in both Britain and India, was to mount expeditions against Egypt. In India the new Governor-General, Lord Mornington (later Marquess Wellesley), who took up office during 1798 as the successor to Sir John Shore, at once ordered two expeditions to be prepared. The first was to suppress the Mysore kingdom, for it was clear that Tipu would be the automatic ally for any arriving French forces. The second was a seaborne force which would be sent to secure control of the southern entrance to the Red Sea. He followed this up with still another expedition which was to gain control of Red Sea ports which might be used by the French.[6]

In Britain, Secretary of State Henry Dundas also organised an expeditionary force to attack the French in Egypt from the Mediterranean side, commanded by General Sir Ralph Abercromby (Robert Abercromby's brother), with Admiral Lord Keith in command of the fleet. Quite possibly because they were both Scots – the choice of commanders was that of Dundas – these two commanders were able to cooperate successfully, and the navy landed the army in Egypt in March 1801.[7] More relevant to this story, Dundas also organised a naval expedition under Captain John Blankett which was to sail from Britain to take naval command of the Red Sea.[8]

In India the war with Mysore – the Fourth Anglo-Mysore War – ended with the capture, sack, and partial destruction of Seringapatam, and the death of Tipu, in 1799. Major General Sir David Baird had returned to India from the Cape when he heard the news of the outbreak of the Mysore War and had taken a prominent part in the storming of the city, as had the younger brother of the Governor-General, Colonel Sir Arthur Wellesley.[9] These two were now rivals, if not worse, especially when Wellesley was appointed Governor of Seringapatam by his brother instead of Baird, who was his senior in rank, and who had expected the post. On being told this at his breakfast Baird stepped out of his tent, leaving his meal unfinished, apparently an unprecedented action.

The victory in India left the way open for the dispatch of the Indian expedition to Egypt. The first expedition had seized Perim Island at the southern mouth of the Red Sea, and the arrival of Blankett's squadron brought British naval forces further north, well into the sea itself. This was a classic exercise in sea power, since the presence of a squadron of ships at the southern end of the Red Sea effectively blocked the French route to India. This was a ploy which had occurred to those in London and those in Calcutta at much the same time.

Blankett, with the local rank of Commodore, had sailed in July 1799 with the 50-gun ship *Leopard*, a frigate (*Daedalus*) and a sloop (*Orestes*), and arrived, after a slow and difficult voyage, in April 1799. He found that ships from the Bombay Marine and two Royal Navy ships from the Indian Ocean squadron commanded by Admiral Peter Rainier, *Centurion* (50) and *Albatross* (18) were already there. In total this could be reckoned no more than a mere squadron in the seas west of Egypt and in the Atlantic, but in the Red Sea the two 50-gun ships were dominant. By early 1799, therefore, there was a substantial naval force in the southern part of the Red Sea, which was quite sufficient to block any French move by sea which might be made. This was actually all that needed to be done, but not all that was done. It may be that the ships prevented any further eastward movement by the French, but they could not eliminate the threat entirely; this had to be done by the army.

Once he had secured Cairo, Bonaparte sent General Bon with a detachment of troops and some sailors to secure the port of Suez at the northern end of the Red Sea. Bon reported that there were in the harbour four merchantman and several smaller vessels. His orders were to send out a couple of ships to cruise the Red Sea, making contact with the Arabian authorities at Jeddah and in the Yemen; when Bonaparte himself came to see Suez at the end of December 1798 he repeated and reinforced that order.[10] In this he was well ahead of the British response. Only in April had the small expedition from India occupied Perim Island, after which two of the Indian ships, *Centurion* and *Albatross*, made their way to the neighbourhood of Suez. Their arrival blocked any naval move out of Egypt; Bonaparte had had just four months or so to exploit his Egyptian position for an attack on India, but he had not used it – he had been very busy, of course. In effect, the resistance to his expedition into Syria mounted by the Ottomans and the local Palestinian chieftains, with British help, had so preoccupied him (and led to his defeat) that he could spare neither time nor resources for the Indian Ocean, and the chance would not come again.

Another possibility for the French was that their ships could, like the British from Britain and India, enter the Red Sea from the south, from the French island of Mauritius or from Europe. But the French squadron at Mauritius was being gradually worn down in a series of minor actions with British ships, and rarely being reinforced from France – the British conquest of the Cape largely blocked the route while the fate of the fleet

Bonaparte took to Egypt was a powerful deterrent to any ships being sent from Europe. The arrival of the several British and Indian ships in the Red Sea was therefore quite sufficient to block any French expedition sent from Egypt getting far to the eastward. And so Tipu of Mysore went down to destruction and death without any significant French help. Whatever plans Napoleon had with regard to India had been rendered unviable.

The number of British ships in the Red Sea was now impressive, especially as they had no opponents. *Centurion* and *Albatross* reached as far north as Suez, where the French shipwrights had built three gunboats and brigantine out of locally available supplies, including dismantling several local merchant ships, but the approach of the two Royal Navy ships put an end to any French ambitions by sea; two other ships found that Cosseir (Qusayr) was in French hands and bombarded the fort there into ruin; the French left.[11] Contact was made with the Sharif of Mecca through Jeddah. The Sharif was particularly interested in securing an ally, but for his own purposes. Meanwhile, Blankett inspected Perim and did not like it; he suggested that Mocha in Yemen would be the best base for the troops, but the Perim detachment went to Aden, where the Imam Ahmed was as interested in securing British assistance for aims of his own as the Sharif.[12] It was not going to be easy to stay out of these local quarrels and ambitions. Given that, with the elimination of Mysorean power, the British had now established an effective domination of all western and southern India, and its navies controlled the Red Sea, so there was clearly no danger of any French expedition reaching India.

And yet the French still controlled Egypt, even if Bonaparte himself had been defeated in Syria, and had then left Egypt in August 1799. This rather suggested that little further enterprise could be expected from the remaining French forces, yet their control of Egypt was a standing threat, and the British in both Britain and India felt that they had to be removed, if only to free up the ships standing guard in Egyptian waters. And so to the British the French in Egypt ceased to be a threat, and instead became an opportunity. Here was a large French army marooned far from home, and amid a hostile population – the account by Captain Moiret makes it clear that there were repeated 'rebellions' by various Egyptian groups throughout the French occupation – so that its isolation eliminated it as an immediate threat to anyone else. The opportunity certainly existed of simply leaving it to decay, useless for military purposes, a significant reduction in French military power; alternatively, and better, it provided a target which the British Army could attack and defeat. In any peace talks the French occupation of Egypt would be a useful item on the French side; if peace was made and the French were still in Egypt they might stay there and then could be reinforced, their peacetime navy could reach into the Red Sea, and the threat to India would revive in an increased form. Remove the French Army by gaining a military victory over it and the British would gain prestige, would show that they had an efficient and capable army (something which had been in doubt for several years), and at the same time they would strike away both that particular French political advantage, and the potential threat from Egypt to British possessions in the Indian Ocean.

London and Calcutta, once again operating independently but in effect in tandem, reacted in very similar ways. An expedition was organised from Britain, and was eventually ordered to invade Egypt, its commander, after some changes, being Lieutenant General Sir Ralph Abercromby, Sir Robert's brother. And just in case the French in Egypt simply retreated up the Nile, an expedition was organised from India as well. This was to land on the Egyptian Red Sea coast and block the French retreat, or maybe attack their forces in Lower Egypt from that direction, so taking them from north and south simultaneously. The main expedition against the Mediterranean coast had 15,000 men; the Indian expedition was a third of that in size, about 5,200 men, and was commanded by General Sir David Baird (after Major General Arthur Wellesley became ill – to Baird's considerable satisfaction).

The expedition from Britain landed at Aboukir Bay in March 1801 and soon achieved a notable victory over the French forces. Abercromby had taken his time. The expedition had been at sea for several months, being successively directed to attack Ferrol, then Cadiz. Eventually it reached Gibraltar, and from there it was finally directed to go into the eastern Mediterranean. By that time the Ottoman Empire had finally realised that Bonaparte's diplomatic smoke screen – he had claimed that he was operating in effect to eliminate the rebellious and disobedient Egyptian Mameluke government on behalf of the Ottomans – was nonsense. Abercromby and Admiral Lord Keith were then able to make use of Ottoman territory in southern Anatolia to land and rest the troops after their long confinement in the ships, and in particular to give them training in an opposed landing from the sea. As a result when the landing took place at Aboukir it was rapidly successful, despite early and strong French opposition, and when a sizeable French army was sent from Alexandria against the landing force it was defeated.[13]

Abercromby's training methods were thus seen to be successful, though the man himself was killed a few days later in the next battle. He was succeeded by General Sir John Hely-Hutchinson who brought up his forces first to mask Alexandria, which was held by a substantial but quiescent French garrison, then, in concert with an expedition of Ottoman forces sent from Syria, to lay siege to Cairo.

Meanwhile a detachment from the Royal Navy squadron in the Red Sea under Commodore Blankett sailed to secure control of Suez, and landed the 86th Foot there. Then the main force from India under Baird arrived and landed at Cosseir on the Egyptian side of the Sea. This was the Red Sea port which was nearest to the Nile in Upper Egypt, to which it was linked by an ancient and well-travelled road (which the French had used earlier), through the Wadi Hammamet.[14]

Yet another British force then arrived, this one commanded by Colonel Samuel Auchmuty. He had been promoted to colonel by brevet at the beginning of 1800 and made Lieutenant Colonel of the 10th Regiment of Foot soon after. This was a clear mark of approval from the War Office, and it is evident that his organisational and administrative skills had come to be fully appreciated. When it was decided that a small expedition would be sent from Britain to block up the Red Sea ports – he had only 1,000 men so he was scarcely expected to do more than hold on to these poor and thirsty ports – Auchmuty was available, had the right rank, and the appropriate experience. Auchmuty's task was first to take the 65th Foot to the Cape, and there to exchange it for the 61st Foot and take that regiment on to the Red Sea. The purpose of this arrangement was to take advantage of the fact that the 61st had been 'seasoned' by its time at the Cape, implying that those who were likely to succumb to the diseases of Africa and Asia had already done so, and that the survivors were capable of withstanding the heat of an African climate; it was now the turn of the 65th to undergo such a process. He had been convoyed by a squadron of ships commanded by Captain Sir Home Popham (the brother of Colonel William Popham, so recently deeply implicated in the mutiny in Bengal – Sir Home was just as liable to disobedience and unauthorised initiative as his brother). All these men

Baird, Popham, Auchmuty were already known to each other from service in India. Also among the officers in the force sent direct from India were Major Macquarie and Lieutenant Colonel Montresor, the first Auchmuty's friend from India, the second his brother-in-law.[15]

As soon as Auchmuty turned up he joined with Baird's force and Baird appointed him as the Adjutant General for the whole force – or so the Auchmuty family legend appears to have had it.[16] But a letter which Auchmuty wrote from the camp of the army at the Nile in Upper Egypt later puts the events in a different light. He wrote to the Governor of Bombay, Jonathan Duncan, some of whose forces were part of Baird's expedition. (He knew Duncan, who had been Resident at Benares during the Rohilla campaign, where Auchmuty had stayed for a time.) He commented that he had commanded the small force from England at the appointment of the Duke of York, the Commander-in-Chief of the army, but he could not expect to command a larger force since his rank would not permit it. So the duke had given him a commission as Adjutant General for the Red Sea force. He commented that 'it has been to me a most pleasing circumstance that the Commander-in-Chief (i.e., Baird) is an old and valued friend'.[17]

Reading between the lines it was clearly also fortunate that the two knew each other, for neither Auchmuty nor the Duke of York knew in London who would be placed in command of the expedition from India when the English contingent set out – nor in fact whether any such expedition would take place. His orders do not seem to survive, but he must have been given alternatives, since if no military expedition (as opposed to naval) had been sent from India, he would need a different set of objectives, perhaps the occupation of Suez, which is what Blankett had expected the Indian force to do. So Auchmuty's appointment was in the nature of a precautionary one, just in case a larger expedition had been sent from India; the duke was clearly anxious to install a man of his own in a senior position in such an expedition. That Baird was capable of working with Auchmuty was thus the 'most pleasing circumstance', and Baird was sensible enough to accept Auchmuty and his appointment and make use of him. It meant disappointing Macquarie, to whom Baird had promised the Adjutant General's position in the expedition, but the duke's appointment superseded Baird's promise. In fact Baird in command was not merely pleasing for Auchmuty, but it was also fortunate for the expedition as a whole, which was the gainer by their agreement. Baird was a ferocious trainer of soldiers, but was less than adequate as an organiser and administrator. The arrival of Auchmuty allowed Baird to delegate that task, no doubt with some relief, to one who he knew could perform it competently.

Baird also used Popham as his man afloat in the Red Sea. Commodore Blankett had set up the blockade at the southern end of the sea, but he was both unenthusiastic about that task and ill – he died not long after the army's arrival. Popham had been given a second task besides that of convoying Auchmuty's little army. He was to negotiate with the local powers in and around the Red Sea to allow British merchants to purchase supplies of coffee, and presumably other local products, if there were any. His was therefore essentially a diplomatic mission, something Popham was usually quite good at, but it was also a cover for espionage, for he was expected to discover the disposition of the local potentates in view of the French occupation of Egypt.

The Red Sea was at first the main object of the expedition. Contacts had already been made with the Arab rulers at Aden, at Mocha in the Yemen, and at Jeddah and Mecca. The Imam Ahmed at Aden, no doubt for his own purposes, had allowed the detachment on Perim Island to move to his city when it proved impossible to victual the men on the island, which was waterless. Popham negotiated through Mocha – the source of the best coffee in the region – with the Imam of Sana'a, but could reach no agreement. He found more agreement at Jeddah and there he was sold supplies for the ships and for the army. The Sharif was happy to see the French in Egypt being evicted, but he was also looking to get political support from the British. That the 86th Foot under Lieutenant Colonel Lloyd had sailed all the way up to Suez, landed there, and, when the main army from the Mediterranean was victorious, had marched to Cairo, was a clear indication of who controlled the sea and its coasts; this was sufficient for the Sharif for the moment. (On the other hand, Lloyd had marched his men in the heat of the day, in summer, through a waterless desert, with the result that his small force was rendered wholly ineffective for some time after it reached Cairo.[18]) The contrast with the march of Baird's force over a longer distance and through an even more forbidding desert is marked, and it was planning and organisation – and imagination – all of which Lloyd failed at, and which was Auchmuty's strength, which made the difference.

Baird had a fairly substantial force under him. Popham and Auchmuty had brought the 61st Foot from the Cape; from India came four other king's regiments of foot. These included the 10th, of which Auchmuty was the recently appointed Lieutenant Colonel, and which had only arrived at Madras in April 1799 to be almost immediately sent to Egypt.[19] Also the 80th, the 86th (now comatose with Lloyd in the north), and the 88th – plus the 8th Light Dragoons; he also had three battalions of Native Infantry, the Bengal Volunteers and the 1st and 7th Bombay Battalions. To these were added some horse artillery and several artillery detachments from each of the three Indian presidencies. The total rank-and-file strength at the point of disembarkation (which included the 86th at Suez) was 5,227 men, plus officers, NCOs, lascars, and 'followers' – over 6,000 people all told.[20] It was a nicely balanced force, but it was scarcely going to be enough to reconquer Egypt from 30,000 Frenchmen, so Baird from the moment of his arrival was in dire need of information from the north.

This force was landed at the port of Cosseir on the Red Sea coast, a place as dry and desolate as Perim Island; the small French force which had occupied the old fort until the British bombardment which destroyed it, had long since left. (Just so had the French detachment at Suez: the British landing there had compelled a French concentration and the withdrawal of these more distant detachments.) Baird's force had then to be marched to the River Nile with the intention of transporting it northwards to fight the French Army in the Cairo region but only if Baird could be sure that it was only to be a reinforcement for a British force already there. It was fortunate, though Baird and his men did not know any of this, that Bonaparte had deserted his army, that a much larger British Army had landed near Alexandria, and that the French Army in Egypt – much larger than the two British forces put together – was suffering from demoralisation and disease, and from inadequate and incompetent command. It outnumbered the British forces, even when the latter were fighting alongside the Ottoman Army, all the time and in every engagement.

As it happened, the main force, under Abercromby, had won the first battle, at Aboukir, even before Baird's force had landed at Cosseir, though Baird did not get to know of this for quite some time. He and Popham and Auchmuty had in fact arrived in the Red Sea at the wrong season. The ships which took the 86th Foot to Suez managed to get through, but soon afterwards the winds changed and blew from the north for three months, so that it proved to be impossible to get messages through to Colonel Lloyd at Suez; further, even though he was able to contact and join the army in the Delta, it seems that Lloyd also failed to report to Baird, which, with northerly winds at Suez, should have been possible. Abercromby had been killed three weeks after the landing, and his successor, Major General Hely-Hutchinson, does not seem to have paid any attention to Baird's expeditionary force for a time; he did not send news of the situation in the north until 15 May, a message which did not reach Baird for another month – but then Baird's force had only arrived in mid-May, so Hutchinson's message was hardly delayed by him. Baird made much complaint about the lack of information from the north, but Hutchinson could hardly have sent any much earlier, though greater speed in its transmission was surely possible.[21]

Baird had to assume that he and his force were required in the north, and certainly it was not until 28 June that the French forces holding Cairo agreed to capitulate, and not until August that the final French force, holding out in Alexandria, surrendered – and both of these French forces were considerably greater in number than Hutchinson's army – together they would have been over twice its size. But Baird was a cautious commander for all his bluster and noise, and he was faced with a difficult problem. He had 5,200 men on shore, and 800 wives and children and servants as well, on a desert coast, and he was expected to get most of them through that desert, a journey of about 120 miles, to the river, and then down the river, possibly marching, unless he could find boats. It was June already and getting steadily hotter. Anywhere else it would certainly be possible to march a force of 6,000 people that distance in no more than a week, or less; in Egypt in June the problem was heat and water, too much of the former and very little of the latter.

The crossing of the desert is generally skipped over with the odd comment about its difficulty, which is accurate enough, but hardly specific.[22] In the first place it had not been intended to land at Cosseir at all. The difficulty of the passage from the coast to the Nile was well understood, and the bombardment of the fort had hardly improved matters at the landing place. The original aim had been, as with the 86th Foot, to land at Suez, whence a well-used road could be followed to Cairo, marked by five regular stages, and which was considerably shorter than the Wadi Hammamet route. But before the main force of the expedition arrived, Lieutenant-Colonel Murray, the

Company's agent at Mocha, had pre-empted the decision on where to land. The Sharif of Mecca had occupied Cosseir when the French had left, and Murray had moved to Jeddah to set up a forward post for the British forces as they arrived. It was perhaps this connection, and so the likely assistance available from the Sharif in the way of supplies, that led him to make Cosseir the landing place. The only obvious alternative was Suez and since that port became unattainable from soon after Lloyd's landing, due to the adverse northerly winds, a climatic regime which lasted three months, Murray's decision was reasonable.

The first detachment of Indian troops there, dispatched by Governor Duncan from Bombay, arrived at Mocha on the Yemeni coast on 21 April, and was then directed on to Jeddah by Murray. Baird with the main force arrived on 18 May, and Popham with Auchmuty's contingent a day or so later. The first thing to do was to sort out the competing claims of Auchmuty and Macquarie to be Adjutant General of the expedition. Auchmuty not only had a higher rank but had an appointment from the Duke of York, and he had experience in the post, so these factors clearly trumped Baird's promise of the job to Macquarie, but the dispute no doubt soured relations between the two men. Baird had to explain the contretemps in a long letter to Governor-General Mornington; Auchmuty did the same in his letter to Governor Duncan.[23] It is likely that the installation of Auchmuty, a steadier, less emotionally ambitious, and less obsequiously petitioning soldier, helped the expedition to run more smoothly than it would have done if Macquarie had been its administrator. Macquarie was made Deputy Adjutant General, and he took charge from the early period at Cosseir.

The passage from Cosseir to the Nile was essentially a problem of logistics, though there was a faint possibility of armed opposition from some of the Mamelukes or the local Arabs. What was required was to find water, suitable food, and transport animals to assist the men on the journey – and the animals required food and water as well. An early blithe attempt nearly came to grief when Colonel Murray sent a force on ahead without sufficient supplies, and the difficulty was not helped by Baird underestimating by 20 miles the distance to be marched. It was necessary to establish a series of staging posts at which the marching troops could rest and recover during the sequence of marches. Detachments were sent out in advance, partly to stockpile food supplies – food is as essential to desert travel as water – and partly to locate water supplies, or indeed to dig new wells. It turned out that the water supply at Cosseir was bad, which a number of men found out the hard way when they fell ill after incautiously drinking from it.

The details of all this can be followed in a collection of letters made by Macquarie in a letter book he compiled as Deputy Adjutant General, a position which was his consolation prize. He remained for the early part of the expedition at Cosseir with the headquarters there, while Auchmuty moved along the land route in stages. Some of the letters were written by Macquarie himself, but most were by Auchmuty, who was more likely to have been in control.[24]

From Cosseir detachments were sent ahead along the track to locate the existing wells, at places which the British called Moilah and Legetta (actually al-Muweih and Leqeita). The former was a little over halfway along the route from Cosseir to Kenna (Qena), where the track reached the Nile, and the latter was a little over a day's journey further west. These were reasonably well-established posts, so the main problem was the 55 miles between Cosseir and Moilah, far too long for unaccustomed men to march.[25] On 15 June Auchmuty wrote to Captain Mahoney of the 1st Native Infantry, who was already at Moilah, and referred to water which 'has already been found about ten miles from here' (i.e., Cosseir), and he now wanted Ensign Wilson of that battalion to investigate another site a further dozen miles on to see if a well could be dug there as well. Wilson would need men from Mahoney's detachment for the work, 'provided you can supply them with water'. On the same day he demanded reports of progress from Lieutenant Stirling of the 7th Native Infantry, who was digging wells at another site, which was hopefully named 'New Wells'.

Stirling was also warned to be alert 'to guard against a surprise', and to watch out for 'the movement of a large body of Arabs'. The presence of small armed groups of soldiers along the track could well be a temptation to the locals. If any threat appeared 'you will of course retreat with your detachment' – an instruction which was probably necessary so as to prevent eager young officers from chancing a battle in order to gain a name for themselves. This issue did not in fact arise, partly because the British resorted to hiring the camels and asses belonging to those Arabs to assist in moving the stores and water – and in carrying soldiers who were weakened by sickness – so that the Arabs who might have raided the British columns instead made money from them peaceably. The animals were hired for hard cash, half now, the other half on the completion of the set task; this brought in more than enough of them to transport what was needed; for the Arabs it was clearly more profitable to help the British than to attack them.

Macquarie at Cosseir was organising the construction of water casks, for which it was first necessary to make rivets. It had soon became clear that the water bags the troops had with them, which were perfectly adequate in India, were not good enough in the desert and had to be replaced by the casks, from which less evaporation took place. No detail was too small for the attention of Baird and Auchmuty. A cart broke down in Cosseir and this brought an instruction from Baird to Auchmuty to write to Captain Burr, 'the commissary for cattle', that he must 'send on the provisions by some means or other, as very serious consequences may result from their not reaching' the 88th Regiment. That day (17 June) Captain Mahoney was ordered to move on from Moilah to Legetta, while Lieutenant Kenny of the 7th Native Infantry was to move on to Moilah behind him. Several of Auchmuty's letters included demands for frequent reports on progress, but it is clear that these were not always complied with. It was still not certain, on 22 June, for instance, how successful Lieutenant Stirling had been at digging the 'New Wells'.

By that date the procedure for moving the troops forward had been worked out, and it was decided that they should march by night to avoid the daytime heat. It was explained by Auchmuty in a letter to Colonel William Carr Beresford, who was in command of the 'Left Brigade'.

> The general intends sending 200 camels on which you will mount 400 of your weakest men and officers and send them to make a forced march direct to Moilah. These men should leave you by 4 o'clock at furthest. They will take with them their canteens and four camel loads of water in casks which should if necessary be delivered to them during the night, or early in the morning. A trusty officer should command these. The remainder of your detachment will endeavour by every means in your power to reach Moilah the second day.
>
> Two days' wine for 1100 men is sent tonight to your post. You will see that your men cook enough [food] to last them two days and as much congee water as their canteens will hold to take with them. A sufficiency

> of wine for the march at a pint a day per man will also accompany you, one half to be put into their canteens with their congee, the other half to be given them on their coming to their ground. You will not suffer any salt meat or spirit to be used on the march.

Prospecting for water continued, with the headquarters apparently receiving the information about possible sites for sinking new wells before it reached any of the men in the field. It is not clear where this information came from, but the obvious possibilities are the local Arabs or scouting parties – who, now that the Arabs were friendly, could range more widely. Lieutenant Kenny at Moilah was directed to investigate two possible sites west of his station:

> [I]n the event of your having reached Moilah you will dispatch a company of your corps under an active officer to a place about 7½ miles from thence and about half a mile from the road. It may be found by the camel march that leads to it and must not be mistaken for a place where there is water about four miles from Moilah. The company will immediately dig wells and I trust that you will inspect their progress and add to their party if there is a prospect of succeeding to as great an extent as at the New Wells.[26]

The expeditionary force therefore made its way through the desert slowly and in batches. The water supply on the route was sufficient only to maintain a small party at each halt, so the men moved only when the wells had been able to provide sufficient supplies for its next stage. Recruiting camels and asses helped to transport the heavier items, which included the water casks, and as Auchmuty had noted, men who succumbed to the heat or disease. The newly dug wells were not capacious, and the men had to be trained not to drink too much or too quickly. 'It has been recommended that the men should march with one or two pebble stones in their mouths to preserve them from thirst. The general desires you will try if it will answer.'

It was also necessary to move the guns of the artillery, the horses of the dragoons and the horse artillery, and the ammunition for the artillery, as well as the soldiers, their weapons, their supplies, and the women and servants. And money, in cash and in local coin, had to be available at each station for the camel-men and the ass-drivers. And the women and children who always accompanied an Indian army had to be disembarked and transported to the Nile as well. It was not simply a matter of men marching.

Baird decided to gather a fairly substantial force at Legetta before moving the last 28 miles to the Nile. He knew that there were no French forces in Upper Egypt – the Arabs were evidently free with information – but he was also aware that many of the surviving Mamelukes and their men, after their defeat in the north, had moved upriver to escape the French, who had followed them, but had then withdrawn. These were the ex-slave soldiers who had ruled Egypt since the thirteenth century, first on their own and later under Ottoman suzerainty. They were now one of several armed elements which were contending for control of the country – the British, the French, the Ottomans, more than one Mameluke faction, even the Sharif of Mecca, were all separately interested and at least potentially mutually hostile. Baird had to have a care not to become too involved in the local quarrels, and not to make any commitments which might have to be disavowed, or even honoured, later. The Mamelukes on the upper Nile were for the present as hostile to the French as were the British, but they were pursuing their own ambitions above all – as was the Sharif of Mecca – and their hostility might easily switch towards the British. Service in India will have provided all the senior British officers with a good grounding in such political manoeuvres.

At the end of June the General Headquarters of the expedition moved forward to Moilah, leaving Lieutenant Colonel Montresor, Auchmuty's cousin, in command at Cosseir with Macquarie as his Deputy Adjutant General. Colonel Murray was sent forward to Kenna to investigate the situation at the river end of the march, and perhaps to contact the Mameluke chiefs in the area. The scale of the logistical problem is suggested by a letter Auchmuty sent to Murray from Moilah. There were 1,300 camels at Cosseir. Each owner had been paid 2 dollars per camel; they were to go, now, to Kenna, where Murray – who had clearly taken a force of soldiers, supplies, and equipment with him – was to pay them another dollar. The camel drivers were unhappy since the supplies for the animals were low; therefore the camels were to return at once to Cosseir (where there were presumably supplies available). All this had been arranged with 'Sally Aga', the local entrepreneur, a name and title which just might be Mameluke. More revealing is the final comment that '50 asses' were carrying '100 kegs of spirits to Kenna. They left Cosseir yesterday and arrived here (Moilah) this morning.' It is clear that the most efficient transport animal in the desert was a donkey.

Not everything went smoothly. The 10th Foot moved on from Moilah on 2 July, marching, as usual, at night, but when they were met by Lieutenant Warden, the commissary of stores, they were 'straggling greatly and getting on badly'. This observation was in a letter by Auchmuty at Moilah to Montresor at Cosseir which was peppered with comments and instructions:

> Order the cavalry to send on board there painted cloths which are too weighty for the horses. Order to Moilah twelve camel loads of rice, the camels to lodge their rice here and go on with two Bengal companies to Kenna. If they are marched the camels will assist the 86th. Continue mending mustact and making casks. Speak to Lowe about the latter, it is a matter of great consequence. Enquire of the paymasters whether they can tell the amount of the treasure with you and let me know. You must send a surgeon's mate to remain at Moilah. [Doctor] Shapter must find one.

And so on. He wrote much more familiarly to Montresor than he did to anyone else, including Macquarie. 'We are certainly in a foul scrape,' he said in an unprecedented slide into slang, in the same letter. 'We can hardly get on or go back, and the prospect does not brighten, but we must not despair.'

One matter which was preventing decision and promoting indecision in Baird was the continuing and almost complete ignorance at his headquarters of knowledge of the situation of the army in the north. Baird knew that Abercromby was dead and had been replaced by Hely-Hutchinson, because Commodore Blankett had finally returned from carrying the detachment of the 86th under Lieutenant Colonel Lloyd to Suez. Blankett had waited there until Hutchinson had at last asked that Lloyd and his men should join him at Cairo. (Twenty-three of them died on the march along a well-used road, travelling in two days what normally took five, and in a temperature over 110 Fahrenheit; Baird's much larger force did much better on a longer and drier march.) Hutchinson had heard of Baird's arrival by 15 May when he wrote to him – the letter was probably carried by Blankett, who had delayed for weeks before leaving Suez and only reached Cosseir on 15 June, just when the Red Sea expedition was disembarking. But on 2 July Auchmuty commented to Montresor that 'among other causes of uneasiness is the not hearing from Hutchinson'. In fact, Hutchinson had other things on his mind. His army and that of the Turkish vizier had begun the siege of Cairo at the beginning of June, and it was not until the 22nd that the French forces in the city surrendered. In such a situation the far away (and possibly out of mind) Baird scarcely counted.

By the end of June Baird had gathered part of his force at Kenna on the river, but had delayed bringing the 'second division' forward until he knew whether he should move on northwards or back to the Red Sea coast. Some of the troops would be left to hold Cosseir, either sick or in garrison, but he did not feel he could move north from Kenna until definite news of the situation there arrived from Hutchinson. Montresor at Cosseir passed on a letter to Commodore Blankett from Major Holloway, who had accompanied the Ottoman forces through Syria, and was with Hutchinson's force, but this was hardly official news of Hutchinson's situation, as Auchmuty pointed out on 9 July. At that point Baird was still undecided whether he would be 'advancing or returning'.

Hutchinson had in fact threatened Cairo, along with the surviving Mamelukes and a Turkish army commanded by the Grand Vizier, for only a few days after the allies' forces arrived at the city. On 22 June, even before Hutchinson had formally set the siege, the French in the city surrendered on the condition that they should be evacuated to France. One of the major factors in the collapse of the French morale in Cairo was the prospect of being butchered by the Mamelukes and the Turks in the event of a storm of the city, a possibility Hutchinson did nothing to decry. In the city General Belliard was as short of news from the French overall commander General Menou, who was in Alexandria, as Baird was in the south of news from Hutchinson. But another factor in Belliard's despair was the reports of Baird's landing at Cosseir and his force's advance to the Nile. This closed off a possible final retreat upriver.[27]

Baird at last received official news from Hutchinson on 14 July, reporting the capture of Cairo and the restriction of the French to Alexandria, but nothing more. Next day, Auchmuty wrote to Montresor at Cosseir summoning forward the second division, which was strung along the route back to the port, and more letters went to the officers at Moilah to spur them on.

But now the river became difficult. The shortage of water in the desert was replaced by overmuch water in the river. 'The Nile has risen so much that it is too late to march on the banks', Auchmuty told Montresor in a second letter that day (24 July). Parties had been out seeking boats, but this was taking time to produce results. Again it was intended to spread the force out, 'leaving the 7th at Cosseir and the desert [posts], and the 1st Bombay Regiment at Kenna, at least for the present'. And Auchmuty's letter ended the frustrated cry: 'We have not a word of news from the lower army more than I have mentioned. Has Macquarie any?'

A week later, the 'boat committee' having gathered some boats and seen to the repair of others, Baird was 'now most anxious to get away'. But there were not enough boats for everyone. With the river rising the road alongside it would have to be used as long as possible. Auchmuty sent Montresor detailed instructions for the disposition of the troops, treasure, and artillery which had still not reached Kenna; next day he sent orders to Lieutenant Colonel Quarrell, commanding the 10th Foot, to begin the march along the riverside road; arrangements had been made to collect supplies along the route. His initial destination was 'Gingie', and if conditions permitted he should move on to 'Scorf', and then onwards. The rising river was liable to flood the road, so that 'when you can proceed no further you will encamp on some high ground and await the arrival of the fleet under the commander-in-chief'.

Three days later, Quarrell was told that more boats than expected had been collected; a later reference suggests that the purse-strings had been loosened again to hire the boats; but the Mamelukes may also have exercised their usual brutal requisitioning methods. Quarrell was now to wait at 'Gingie', and the boats would collect his forces there. The 'cattle', which were making their way on the same road under Captain Burn, the 'commissary for cattle', would follow and Quarrell was to hand over his own cattle to Burn's care. The 88th Foot was being put on boats to follow on. And Auchmuty could now write directly to the headquarters of the main force at Giza, outside Cairo, to report that the southern army was embarking and would soon arrive in the north.

Baird followed the 10th and the 88th, intending to move on 24 July, though in the event he did not do so for another week. Auchmuty at Kenna made the arrangements which were to be left in place in the south. Colonel Murray was to remain in command at Kenna, and a long letter to him detailed the things he had to do. Appointments at Cosseir and Legetta and Moilah were made. He left with Baird on the boats with the last part of the 80th Foot. The journey from Kenna to Giza of the whole force was apparently trouble-free, for which the likely willingness of the British to pay for hiring boats and to purchase supplies (the Mamelukes usually merely seized them) was probably responsible. By this time Cairo had capitulated on 22 June. The whole journey from India to Egypt, across the desert, and along the Nile could have been described as unnecessary.[28]

By 8 August Auchmuty was reporting to Holloway, now a lieutenant colonel, from Giza, below the Pyramids, but out of Cairo, which was liable to be disease-ridden. Baird's force at their new camp would be 5,000 men, he reported, 'when the different detachments of his force are collected', and they should be provisioned in the same way as Hutchinson's own force. It turned out that the Reis Effendi (commander) of the Turkish forces was responsible for the provisions: Auchmuty promptly sent Holloway an estimate of what was required, to be passed on.

The long sequence of letters produced by Auchmuty on this march from Cosseir to Giza gives a view of his unceasing resource in his post. There are references here and there to Baird's instructions and intentions, but most of the letters are simply Auchmuty telling someone what to do on his own responsibility. It is clear that he had all the necessary information to hand, about water supplies, distances, directions of march, and so on, and was able to give clear instructions to commanders at some distance, so from Kenna to Cosseir, or from Kenna to Gingie. His tone becomes increasingly assured over the period of these letters, and it seems clear that not only did Baird leave much of the organising to him, but that the recipients of the letters were quite willing to accept his system and his instructions because they were able to trust him. The relative lack of casualties is a testimony to his efficiency. It was, in fact, he who organised the march, though, as usual, the credit went elsewhere.

With the two British armies now camped close to each other geographically, presumably a good deal of communication took place orally, for there are large gaps in Macquarie's archive between letters of 9 and 19 August. (He was also presumably travelling in that time.) Hutchinson, as it turned out, did require Baird's force for two main reasons: once the last of the French were defeated and evacuated it was Baird's army which was to remain as the Egyptian occupation force; but these troops were also needed for the last stage of the fighting, the capture of Alexandria.

The reason was that when Cairo surrendered, the British were shocked to find that the surrendering French, whom they had assumed to number about 6,000 men, were actually claiming a ration strength of 17,000 – the total besieging force had been only half that – Hutchinson's British force had been only 4,000, with as many Turks and Mamelukes – a clear sign of the demoralisation of the French. This suggested that the French in Alexandria would also be more numerous than had been thought, though possibly just as demoralised: Hutchinson therefore needed all the troops he could collect. But the first necessity was to remove the French from Cairo, and they were marched, carrying their arms and moving with their artillery in accordance with the surrender terms, along the Rosetta distributary of the Nile to the coast west of Alexandria. They were accompanied by a strong escort of British, Turkish, and Mameluke troops – just in case they chose to disregard the terms of surrender and decided to break away to join their fellow troops in Alexandria. The British were commanded on this march by Major-General Sir John Moore, who finally got to count them as they passed through a narrow defile: 8,000 marching troops, 2,000 men in boats, and 3,700 others – plus women and children and slaves and servants.[29]

Hutchinson could therefore expect to face just as substantial a French force at Alexandria, which in turn was a more defensible city than Cairo had proved to be. He ordered Baird's force to come forward, and received further reinforcements by sea. The Cairo French sailed from Rosetta in early August, just as the forces from the upper Nile were finally gathered at Giza. It took another week to assemble a force at Alexandria which Hutchinson thought sufficiently strong to make a serious attempt at capturing the city.

It also took that length of time for Baird's last detachments to arrive, and in the event his force was left in garrison near Cairo during the siege. Hutchinson in fact did have enough soldiers in his own forces at Alexandria, in part because the fighting was concentrated into two narrow areas on either side of the city and between the sea and Lake Mareotis (which had been flooded when British engineers breached the dike on the river; this reduced the scope for French sorties by land, and allowed the navy to exert pressure from armed boats in the newly flooded lake – the French, of course, did the same, but had much less naval expertise than the British).[30] So even though, as it proved, Hutchinson's besieging force was once again seriously outnumbered, his effective force in the attacks was quite sufficient, since its fronts, either side of the city, were so narrow. The siege lasted nearly two weeks, until 28 August, and surrender terms were agreed by 2 September. A count of forces at that time showed that General Menou had a force of 11,200 men, and Hutchinson 9,600. Once again a French army had been defeated by a smaller British force; demoralisation was the basic reason again, but the British forces had certainly defeated the French more than once in open combat.[31]

Baird and his troops had been left out of it. Plans were being made on 16 August to move forwards towards Alexandria, but the force's headquarters remained at Rhoda Island at Cairo until the siege ended. Colonel Ramsay was appointed to command the forces left at Giza, a posting he greeted with annoyed complaints. A detachment under Colonel Lloyd was sent to garrison Damietta, the point at which the road from Syria reached the Nile. On 26 August Ramsay was finally told the full details of his command: Lloyd and the 86th and four companies of the 7th Bombay Regiment, which were at Damietta; two more companies of the 7th were at Kenna; six companies of the 7th and 1st which were still spread between Kenna and Cosseir; and there were seventy chests of treasure at Giza which had to be guarded. All this, together with instructions to maintain good relations with the Mamelukes in Cairo, seems to have quietened Ramsay's hurt feelings, and gave him plenty to do. His main grumble was that he was not included in the force marching to Alexandria, but the fighting there came to an end soon after, curtailing the opportunities for glory he may have envisaged, and this must also have quietened him. Baird's force, therefore, arrived at Alexandria, as it had at Cairo, after the siege was over, so Ramsay's desire to get involved in the fighting was now irrelevant. Baird and Auchmuty reached Hutchinson on 1 September, according to Wilson's account.[32]

By 8 September Baird's headquarters were at Rosetta, and most of the French troops had been evacuated from Alexandria. Auchmuty spread the news of the capitulation of Alexandria to the officers at Kenna and Cosseir, and to the sailors on the ships at Jeddah – to the latter he also gave news of the battles of Algeciras, a tactful gesture to the sailors. His letters continue to discuss minute details of administration – the asses used by the 10th Foot, officers requesting sick leave, Captain Burn's cattle.

The arrival of the forces from India in the north near Cairo provoked amusement and some scorn among the force from Britain, who saw the Indian officers dining in palatial tents, their great quantities of wine, their servants, and their regular and substantial pay – pay which was actually paid. (This puts in some perspective the complaints of the officers in India, who actually were better off than the royal regiments – their lavish lifestyle was the product of their *batta*.) The amusement and scorn were, of course, the product of jealousy, and the false bravado of living hard. Hutchinson kept the two forces in well-separated camps, knowing full well that such jealousy could easily feed enmity. He hardly wanted inter-British riots to ruin his time in command. Baird conducted elaborate drills and manoeuvres with his force, and their professionalism somewhat quietened the initial jealousy and contempt.[33]

The problem subsided quickly, for the forces from Britain were removed fairly rapidly after their victory, and once the French in Alexandria had also been removed, just as had those from Cairo, in British cartel ships. The British troops were sent back to Britain, or to the West Indies, Malta, or Minorca, and they had mainly all left between September and December. Baird's force remained as the occupiers of Egypt.[34] General Hely-Hutchinson left in October, and General Moore, who had been appointed to take over the command, took himself back to Britain on self-awarded leave, not being willing to hold still when there might be action elsewhere. The command-in-chief fell to Lord Cavan, another Major General. The reduction in the British force was accompanied by a reduction in its power and its importance – and the rank of its commander – and, of course, therefore also its political clout was diminished.[35]

This weakening of the British presence was therefore also accompanied by a growing inability to control the local situation. Hutchinson had been clear that the Mameluke beys had been very helpful in the campaign and he had aimed to see that their control of Egypt was safeguarded. The British, however, were technically the allies of the Ottoman Empire in this enterprise, and the Mamelukes were technically Ottoman subjects; they were also divided into two main parties, which made it difficult. One group, following Murad Bey, had retreated into Upper Egypt, but had then made a peace of sorts with the French. His rival, Ibrahim Bey, had escaped to Syria and had participated in the fighting against the French there, and had returned with the Ottoman

Army. Neither of these groups was any longer acceptable to the Turks, whose army and navy had also fought the French, and had provided more troops than either the British or the Mamelukes. Whereas the Mamelukes wanted to regain their earlier power in Egypt, the Turks' ultimate aim was to recover control of Egypt from both the French and the Mamelukes. To add to the confusion, British intentions as articulated in London were unclear, and were subject to conflicting advice from Lord Elgin, the ambassador in Constantinople, and from General Hutchinson, when he reached Britain.[36]

Hutchinson had generally supported the Mameluke beys, perhaps because he was grateful for their assistance, more likely because he disliked the Turks – and they were all anti-French, which the Turks might not be, in the future. And, if the object of British policy was to weaken the Ottoman Empire, detaching Egypt from the Turkish government and putting it under the beys once more would be a good way to go about it. All the better would it be if the beys found that they needed British support to maintain their rule – against French or Turks or anyone else. Also the recent campaign had shown that Egypt was relatively easily accessible from India. Even if the journey from Cosseir to the north had been slow and awkward, the route from Suez to Cairo was easy, so long as someone like Colonel Lloyd was not in command. Some sort of British protectorate over Egypt might have eventuated. From London, however, it was the access to Egypt from Europe, specifically from France, which was the real problem, and this could well be achieved if the Royal Navy was once more removed from Mediterranean, and over the next two years several French squadrons came near to reaching Egypt again. Once peace was agreed with France in October 1801, there was no guarantee that French influence would not suddenly and clandestinely return to Egypt in force – the French attack had been in a time of peace with the Ottoman Empire, after all, and if Bonaparte was in charge in France such a ploy could well be repeated. Nelson's long search for Bonaparte's fleet, and his regularly missing of it, showed clearly enough that even with the navy freely roaming the Mediterranean, a hostile force could make the voyage without being detected. In that case, either a strengthened Mameluke regime, or a firm Ottoman government, would be preferable. The problem therefore was still how to decide between these alternatives.

Peace with France was made in negotiations at Amiens – conducted by Lord Cornwallis – while the British Army was still in Egypt, Auchmuty and Baird included.[37] What internal security there had been in the country was fast breaking down in the absence of a government in control. On 27 October Auchmuty passed on orders to Colonel Lloyd to take the 86th Foot and some artillery to Giza by boat to assist Ramsay, and added 'the general desires that you will be particularly on your guard during the passage … and be careful to avoid any disputes between your people and the Turks'. But Lloyd was also told to stop and examine any boats he met coming from Cairo, and if he found any beys imprisoned on them, to 'take them with you and deliver them to Colonel Ramsay'. The contradiction between these two instructions shows how British detachments risked being caught between the various factions.

The dispute between several parties over the future of Egypt continued throughout the command of Lord Cavan, and into that of his successor, Brigadier General Sir John Stuart, who had also participated in the original campaign of conquest. Having returned to Britain with his brigade, he had been commissioned by Lord Hobart, the Secretary of State for War, to return to Egypt to take over as Commander-in-Chief from Lord Cavan. He was to travel by way of Constantinople to attempt to organise a compromise between the Ottomans and the beys, but with a much-weakened army in Egypt he had little leverage. The Ottoman government, which claimed to be the rightful rulers of Egypt, the Mameluke beys being in rebellion, required the beys to leave, going into exile. Needless to say the beys had no intention of doing so, being confident of recovering control from the Turks when the British left.

The army under Baird thus largely remained in Egypt, though some units, like the 86th under Lloyd, were withdrawn back to India. Auchmuty himself stayed on; his appointment had been by the War Office, and so he was not subject to being sent to India. He continued to act as Adjutant General of the whole force under the successive commanders, his evident importance rising as the upper ranks thinned out. By the time Stuart took over in October 1802 Auchmuty was close to being, in effect, the second-in-command.

The experience had clearly been of great value. His administrative ability had been demonstrated to a series of generals, and, more important, had been confirmed to the War Office in London. His ability also to get along with everyone had been clear. Hutchinson was not difficult to serve with, but Baird had a rich temper, and Stuart was a pernickety and quarrelsome character. All of the various men had had no dispute with the efficient Adjutant General.

By the time that Stuart took over from Cavan in October 1802, a condition of peace between Britain and France had been concluded. This meant that French travellers and envoys were able to visit Egypt, and one who did so, arriving almost simultaneously with Stuart, was Colonel Horace Sebastiani. He was on a tour of investigation which was so open that 'spying' is an inadequate and inaccurate term. He returned to France in January 1803, and his report was published in the *Moniteur*, the official French government organ. It was so obvious and blatant in its advocacy of French aims that it must have appeared with Bonaparte's blessing, if not at his instructions, no doubt as a way of preparing French opinion for the possibility of another Egyptian expedition. Sebastiani laid out a series of ambitions for the Napoleonic state, for conquests in North Africa, Syria, and the Ionian Islands; and he claimed that 10,000 French troops could reconquer Egypt (once the British had left). Sebastiani was, so he claimed, greeted by the Egyptians as Napoleon's agent during his visit, and everyone he met seemed to be pro-French. He was, of course, deluding himself, and possibly Napoleon, in all this; it is clear that the French would not be welcome in force, even if individuals could be treated in a friendly and flattering manner. But his report did emphasise the vulnerability of Egypt, and revealed the ambitions of the French, and drew attention to the vanishing size of the British forces there.

To the British – who clearly understood what he was reporting and advocating – this could well mean that a French force might arrive unexpectedly, perhaps in alliance with the Ottomans in a joint invasion to suppress the Mamelukes now that the peace had been signed, and the Royal Navy could not officially intervene. Given the reduction in the British forces in Egypt and the destruction of much of the Mameluke armed force, 10,000 French troops might well be quite adequate to defeat the British Army in Egypt even if it had stayed.[38]

The British had already determined not to evacuate Malta as required in the peace with France, for if Malta was retained they could dominate the entrance to the eastern Mediterranean, just as Gibraltar held the western gateway. That would mean they could leave Egypt, and let the local disputants arrange matters for themselves, and any French attempt to intervene could be at least watched. Therefore, Baird and many of the Indian troops left in mid-1802, and in March 1803 the last of the forces from Britain also left.[39] (Macquarie had gone to Britain at the end of 1801, so we are deprived of his assiduously collected copies of letters.) Auchmuty, however, remained in Egypt to the end.

Even before the British left, indeed even before Hutchinson left, the dispute between the Mameluke beys and the Ottomans had produced violence. At one point the Ottoman commander had invited some of the beys to a conference only to murder several of them and imprison others. Hutchinson had intervened and got the prisoners released.[40] But once the British had gone, or even while Stuart commanded the few British troops who remained in the last months, it was clear that the situation in Egypt was out of control. A new Ottoman governor, Khushraw Pasha, had been appointed, but found that his authority was very limited. Of the beys who had survived, there were at least two factions in arms, including one which had been persuaded by Stuart to withdraw to Upper Egypt under the leadership of Alfi Bey, who proved to be a ferocious oppressor of the Egyptians and an avid tax collector. Cairo was occupied by Ottoman troops whose oppressions were even worse than those of the beys, and went as far as evicting householders, burning anything that was burnable, and then moving on to another household, meanwhile extracting any money they could find. They intercepted incoming supplies of food, forced the peasants to sell their produce at a low price, and then sold it on to the merchants of the city at a handsome profit; and still they demanded their pay.[41]

The British were, by late 1802, incapable of seriously affecting the situation inside Egypt. They were told of a battle which took place between Turks and Mamelukes at Damanhur, not far from the British headquarters at Alexandria. If they could not stop such an event there was no point in staying on. This Stuart reported to Lord Hobart in London on 24 November; two days later, and so conveying a decision which had been arrived at separately from this information, Hobart sent orders to Stuart to withdraw from all of Egypt.

Stuart did not really wish to withdraw. He interpreted Hobart's orders as 'preparatory' to the withdrawal, and decided that he was finding it too difficult to disengage. The British force was still in position in February, but his numbers gradually fell; he finally reported that the last units were withdrawn on 28 and 29 March 1803.[42]

In the midst of all this one man, Muhammad Ali, originally the deputy commander of a group of irregular Albanian soldiers in Ottoman pay, gradually rose from that minor position to the command of the whole Albanian group of soldiers, perhaps 6,000 men; more importantly, he appears to have quickly identified himself with, and gained the trust of, the Cairene population, who were thoroughly alienated by the behaviour of the Ottomans, and hardly more pleased at the possible resumption of Mameluke rule. He also made allies of the *ulama*, the Muslim hierarchy who were centred at the al-Azhar mosque. A new Ottoman governor was appointed, Kurshid Pasha, but he found he had no control whatsoever over any troops in Egypt. He called in a group of irregulars from Syria who proved to be even more oppressive and unpopular than any of the others. The beys, much weakened in numbers and authority, demanded that their traditional authority be restored; the Ottoman governor aimed to restore Ottoman power; neither had any real authority other than over the force they claimed to command, and so they exercised power over the population only by the violence they could exert, both in the countryside or in the cities.[43] In all this unpleasantness, Muhammad Ali stood out, at least as the least bad alternative.

It gradually became clear to the Ottoman government in Constantinople that one of the major blocks to the restoration of Ottoman authority was Muhammad Ali and his forces. He was appointed to the rank of Pasha and was made governor of Jeddah in Arabia, with the intention of removing him from Egypt. This was too transparent a ploy to succeed. He took the title and ignored the office. When in mid-1804 the situation in Cairo descended into a civil war between Khurshid Pasha's force of irregulars and the Mamelukes, Muhammad Ali emerged as the one man with any real authority over the population. It took him several more years to persuade the Ottoman government to accept his authority as Egyptian ruler, and to eliminate the beys – it could only be done by massacre, since they were obdurate.

For over a year after the British finally left, therefore, Egypt went through a process of revolution which was as violent as anything seen in France, and in fact the situation was compared by the French consul, Bernardino Drovetti, to the French experience.[44] It would be easy in fact to blame the situation on, first, the French invasion, then the British counter-invasion, and then the British negligence in leaving without setting up any viable government. Yet these interventions did no more than aggravate the situation which was already sliding out of control before the French arrived, and in actual fact, both French and British were operating in Ottoman territory, and if anyone had responsibility for the situation in Egypt it was the ineffective Ottoman government in Constantinople. Muhammad Ali, when he finally gained control over Egypt, was in fact the successor of an earlier attempt fifty years before by another man, Ali Bey al-Kabir, to do exactly that: remove the Mamelukes and reduce Ottoman authority to nil, and then impose a government which was distinguished by its application of law and order, which was in fact Muhammad Ali's programme.[45] This development had therefore been on the local political agenda for decades. For the last century the Mameluke beys had exercised authority only by violence and fear. Captain Moiret has a revealing anecdote on this: in a fight between a Mameluke force and a local force of French and Arabs, the Mameluke commander charged directly into his enemies and was killed by one of the Egyptians; the Egyptians fled into shelter, for they had killed a bey, and they understood that the penalty for such an act would be a massacre, probably indiscriminate.[46] The intervention of Ottoman governors was in fact seen locally as yet another foreign invasion along with that of France and Britain; in view of local attitudes to the Mamelukes, and of the Mamelukes to the Egyptians, whom they regarded only as prey, however, any alliance between Mamelukes and Egyptians was probably out of the question.

For Britain, the experience was in the nature of a revelation. Given the geography of the Mediterranean it was clearly much easier for France to intervene in force in Egypt than it was for Britain; hence the decision to annex Malta by both the French and the British. The annoyance Napoleon displayed at the decision by the British to maintain their hold on Malta was to the British a clear confirmation that he intended to seize it for himself once more at the first opportunity, and then to use it as a base to dominate the eastern Mediterranean, and perhaps to dismantle the Ottoman Empire on the lines suggested by Colonel Sebastiani's report. If the French could gain control of Egypt once more, they could mount a standing threat of French intervention against the rest of the Ottoman Empire, and to British control of the Indian Ocean.

The eastern Mediterranean therefore became for the first time a standing area of British concern. They made a new intervention in Egypt in 1807, humiliatingly defeated. After the Napoleonic wars considerable numbers of Frenchmen went to Egypt to offer their technical services to Muhammad Ali, which he welcomed, but as soon as Muhammad Ali began expanding his authority out of Egypt, Britain became increasingly concerned, and in the end used force (in 1840) to drive him back into Egypt. For the rest of the nineteenth century, therefore, Britain became increasingly entangled in Egyptian affairs, an entanglement which lasted until the 1950s and the Suez crisis.

One of the major sources of Egyptian vulnerability to Europeans was its past. The great monuments of pharaonic power which littered the Egyptian landscape were of little interest to the Egyptians, whose Islamic beliefs disdained their past as infidel. But to Europeans they were fascinating, and they were drawn to Egypt in their thousands to inspect, excavate, or simply to look at them. This was, in large part, Napoleon's doing, for he took with him 150 '*savants*', who spent their time exploring this strange land, and then produced huge and magnificent printed accounts of what they saw.[47]

And yet it did not need Napoleon's *savants* to interest the British in the Egyptian past. The occupation of Alexandria between 1801 and 1803 saw many minor investigations of local monuments. This might be done by the commanding generals, but it was also something which drew the attention and investigations of the ordinary soldiers and sailors. The monument called Pompey's Pillar was explored by officers and men, and British sailors agilely climbed it. Cleopatra's Needle was admired to excess, on the erroneous assumption that Cleopatra was beautiful, and that the Needle had anything to do with her. The site of the lighthouse on Pharos Island was repeatedly examined. The extent of the city founded by Alexander was emphasised in the re-flooding of Lake Mareotis which helped by reviving the geography of Alexander's time.[48]

In the more or less idle last months of the British occupation several of the British officers formed themselves into a 'committee', with Major General Lord Cavan as president and Colonel Auchmuty as treasurer. Their aim was to raise money to finance the extraction of Cleopatra's Needle and transport it to Britain as a monument to the success of the British expedition. This committee was formed as early as January 1802, and by late February it had received pledges of £4,000 for the task. Cavan promised to contribute £200 and Baird £150; Auchmuty chipped in £100 as did Colonels Hope and

Beresford. But it was not enough, and the project was abandoned, probably wisely, since this was one of those projects which was always going to be a lot more expensive than any advance estimate.[49]

There is no indication that anyone's permission to remove the huge stone object was sought, nor indeed that this was felt to be necessary. Lord Keith, the naval commander, refused to have anything to do with the scheme, which effectively would have killed it had it not died already of financial starvation. But it, and the confiscation from the French of the Rosetta Stone (which was recognised as culturally vital for understanding the past by both British and French soldiers as soon as it was found, but not by the Egyptians) and other souvenirs picked up by individuals, was a start in the wholesale despoliation of Egypt which began soon afterwards. Drovetti, for example, took back to Turin a museumful of Egyptian antiquities and papyri.

The political and military shrinkage of the British presence which enabled the Turks, the Mamelukes, and Muhammad Ali to indulge in their mutual contest for power, had rendered the British presence irrelevant. Colonel Auchmuty probably did not see much further than his immediate problems of administering the British forces in Egypt, but he cannot have been ignorant of the fact that their presence was not wanted by any of the factions involved in the struggle for control of the country. In this his experience in Egypt replicated that he had undergone in his homeland in North America, and in India, and he was not yet finished with such experiences.

Chapter 5

United Kingdom, 1803–6

On his return to Britain in early 1803, Samuel Auchmuty, if he had not done so before, bought (or possibly rented) a small country house called Syndale, close to Ospringe, south of Faversham in Kent. He was clearly now fairly wealthy from his prize money in India, and more prize money was arriving as a result of the Egyptian expedition. (He had been able to promise £100 to transport Cleopatra's Needle, not a small sum.) More important for his future, he had made a considerable impression on his superiors by his administrative efficiency as Adjutant General for Baird's force in Egypt. He had already been noted by the Duke of York by being selected for the independent expedition round Africa to the Red Sea and Egypt; he could clearly expect further promotion.

It did not hurt, in his new search for promotion and command, that his old Indian commander Sir Robert Abercromby had nominated him to stand in for him as his proxy at a ceremony of the Knights of the Bath. Abercromby was going blind and lived in Scotland, in Perthshire, so presumably the journey to London was now too awkward and arduous for him. His nomination of Auchmuty implies a strong friendship between the two men, based on their several years' association in India. For Auchmuty this also brought a pleasant increase in prestige, since one of the rewards for acting as a proxy at the ceremony was to become a supernumerary Knight of the Bath himself. So he was now Colonel Sir Samuel.[1] He performed the same service for his nephew some years later.

The place he lived in was not far from several of his relatives, who had also settled in Kent.[2] His mother had lived with her youngest daughter Jane and her husband the Revd Richard Tylden at Milsted, a few miles south of Faversham, where Tylden was vicar; they had two sons. The Montresors, who included Frances Tucker, Samuel's half-sister, were by then deeply involved in the problems of repaying, as slowly as possible, Captain Montresor's illicit acquisition of wealth through his corrupt administration as military engineer in America; they had lived at Belmont, also to the south of Faversham, though General Harris had used his prize money from India to buy the place some years before. (Captain Montresor had died in 1799; his son was in India, and had been with Auchmuty in the Egyptian expedition.) Another sister, Isabella, and her husband William Burton lived elsewhere in Kent and had died there in 1792. Mary Julianna had married another Royal Engineer, Frederick George Mulcaster, who had connections with the Royal family; they lived at Sittingbourne.[3] Their daughter Mary had married Thomas Gage Montresor of Ospringe.

It is scarcely surprising that Samuel settled in Kent – if settled is the right word for a professional and ambitious soldier. He had had little experience of Britain. He had lived there for a few years in the 1780s when he had served at Nottingham as a young lieutenant in the 45th Foot, and then and only briefly in 1798–9; at that time he had probably had enough wealth to buy property, but he may well have expected to be posted elsewhere soon and may not have bothered. In all this he had seen a good deal of England as his regiment had moved about, and perhaps Scotland, if he had visited Abercromby there, but Kent was clearly his preferred choice, no doubt for family reasons – though it was also convenient for London, the source of patronage and promotion. His residence in Britain from 1803 was clearly expected to be longer than before, and as a full colonel having sold two of his earlier offices and collected prize money on at least two occasions, he had the wealth to buy; on the whole it seems more likely he bought Syndale in this period of British residence, and expected to stay for some time.

Not long before his return to Britain, it had become clear that the peace agreement secured by Lord Cornwallis at Amiens during 1801–2 would not hold.[4] Britain, having promised, on conditions, to evacuate Malta and return it to the Knights Hospitaller, from whom Bonaparte had taken it, was having second thoughts, partly as a result of Sebastiani's revelations of French ambitions in the Mediterranean, which fitted all too well with the current steady expansion of French power into Italy and Germany. Napoleon Bonaparte, now First Consul of the Republic, was demonstrating that, whether he was involved in either peace or war, he could extend his power over any neighbouring weaker state – and the Mediterranean was ringed by weak states.

The Maltese had accepted British direction of the fight to drive out the French, and in view of its clear usefulness to the Royal Navy, it was resolved to retain control of it, a decision which the Maltese acquiesced in. Bonaparte's expedition to the eastern Mediterranean had opened up that area to naval enterprise, and Malta was ideally placed to block, or to watch and detect, any further French adventures in that direction. Bonaparte cannot have been surprised at British intransigence over Malta; after all, he had himself seized the island for that very purpose; he protested nonetheless, of course.

Bonaparte's move further into Italy was assumed to be a preparation for another lunge at Egypt and therefore India. Annexing areas of both Germany and Italy gave him access to greater manpower resources for his wars, and to large numbers of ports and shipbuilding facilities, so he was expanding at sea as well. Mutual accusations of bad faith and treaty breaking were made, and in both cases were fully justified. In March 1803 the British government seized the moment and declared war when Napoleon was not ready, reaping a useful harvest of intercepted French (and Italian and Dutch) ships and their cargoes. This was the month in which Auchmuty and the last of the British troops in Egypt returned to Britain.

Napoleon set about organising a new attempt at an invasion of south-east England, gathering his army at the Channel ports, with his headquarters at Boulogne.[5] It was all a fairly slipshod operation, with unseaworthy barges which were expected to cross the water almost instantaneously; exercises showed their unsuitableness and an elaborately planned set of sea manoeuvres intended to bring an overwhelming French fleet (with Spanish and Dutch contingents) to control the English Channel for long enough – a week was thought to be sufficient, even, it was claimed, a day, 'six hours', Napoleon claimed – for the barges to get across. It was so badly developed as a plan that doubts exist as to Napoleon's seriousness.[6] On the other hand, he must have known that the conquest of Britain would open the way to much greater things, both in Europe and in the wider imperial overseas world, and the sheer quantity of preparations he made suggest a powerful determination. Surely it was all serious.

The target for the invasion would obviously be the coast of Kent and Sussex, the shortest sea crossing. These regions included the two great naval complexes at Chatham-and-Sheerness and Portsmouth and its neighbourhood. These were clearly major targets, and these two fortresses in effect marked the geographical limits of the possible landings. At St Helena fifteen years later Napoleon did suggest that he could have landed between Deal and Margate, but the more obvious landing places would be along the Sussex coast – the area targeted by William the Conqueror and the Nazis. This was all, of course, a repeat of the threat which had existed in 1797–8, when General Bonaparte, as he then had been, commanded in the same place for the same purpose and with many of the same soldiers. His plans had been somewhat refined and improved since then; there was a second French force which was assembled at Cherbourg, perhaps for a landing intended at Portsmouth or even Plymouth; one alternative, or addition, was to make a landing in Ireland, though such adventures had been disasters for both French and Spanish invaders in the past. In the War Office the old plans for defence were brought out of the files and adjusted slightly, though they were deemed still adequate.[7]

The essential first part of the defence plans was to embody sufficient soldiers, and second, to bring them to the target area so as to fight the French close to the coast. The Kent-Sussex area was already well stocked with regular soldiers, who were posted at the most vulnerable points – that is, now, the coast and the ports. In the rest of the country the militia and the Volunteers could be quickly brought to arms. The main part of the plan, to be implemented when the invasion came, centred on bringing the forces which were north of London in the rest of the country into the invaded area as quickly as possible.[8]

The militia was the traditional system whereby it was part of the civic duty of every (male) citizen to turn out in an emergency to defend his country. It could be embodied by a proclamation, and was organised by the Lords Lieutenants in each county. But it was unprofessional in the extreme, the men were originally not supposed to serve outside their own county, and most men could scarcely be persuaded to bother to turn out at the training days; they were certainly not an effective military force. The threat of invasion, however, certainly brought their numbers up, and being armed they would certainly have been a threat to the French.

An alternative source of soldierly manpower was the Volunteers, a much more recent, if still to a degree amateur, group, whose terms of engagement meant that they could be sent to serve in other parts of the country without difficulty; they were paid for the days they turned out for training and exercise, a useful incentive, and so they did have some useful basic military training. Plans were laid for the directions of march for the many volunteer units, and assembly places north of London were designated for the Volunteers from the northern regions where they were to be formed into larger units, and the militia similarly.

General Sir John Moore, encamped at Shorncliffe between Folkestone and Rye, who was also appointed commander of the forces in Kent, described in a false alert in October 1803, how the 'Volunteers, Sea Fencibles, and all were turned out … – not at all dismayed at the prospect of meeting the French.' He did not say, because it was clearly understood, that the alarm, though given by mistake, had successfully brought out all the required forces, armed and in position, well before the French could have arrived.[9]

(The volunteers were the butt of jokes and cartoons, and were derided by political opponents of the Tory government at the time, and by historians since, as amateurs and likely to fail in the face of French attacks. But it may be noted that it was the Volunteers who provided the recruits for the British Army after 1807, with Castlereagh's reforms, and thus they were the men who were commanded by Wellington in the Peninsula, where they consistently defeated the supposedly superior French – who were almost invariably superior in number, as in Egypt. A French invasion of England faced by the Volunteers would not have been a pushover.[10])

It was generally understood in the War Office that the invasion, if it came, would arrive at the low-lying part of Kent and Sussex as the point of landing, and indeed this was the French intention – little serious attempt had been made to keep it all a secret. This would give the invaders a reasonably extensive area of level lowland on Romney Marsh in which to collect themselves and sort themselves out after the crossing. To counter this the Royal Military Canal was planned. It would isolate Romney Marsh from the rest of the country, and plans were laid for flooding the marsh as well. The canal, a deceptively simple idea, would in fact be a major obstacle to an invader, and was so located as to be overlooked by higher ground from inland, and at places by ramparts, all well within musket shot of any man attempting to cross it. At 30ft wide, it was impossible to cross in force in the face of obstinate resistance, and being overlooked a surprise attack would be extremely difficult to execute.[11] Bridges which were built to cross were all within easy range of defensive forces, and could be broken without difficulty.

On the other hand, work was only started on it in September 1804, and was not completed until 1809, so its value in combating an early invasion would be small. (Yet there were intermittent revivals of the invasion threat right up to the outbreak of Napoleon's Russian war in 1812, so the canal was hardly wasted effort.)

This preference for the south coast as the invasion target did not mean that the rest of the coastline could be ignored, and the War Office officers were apprehensive for the rest of Kent, for East Anglia, and even for Lincolnshire, all of which had long stretches of low-lying coast, and were to be protected during the years 1805 to 1812 by the building of a series of Martello towers, protected gun platforms overlooking vulnerable points of the coast. Once again, these defences were built too late to affect matters in this early phase, but the fact that they continued to be built shows continuing fears of invasion.[12]

One of the disputes within the military – and this issue was repeated in 1940 – was where to meet the enemy invaders if they landed. Should the fight take place on the beaches, or should the army wait somewhere inland and then strike back powerfully and with great force. There were good arguments on either side: beating the invader as he floundered ashore, dizzy from the sea, weak from seasickness, perhaps with useless dampened powder, and disorganised, could surely be effective – but only if the defenders were in sufficient numbers to drive all the invaders back. And it was unlikely that a large enough defensive force could be on the spot, for a long line of coast had to be covered; some invaders would certainly land and would organise themselves. Instead the defenders might wait until they had done just that and then strike with a properly constituted army. But as soon as the question was properly formulated it became clear that it would be best to use both methods: to fight at the landing places, even if it was not possible to stop the invaders completely, and at the same time to hold in reserve a large army to deal with whatever groups managed to break through. Making them fight for every inch of territory, inflicting casualties on them all the while from the start, would reduce their effectiveness and would probably keep them disorganised, and this was clearly a worthwhile approach. But the defenders would also suffer casualties, and while they would delay the attack, even possibly driving some of the invaders back into the sea, it would still be necessary to gather a force in reserve in case the initial defence failed.

And for any invader, Kent was a seriously difficult target. The county of Kent was replete with military and naval fortifications. Apart from the great fortress which was Dover Castle, Chatham was well defended by several fortifications and a substantial garrison, military and naval. Faversham, close to Auchmuty's home at Syndale, had important gunpowder mills; a barracks was built for a garrison at Ospringe. Every castle around the coast, of whatever age, was spruced up and put into a state of defence, and the Martello towers then added to this system. These castles included one at Deal, on the coast north of Dover, where was the terminus, or start, of the telegraph system which would carry the news of an invasion to London and beyond; Walmer Castle, a little further south, was the home of the Lord Warden of the Cinque Ports, the former Prime Minister, William Pitt, a powerful local presence.[13]

The coastal areas were subdivided into sections, each of which was assigned to a commandant. It was clearly necessary to have experienced commanders in position in each area in order to supervise the distribution of the forces and to command them in action if it became necessary, and it was best if these men could be on the spot beforehand to become familiar with the issues, and if possible with the men as well. Auchmuty fit this bill perfectly, an experienced commander of rank, and already living in Kent. He would be able to examine the ground, become familiar with the local forces, and he would also be defending his own home and those of several of his relatives. He was placed in position as commandant of the Isle of Thanet; he was in office probably as early as May, perhaps as soon as he had arrived in England, and in August he was already issuing orders to his subordinates. Therefore he had probably been investigating the situation on the ground for some time already.

The Isle of Thanet included a series of small ports along its coast which were separated from one another by white, vertical, chalk cliffs. It was no longer technically an island, though it was separated from the rest of Kent by the wet flatlands of the valleys of the Rivers Wantsum and Stour. If the French did not in the end choose to land between Folkestone and Eastbourne, as was their actual plan, the coast of Kent north of Dover was clearly a likely alternative place where they could attempt to invade.

The defence of the Isle of Thanet centred on its geography. It is an uplifted block of chalk, dipping gently to the south. The coast is therefore lined with those vertical chalk cliffs along the north and east sides; these are penetrated at intervals by narrow breaks in the cliffs formed by streams or faults in the rock, and fronted usually by sandy beaches. These were usually locally called 'gates' and many of the ports have that term in their names – Margate and Ramsgate, most notably.[14] Each 'gate' is narrow, with a sandy beach, so that moving from the sea to inland requires a climb – one such place is Broadstairs, which, despite the name, is one of those narrow 'gates', and, as the name says, the way inland is steep.

The southern edge of the block dips away to the valley of the River Stour, which by Auchmuty's time was more or less dry, but it had been a sea channel earlier, whereby river craft and small seagoing ships could sail almost to Canterbury. This flat land was, and still is, seamed with streams and drainage ditches, often attended by levees. The western edge of the Isle was another 'level', drained by the River Wantsum, successor to the saltwater Wantsum Channel – together these valleys had once made the Isle of Thanet a real island. In winter and in excessively wet weather these levels were waterlogged, even flooded. Even in dry weather men and animals could find themselves floundering in mud.[15]

That Thanet had originally been separated from the mainland of Kent had made it a convenient point at which an invader could land in preparation for an attack on the mainland, and this meant that it made the mainland even more vulnerable than it was in 1803. The island could be seized with little apparent difficulty by a seaborne force, and it is no accident that it was here that tradition had it that the original Saxon 'invasion' of 'Hengist and Horsa' began; more certainly it is known that more than one Viking army had used it as a convenient winter camp. In 1588 the 'Cape of Margate' was one of the points on the coast which Philip II of Spain noted as a good rendezvous for his fleet from Spain and his army from Flanders – and, unlike his commanders (or the French in 1803), he had actually seen the area, during his time as consort king of England. One can be sure that had Thanet still been an island in Napoleon's time, he would have seized on that as the first objective for his invaders – and indeed he recalled later that he had considered such a move, though one must here emphasise the word 'later', since hindsight was clearly operating. As it was, the digging of the Royal Military Canal had converted Romney Marsh into a new island, and this may well have presented the invader with a similarly safe preliminary landing place – though the original intention was to pen him into that new island rather than to give him a secure base. But if Thanet, even though it was no longer an island, was seized, the effect might have been much the same, so long as the commander could get a large enough force ashore. Having gained any sort of foothold – and this would clearly involve acquiring the use of a port, of which Kent had many – it would certainly be possible for the invader to consolidate his early position, sort out his men, reinforce them, and gather supplies – the Royal Navy permitting, of course.

But, with the navy intervening – and several attempts were made in 1803 and after to prevent the collection of the necessary boats in the French courts – no army could land in quantity along these coasts.[16] The men might get ashore at the beaches, but in Thanet most of these beaches were small in extent, the sands were soft and difficult to get through, and every beach became steadily smaller as the tide rose. To get away from the shore, through the gates in the chalk, would be a difficult task in the face of a defence which was conducted with any real determination. Even small defending forces at each of the gates would be effective. A landing south of the Thanet cliffs, at Pegwell Bay or at Sandwich, presented the invader with a great, wide, long beach ('Sandwich Flats') where he would have to be decanted into shallow water a mile or more from the actual shore, and if he reached that shore he would move at once into the Stour valley's swamps and ditches, with the river to cross as well. (If he timed it wrong, of course, he would be chased ashore by the rapidly incoming tide.) Once ashore, it would not take much time or effort for the defenders to open the dikes and break down the levees and flood the whole valley. And to the south there was the great fortress of Dover, beyond which were still more white cliffs. Pegwell Bay is, in effect, a large 'gate', unlike those in Thanet and south of Dover, and would likely be a trap for an invader.

Out of office since 1801, the former Prime Minister William Pitt had retained his position as Lord Warden of the Cinque Ports with his seat at Walmer Castle, south of Sandwich and Deal, on the coast looking across the Channel at France. He threw himself into organising matters in his end of Kent. As early as March 1803, within a fortnight of the beginning of the new war, he had ordered the constituent towns of the Cinque Ports to arrange for the impressment of sailors. In September he was at a meeting of the Ports at Dover to agree on how the government's requisition of 400 men for the

Army of Reserve should be divided among them. A month later the Ports held a meeting at Margate (which was not a member of the 'five' towns) to discuss transport plans. Although he is not mentioned in the minutes, it is probable that Auchmuty was present at that meeting: he had given out his orders and plans of defence several days earlier, and some of the Volunteer units of the Cinque Ports were involved and came under his command.[17]

A survey had already been conducted in each parish to determine the extent of the local military reserves, and in Thanet that for the parish of St Lawrence in Ramsgate survives. The churchwarden, Mr W. Peake, and the two overseers, reported that there was in the parish just one man willing (or able) to serve on horseback – providing his own horse – and five on foot. The parish had just two swords, two pistols, and one firelock musket. This enumeration, of course, ignores those already enlisted in the militia and the Volunteers. There were also fifteen men willing to act as labourers for such tasks as digging fortifications, or perhaps breaking levees, and there seems to have been plenty of implements for them to use – axes, pickaxes, spades, and shovels are all counted. Further, there were another eighty-six men who were willing to act 'as servants with cattle', and 'servants with teams' of horses, and no doubt these could be drafted as labourers if the need arose. One of the intentions if an invasion came had originally been to remove all farm animals from the area – to 'drive the area' in the jargon – so as to deprive the invader of supplies and transport; it was well known that the French Army tended to rely on the theft of local supplies. The idea was soon dropped from the plan since no provision could be made to feed and house the thousands of animals who would need to be moved out of Kent. But the return does provide a detailed breakdown of the 'livestock' and 'dead stock' in the parish, and it seems highly likely that the inhabitants of an invaded area would move out of their own accord, taking many of their animals with them.[18]

This is just one parish, and there were half a dozen other parishes in Thanet. There was also another return, dated 1805, listing the officers of the Volunteers made for the Home Office.[19] Kent, the county most immediately threatened as the first target of an invader, had produced a large Volunteer and militia force. It was, of course, much divided among a host of local units, but the Home Office list in 1805 counted 742 officers in the militia in Kent, to which must be added perhaps 30 or 40 times that for the private soldiers.

Thanet had an 'Isle of Thanet Cavalry', with three officers, commanded by Captain Thomas Garrett who lived at Nether Court, close to Ramsgate. In addition there were a group of units of almost equivalent size which were produced separately from the counties of Kent and Sussex, and among the Cinque Ports of the coasts; these overlapped with those from the rest of Kent and from Thanet, and included a series of units from the several towns and villages of the Isle. The number of units looks confusing, and it was clearly one of the tasks of each commandant to make use of them where he could.

Such a force was clearly numerous, and even the men of Kent and Kentishmen alone may well have outnumbered the French invaders, had these ever come. But though they had undergone some training, they were entirely unblooded, and may not have put up a serious resistance to the swift and ruthless moustachioed *grognards*, yet their very numbers, of the Volunteers especially, made them formidable, and this was only one county. Furthermore, the defenders were fighting almost literally close to their own houses and families – Captain Garrett's house was within musket shot of the beach at Ramsgate. The reputation of the French Army for violence against civilians and for indiscriminate destruction and theft of property was well known and well deserved; the Volunteers and the militia were fully aware of the dangers they faced in fighting such men, and of the consequences to their families if their defence failed.

To some extent the Volunteers were regarded, by the sophisticates of the Whig party, as a joke (and also by some later historians), but on examination some of these units were clearly capable, and some were properly trained. They may not have been able to march and manoeuvre, but they could all clearly be effective, especially if placed inside fortifications. The construction of Martello towers soon began, exactly the sort of fort from which half-trained artillerymen could be most effective. These were built along the south and east coasts (and as far north as Orkney), but Auchmuty's Thanet command did not need them. Such minor forts were especially useful in blocking open beaches (such as those Napoleon proposed to use for his landing), and Thanet did not have these. Instead he – and Thanet – had the cliffs and the gates. A document sent to Captain Garrett, commander of the Thanet militia, gave an idea of how the defence of the Isle was to be organised. It is dated 7 December 1803, and was composed by Major John

G.D. Tucker, Major of Brigade – that is, a regular soldier, and Auchmuty's chief of staff – in the name of Colonel Sir Samuel Auchmuty, 'commandant of the Isle of Thanet'.[20]

Major Tucker is probably the same man who is listed in Mrs Townsend's collective biography as 'T.G.T. Tucker', who is also noted elsewhere as 'John Tucker' – 'T' and 'J' can be easily mistaken in manuscript. He married Anne Mulcaster, the daughter of Auchmuty's sister Mary Julianna. Their first child, Auchmuty Tucker, was born in 1803 and his name presupposes that Sir Samuel was his godfather.[21] Major Tucker was therefore Auchmuty's nephew. This is not the first or last instance of his favouring a relative in his career; nor is it the first or last instance of previous parts of his career providing a useful connection.

(Note that within a month of Auchmuty's return to Britain he had become a godfather, a Knight of the Bath, and the commandant of Thanet, a series of appointments suggesting a wide appreciation of his character and skills; he had also in all probability bought himself a house.)

If an invasion came, the first event would be an alarm, based on either an actual enemy landing somewhere, or a report that one was imminent, which would presumably come as a result of a report by the navy. Such a report would come first of all to the maritime anchorage of the Downs and so to Dover, and on to Deal where the telegraph would send it to London. It would reach William Pitt at Walmer just as quickly, and Thanet and then Auchmuty at Syndale within a few hours at most, though it is more likely he would be closer to the coast at the time. The navy was keeping a close eye on events in the French ports; the sortie of the thousands of French ships involved in an invasion would hardly come as a surprise.

As the alarm spread the Volunteers would be alerted and man their posts. The local militia were to take up arms and assemble at their designated places, but they were then to wait for orders as to where they were to go. (The document makes it clear that regular reports were to be sent to Auchmuty giving locations and numbers.) The commander of the Southern District, General Sir David Dundas, was based, it seems, at Canterbury, and Auchmuty would first go there for information and orders on his way from his home to Thanet, but certain defensive posts were to be occupied and prepared at the very start, and even before he had reached Thanet (if he was not already there). That is, the potential landing places had been located and designated well in advance and these were to be immediately garrisoned by the Volunteers; the main part of the militia, who were significantly less effective than the Volunteers, were to act as a reserve.

The first line of defence would be thus taken up by a number of local Volunteer forces. There was to be only one regular unit in the Thanet area, the 15th Light Dragoons; this was probably already in post at or near Ramsgate, from where it could move to any of the threatened landing places. The defences of individual ports and gates were allotted to the local Thanet Volunteer units and the Cinque Ports Volunteers.

The Cinque Ports units had been raised by William Pitt, who was their Colonel. It was a powerful, or at least a numerous force, composed of no less than 3 battalions, comprising 138 officers who would presumably command something up to 3,000 soldiers. These were infantry, and Pitt himself had famously organised, or at least supervised, some of their drill. (As Warden of the Cinque Ports, living at Walmer Castle, he was directly on the coast and close to Deal; this gave him local authority, quite apart from his personal prestige as a former (and potential) Prime Minister, and membership of the House of Commons and the Privy Council; he was out of office, but hardly out of power.[22])

Several professional soldiers were impressed by the results of the training of these Volunteers, including General Lord Mulgrave and General Sir David Dundas. Major General Sir John Moore was less impressed, but then he was busy training his own men in his own way at the Shorncliffe Camp, near Folkestone, in the south of Kent, and he disdained any forces he had not taken in charge personally. When Pitt visited the camp and asked him how he would use the Volunteers in the event of an invasion, he pointed to a hill where they would stand looking menacing and numerous while the real soldiers fought it out on the beach. (Pitt laughed.[23]) Fortunately this was not the attitude of men like Auchmuty, who would not have a numerous and highly trained regular force to use as their first line of defence. Instead they would need these Volunteers to form the main defence of their command. If ever Pitt wanted to examine what Auchmuty was doing in Thanet – and given his activity and interest, and his proximity, it is very likely that he did so, though no record seems to exist – he would have found that the Volunteers he had so busily recruited were being put into the front line with a vengeance.

Moore, apart from his camp at Shorncliffe, was also in overall command of all the forces in Kent. He therefore commanded, at some distance, Auchmuty's forces, and will have had to approve his plan. But Auchmuty also had another means of communication with Moore if he chose to use it. His nephew, John Maxwell Tylden, the son of his youngest sister Jane, was an ensign in the 43rd Rifles, who were in the Shorncliffe camp. He had only recently joined, but had swiftly been promoted from Fifth to First Ensign, and hoped to become a lieutenant soon (this was in 1804). It is not clear if Moore knew of the connection with Auchmuty, but Auchmuty could certainly have used it if he had needed it.[24]

In addition to the large force of Cinque Ports Volunteers, some of whom were allocated to Auchmuty's command, there were a number of other volunteer forces, each much smaller in number, who had been recruited from all the towns of coastal Kent, including those which were not part of the Cinque Ports federation: the Broadstairs Artillery, the Deal Artillery and Deal Infantry, the Dover Artillery and Dover Infantry, the Margate Riflemen and Margate Artillery, the Ramsgate Rifleman and Ramsgate Artillery, and other artillery units recruited at Ringswold, Sandwich, and Seaford. The names these units adopted (or were given) indicate quite clearly they were specialised units of gunners and riflemen. Such men will have been given much better training than the ordinary infantry, or even perhaps than the cavalry.

The artillery units were usually of three officers and perhaps forty soldiers in each unit, and were clearly picked men who were given special training. Those who had no aptitude for the big guns were no doubt soon moved to the infantry, or were placed in the reserve. But the gunners were the men who would have to be stationed to block the landing at the possible danger points; they were the actual front line of defence. Hence the curious, even comic names they acquired, such as the Broadstairs Artillery – but these were only comic in retrospect (like 'Dad's Army'); in action these would be formidable indeed, men who knew perfectly well that their homes and families would be the first to suffer if the enemy invaders broke through their line of defence. There was no question here of half-trained amateur militiamen, got up in gaudy uniforms and preening themselves on occasional parades. Gunners had to know what they were doing, and had to have been trained. They may not have been able to move the guns, or go on campaign with them, but they were able to load them and fire, and obey orders.

The dual nature of the recruits from Deal, Dover, Margate, and Ramsgate – units of both artillery and infantry in the same places – was quite deliberate, since in order to operate effectively the artillerymen had to be protected from attack, and this was the function of their attached infantry. So while the artillery volunteers would service and fire their guns to defend the 'gates', the infantry and rifleman were an integral part of the operation, defending the gunners and supplementing the fire of the artillery.

These artillery units were recruited from the neighbourhood of, and stationed at, the 'gates' which broke up the blank cliffs of Thanet at intervals. Sandwich, behind its long sands and its winding River Stour was at the southern end of these defences. If the enemy got ashore there it would be only slowly, for the men would have to struggle through water and sand to reach the coast, and they would be easily spotted from the higher land at Thanet and Deal to the north and south a similar situation as that which was intended at Romney Marsh. They would be heading essentially into a cul-de-sac formed by the valley of the River Stour, menaced by forces in the hills on either side if they penetrated into the valley for any distance.

Thanet itself presented several opportunities for an invader, with its several gates – Ramsgate, Dumpton Gate, Margate, Kingsgate, Broadstairs – but Ramsgate, for example, presented only a very narrow and steep entrance, if one could actually land. The harbour had been developed recently and was being further improved even then; if it could be seized, it might provide a sheltered landing place, but behind it were the cliffs and the town, with no easy way through. In fighting in the narrow streets of the town a relatively few men would be fully capable of holding up hundreds of men in an attack, if they had survived the artillery and riflemen which were placed to fire on them as their boats approached and unloaded.

And, of course, the artillery was not the only force in the front line. There was a detachment of the 15th Light Dragoons to be located at their 'private parade', that is, their designated assembly point, near Ramsgate. This cavalry unit would be hardly of any use in the town or at the harbour, but could be used when enemy horsemen were seen, or when (or if) the invaders broke through. The invaders would be almost entirely infantry, at least at the start, and would be disorganised if they got through the harbour and the town, and so could be an easy target for cavalry. A detachment of Mr Pitt's Cinque Ports Volunteers was to be located 'at the entrance to the pier' of Ramsgate, that is, where the enemy could be attacked while still in their boats. This was in addition to the artillery. The guns were in batteries, one of which was on the East Cliffs, above the harbour, and the guns were to be protected from attack by a detachment of the Royal Surrey militia. Also at the pier were the 'volunteer riflemen', another group who had evidently undergone some special training – the use of a rifle was a specialised matter, and rifled muskets were fairly scarce; they would not be handed out to men who did not know how to use them. The enemy would therefore face artillery, riflemen-marksmen, massed infantry who were no doubt trained to fire in volleys, at least at first, and if any of the enemy got through they could be attacked by the cavalry of the Light Dragoons. It was on a fairly small-scale, as was suited to the narrow battlefield, a defence in depth.

Finally, 'at their private parade', the Nottingham militia were to be stationed somewhere in Ramsgate. It would take some time for these men to arrive from the North Midlands and their positioning took this into account. They were included in the planning, however, suggesting that it was assumed that the defence of the port might have to last for some time, for they could hardly arrive in less than a week from their assembly at Nottingham, and probably would take longer. Alternatively they could also be used elsewhere, if the fighting at the port was over, or if it had not been attacked. The 'private parade' – the term was also used for the station of the dragoons – was clearly the place which they were to occupy to rest up after their march, at which point they could be directed elsewhere if necessary.

It is of some interest that it should be a militia unit from Nottingham which was to be sent to Auchmuty's command. He had been stationed in the city himself, of course, when he first came to Britain with the 45th Foot, and even though he had left the city twenty years before, it is highly probable that he would be personally acquainted with some of the militia officers and men. The officers in particular were exactly the sort of men who had urged recruiting into the 45th. This was the city and county which had petitioned to have its local regular unit named for it, promising to ensure sufficient recruits, and Auchmuty had been with that regiment at the time; indeed as regimental adjutant he will have been deeply involved in these plans. One wonders if someone at the War Office, or perhaps Auchmuty himself, had pointed out the Nottingham connection. It is not in fact the only such connection (note the Tucker connection mentioned earlier) to be found in these events.

It is worth pointing out, while on the subject of connections, that Auchmuty's position as commandant in Thanet was bringing him still more, and still more exalted, useful political and military connections. He was already noted by the Duke of York as a competent soldier both in operations and in administration, and he had his contacts with Lord Cornwallis and Lord Cavan. Now he was working with the former Prime Minister William Pitt – who became Prime Minister again during 1804 – for he was disposing of several units of Pitt's pride, his Cinque Ports Volunteers, and would command these units if an invasion came; it seems probable that they had met in 1803 at the Margate conference. Other notable men involved in the defence of Kent through the militia and the Volunteers included Lord Carrington, while Lord Hawkesbury (the future Lord Liverpool) was involved with the Sussex militia; Lord Camden, another Cabinet minister, was Colonel of the West Kent militia; and the Earl of Thanet was Lieutenant Colonel of the East Kent militia – several of these were in government again from 1804 onwards. Auchmuty would no doubt have to work with all of them during his Kent command. And then there were Auchmuty's military superiors, Sir David Dundas at Canterbury, and Sir John Moore. Moore had been in Egypt at the same time as Auchmuty; they had perhaps never met, but Moore would surely have been aware of Auchmuty's well-organised movement of Baird's army. Given his efficiency, and what seems likely to be his general attitude of modesty and self-effacement, Auchmuty no doubt made a good impression on such politically powerful (and ambitious, egotistical, and therefore jealous) political men and commanders; he probably came across as a useful administrator and competent commander who was no political threat, and therefore would be easily accepted.

The reverse of this apparently favourable situation, of course, was that if he failed in any way, producing an incompetent plan, for example, or failing to command his men satisfactorily, he would be rapidly discarded, and his career would be over. These powerful men would not accept either failure or incompetence. The defence of the country against invasion was not something they were prepared to trifle with, and men such as Auchmuty, commanding in an already sensitive place, will have come under searching scrutiny. He clearly passed the test.

The plan for the defence of Ramsgate is rather more detailed than for other posts, but this was because it was perhaps the most likely landing place in Auchmuty's area. In other vulnerable ports and 'gates' much the same arrangements were made, but adapted to each local situation. Ramsgate and Margate were the most obvious points at which an invasion might come in this part of Kent, but the other 'gates' had to be guarded as well. At Margate there were to be two batteries positioned so as to dominate the seaward approach. East of the town, on an elevation (now partly occupied by the Turner Museum), one battery was located above the town, looking down on the beach and its approaches. There are at present two rather lonely cannons there, on a pedestrian pathway called Fort Hill, and beyond that is Fort Crescent, though there is no other sign of the erstwhile fort any more.

Guns stationed at that point commanded the harbour and the beach, and the approach from the north and east by water. The second battery was placed west of the town, again commanding the beach, but perhaps not quite so decisively as that on the east – but the two batteries clearly enfiladed the whole approach by sea, and commanded the beach. To the east battery was allocated a detachment of the West Surrey militia (as at Ramsgate); to that on the west was allocated a group of volunteer marksmen, which might suggest that the position of the lower western battery provided a better set of targets for riflemen than that on the east – or that the battery was more vulnerable than that in the fort. Between the two batteries a battalion of the Cinque Ports Volunteers was to be placed in front of the harbour, commanding the beach. They could operate from the buildings which faced the harbour and the beach, which was larger than others in Kent, hence the need for a full infantry battalion there. (Margate had been developing as a beach resort for the previous half-century or so and there was a whole series of substantial buildings, some designed originally for sea bathing, which lined the front – useful places for the defence.[25])

Broadstairs had produced its own unit of Broadstairs Artillery, and this was to be supported by more of the Royal Surreys and Cinque Ports Volunteers, the former at the battery itself, the latter on the terrace above the tiny harbour, so firing down into the invaders coming ashore. That part of the coast had several small breaches in the cliffs to either side of Broadstairs – at Kingsgate to the north, or Dumpton Gate to the south, for example, both very narrow gaps – but they were clearly not thought to be a source of serious danger. Nevertheless, officers of the Royal Staff Corps were to be deployed at 'the different gateways', just in case; their task would be to observe and report: fighting back would be the task of the mobile units, such as the dragoons and the militia; armed with Auchmuty's delegated authority, the Staff Corps would be able to call up these forces if required.

The beach at Pegwell Bay, south of Ramsgate, was to be watched by a part of the Nottingham Volunteers, who were presumably there to support the men of the Sandwich Artillery (who are not mentioned as part of Auchmuty's command and were presumably under the commander who was in charge of the higher land south of the Stour Valley). Since these Nottinghamshire men would not be able to get into position until several days after the alarm, this is another area which was clearly regarded as an unlikely point for the invasion. A second group of Cinque Ports Volunteers, recruited at Sarre, a village at the east end of Thanet, but only 6 miles from their post and therefore likely to be in position very quickly, were to be put at Cliffs End, at the point where the Ramsgate cliffs sink to the valley of the Stour and Pegwell Bay; there they overlooked the whole of the bay, but they could also act as an outlying point of defence for Ramsgate, 2 miles away to the north.

A second, updated, version of this plan of disposition of late 1803 is given in another letter to Captain Garrett, dated two years later on 9 August 1805.[26] It is essentially the same as the first version; there were, of course, very few places where an invasion of Thanet could take place, and these had been covered in the first planning. This document was dated ten weeks before the Battle of Trafalgar, at the point of the greatest tension in the naval campaign, and of greatest threat of invasion. A local diarist, Thomas Pattenden of Dover, noted on that very day, 9 August, that there was a rumour that the French at Boulogne were putting to sea. 'The Regiments' – either the Volunteers or the regulars, or both – had been issued with extra ammunition. Three days later he could hear the French guns firing at Boulogne, presumably at encroaching British ships.

But a month later, on 6 September, he could record that the camp at the Boulogne was visibly breaking up – this could be seen by telescope on a clear day from Dover, quite apart from the naval patrols which were constantly sailing off the French coast to within gunshot of the French batteries. And a month later still he knew of the result of the Battle of Trafalgar.[27] But the invasion scare was over at the beginning of September.

The annual militia list issued from the War Office was dated 14 October 1805; Trafalgar was on 21 October, both of these therefore well after the immediate threat had ended. By this time Auchmuty was a brigadier general, but Tucker had been replaced as his Major of Brigade by Major W. Ellington. The disposition of the troops as set out in the detailed instruction issued in Auchmuty's name in August was to be much the same as two years before, and the local militia companies of artillery and riflemen recruited in the various towns had the same stations all around from Margate to Pegwell Bay, and the Cinque Ports Volunteers likewise; probably the Volunteer marksman were the same men as two years before, serving in the Margate Riflemen and the Ramsgate Riflemen.

The supporting forces from elsewhere, however, were now different. The 15th Light Dragoons had been replaced by the 13th Light Dragoons, but they were still to take up their posts at the dragoons' 'private parade', somewhere in or near Ramsgate. The militia regiments in support, however, were different. This time Auchmuty was allocated two Scottish militia forces, the Royal Perthshires and the Renfrew militia. (Once again, one must point out the possible coincidences here. Perthshire was close to where Sir Robert Abercromby now lived, and it is certainly curious that Auchmuty should have been allocated exactly that regiment.)

Ellington refers to the 'Royal Perthshire' militia, which would probably be a regiment which had been raised by the Earl of Mansfield. This was a substantial force with a full list of forty-three officers and so probably comprised a large battalion of about a thousand men. There were also two 'Perth Brigades', though Ellington's letter refers to Perth*shire*, which would tend to exclude these, who were probably recruited from the city. The Renfrew militia, however, is even less easy to identify. The 'Renfrew militia' had been raised by the Earl of Glasgow, but there were also two other militia units raised in the county and they had the same name. Perhaps Lord Glasgow's unit was recruited from the county, and the others from the town. It is also clear that neither Ellington nor perhaps Auchmuty much cared about the precise origins and names of these units. It would take them at least two weeks to reach Thanet from Scotland: by that time their positioning in the ports would likely be purely theoretical.

The Perthshires were well enough trained by now to have a light company. This was probably composed of the more adept and agile soldiers, perhaps armed with rifles, and was to operate from, and in defence and protection of, the battery on the East Cliff at Ramsgate. The Renfrew militia was to defend the east battery at Margate – that is, they were to be stationed at the cliff-top fort. The second part of the Perthshires was to go to Broadstairs to support the local Volunteer artillery, and a section was to be given charge of the guns at Pegwell Bay, where they were to practise the gun exercises and 'fight the guns when necessary'; once again, it is clear that this was not seen as a particular point of danger – but it was assumed that the Perthshire detachment would have some familiarity with the guns; it would be expecting a disaster to put untrained men in charge of artillery.

As before, the local militia, commanded by Captain Garrett, was to assemble on the road leading out of Ramsgate towards the village of St Lawrence, the parochial centre a short distance away. There they were clearly intended as a reserve if the French broke through the initial defences. Their positioning suggests strongly, as does the heavier military presence at and about Ramsgate, that this was still expected to be the invasion point along this part of the coast, if an invasion actually came to this area. It never did, of course, and by the time that Auchmuty's newest version of his disposition of troops had been sent to the commanders of the units, Bonaparte had begun to march his army away from the Boulogne camp so as to deal with the new war in Eastern Europe. Clearly it was diplomacy and British gold, which had lubricated the formation of the 'Third Coalition' constructed by William Pitt once he returned to power in 1804. This was the most effective defence against invasion from across the Strait of Dover, assisted by the destruction of the Franco-Spanish fleet at Trafalgar and its associated battles. On the other hand, the reception of any French Army which attempted an invasion, as the troops arrived wet, weary, and seasick, was likely to have been hot and the fight tough.

It is assumed here that Auchmuty had a relatively free hand in positioning the troops placed under his command for the defence of Thanet. No doubt his measures were subject to approval by the higher command, though who this was is unknown – perhaps Sir John Moore, or Sir David Dundas, possibly even the Duke of York, but certainly a senior general. If so, they appear to have been accepted (as suggested by the fact that the same dispositions were laid down in both the 1803 and 1805 directives, and no obvious changes were needed), and they indicated that Auchmuty was an adherent of the school of meeting the invaders on the beaches and defeating the attack at the water's edge, rather than holding back his forces at some central location until it was clear where they were landing. But then his area had a series of very obvious landing places for him to supervise, so geography had laid out the clear means of defence, and it would plainly be dangerous to let the French breakthrough into the flat and open country behind the coast. His plan was in fact very obvious, but that is no fault. If the French had information about its geography they would understand that landing there would be difficult and costly – a very effective deterrent. He had command here of perhaps 2,000 troops, and with another 2,000 militia due to arrive several days after the landings, but his dispositions indicate clearly that he expected to have won the battle by the time they arrived.

All this, together with the connections he had formed in Kent among the prominent men, will have done him no harm at all in his military reputation among the senior generals. It is no surprise that, given his experience at organising forces, and his overseas campaigning, he was soon employed once more.

Chapter 6

South America, 1806–8

The new task given to Brigadier General Sir Samuel Auchmuty came in October 1806. The danger of invasion from France had passed, at least for the moment, from early in September 1805, and Napoleon and his army were busy in Austria and Prussia and Poland until 1808, and then first in Spain, then in Austria again. The Third Coalition was thus successful in deflecting him from the British problem for several years, though Britain's coalition partners may well have been less than pleased. As a bonus the Franco-Spanish joint fleet had been all but annihilated at Trafalgar, and it would clearly take some time for the French emperor to redirect his energies westward again. (At the same time his ports, from Hamburg to Venice, were busy rebuilding his navy, though the ships could never gather to form a fleet in the face of British opposition.[1])

Auchmuty, having set up the defensive system in Thanet, was clearly now no longer the necessary commandant; all that was needed was a competent soldier to conduct any defence that was required. He was therefore available for command employment elsewhere and, against the background of the general shortage of British commanders of real talent, it was guaranteed that such employment would quickly be forthcoming. It turned out to be in South America.

A year earlier, in 1805, two of Auchmuty's earlier colleagues from India and Egypt and the Red Sea, Captain Sir Home Popham and General Sir David Baird, had been sent with an expedition to recapture the Cape of Good Hope from the Dutch. This had been taken from them in 1796 and then returned in 1803, after a long delay, as part of the terms of the Treaty of Amiens. The return, in fact, took place not long before news arrived that war had begun again in Europe – and the Dutch, as French satellites, were automatically included in the British declaration of war. As an enemy base the Cape had not so far been very effective, but in the conditions of 1805, if it had held a substantial enemy naval force, it could have been a powerful block on communications between Britain and India, whence came much of the wealth which fuelled the British war effort. Captain Popham pointed this out to two of the most powerful British ministers, the Prime Minister William Pitt, and Lord Melville (the former Henry Dundas) the War Secretary and President of the (Indian) Board of Control. A force of troops and ships was organised. Popham was, reasonably enough, given the sea command; the command of the soldiers went to General Sir David Baird – who had some experience at the Cape several years before. He was given a commission to be Governor and Commander-in-Chief of the Cape once he had captured it; these two, of course, had been colleagues in the Red Sea expedition, along with Auchmuty, five years before.[2]

Both men argued that a larger force than they were originally allocated was required and received more men and more ships. Baird had a total of over 6,000 soldiers, Popham 4 line-of-battle ships and 2 frigates. The expedition sailed for the Cape from Cork on 1 September, voyaging through seas which were busy with French and British fleets searching for each other in the beginning of the Trafalgar campaign. But Popham and Baird bore charmed lives and, despite coming almost within sight of one French fleet – that under Allemand of Rochefort – he successfully navigated the whole force and convoy to the Cape. There Popham landed the troops, and in a few days Baird fought the Dutch forces, which consisted mainly of German mercenaries, Hottentots, and 'Malay' (probably Javanese) gunners, and defeated them. The Dutch Governor-General, Lieutenant General Jan Willem Janssens, made an attempt to retire inland with his surviving forces to carry on the fight from the interior, but he had lost most of his better soldiers as prisoners, and the local militia forces were unwilling to move away from their homes in the Cape area. The earlier British administration had been mild enough to bring the Dutch population to acquiesce for a second time, especially as under the recent Dutch control they were being harassed into reforms they did not like: the Republican regime in the Netherlands was not well liked. With British rule they also knew they could have access to a much wider market for their produce, and the naval blockade would end. After a short time Janssens himself surrendered with his remaining soldiers at the Cape. (He will enter this story again later.)

The conquest had been much easier than Baird had anticipated, and he therefore now commanded a much larger force than he really needed, either to capture or, now, to garrison the Cape Colony. At least for the moment, the Cape was utterly quiet. Not only that, but he recruited a new regiment out of the captured Dutch mercenaries by the effective expedient of locking them in one of the noisome gun batteries at Cape Town and promising that they could come out once they agreed to join the British Army; most did so, being assigned to the 60th Foot, though they were universally reluctant recruits; many of them were German Catholics, and did not appreciate having to fight for British Protestants while their homelands were under French rule. Meanwhile Popham had also successfully captured a French frigate which turned out to be carrying about 200 men of the Queen's Regiment as prisoners. They had been reduced to extreme starvation during their unwilling voyage from near Spain to the Cape, but once those who survived recovered they were incorporated into Baird's forces.

Furthermore, Baird began to recruit Hottentots (Khoi khoi) into a battalion for local use. He therefore ended up with an even larger army – now up to 8,000 men – than the one he had brought with him, which was already larger than had been planned, thanks to his insistence on needing more men. He had far too many for the local garrison, and this fact is one of the sources of the following events; had he had only half the force he now commanded, no further adventures are likely to have been undertaken. (The usual garrison in the Cape during the next half-century or so was between 3,000 and 5,000 men.)

Popham met an American merchant, Wayne, who had come to Cape Town, and who provided interesting information about the state of the defences and local opinions in the Spanish viceroyalty of Buenos Aires. He claimed that the merchants at least were much discontented at their inability to trade with Spain, thanks to the British blockade. Whether Wayne also commented on the block of the passage of silver through Buenos Aires, also a result of the blockade, is not known, but it did not take much imagination – and Popham had plenty of imagination – to realise that if the silver, which was brought from Potosi in the Peruvian viceroyalty, could not be sailed to Spain it must be accumulating at Buenos Aires. Given this information and speculation, it proved to be an easy task for Popham to convince General Baird that he could spare a part of his enlarged forces for a raid on the city of Buenos Aires. Both men were avid for prize money at all times.

Taking 1,500 men from the Cape forces, therefore, Popham took most of his ships to South America. (Baird was not being overly generous: he still had a larger force than he had begun the expedition with.) Popham called at St Helena on the way and persuaded the governor to let him have men from his garrison, particularly some gunners, so he reached the River Plate with about 2,000 soldiers, in several ships. In the estuary – his luck was always good – he captured a ship which was being piloted by a Scotsman called Russel, who was easily persuaded to con the fleet up to Buenos Aires. The expedition landed a few miles from the city, near the village of Reduction, 3 or 4 miles from Buenos Aires, under the command of Brigadier General William Carr Beresford, who had been given a commission as a local Major General by Baird. (Beresford had, of course, been one of Auchmuty's – and Baird's – colleagues in the invasion of Egypt from India.) Popham himself had earlier, without any authorisation, assumed the rank of Commodore; Beresford's new rank, which he only revealed when the joint force reached the River Plate, made him Commander-in-Chief of the expedition, to Popham's annoyance. To contest the landing, the local Spanish force came out of the city, but this was briskly defeated, and the city was captured.

If Popham had kept to his original intention of merely making a raid, he could have looted the place and then left, probably within a week. But it turned out that, when the news arrived that the British ships were in the estuary, much of the treasure had been removed to a village to the west of the city. While searching for it the British forces began to settle down in the city, where they seemed for a time to be welcome. Popham wrote a report to the government in London about what he had done, and at the same time he sent letters to the Lord Mayor of London and to the mayors of the great manufacturing cities – Birmingham, Manchester, Leeds, and others – pointing out the commercial possibilities of the conquest; in effect he was claiming that this part of South America was no longer under British blockade.

It was widely believed in Britain that the Spaniards in South America were so wholly disenchanted with their political, economic, and commercial situation that they were longing for an opportunity to become independent. It was for some in Britain only one further step from that to believing that they would be pleased to be incorporated into the British commercial system, and become part of the British Empire. It was also believed that the continent of South America was teeming with wealth, a legacy of the transport of great quantities of silver cross the Atlantic over the past two centuries and more. Popham's news, therefore, was greeted with acclaim, especially as the possibilities of trade in other directions and to other destinations was closing out because of the war, and the institution of Napoleon's Continental System of excluding British goods from Europe. Popham's letters to the cities ensured that the conquest was widely publicised. Had the government (now in Whig hands under Lord Grenville as Prime Minister) wanted to disavow his conquest, it was no longer possible once it had become known. *The Times* blared out the news under the headline 'Buenos Aires is part of the British Empire'.

This is misleading in every single particular. First, the place had not been annexed; it was simply, for the moment, occupied enemy territory. Second, 'Buenos Aires' referred to two distinct political entities: the city, which Popham and Beresford had captured, and the viceroyalty. The city was a major settlement, with about 70,000 inhabitants, which Beresford was now occupying with just 1,500 or so troops and some of Popham's sailors and marines. The viceroyalty was a huge territory which included the modern states of Argentina, Uruguay, Paraguay, and Bolivia, no part of which had been reached by any of the British forces. The western border was 700 miles from the city, the northern nearly 2,000.[3] *The Times*'s headline implied that the viceroyalty was now British, whereas the small British force had gone no further than a few miles out from the city, to seize the evacuated treasure, and had then withdrawn back into it. The third misconception was that, by the time the news reached Britain, the local Spaniards had reacted to their humiliation and had retaken their city; the British troops who had captured it became prisoners of war. The Spaniards of Buenos Aires city, and the viceroyalty, demonstrated quite clearly that even if they were unhappy at being ruled from Spain, being ruled from London and garrisoned by British troops was an even more unpleasant condition to contemplate.

Even before this news reached London – and Popham delayed sending home the news of the loss of the city as long as he dared, while making desperate attempts to secure the release of the prisoners – the Grenville government decided to reinforce the expedition, ignoring their first reaction, which was to condemn the commanders for acting so unofficially. So Popham's publicity was so far successful.

In addition to Popham's and Beresford's reports of the original capture, they sent the captured treasure to Britain. This amounted, when it reached London, to about a million Spanish dollars, though how much more had stuck to greedy and sticky British fingers before it was shipped out is not known. It was paraded through southern England from Portsmouth to London, and through the city's streets, with wide publicity and to much popular acclaim. This seems to have finally convinced the government to accept and retain the conquest.

Popham had, of course, sent the news to Baird, and had asked for more troops, as did Beresford. Baird had already decided that he could send the former Dutch mercenaries, now members of the 60th Foot, together with those men of the Queen's Regiment retaken from the captured French frigate who had now recovered, and another regiment, the 47th, which had been on its way to India and had stopped at the Cape to refresh. Baird decided it was not needed in India and diverted them to South America. This was a total of about 2,000 soldiers. (He was wrong in his assumption about India, for soon the news arrived of a nasty mutiny at Vellore, and he had to send some of his remaining troops on to India to assist in putting it down.) Also, he sent a further regiment to the Plate, 400 men commanded by Colonel Backhouse. When this contingent arrived, it was joined by the second group under Colonel Vassall (especially asked for by Popham). Backhouse, who was the senior colonel, gathered up all those troops in the Plate who had not been captured, and seized the small town of Maldonado, at the northern entrance to the estuary, supposedly as a base for either a new conquest, or to receive released or escaped prisoners.

In London the government also gathered a force of about 2,000 men to send to secure the city; this was the force which was put under the command of Brigadier General Auchmuty. He brought along his nephew, John Maxwell Tylden, as his aide; there was a Tucker in the contingent also, apparently the relative who had served with him in Kent in 1803. They also sent out General Sir George Grey as the new Commander-in-Chief and Governor for the Cape to replace Baird; Popham was to be recalled as well, and replaced by Rear Admiral Charles Stirling. There were far too many ambitious officers who were too ready to act independently in the South Atlantic for the government's taste. Both of the recalled men had quite deliberately flouted their instructions to pursue their own personal ambitions. Baird escaped punishment, but Popham was court-martialled and reprimanded. On the other hand, both were talented and were soon re-employed. (Grey was a relative of Charles Grey, the First Lord of the Admiralty, by no coincidence.)

Auchmuty was to take over command of the army in the River Plate but, having appointed him, the government took away his troops when the news of a possible crisis in Portugal arrived, though then his force was increased to 3,000 soldiers. Stirling had already sailed to replace Popham, and now Auchmuty at last sailed to replace Beresford. And meanwhile Popham's letters, publicised in local newspapers, persuaded large numbers of British merchant ships and merchants to set out independently to profit from this new conquest. Strange ambitions were stirring, including a plan by one optimistic merchant to sell ice skates in Brazil – such was the general ignorance of the country, even though clandestine and neutral trade had long been conducted by British merchants into South America.

The government was not immune from the excitement. Besides the reinforcements for Buenos Aires going out with Auchmuty, and the ships with Stirling, a new scheme was concocted by which a force of about 4,000 men was to sail by way of the Cape to Botany Bay in Australia, and then to cross the southern Pacific and invade Chile, where it was intended to link up with the force in Buenos Aires. This was under the command of Brigadier General Robert Craufurd, an expert in Light Infantry warfare but a commander who usually needed careful direction. The likely condition of the troops after such a voyage does not bear thinking about. Then, seeing the size of the forces now headed for the city and already there, a new Commander-in-Chief, Lieutenant General John Whitelocke, was appointed for the whole command. He was sent with yet another small reinforcement.

The men who had been taken prisoner in the recapture of the city became pawns in the contest. The *portenos* (the slang name for the people of Buenos Aires) wanted their looted belongings back, and they wanted the whole British force to leave. The British, at first Popham, but later every other British commander, wanted the prisoners released first of all, and to reconquer the city, if possible. The two sides agreed that the prisoners should be liberated, but they could not agree on how. On the *porteno* side the leading figure was Colonel Santiago Liniers, a French soldier, trained by the Hospitallers in Malta, who had made his career in the Spanish colonial administration. He had organised the forces which retook the city in combination with an uprising by the citizens. His French origin made him doubly suspicious to the British, and he was buffeted on the Spanish side by strong popular feelings of annoyance, first at the ease with which the British had taken the city, then at their unwillingness to leave, but also at their own government, who was personified by the Viceroy, the Marquis de Sobremonte.

As the British fleet stayed on in the estuary, and then landed soldiers to take control of Maldonado, the Buenos Aires government moved the prisoners out of the city and sent them in batches to a series of inland cities, several of them close under the Andes 500 miles away – to Mendoza, San Juan, Tucuman, and several other places – spreading the men out in groups to prevent any trouble; they were frequently billeted on wealthy landowners, who were usually generous and friendly. The Spaniards feared a new joint operation, of course, but this dispersion was seen by Popham and the other commanders as a sort of treachery. The issue of the release of the British prisoners became one of the more intractable elements in the dispute.

Of the several commanders now in or approaching the River Plate, only Auchmuty had had any serious command experience. Beresford was a prisoner, though he soon escaped; Popham was about to be sent home, when Stirling could finally persuade him to go; Whitelocke was an administrator, and had not commanded troops in action for at least ten years, and then only briefly in the West Indies. There is a powerful suspicion that he was only appointed in order that his post as Inspector General could be abolished as a minor money-saving gesture.

Auchmuty arrived in the estuary on 5 January 1807, four months before Whitelocke. The British soldiers who survived from the original invasion, and those sent by Baird from the Cape, were concentrated at Maldonado under Colonel Backhouse. They were not strong enough to make any progress against the clouds of Spanish light cavalry who beset them, and so they were effectively marooned, though the Spaniards could not attack them in Maldonado. Auchmuty's arrival with his force broke this deadlock, and he quickly arranged with Stirling to transport his whole force to attack Montevideo. Stirling was generous with supplies of food and ammunition from his ships.[4]

Montevideo was a reasonably well-fortified town. The Banda Oriental, the region now forming the country of Uruguay, was a disputed territory between the Spaniards in the modern Argentina and Portuguese Brazil, and this had required the town's walls to be kept up to a reasonable condition, though they were also somewhat old-fashioned by European (or even Indian) standards. Auchmuty was able to bring up guns to bombard the walls and prepare to assault the town. But that was only after fighting off attempts by the Spaniards to prevent his approach.

The Marquis of Sobremonte escaped from Buenos Aires city when it was captured, and he had then gone into the interior of the viceroyalty to gather the forces of the regular army which were stationed there, apparently under the impression that the British were stronger than they were. It was while he was doing this – a sensible military move – that the *portenos* finally understood the small numbers of Beresford's army, and meanwhile, Colonel Liniers organised the locals into a force strong enough to overwhelm the British force in the city.

One result of these actions was to create a strong feeling of viceregal betrayal among the *portenos*, who felt that by leaving the city he had abandoned them; he was excluded from the city by popular feeling. Liniers commanded there, somewhat uneasily. When Auchmuty attacked Montevideo, therefore, he found there were four enemy forces opposing him: first, those in the town itself, somewhat depleted because some of the local forces were still in Buenos Aires, where they had gone to help with the recapture of the city; then there was Liniers commanding the Buenos Aires forces, who gathered themselves rather slowly, but did eventually march to the aid of the besieged; the third group was the Spanish amateur forces which had been harassing Backhouse in Maldonado, mainly mounted men of the gaucho type, among whom Jose Artigas was emerging as the leader; the fourth group was the regular army forces which had been collected together by Sobremonte in the interior, at first with the aim of recovering Buenos Aires, but now approaching to relieve Montevideo.

These forces were either largely ineffective (the local guerrillas) or were approaching only slowly. Their slowness was partly due to mutual enmities. The *portenos* saw Montevideo as a commercial and even a political rival, and also feared that if they left Buenos Aires it might be retaken while they were away – the British ships still commanded the estuary and could have landed an army on the southern shore. The first enemy which Auchmuty's army had to tackle was the force gathered by Sobremonte from the interior. This reached the town first, and joined up with the city's own forces. This joint force was therefore prepared to defend the city even before the siege began, and it was this force which confronted Auchmuty's army as it landed near the town.

Auchmuty was thus under considerable pressure, and not only from the enemy forces, for he was also generally short of everything he needed. The guns he was using were naval guns from Stirling's ships, manned by sailors. He had to forage for food in the surrounding territory, and once this was realised, not only were the cattle driven away, but his foraging parties could be harassed by the guerrillas. Otherwise his supplies came from the ships, or were bought from the merchant ships which had arrived in the country and were now waiting until they could begin trading; meanwhile they made a profit from the British Army. All this added to the pressure of time, for it would not be long before the supplies ran short, or the enemy gathered in overwhelming numbers, or both.

In the advance on the city the army was transported in Stirling's ships from Maldonado to a landing near Montevideo, then the troops were to march on Montevideo in two columns. The Spaniards came out to prevent this. The right column was menaced by a Spanish force consisting mainly of cavalry, but with some guns; this was driven off by an infantry charge, and then the second part, the infantry column, also retreated.[5]

An account is given by Sergeant Landsheit of the 20th Light Dragoons in his ghosted memoirs thirty years later. He remembered a small incident during this advance, which throws some light on Auchmuty and on the soldiers' attitude towards him. At the threat of the enemy force, says the sergeant, 'Sir Samuel examined the array carefully for a moment, then ordered the advance, which the troops obeyed with … alacrity'. This was essentially an infantry attack. A little later the dragoons' commander led his force forward, but then halted his men on a hill in full view, and within range of, the enemy's cannon; he lost several men and horses killed and wounded as a result. The sergeant describes Auchmuty's reaction:

> Sir Samuel rode up. He rebuked our commandant in good round terms, desired him to move down into the hollow, and keep his wits about

> him, as he would be needed very shortly. The old man was yet speaking when a shot took his horse in the hip, and knocked the leg to shivers. Of course, Sir Samuel fell to the ground as if slain and his staff … crowded round him to ascertain whether he was hurt. 'There is nothing the matter', said the gallant old soldier. 'I'm not hurt in the least. Just help me get up from under this horse; and John' – calling to his groom – 'fetch my charger'. It was done in a moment, and I need hardly add that the perfect unconcern of our brave chief was not without its effect on the courage of his followers. For, no sooner was he on his legs than he gave us some work to perform. 'Charge that gun, and that, and that,' said he, 'they will annoy the infantry as they come up.' On we rushed at a gallop; and sabring the cannoniers, were in possession of three pieces e'er another shot had been fired.[6]

The picture of the 'gallant old soldier' is perhaps a little overdrawn by the sergeant's memory – and perhaps by his 'ghost' – but in essentials it is clearly true. It is, of course, exactly the sort of incident which sticks in the memory.

This had been Sobremonte's force, together with the town governor and the town militia, and perhaps some of the gauchos, which was now therefore defeated and driven back. Sobremonte's reputation, though he had not commanded in the fight, was further damaged. The force retreated to the town, and the Viceroy gathered his troops once more to make another stand outside it as Auchmuty's force approached the walls. They advanced against the British force in two columns. One was attacked by three companies of the 40th Foot and stopped, and was then taken in the flank by the companies of the 95th (the Rifle Brigade) and the combined light companies from the other regiments. The column broke and fled into the town: the other column retired at once. Casualties among the Spaniards were considerable, though numbers are vague, but this new defeat was sufficiently unpleasant to deter any further attacks.[7]

The Montevideans were still not prepared to give in. Sobremonte left the town, possibly with some of his troops, when the siege became inevitable. This, of course, made good military sense, as had his attempt to stop the British advance on the town. But his defeat, and the naval blockade, made him as unpopular in Montevideo as he was in Buenos Aires. When he left, once again intending to gather forces for the town's relief, even though this was the correct military decision, his unpopularity further expanded.

Auchmuty set up his guns before the walls, at a distance at first of 600yd. His forces occupied the suburbs, which had been evacuated. (Part of his camp was on the town rubbish dump, which resulted in some cases of disease later.) He opened communication with the town governor, Colonel Don Pasqual Ruiz Huidobro, and offered to return the Spanish wounded, so long as they were regarded as prisoners of war and so unable to fight. The governor refused such terms, but he did accept Auchmuty's offer to allow the Spaniards to bury their dead. Meanwhile, of course, both sides were busy preparing for the next round of fighting.

Auchmuty began the bombardment on 28 January, a process which looked as though it would be slow work. Both Liniers from Buenos Aires and Sobremonte in the Montevidean hinterland were preparing to intervene, but were not willing to link their forces. Sobremonte was close enough to block the foraging attempts by the British; in this he was assisted by the Uruguayan gauchos, but he was apparently not strong enough to intervene in the siege. Liniers was forced to march his men a fair distance inland along the estuary coast in order to cross to the north bank. Meanwhile, Montevideo was able to bring supplies and men into the town across the harbour, which the British ships could not enter because it was too shallow. Two of the smaller British ships ventured too far into the harbour, and were badly damaged by fire from the walls, to Stirling's annoyance – a curious echo of Auchmuty's reaction to the carelessness of the dragoon commander in getting too close to the enemy.[8] It was Sobremonte who organised these supplies from the land side, though he does not seem to have been given any credit for it.

Liniers sent a force of 500 men under Brigadier Pedro de Arce in advance of his main force, and then followed up with 2,000 men under his own command. Arce's force got into the town across the harbour, though whether this was also arranged with Sobremonte is not clear. Auchmuty was therefore now menaced by the town's reinforced garrison, by Sobremonte's force (though this was now fairly small, most of his original force having been left in the town), and by Liniers' force; meanwhile, the gauchos menaced the British foraging parties, though they could usually be driven off in any fight; later Sobremonte's regular Spanish troops did effectively stop much of the foraging. It was not at all clear, however, that these three Spanish groups were capable of cooperating effectively with each other.

The bombardment went on for four days, with little obvious result, but then on 1 February Stirling came ashore with the worst news of all. He said that, though he intended to provide ammunition until the ships had been reduced to ten rounds per gun, gunpowder was now very short; he had been collecting it not only from the naval vessels, but from the armed merchantmen as well. He now set a limit of three days for the provision of any further supplies; after that he would be reduced to a bare minimum for the ships to be viable as men of war. He says in his journal that he was confident in the ability of the troops to defeat any attack, but without supplies of ammunition their survival was clearly in question. Even food was becoming short. Foraging was failing in the face of the successful intervention by the Viceroy's forces, whose detachments could always outnumber the foraging parties, and buying supplies from the merchant ships had merely forced the prices up. He did not need to point out that at the end of three days it would be necessary to evacuate all the forces.[9]

The Spanish relieving forces were approaching. Arce's troops had got into the town, though this was probably a mistake, since it significantly reduced Liniers' relieving force, and he and the viceroy were not cooperating after all. But Liniers' force was large enough, in combination with a sortie from the town, to be a serious menace. Liniers sent in a message – they could have coordinated attacks without difficulty – that the town must hold out for four days, that is, until 3 February. It is not clear that Auchmuty appreciated the particular deadline of his enemies, but he did know where Liniers' force was at any given moment, and that it would need some days to get to Montevideo.

Both sides had deadlines, therefore. With just two or three days available, Auchmuty decided that an assault must be made on the town, even though no obvious breach had yet been made on the walls. He concentrated the bombardment on a section of the wall between the South Gate and the Citadel, and brought up a new battery of six guns to increase its power and shock effect. During the next day, after an all-night bombardment, a small breach did appear in the wall. Normally nobody would have considered it more than the beginning of a possible way in, but unless the town was stormed within the next day-and-night period, Auchmuty would need to begin withdrawing his forces to the ships. Then, wherever the ships went, they would face a long voyage on short rations, with a thoroughly demoralised army, and the prisoners would have been left behind; alternatively, he could go back to Maldonado, which nobody wanted to do.

The assault was timed for 3 am on 3 February, the morning of the day Liniers thought he could reach the town. The previous evening Auchmuty sent in a flag of truce demanding the town's surrender. Given the situation the reply was inevitably in the negative, but Auchmuty was always careful to follow the correct customs of war. (It is not known if Liniers knew of this; he certainly did not speed up his approach.) Colonel Ruiz Huidobro in the town knew he was in a strong position. The breach was not considered good enough to be threatening, and anyway his men were blocking it with materials already prepared; there were two relieving Spanish forces within 5 or 6 miles of the town; and he must have known that supplies for the British were running short – communications with the relieving forces were still maintained, and he clearly knew that Sobremonte was blocking all the British foraging efforts. If Sobremonte's force was hardly large enough to mount a relieving attack, that of Liniers' certainly was, and it is possible that Huidobro was in contact with both. The Buenos Aires forces owed a debt to Montevideo, which had sent some of its own troops to assist in the recovery of the larger city, and Huidobro certainly expected Liniers' force to menace the British. Sobremonte was Huidobro's superior in the Spanish gubernatorial hierarchy. He had received reinforcements in the city from both men. If the two approaching forces did not actually attack, they could nevertheless distract. Further, a British assault must come at night, and he would have known well enough that such night attacks are always accompanied by confusion. Auchmuty's demand for surrender, therefore, may have seemed to him to be a bluff; but he concentrated his forces around the breach in the wall, just in case.

If Huidobro thought the summons was nothing but a bluff, he was wrong. Hindered by confusion in the dark, by Spanish supplementary blocking of the breach, by Spanish fire, though this was inaccurate in the darkness, the assault was marked by a plan which went almost comprehensively wrong, but nevertheless succeeded. Most British troops were actually posted to block any intervention from the relieving forces, since Liniers and Sobremonte were each only a few miles off. Only half of the British force was thus available for the storm. The 95th and the light battalion were once again to lead the assault, behind a forlorn hope of 200 volunteers; the three largest of the battalions were to follow up, supposing the breach was actually penetrated. A secondary attack was also planned, against the North Gate, hoping to take advantage of the necessary Spanish concentration on defending the breach.

The breach, such as it was, had been blocked up by bales of hides filled with earth and the approach was dominated by the overlooking Spanish guns and gunmen. The troops of the forlorn hope were discovered by the Spaniards well before the men reached the wall, and suffered casualties in the approach. Nevertheless, once close to the wall, they were less vulnerable. They climbed into the breach and threw down the blockading materials, which then, of course, allowed the following troops to gain access more easily. The fighting in the breach went on almost until daybreak, at about 5 am, the attackers facing fire from the wall on both flanks, from the Citadel, and from within the town.

At the North Gate the 87th Foot was supposed to wait for news of success at the breach. Probably because the Spanish forces at the gate had been drawn away, some of the men of the 87th were able to scale the wall and the gate themselves, and then opened the gate even as the successful breaching party approached along the wall. It seems clear that even if the breach had been successfully defended, the party at the North Gate would have got into the town.

The follow-up activity, once the troops were inside, suggests that some careful preliminary planning had been undertaken. The invaders at once fanned out along the wall in both directions to clear it of defenders, one group joining the 87th at the North Gate; another group blockaded and attacked the Citadel, some men firing from the roof of the nearby cathedral; still other parties moved systematically through the streets eliminating opposition there. By daylight the Citadel had surrendered – the last Spanish post to do so – and, as Auchmuty noted in his report with pardonable satisfaction, 'early in the morning the town was quiet and the women were peaceably walking the streets'.[10]

Governor Ruiz Huidobro was captured and brought to Auchmuty at about 5 am. He offered to surrender the town if his forces were granted the honours of war, that is, to the able to leave the town, carrying their arms. Auchmuty refused, for this would release his prisoners, who could then join Liniers or Sobremonte, and he did not trust either of those men – Liniers in particular was accused of having broken his own parole when he was in control of Buenos Aires, and of having broken a similar agreement at the surrender of Buenos Aires; nor would it recover the British prisoners, even on an equal exchange, for the governor did not have the authority to agree to such an exchange.

Casualties had been fairly heavy on both sides. Auchmuty's army suffered 120 killed and almost 300 wounded, and many of the wounded later died, including 2 colonels. Spanish losses were much worse, though less accurately tabulated: possibly 500 were killed, and 300 wounded, and about 1,400 had been made prisoner. At first Auchmuty estimated that 1,500 Spanish soldiers had escaped or were still in hiding in the town; this was never authenticated, though it is quite possible it was correct, certainly considerable numbers left during and after the assault.[11]

There are several remarkable aspects to this story. First, it took only two-and-a-half weeks from the landing near the town until its conquest, and this was using a force composed of the remnants of the original (defeated) Buenos Aires force, troops from the Cape, including the recovered former prisoners of the Queen's Regiment, and the former Dutch mercenaries, most of whom were Catholics and were unhappy at the prospect of fighting other Catholics. To these had been added the latest contingent from Britain, brought by Auchmuty, and both of these late arrivals from Britain and the Cape had travelled a long ocean passage. This was, that is, a motley collection of units, some of them almost actively disloyal, and many more probably weakened by their long travelling. There was plenty of scope for desertion and malingering.

Second, all of the three fights from the landing to the storm had been conducted in the face of superior numbers, and in every case the victory had come from attacking the enemy with a selected but small part of Auchmuty's army; infantry and the dragoons in the first battle at the landing place, riflemen and the light battalion in the fighting before the town and in the breach. The initiative of men of the 47th at the North Gate was clearly expected, presumably because Auchmuty encouraged such action. Auchmuty had clearly got to know his heterogeneous forces quickly, and had detected the most effective units for the different tasks.

Then there was the way the victory outside the walls of the town had been achieved. Sobremonte had a force of several thousands of men, mostly military professionals, together with local militia fighting for their homes; he had military training, having been an officer in the Spanish Army before being posted to Buenos Aires. (This, given the demoralised and barely trained condition of much of the Spanish Army after two decades of the negligent administration of Godoy, may not mean much, but the Viceroy surely knew at least something of the military art.) The Spanish tactics were essentially those of the French since the revolution. They attacked in two columns, intending presumably to punch through the British line by sheer weight.

There is no indication in his earlier military career that Auchmuty had encountered such an attack, nor had he ever commanded a British army in a battle of any size, though he had certainly gained experience of fighting and commanding in North America and India and Kent. And yet he appears to have understood at once how to counter the columnar attack launched against him. He will have known of the successes and methods of the French Army. In the previous eighteen months there had been the great battles of Ulm, Austerlitz, Jena, and Eylau, with Friedland being fought almost at the same time as Montevideo. So he was, no doubt, as an educated soldier, fully aware of the French methods. His defeat of the two Spanish attacks at Montevideo would therefore seem to have been a result of thinking through the issues involved in advance, and arriving at a means of tackling an attack by such columns.

(The method used by Wellington in the Peninsula and at Waterloo – utilising a reverse slope to hide his men from the approaching columns and then confronting the columns, already winded by the climb, by British infantry fighting and firing in line – had not yet been put into effect, though since he used it in his very first fight in the Peninsula at Vimiero, it seems probable he had already worked it out. The earlier belief of Sir Charles Oman that the Battle of Maida in July 1806, which Auchmuty would have known about, was the first success of 'line' against 'column', is now seen as incorrect.[12] But the fighting at Montevideo really was of a British line facing and defeating an attack in column, first stopping it by volley fire, and then driving it back by attacking from the flanks. This was at the beginning of 1807; Wellington first used this method eighteen months later in August 1808; could it be that Wellington heard of it from Auchmuty's experience? The two men overlapped for a few months in India in 1797, and Wellesley returned to England in 1805, so they were England at the same time in 1805–6, but there is no record of their meeting: an encounter in the War Office is possible, a discussion of how to counter French battle tactics seems unlikely.)

In the first fight, against the force of cavalry occupying higher ground soon after he had landed, Auchmuty's response was to order a charge by the light battalion – infantry only – which 'dispersed' their opponents, with the dragoons moving in later. Starting from close enough a British infantry bayonet charge was often successful by its sheer ferocity; it rarely came to an actual conflict. The rest of the Spaniards then retreated. The bayonet charge was delivered into a 'heavy fire of round [shot] and grape', and the reply to this of a rapid charge was no doubt directed partly at the cavalry, but also at preventing further fire from the guns – one gun was captured; the others were presumably removed rapidly, thus proving the effectiveness of the charge. An attack by a party of swift and well-trained infantry was a normal British response to stationary cavalry. The Spanish tactics appear to have been using the guns to disorganise the British, intending to follow this up with a cavalry charge – a traditional method. This suggests that the Spanish infantry were unreliable, at least in an open fight; behind walls and in the streets (as later shown in Buenos Aires) they were formidable.

The second fight, outside the town, was an attack by two Spanish columns, one of cavalry, the other of infantry. The aim appears to have been for the infantry to pin the British down by their advance, while the cavalry column attacked the British flank. This was, as in the earlier fight, all too obvious, but was threatening nonetheless, and a militarily correct procedure. The infantry column did reach as far as the picquet posted in front of the British main force. The picquet perhaps retreated a little way under the weight of the attack, but was then joined by 3 companies of the 40th Foot – a total of perhaps 800 men – and this joint force charged the head of the Spanish column and stopped it. Auchmuty was on the spot and had already ordered up the light battalion and the riflemen of the Rifle Corps, something he must have arranged even before the picquet was attacked. When the attacking column was seen to have been stopped by the picquet and the 40th and was about to give way, Auchmuty sent in the lights and the riflemen to charge their flank. The column collapsed and the men ran back towards the town. At this the cavalry column turned back also.

Auchmuty had, therefore, detected the weakness of the column attack. The infantry column was about 3,000 strong, and was stopped by the picquet, perhaps 200 or so men, and 3 infantry companies, maybe 800 men in all; this was large enough to deal with the head of the column on more than equal terms and to bring the whole to a halt. The attacking force which took it in flank was not much stronger. Hardly any of the 3,000 Spaniards in the infantry column came into serious action. Only the head of the column was engaged by the defenders, and when the lights charged they clearly took an already beaten column by surprise, and it broke and fled before the British charge could close with it. Auchmuty had clearly worked out a satisfactory method of defeating an attack in column by defending line of infantry.

'It required some nerve to pass the breach', commented Lieutenant Colonel Richard Bourke, in a letter to the politician William Windham, who had been a member of the government which sent Auchmuty and Craufurd and Whitelocke on their several journeys to, eventually, South America.[13] (Bourke was acting as Quartermaster General in the Montevideo force, and later served as Governor of New South Wales, following, as it happened, Macquarie). His comment is an indirect compliment to Auchmuty, whose judgment that the poor breach was sufficient was justified, even if it was a decision forced on him by constraint of time and resources. He had thus exercised, both at the breach and in the preceding battle, that fine judgment of timing and decision expected in a battle commander.

Perhaps the most surprising element of this series of fights is the result in the town on the morning after its capture. The capture of a town which had refused two summonses to surrender and had then been taken by storm, left it open to a sack, particularly when the fighting had been fierce, and considerable casualties had been incurred among the attackers. The history of Europe in the very time of the siege of Montevideo was replete with such events, and British troops were as unpleasant as any, though perhaps it was the ruthless brutality of the French which was most feared. Yet Montevideo, which had fought to the very end, was basically untouched by the capture, and in the morning of the capture the 'women were peaceably walking the streets'.

This is not just a complacent comment by a self-satisfied commander, and possibly exaggerated, for it is confirmed by remarks by other participants. The anonymous author of an account of these events, published in London a year later, explained that 'one of the singular things, and, I may say, that adds a feather to the cap of the troops employed in the attack, is that it remains perhaps the solitary instance of a town taken by storm in the night, in which no instance of plunder or outrage took place'.[14] In addition Captain Jennings of the 40th, who had been involved in the actual storm, where several of his colleagues and men had died, noted that 'the moment the town was in our possession all further hostilities ceased on both sides, and in the course of that day everything appeared quiet within the walls as in a time of perfect peace'. All was not quite as peaceful as that, for Jennings also noted that a 'few instances of pillage and disorder occurred ... [but] ... the authors were punished on the spot'.[15]

The faint air of surprise which seems detectable in Auchmuty's report is magnified in those more private comments. Clearly violence and a sack had been expected. And clearly it did not occur. Jennings's comment on instant punishment given out to offenders suggests that all was not quite as peaceable as some claim, but also that plans to suppress such 'outrages' had been laid in advance. One may ascribe this 'good conduct' of the British troops to Auchmuty's influence and planning, and to the fact that the officers who had to act to prevent and punish these 'outrages' were present all through the town from the moment of capture, no doubt at his insistence. It all implies that Auchmuty's influence over the soldiers was very powerful.

The capture of Montevideo forced all parties to review their situations. Liniers turned his force around at once, and returned to Buenos Aires, making no attempt to contest the occupation of Montevideo, no doubt rightly fearful of an immediate British attempt on the major city. Auchmuty made two moves: he made an attempt to negotiate with the Viceroy, but this was quickly scotched by Liniers, who arranged for Sobremonte's arrest and detention at Buenos Aires. This, however, assisted Auchmuty's second move, for he sent out parties of his soldiers into the surrounding countryside to expand his area of control to up to 20 miles from Montevideo, and the same distance along the estuary coast. With Sobremonte removed, his force's harassing of the foragers ceased. Auchmuty hoped this would also encourage the revival of the local market, so producing supplies for the town and for his forces.

Auchmuty did not have the military strength to do much more. Out of his 5,000 men, he had a sick and wounded list approaching 1,000, and he was stretched to keep control of the northern coast of the estuary. He was in fact in the same condition as at Maldonado, where manpower had only been sufficient to hold on; so it was after Montevideo was captured. Considerable supplies of ammunition and gunpowder were captured in the town, however, so easing his and Stirling's problem there. There was, however, a possible source of reinforcement locally. He opened communication with the Cabildo (the town council) of Buenos Aires. His main aim now, being unable to continue further operations, was to recover the British prisoners, and with a substantial number of Spanish prisoners in his hands he thought he had a lever to induce an exchange. He threatened that he would send his prisoners to Britain if such an exchange was not agreed, a rather more drastic evacuation than the Spaniards had enforced on Beresford's troops so far, but not in essence different. His negotiating position, however, was not helped by the escape of Major General Beresford from captivity, together with Colonel Denis Pack of the 71st Foot, whose men had constituted the greater part of the original expeditionary force. Beresford claimed to have had a promise of liberation from Liniers, who was one of the few in Buenos Aires who appreciated that holding the British prisoners meant that British attacks would continue – many *portenos* thought the opposite, that holding the prisoners would deter an attack. The scheme for their liberation was discovered, however, and Beresford had to make his escape without the consent of the Cabildo, which then accused him of breaking his parole. Negotiations were halted all round, and Auchmuty's suggested solution of an exchange failed (though it would probably not have succeeded). Beresford had been held not far from Buenos Aires; one result of his escape was that those prisoners still within reach of the city were moved further away; they did not blame him, however, seeing clearly that they were subject to Spanish whims, and changes of policy enforced by surges of popular anger. The *portenos* were understandably liable to communal hysteria. On the British side no one was really clear who was in control in Buenos Aires.[16]

Beresford, though his rank was brigadier general in the British Army, had been given the local rank of major general by Baird. He was thus superior in rank to Auchmuty, whose original instructions had also made him subordinate to Beresford as the commander in the region. Auchmuty offered to serve under Beresford, correctly, but the latter, who may well have appreciated his own toxicity with the Spaniards, decided it would be better if he returned to Britain. Pack, however, most of whose soldiers in the 71st were still prisoners, decided to remain. (The *portenos* always noted where Pack was, and regularly insulted him, so Beresford's decision made sense.)

Auchmuty set about expanding his conquests. Liniers had returned to Buenos Aires, and Sobremonte's force had evaporated after his arrest, so he could operate without much opposition in the Banda Oriental. He sent Colonel Pack further along the coast to the west to take the old settlement of Colonia de Sacramento, which was directly opposite Buenos Aires across the estuary, and he proposed to take control of the fort of Santa Teresa, on the frontier with Portuguese Brazil on the Atlantic coast. An examination of the fort from the sea, however, produced the conclusion that it was probably too strong to be attacked; the size of the garrison was not discovered, but the sheer distance of the fort from Montevideo, and the likely difficulty in taking it, in the end made its capture unnecessary.

Auchmuty's force was now spread from Colonia to Maldonado, and could do no more than hold what he already had, as the decision that Santa Teresa was a fort too far, demonstrated. A few reinforcements, part of the 9th Dragoon Guards, joined him in February, but this was not enough to make any difference. He knew full well that the inhabitants of the territory under his control were sullenly hostile, so he could not relax his grip anywhere; he thus had no troops to use for further adventures. Colonel Bourke fully appreciated Auchmuty's problem. He investigated if, as was the general opinion in Britain, the Spaniards of South America were willing to become 'part of the British Empire', as *The Times* had put it. If they were, then Auchmuty's small force could extend itself without fearing a rising in its rear.

> I was assured that the prejudices of religion were not to be overcome, and that whatever commercial benefit might be derived from such a charge, still it would not render it acceptable. That it was true the great mass of the people were heartily tired of the Spanish yoke, but that their wishes were entirely turned towards independence, and the establishment of a republic or federal government similar to that of North America. That the submitting to an English master would be the greatest possible blow to this project, and that on this account as well as others they would strenuously resist us.

The local suggestion was that the 'English' should assist in establishing that local independence, and 'that you [the United Kingdom] then would be required for the purpose, but that the country could not be conquered without a large army, nor preserved without a greater'.[17]

In a nutshell, this was Auchmuty's problem, and one which would face General Whitelocke when he and his larger army arrived. If Auchmuty relaxed his grip on Montevideo to go on campaign to take more territory, the Montevideans could well rise up behind him. Auchmuty could do no more without more troops. And when they arrived, with a new commander-in-chief, he would be trapped in the same problem. (And next year the French in Spain would repeat the experience, as they would in Russia from 1812.)

The news of the capture of Montevideo, on the other hand, had a cheering effect in Britain. Almost as soon as the news arrived, and capitalising on the news of Auchmuty's success, both Houses of Parliament carried votes of thanks to him on 17 April, though he only heard about it on his return to Britain several months later; the Patriotic Fund voted him a silver vase worth £200.[18] The capture of the town – 'fortress and city', according to the Patriotic Fund – can only have persuaded many in Britain that further South American conquests would be, if not easy, then certainly possible. By mid-1807 there was certainly no possibility of any success for British arms in Europe.

Reinforcements were now on their way, but they were spread out and wandering. Bourke himself had arrived in advance of any of them. Apart from the 9th Dragoon Guards, who arrived in February, Lieutenant General John Whitelocke, the new Commander-in-Chief, was supposed to bring a force of another 1,600 men with him, but he took passage in a fast frigate, and the troops sailed in much slower transports. Most of them never did arrive in time to participate. The force of 4,000 men under Brigadier General Robert Craufurd which was supposed to invade Chile by way of Australia and the Pacific Ocean moved equally slowly. It had to wait at the Cape Verde Islands for a month for the naval escort under Rear Admiral George Murray, who had difficulty in getting away from Portsmouth. Craufurd persuaded the convoy commander, Rear Admiral Robert Stopford (who we will meet again later in this book), to sail on, hoping the errant admiral would catch up, or perhaps hoping to avoid him altogether. And a sloop, *Fly*, was also on its way with a set of new instructions for Craufurd.

All these ships and forces and commanders sailed by the same oceanic route, but none of them met up with the others until they all arrived at the Cape in a single week in mid-March. A frigate sent from Montevideo by Rear Admiral Stirling arrived with news of the town's capture, when the loss of Buenos Aires became known also. Then successive arrivals from Britain forced repeated re-considerations of the situation by everyone involved, but it eventually became clear that, with Buenos Aires retaken by the Spaniards, and with Auchmuty at Montevideo stretched to breaking point, and a new Commander-in-Chief on his way, the Chile expedition would have to be redirected to the River Plate. General Sir George Grey, Baird's successor as Governor at the Cape, was already intending to send provisions and powder to Auchmuty; the men of the several expeditions went there also.[19] The sailors and soldiers appreciated the virtues of concentration, while the politicians had spread their aims too widely, and ineffectively. It remained to be seen if the concentration was sufficient.

Auchmuty was superseded in command by Whitelocke when the latter arrived in May, but little could be done at first. Only when Craufurd's force arrived in June was Whitelocke able to make an advance, and it is not clear that he knew for some time that Craufurd was being redirected. He did, however, undertake such activities as he could, including starting a bilingual newspaper, *The Southern Star/La Estrella del Sur* (which is a useful source for discovering the commitment of British commercial activities in the town, as well as the tone of British propaganda, essentially false enthusiasm and confidence, as might be expected); he also issued new customs regulations, and generally encouraged the market, all aimed at convincing British and Spaniards alike that the conquest was permanent and substantive.

Whitelocke clearly knew how to govern on these lines, and he would have been a competent colonial governor. When Craufurd's force arrived Whitelocke swiftly organised the embarkation of most of the troops already in Montevideo and launched a new invasion of the southern coast, aimed at Buenos Aires. He also got many of the British merchants to organise themselves into a militia battalion commanded by Colonel Browne of the 40th Foot which was left to garrison Montevideo, so allowing him to take as many of the professional soldiers with him as possible. Whitelocke the military administrator could certainly do all this competently, but it turned out that he had little idea of planning an attack or of command in the field.[20]

The situation in Buenos Aires was now very excited and militaristic. Large numbers of men had been enrolled into numerous military units, many of which had already existed as part of the normal militia forces.[21] (The British should have understood all this – it was essentially how the British at home had reacted to the threat of invasion.) Liniers was in overall military command, but the Cabildo acted as the government both of the city and the whole viceroyalty – though this was not at all pleasing to many of the more distant territories. (Federalism was already a political force in the region, as well as an overall wish for independence.) There was thus a good deal of tension on the Spanish side. Liniers was not entirely trusted, being thought to be a Royalist and a Loyalist as well as French, while the wide social sources of the new recruits to the army were much disliked by the conservatives, who feared that their social inferiors might use their new military power in inimical ways. Liniers' French origin made him suspect to the Spaniards (as well as among the British) and he was under suspicion as a result of the escape of Beresford and Pack, but he did have better military training than anyone else on the Spanish side. He was allied politically with Martin de Alzaga, who for the moment dominated the Cabildo, and both were assisted by the arrival of Colonel Javier de Elio direct from Spain. Reinforcements were arriving for the citizens' forces from the interior, including 3,000 men from Paraguay – 'Indians', to the British – and when Whitelocke launched his invasion force, with 8,500 men, he faced a city determined to defend itself, and containing as many armed men as he commanded, who were also reinforced by angry, and often armed, citizens.

Auchmuty was placed in command of the Second Brigade, with the First under Brigadier General Lumley, who had been in the fighting at Montevideo (and shared in the thanks of Parliament along with Auchmuty); the light troops were placed under Craufurd. Whitelocke marched with Auchmuty. The other two sections, the First Brigade and the lights, were eventually united under the command of Major General Leveson Gower, Whitelocke's second-in-command, who had come out with him. It is notable that Auchmuty, the only senior commander with experience in the area, was now some way down the chain of command. Not only that, but the order of march put the Lights and the First Brigade in advance, and so Whitelocke, with Auchmuty, was bringing up the rear, technically with the main body, but actually out of touch when the enemy was eventually met.

The landing took place at Ensenada de Barragon, 10 miles east of Beresford's landing place, on 28 June, a year and three days after Beresford's and Popham's landing. The Rio Chuelo stream was crossed at an unexpected point, which forced Liniers' defence force to move back towards the city. The two opponents met at a butchering area, the Corral de Miserere, and Liniers' force was driven back into the city in defeat after a swift attack by Craufurd and the Lights. Whitelocke was not involved in any of this, for the Second Brigade had been marching well behind Gower's force, and eventually took a longer and different route. The whole march was very slow, taking four days to cover less than 20 miles. After the fight at the Corral, the First Brigade halted to await Whitelocke's arrival, though Craufurd wanted to rush on to take advantage of the confusion and demoralisation caused by his victory. When Whitelocke came up it became clear he had no plan for conquering the city. One was produced by Gower, and Whitelocke accepted it, perhaps because it was the only one offered.

The city before them was laid out as a grid of streets at right angles, forming square blocks. The street layout was extended a good way beyond the most densely populated areas in anticipation of expansion. The public buildings were concentrated close to the river, clustered around an old fort and spread along the two streets closest to, and parallel with, the river. Gower was perhaps influenced by the report of Beresford's capture of the city in producing his plan, for Beresford had marched straight into the city along those main streets parallel to the river, meeting no resistance after defeating the city militia outside the city, just as had happened at the Corral. So Gower's plan was to divide the army into its regiments, spread them along the inland boundary of the city, from whence each regiment would advance along the streets – two streets per regiment as far as the river shore, sweeping any opposition before them. Having reached the river they would then have taken the whole city. On paper, it looked logical and simple. In practice it relied on the enemy doing what was expected; it divided the army into small sections, each of which could be defeated in isolation from all the rest.

The plan was presented at a meeting of senior commanders, but no objections were made other than requests to make a reconnaissance first; Auchmuty and Pack both suggested that the opening of the attack would be better at daybreak rather than at noon as originally suggested. This all meant, in effect, a delay of two days before the attack was launched. A resident of the city, William White, an American merchant in whose house Whitelocke was staying, provided some local information. He described the conditions in the city, explaining what he knew of the disposition of the Spanish forces, which turned out to be accurate, but he also made it clear that the defence was concentrated in the area around the Plaza Mayor and the Fort beside the river, and that little in the way of opposition would be likely until the British forces reached the centre of the city. But they then would be faced by entrenched positions, with guns placed to fire along the streets. This information does not seem to have affected the plan in any way, but if the enemy was concentrated in one place, the division of the army into its separate attacks was scarcely necessary.

The delay for discussion and reconnaissance was occupied by the Spaniards in preparation. If Whitelocke had had his plan ready and had sent his forces directly into the city along the streets two days earlier, he would have caught the Spaniards unready – which is not to say there would have been any the less of a fight, but by ignoring the chance of a speedy attack, Whitelocke (and Gower) threw away their only real opportunity of winning. And a sensible commander would have been up with the advanced forces moving into an attack; both Whitelocke and Gower seem to have expected everything to go as planned, like clockwork.

Auchmuty commanded on the left, where the 5th, 87th and 38th Regiments would attack along six of the streets. The rest of the attack was under no single commander. The central street was to be the line of advance for the 9th Dragoon Guards, moving on foot. The Light Brigade under Craufurd was next, along with the 88th, then the 45th on the right, each moving along two main streets. Whitelocke and Gower and their staffs took no part in any of the attacks, remaining all day at White's house, completely out of touch with every regiment. There was, in fact, little they could have done, for, having so subdivided their army, they had foregone any opportunity to affect events – not that they ever seem to have felt that they should. It was a clear abdication of responsibility.

All of these columns, each street taking half a battalion, advanced almost all way to the riverside. Initially they faced no opposition but this was due to any Spanish forces in these outer areas having been withdrawn to concentrate and occupy – or perhaps hide in – the houses and substantial buildings which the British simply by-passed. They came out after the British had marched past, followed them at a distance, and then joined in the fight near the river. Auchmuty's regiments mainly performed their tasks, and occupied the northern part of the city, an area called the Retiro, which included the Plaza de Toros, and this area became his command post. The northernmost streets these troops had moved along had hardly been defended, but one regiment, the 5th, under Major King and Lieutenant Colonel Davie, came up against powerful opposition as they approached the river. After taking heavy casualties both sections turned away from the city centre northwards and joined the 87th and the 38th with Auchmuty around the Plaza de Toros in the north.[22] The result was a concentration of part of the British forces in the Retiro, but they had established no real command of any part of the city beyond that area. Nevertheless they provided a threat of an advance along the riverside region just by being there.

In the southern area matters were much more fragmented and confused. Half of the 45th marched as far as the riverside, but then occupied a large building, the Residentia, on the southern edge of the town (just as the Bullring was on the northern edge), well away from the main action. Like Auchmuty's forces in the Retiro, having accomplished their set task, this group then stayed put. Orders were needed for any further action. Clearly Gower's and Whitelocke's planning hadn't gone any further than getting to the river.

On their left, on the other hand, the other half of the 45th and the light troops under Craufurd met disaster. Craufurd and some of his men took refuge in, or were besieged in, the Church of Santo Domingo and suffered many casualties from Spaniards firing through the windows.[23] Half of the 45th under Colonel Cadogan, met strong opposition as it neared the river, and turned away towards the north, towards the city centre, but they were then blockaded in another building. Both of these forces were surrounded, and many of the men were shot down by enemies firing through the windows.

In the centre, the 9th Dragoons advanced on foot but only got about halfway along their chosen street before being stopped, and they then failed to make any further progress – they were only a small unit, and were thus relatively easily stopped. The two regiments between the dragoons and Auchmuty's forces, the 88th and the 36th had, like others who came close to the city centre, marched most of the way and then met sustained and determined opposition in the area close to the river. The 36th, with Lumley, turned off towards the north, and retreated to join Auchmuty's assembly near the Plaza de Toros.

Both parts of the 88th were forced to surrender. To their right, Craufurd and the Lights and half the 45th were also forced to surrender.[24] Of the thirteen columns which had attacked in the morning, five had surrendered by the late afternoon, one was blocked in the Residentia, unable to advance, and the dragoons could not advance any more than halfway into the town; the others had been driven well away from the centre and were concentrated in the Retiro. Auchmuty therefore commanded almost all the remaining active British forces; those in the Residentia were wholly isolated.

Casualties among the British were enough to stop any further fighting: 400 men had been killed, 650 wounded, and 1,900 captured. This figure of almost 3,000 losses was over a third of Whitelocke's total force, a casualty rate quite high enough to disable any army.

Whitelocke remained in complete ignorance of all this. He stayed in White's house all day, occasionally sending staff officers to find out what was happening. Only after Captain Samuel Ford Whittingham reached Auchmuty late in the afternoon, and then returned to White's house, did Whitelocke begin to realise the scale of the disaster; even then he did nothing.[25]

Next morning Liniers, who did understand the magnitude of the Spaniards' defensive victory, wrote to Whitelocke demanding a British surrender, and naming terms. He offered to release all the prisoners held by the Spaniards (those sent into the interior included), and demanded the evacuation of both Buenos Aires and Montevideo by the British forces. He pointed out that the citizens were angry, and that he could not guarantee the lives of his own prisoners if the fighting was resumed. This might have been a bluff, but experience suggested he was not wholly in control of the city. To reinforce the point Whitelocke's reply – a formal rejection – was carried by a strong escort which was fired on repeatedly on its journey even though it was carrying a flag of truce. One result of using amateur soldiers, of course, was that they did not follow, or understand, military etiquette. One of the Spanish complaints was that a Spanish officer carrying a flag of truce had been shot and wounded during the negotiations for the surrender of Craufurd's men at the Santo Domingo church; the confusion there had been very great, in part caused by the realisation by the Spaniards that Colonel Pack was in the church. The culprit in the shooting of the officer bearing the flag of truce was an Irish soldier who confessed later that he did not know what a flag of truce was or what it represented – he called it a 'flag of truth'; it was not only the amateur *porteno* soldiers who did not know, or obey, the rules.[26]

Whitelocke rode to the Retiro to discuss the situation with Gower, Lumley, and Auchmuty. Various suggestions were made as to how to continue the fight, including one from Captain Augustus Frazer of the Royal Artillery that he could mount a deliberate artillery bombardment which would knock down much of the city. This did not meet with approval by anyone. Whitelocke claims to have been more concerned about the British prisoners, whose fate he believed lay in his hands – so far had Liniers' threat that he could not control the citizenry been successful. Whitelocke also realised that even if he succeeded in conquering the city in whatever way he could, and whatever method he used, he still had to hold on to it afterwards, and the scale of opposition among the population made it obvious that this would be impossible without a very large reinforcement of British troops, which he could not expect. Auchmuty had had a difficult task in holding Montevideo and the north shore with an army much the same size as that Whitelocke now commanded (after the casualties and losses) at Buenos Aires – and Buenos Aires was ten times the size of Montevideo, not to mention the huge interior territories. He faced presiding over a ruined city, with half of his own army massacred, or controlling a conquered city with a wholly inadequate force and in the face of an implacably hostile population – or of course accepting Liniers' terms and returning to Britain in disgrace.

It was, of course, not really a choice at all. Holding on in whatever method he chose would leave the British in an appallingly invidious position, holding down a hostile city and country, no matter what they did; and if he allowed a massacre of British prisoners when he had the power to prevent it he could imagine the fury that would greet him in Britain. Knocking down a city, however far from Europe, would be something which would be thrown in the face of every British soldier and diplomat for generations. (As it happened, in that very year a vicious bombardment by the British fleet caused great damage in Copenhagen, and another British fleet menaced Constantinople, though the Admiral there, Sir John Duckworth, found it impossible to get close enough to the city to cause any damage. It is perhaps a sign of the coarsening effect of more than a dozen years of warfare that such actions could be contemplated and/or carried out.) The French did take such a course in Spain, where Saragossa and Gerona were deliberately bombarded into ruin, and Russia, where Moscow was burned, but such actions scarcely produced victory, only renewed hatred.

While Whitelocke was considering all this and pondering his options, the Spaniards resumed firing on that part of the 45th at the Residentia, and others launched an attack on the Retiro. These attacks were not pushed very hard, and were resisted without difficulty, but the British had not been able to mount any attacks at all. Whitelocke at last asked Liniers for a truce, and agreed to accept the terms which had been originally suggested by Liniers. Gower was sent to negotiate for more lenient terms, and, not surprisingly, failed entirely to change Liniers' mind on any of them. They included an exchange of prisoners, the release of all those held in the interior, the removal of all British soldiers from Buenos Aires as quickly as possible, and the evacuation of Montevideo within two months.

The British soldiers in the Retiro area, and at the Residentia, though perhaps not many of the officers, professed to be astonished at this surrender. Like good soldiers, however, they grumblingly obeyed. Gower had witnessed a near riot in the Plaza Mayor among the population when it was learnt that Colonel Pack had been captured and was being held in the Fort; there he was being protected by three priests. In the end he was smuggled out dressed as a Spaniard, and released. If he thus protected Pack it seems extremely unlikely that Liniers would have permitted any sort of massacre of his prisoners, but he was perfectly correct in describing the population as angry, and he may not have been able to prevent it. The Spaniards also made rigorous efforts to recover all the loot taken by the British soldiers, and the British sources often, all too gleefully, describe successful ploys by which the Spaniards were foiled in this. But in one case a missing crucifix was only recovered when the possibly guilty men were credibly threatened with being killed.

It remained to put the terms into effect. Whitelocke's organisational skills ensured that, by early September 1807, most of the men from the interior had returned and had been embarked, and Montevideo was evacuated on schedule. Some of the wounded remained behind by mutual arrangement, and a couple of ships stayed in the estuary to collect them and any laggard prisoners. Several hundred of the British troops remained behind voluntarily, many of them the Catholic ex-Dutch mercenaries who had been forcibly recruited into the British Army by Baird at the Cape. Any man with a useful skill – and many British soldiers did have such artisanal skills – was likely to be welcomed to stay at Buenos Aires, and to be able to set up in business and make a living, and the ladies of the city were often pleased to marry them. More than one British soldier had been wooed by the young Spanish women during the occupation, as part of the Spanish resistance.[27]

The merchants who had come out in hopes of making their fortunes in South America, and who had been recruited into the militia to defend Montevideo, were effectively abandoned by the military. They were often able to get away in the ships, naval and civilian, but the beaches about Montevideo were littered with their abandoned merchandise, which was picked over by delighted Spaniards as their former owners sailed away.

The evacuated soldiers were returned to Britain. The damaged regiments were revived with new recruits at their depots. Sir Arthur Wellesley had been given command of an expedition intended to invade Spanish Mexico – on the same assumption of the willingness of the Spanish colonists to join the British Empire, which had been so clearly disproved at Buenos Aires and Montevideo – and the force he was given included several of these regiments which had returned from Buenos Aires. The expedition was cancelled as it was about to sail, and Wellesley and his regiments were sent to the Peninsula instead when the great Spanish revolt against French occupation broke out. Several of the regiments which had been in South America were therefore part of his forces, this time fighting to free Spaniards, and not to subjugate them. Some of them fought all through the Peninsular War. (The men of the regiments from Buenos Aires had certainly picked up some Spanish, but it might not have been a good idea to advertise where they had learned it.)

But it was not really in Europe that the major effects of this abortive British adventure were felt. The Spaniards in Buenos Aires had fought to expel the invader and had been successful, and this was something they did not forget. They had removed Viceroy Sobremonte from his office for incompetence, as they saw it, and they soon in effect elected Liniers as their new Viceroy. This was accepted by the Spanish government, which was struggling to resist the French conquest, because it could do nothing else. In Buenos Aires it soon became clear that this minor move towards autonomy was not nearly enough to satisfy local aspirations, and that, as Colonel Bourke had detected, it was now independence which was the local political aim. Spain itself collapsed into a chaotic war during 1808, and became powerless to act against this, and wholly unable to exert any sort of imperial control. In effect the *portenos* had been governing themselves ever since they rose up to remove Beresford's rule in 1806; over the next four years this status gradually firmed up into permanence.

The basic political effect of the British attack had therefore been to force the *portenos* to develop a much greater political self-confidence. Whereas before 1806 the members of the Buenos Aires Cabildo had grumbled about Spanish rule and its restrictions, after 1806 they had demonstrated their ability to defend themselves successfully against an attack by one of the great European powers. To the British, or anyone else in Europe, the expedition was a relatively minor matter, employing only a few thousands troops, but to the *portenos* it was their victory which counted. From the failure of the second British attack onwards, it was independence, not simply autonomy, which was at the head of the *portenos*' political agenda.

And this was not only in Buenos Aires. In Mexico and other parts of the Spanish Empire in America as well, the local political sentiment turned to the idea of independence. The example always before the Spaniards was that of the United States, which had freed itself from the British by a war of independence, just as had, so they claimed, those of Buenos Aires. In both areas it took several years for the consequences to work themselves through, and for the conclusion to become clear, but by 1810 it could be said that the viceroyalty of Buenos Aires had moved into complete independence, and had become the Republic of Argentina.[28] Presumably Auchmuty was sufficiently alert to these events to understand, if not appreciate, the irony of his participation in attempting to subdue part of the American continent at Montevideo and Buenos Aires and bring those towns into the British Empire.

But there were casualties. Liniers was one, shot by a firing squad of his own soldiers on suspicion of tending towards either Royalist Spain or imperial France – Liniers almost certainly was a conservative Catholic Loyalist, who had seen that the only way to resist a Protestant British attack was to rouse the people, and his whole earlier career suggested loyalty to the Spanish monarchy. In this he was, therefore in many ways, a Franco-

Spanish version of Auchmuty. (Napoleon sent out one of his own men, the Marquis of Sassenay, as a replacement viceroy, but he did not get any support, not getting any further than Montevideo, which did for a time fall back under Spanish rule.) Independence did not wholly suit all of the (former) viceroyalty, especially as this might mean rule from Buenos Aires by *portenos*. Paraguay detached itself under a local doctor turned dictator. Bolivia successfully resisted an attempted 'liberation' by the invading army of Buenos Aires in 1812. The Banda Oriental similarly fought its own war of independence against both Brazil and Argentina, under the leadership of José Artigas, one of the leaders of the gaucho resistance to the British occupation; it took the country twenty years to secure its independence, eventually as the Uruguayan Republic, the difficult birth of which was assisted by British and French fleets as midwives.

Further, within Argentina there was a long dispute over the form of government to be adopted. There were two aspects to this: the power of the president (or presidents, sometimes there was a tribunal of three), and the design of the constitution. The more distant regions of the (former) viceroyalty, notably those along the foot of the Andes at Mendoza and Tucuman – places where many of the British prisoners had been detained, which may have had some effect on local opinion, had no wish to be ruled from the city, and they enforced their own autonomy even to the point of independence from both Spain and Buenos Aires. It took another war to bring them into the wider republic, if only loosely. The dispute over this has not been wholly resolved yet, and is one of the sources of the repeated resort to dictatorship in Argentina.[29]

There were more personal results of the British invasion. Several of the deserters who stayed behind became soldiers, or even commanders, in the local armies of the independence campaigns. Above all there is William Brown, an Irishman who became an Argentinian Admiral. Then there was James Paroissien, who went out to Buenos Aires as a merchant, stayed on, and enlisted in Jose de San Martin's army of liberation as a manufacturer of gunpowder for the revolutionary army.[30] San Martin gathered his independence army at Mendoza (one of the cities where the prisoners had been held), and marched it over the Andes to liberate first Chile and then Peru from Spanish rule. (The route he used was later given a narrow gauge railway, built by British engineers, but this is now a wreck.) Independence for Chile might have come a dozen years sooner if Craufurd's expedition across the Pacific had actually happened – but he was not intent on making Chile independent. San Martin's army of invasion was, at 4,000 men, about the same size as that which sailed with Craufurd – but San Martin received a good deal of local support; it is unlikely Craufurd would have.

These wars involved large numbers of other Britons as well. British soldiers and sailors fought on both sides in the conflict in the River Plate in the 1820s over the future of Uruguay. It was in part this British involvement which brought intense diplomatic interventions by both Britain and France, long after their wars in Europe had ended.[31] The participation of British soldiers in the South American revolutions extended also to the fighting in Colombia/Venezuela, where, indeed, *el Precursor*, Francisco de Miranda, had made his first attempt at rousing the inhabitants against Spain in June 1806, at the very time that his friend Sir Home Popham was attacking Buenos Aires. (Popham knew Miranda, and knew he was going to make his attempt; this may have been one of the inspirations for his own intervention at the River Plate.) The Foreign Secretary, George Canning, insisted in 1823 that the Spaniards and South Americans be left to sort out their own disputes alone, without European intervention. This in effect recognised their independence, since Spain could not reconquer them herself, and now Britain would prevent anyone else from doing so. He was thus only coming in as the last British intervener, and his words must have rung very hollow in the chancellories of Europe who wanted to give Spain help, and who remembered the attempt by Britain to reconquer North America.[32] Canning's underlying aim, of course, was to see that the former Spanish territories were opened up to British trade, as those merchants who rushed off to the River Plate in 1806 – 1807 had hoped, but which Spain steadily refused to permit; it was to benefit Britain, not South America, that he enunciated his policy.

The consequences of the British invasions of the River Plate were thus wide-ranging indeed. By compelling the development of a strong local resistance to their own attacks, and discrediting the Spanish rulers, such as Sobremonte and, to a lesser extent, Ruiz Huidobro, the invaders had stimulated the latent sentiment for independence, which had already been growing locally ever since the independence of the United States showed the way.[33] It was men who had fought against the British conquest who ruled

Argentina for at least the next thirty years, and it was such men also who led the fight for independence in Uruguay and Chile and Peru. Meanwhile many of the same British soldiers who had attempted to conquer Spanish America had participated in driving the French Army out of Spain and Portugal, by which means the independence of those countries was maintained. They had therefore moved from attempting to conquer a resistant people to assisting in the resistance of a conquered people.

The British did not fail to profit by their intervention in the River Plate region. The expulsion of their soldiers and merchants in 1807 was never complete, for not a few of both groups stayed on voluntarily; British finance repeatedly invested in South American developments during the next century, all too often carelessly. It was above all in Argentina that that development was most productive, in building railways, developing cattle ranches, and stimulating the Argentinian economy, to such a degree that the country has been identified as part of Britain's 'informal empire' – though this is a formulation of a somewhat arrogant aspect, and of which the Argentinians are less than convinced, of course. The real profit for the British came actually in the twentieth century, when Argentina was one of the major sources of food when the British Isles were besieged by German U-boats during the two world wars, and the British investments in the country were liquidated to help pay for British survival (even as Argentina itself was falling under the near-fascist dictatorship of Perón).

Samuel Auchmuty had therefore now fought, but failed, to retain British control of his homeland, fought successfully to extend it in India, fought to defend Britain's own independence against a French invasion, and had fought, but failed, to expand the British Empire into South America, and had seen in the end the return to a Spanish governor (Javier de Elio) of his Montevidean conquest. The later, much more long-term, growth of British influence in the area was to be hidden from him, but not the successful achievement of independence in many parts of the continent, which was well in train before he died. One may be perhaps be allowed to assume that his counsel to Whitelocke in the conference on 6 July at the Retiro in the wake of their joint defeat could have been to evacuate Buenos Aires, but to keep Montevideo.

He sailed back to Britain on one of the Royal Navy ships, the sloop *Saracen*, and a sailor there noted that he spent much of his time in silence, not that he ever seems to have been particularly garrulous. He is said to have been always drinking wine. No doubt he was rightly wary of the quality of the ship's water, which would show a proper caution, but possibly also he was drowning his sorrows.

Chapter 7

India, 1810–11

Auchmuty returned to Britain early in 1808 with the evacuated soldiers from Buenos Aires and Montevideo. One of his first actions was to attend the court martial of General Whitelocke on 28 January, in which he was a witness, but which was over in only a day. Whitelocke was found guilty of a variety of military offences, though incompetence, which was his real problem, was not among them. He was cashiered and dismissed from the service. Such were the results of being defeated.

There was, however, a good deal more involved in the issue of Whitelocke's conduct than mere military carelessness and his inherent lack of command ability. It has been noted already that one of the motives of the Grenville ministry in appointing Whitelocke to command in South America was so that they could abolish his previous post as Inspector General, and so 'save' the money this post would cost. That is, that ministry (in office from January 1806 to April 1807) was using that overseas expedition as a means of pursuing its own policies at home. There was no question of assessing his military competence or otherwise in appointing Whitelocke. And this attitude continued, though less obviously and much less disastrously, after the Grenville ministry fell in 1807 and was replaced by one headed by the aged and somnolent Duke of Portland. The active and vigorous members of this new ministry were Lord Hawkesbury as Home Secretary, Lord Castlereagh as War Minister, and George Canning as Foreign Minister, but they were as susceptible to nepotism as their predecessors.

The fact that this was another 'new' ministry – though it was actually a revival of the Pitt ministry of 1804–6 without Pitt – did not alter the fact that its ministers were fully capable of playing politics with the army, but at least, with Castlereagh to convince, they were much less liable to send small expeditions into far distant regions, commanded by inexperienced or incompetent generals; instead they were actually capable of concentrating on the essentials. Any expeditionary commander appointed by the Grenville ministers was clearly liable to be regarded as politically hostile by the new men, or at least investigated for political reliability above all else, and any soldier associated with a mess like that at Buenos Aires was obviously tainted with Whitelocke's failure. This would include Auchmuty. But the brush of guilt washed over Whitelocke and Gower almost exclusively; the subordinate commanders, even Craufurd and Lumley, were, after a time, deemed to be generally competent and re-employable, and were to be serious commanders, notably in the Peninsular campaigns.

Auchmuty acknowledged the thanks of the House of Commons, voted after the conquest of Montevideo, news of which had reached him by a 'dispatch from the Cape of Good Hope' while he was in South America, and to which he replied from London on 4 March.[1] (He did not acknowledge the resolution of the House of Lords until August, though the two resolutions were both dated 7 April 1807.[2]) He was promoted to Major General later in 1808, which certainly distinguished him from Whitelocke's debacle.

In these fraught political conditions, however, it is not surprising that little or no activity is known for Auchmuty for the two years after his return to Britain. A look at his career must have made it quite clear that he was as apolitical as any soldier of his rank could be, possibly as a reaction to the excessively unpleasant politics of New York in the 1770s. His loyalty to the Church of England, inherited from his parents, in particular his father (and going back several generations), was a commonplace in political circles, but this devotion certainly put him among the Tories rather than the Whigs, if anything. However, his career showed that his priority was always his work as a soldier, and that he was willing to command forces whoever was in office in London.

His career to that point had been not dissimilar to that of Sir Arthur Wellesley, with the crucial difference that Wellesley was fully prepared to descend into the political arena, and he served in the Portland ministry as Irish Under-Secretary. He even retained that position while commanding in Denmark in 1807 and in Portugal in 1808. It was his presence in London, together with his military ability, and his sponsorship by Castlereagh, which ensured that he was employed to counter the French occupation of Portugal in 1808, while Auchmuty, who kept clear of political matters, was in South America. (Of course Wellesley was actually about to sail for Mexico when he was diverted to Portugal, but he was also, as his career always shows, careful to choose his political supporters.)

Auchmuty was apparently not considered for the Portugal expedition in 1808, though he was clearly available once the Whitelocke trial was ended. It may also be that he was tired and disillusioned after the events at Buenos Aires. He certainly did not have such eminent political sponsors as did Wellesley. He would need to make it clear to the War Office that he was available for employment, and that he was keen to be employed. It was never enough to be merely senior in rank. It was necessary also to put oneself forward. This does not seem to have been something Auchmuty generally did. Nevertheless one can see that he was, in fact, regularly employed, and the basic reason must be that he was regarded as both competent and capable. Maybe the Duke of York understood his abilities better than most, and ensured that he was used.

His letter of thanks to Lord Eldon for the House of Lords' vote of thanks is dated from Syndale House in August 1808. This is the first confirmation that this was his home, though it is highly likely that he had acquired it while commanding in Thanet against Napoleon in 1803–6. He would obviously need to be living within easy reach of Thanet during that time. He was near to several other family members, and he described a new appointment in 1810 in a letter quoted by Mrs Townsend to his elder brother Robert Nicholls Auchmuty in Newport, Rhode Island. This was the brother who had remained in the United States, and the letter further demonstrates that he was still in touch with members of his family who lived across the Atlantic.[3] He had also taken his nephew John Maxwell Tyndal, the eldest son of his sister Jane Tyndal, with him as his brigade major in South America, and he was to take him with him again to his new post in 1810.

In early 1810 he was appointed as Commander-in-Chief of the Army of one of the three parts of the East India Company's territories in India, the Madras Presidency. His letter describes the post he was offered as 'a handsome appointment', that 'the salary is handsome', but that the expenses were likely to be considerable. He also knew, of course, that the possibility of prize-money gains would be considerable, that was one of the main reasons why officers transferred to go to India. But what he did not apparently mention – perhaps he did not need to – is that he was going out to command an army which had recently been displaying extreme disaffection, amounting to mutiny. Just as in South America, he was being sent to a new post with the obvious task of clearing up a mess made by others.

The basic problems in British India had not changed since Auchmuty had been there over a decade earlier: the government was a trading company, run by men who had little real idea of how to conduct the government of a huge empire – and they were trying to do so from London, and as cheaply as possible, and at six months' distance. Some improvements had been made in the previous twenty years or so, notably by Lord Cornwallis while Auchmuty was adjutant of his regiment in the Madras Presidency. One of the improvements was that the Directors in London were now under some British government control, and that the actual governors of the three presidencies were men usually appointed at least with the consent of the British government. But the distance had not lessened, and the men appointed as governors were not usually willing to wait for instructions, certainly not in emergencies.

The army which the Company theoretically commanded was composed of mercenaries, both Indian and British (with a leavening of Europeans). A mercenary army is inherently unstable. The men were vigilant in asserting their rights as against the government and against their officers, they were frequently ill paid, and often their pay was in arrears.[4] Mutinies in India were fairly frequent occurrences, and could be mounted by the ordinary sepoys, or by the officers, though they rarely joined together in such a venture.

The Company's armies displayed all these characteristics – that of a trade union, in fact – and the Company reacted with a mixture of annoyance at the ingratitude of their employees, parsimony in their pay, and a speedy surrender to their mutinous demands. Only a few of the senior men attempted to impose their authority on the defiant soldiers. But it is noticeable that mutinies by Indian soldiers were often treated as rebellions to be put down with violence, whereas the British officers' mutinies were never so treated. The officers knew they were in a strong position, since they could not be replaced quickly or easily so long as Britain was the main source of officers.

The British government – as opposed to the Company – had made several attempts to cope with a situation which was only half understood in London, and gradually over the previous thirty years a greater degree of control had been imposed from London, in part by the establishment of much closer control over the East India Company in London, in part by sending out

British Army forces to assist in the Company's wars separately from the Company's army, and in part by using its control of the Company to insert its own officials into the occupation of the most strategic offices. This meant the post of Governor-General, the Governors of the Bombay and Madras Presidencies, and the Commanders-in-Chief of the Bengal, Madras, and Bombay armies; all these men were appointed from London. They might be Company men, but they were always London appointees in consultation between the Company and the British government.[5]

The Company's mercenary army was badly affected by all this. Its officers were actuated more by a will to wealth than by any loyalty to the Company or the government system. There was a steady undertow of corruption, to which the governing officials were also rarely immune, though the riches of India were usually much over-estimated. Any move by the government to reduce corruption, or reduce spending – these amounted often to the same thing – was liable to set off complaints. These complaints were not usually articulated over finance, but over 'principles', or the conduct of senior officers, or what the officers saw as their privileges. And if any of the senior officers took the lead it was taken as a signal by the rest that the grievances were legitimate.

It was this sequence which had occurred in India in the years before Auchmuty went out there for the second time. The preliminary had been a rising at the fort of Vellore by the Indian soldiers stationed there. They had, they conceived, been insulted by new regulations promulgated by the Madras Commander-in-Chief, General Sir John Cradock, who wanted them to shave, wear identical headgear, and remove their caste marks and their jewellery. He did this in complete ignorance of the value which the soldiers placed on these matters, for he had been appointed from Britain and had no earlier experience of India. He had been supported in this by the Madras Governor, Lord William Bentinck, who also appears to have been ignorant of the effect the new regulations would have. Further, and again indicating a failure of imagination, even common sense, in these officials, the men so insulted were cantoned in the very place where the family of the deceased Tipu Sultan was being held. This coincidence helped promote the 'mutiny' which broke out, giving it a definitely nationalistic, or at least anti-British, aspect. Tipu's family was certainly involved in stoking up the sepoys' annoyance, and hoped to use the eruption as a means of restoring themselves to power in Mysore.

The Company government had a great fright, but the rising was rapidly put down, with great brutality, by Colonel Rollo Gillespie, who arrived betimes from a nearby garrison and rallied the surviving local British forces, and some loyal Indian soldiers. Virtually all the mutinous troops were killed – massacred would be a more accurate description – during the mutiny's suppression. The speed with which Gillespie had acted was seen to be the saving grace in the matter, and it was this which allowed the British authorities to imagine that they were really still in relatively easy control, rather than that the issue was local and fundamental, and that the means and ferocity of its suppression were much resented among the Indian troops.[6]

On examination afterwards it became clear that the trouble had originated not with the Indian sepoys, but with the Commander-in-Chief and the Governor, both of whom were profoundly ignorant of the sensibilities of the sepoys. Both men were 'recalled' to Britain, but also went on to other posts. (Cradock had a period of timorous command of the British forces in Portugal between the death of Sir John Moore and the arrival of Sir Arthur Wellesley, and went on to be Governor of the Cape of Good Hope, and to be awarded a peerage, changing his name along the way to Caradoc; the British presence in Portugal only just survived the experience of his command, in effect it was rescued by the appointment of Sir Arthur Wellesley. Bentinck, of the family of the Prime Minister, the Duke of Portland, was for that reason quite untouchable, and went on to command in Sicily and Spain against Napoleon, and to be, of all things, Governor-General in India from 1828 to 1835; at some levels mistakes and disasters had no effect on those responsible for them.[7])

One of the results of their joint regime began the process which led to the next mutiny, this time by the British officers. One of the relatively minor peculations among the officers was the 'tentage allowance'. Tents were issued to shelter the troops while on campaign, and an allowance was made to the commanding officers for this purpose rather than providing the actual tents. But even when not on campaign the allowance had continued to be paid. The Governor-General, Sir George Barlow, had been searching for economies, encouraged from London, and lighted on this. He went through the normal bureaucratic method of arranging an investigation into the matter, which was conducted by Colonel John Monro, the Quartermaster General of the Madras Army, who was nominated for the job by Cradock. Quite predictably, given his office, the source of his appointment, and the origins of his task, he came out in favour of the abolition of the allowance; and on any ordinary reasoning this should have been enough.

That was one problem, and it produced much annoyance among the officers, who also claimed that their honour had been insulted because Monro had pointed out that the existence of the allowance conduced to the officers neglecting their duties. When claims of standing on their 'honour' were made, it usually indicated that the accusation was correct, of course, and that the claim was a means of evading the issue. If anyone was an expert on the matter it would be the Quartermaster General, who had had to administer the allowances for the previous six years. The officers, ignoring the question of the abolition of the allowance, called for Monro to be court-martialled because of his supposed insult to them. This was a good distraction from the real issue.

The second contemporary issue was provided by Colonel Arthur St Leger, who was expecting to be made Inspector of Cavalry in the Madras Army, but saw Colonel Rollo Gillespie given the post instead, in part as a result of Gillespie's speedy reaction to the Vellore mutiny. St Leger complained to Bentinck by way of a petition, claiming the 'right' to succeed to the position, and then also to Cradock, but neither responded. Gillespie had, of course, gained a powerful reputation by his actions at Vellore and once appointed he could hardly be removed; St Leger, however, did not, or would not, see that. He complained further up the official ladder, to the government in Calcutta, and this time, clearly appreciating that a mere personal grievance would not get him very far, he expanded the issue into one covering the relations between the Company's army and the royal forces in India. The two forces were paid and equipped differently; the king's officers also always took precedence over the Company officers of the same rank, which regularly riled the latter, who could claim greater experience in the processes of Indian warfare. St Leger loudly broadcast his complaint(s), and by so expanding them to the relations of the Company and the royal forces he very competently stirred up a considerable fuss.

Meanwhile Barlow was superseded as Governor-General by Lord Minto in 1807, and was made Governor of the Madras Presidency as a consolation.

He was already identified as the origin of both the tentage issue, and the man who rejected St Leger's complaint. Now he had to deal with a prima donna of a Commander-in-Chief as well. The final poisonous ingredient in the mix of complaints came from this man, Cradock's successor as Madras Commander-in-Chief, Major General Hay McDowell. McDowell was annoyed from the start because when he took up the post he discovered that, by an earlier decision which Barlow had implemented when he was Governor-General, the Commander-in-Chief in Madras did not now have a seat on the Presidency Council. This had long been the usual procedure, and had put the Commander-in-Chief in a position to contribute to the Council's decisions, or to thwart them, but when they were implemented he was part of the process; the removal had been agreed by the Directors in London, and was in the process of being reconsidered; in fact, had McDowell been on the Council, it is quite probable that much of what happened next would not have occurred.

McDowell complained, of course, but got nowhere. His timing was incredibly bad. He found that the man he blamed for what he considered to be a demotion, Barlow, was now transferred to Madras as Governor, and was therefore his immediate superior; this annoyed him still more. He complained to Barlow's successor as Governor-General, Lord Minto, but was rebuffed. He then complained to London, where the matter was already being discussed once more, though he did not know this. But then, impatiently, McDowell resigned his post and left India. (In fact Barlow dismissed him, in formal terms, but McDowell had already left, and never discovered this.) Shortly afterwards the news came that the exclusion of the Commander-in-Chief from the Council had been reversed on instructions from London. It was too late for McDowell, who was already at sea. Not only that, but his ship was wrecked in a storm off the Cape of Good Hope on the way to Britain, and he was killed.

Before he left India McDowell had taken the side of the annoyed officers on the issue of the tentage allowance. Barlow had refused to go against Monro, not surprisingly since it was he who had instigated Monro's inquiry, but he also probably agreed with the assertion that the tentage issue had contributed to the officers' lack of diligence. McDowell, however, put Monro under arrest in response to the officers' complaints, and then failed to inform the Governor of this. Nonetheless, Barlow learned about it and ordered Monro's release. McDowell replied with several speeches rousing the level of annoyance among the officers to a higher pitch, and a final General Order to the whole army in which Monro's conduct was condemned in the strongest terms. Barlow replied by suspending the two men who had actually written and published McDowell's General Order (McDowell having now left and so was out of punishment reach) – an action which was as indefensible as the arrest of Monro in the first place. The officers who had already been annoyed now replied by commending Major Bowles, one of those who had been condemned by Barlow, and – of course – they also complained to Lord Minto.

None of this was really serious, of course, to anyone outside the army, except that it was clearly the result of officers having too little to do, and having curious notions of 'honour' in their minds. They had a concept of themselves as a group set apart from, and even superior to, the civil government. This was typical behaviour of a mercenary army, but they also considered themselves to be British officers, though it was not the sort of behaviour to which officers of the royal army would ever have adhered. Had they acted in such a way in Britain they would have been slapped down very quickly, and McDowell and St Leger at least would probably have been rapidly cashiered.

Barlow clearly saw the officers' behaviour as a challenge by the military to his civil authority. In this he was quite correct. He had to act either to head off further trouble, or to meet it head on. The normal reaction of the Company government was always the former, in effect calming down the annoyed men and so evading the need to act; but the only way to actually prevent a repetition of such a crisis, or further trouble of the same sort, was to fight it, and Barlow chose this latter method.

He waited for an opportunity. The officers duly obliged. A new memorial addressed to the Governor-General was produced. By communicating to him directly, of course, they were going outside the accepted procedures, which were always to address their own Governor first. The memorial was being circulated to several regiments and garrisons in order to gather signatures and comments, but it had not been finalised nor delivered when Barlow acquired a copy. He reacted by ordering the suspension of eight senior officers who he knew had been involved in producing the document, and imposed lesser penalties on several other officers involved. St Leger had been one of those concerned in its production, and he was ordered to be sent to Poonevalle on the east coast, as a sort of internal exile, and if he would not go of his own volition, he was to be taken there under guard.

Perhaps if Barlow had left it at that, and maybe let the memorial go up to Lord Minto to be ignored or rejected, like all the other complaints by the officers, the whole pot of problems might have simply simmered on for a time, and then died away, but he wished to assert his and the government's authority over the army, which was what he had done by suspending and punishing the obstreperous officers. So he went one step further, having thought he had detected a division in the officers' ranks. He picked out the troops which were stationed at Secunderabad, close to Hyderabad, as the Hyderabad Subsidiary Force, which was designed to keep the Nizam under control, and to protect him (and was paid for by him). The officers there had not apparently taken part in the various events and complaints so far, and Barlow congratulated them on not being involved. This sparked them to assert that they really were involved, and, perhaps because they had earlier held back over the issue of the memorial, they now not only rejected Barlow's praise of them, but threatened to march on Madras.

Meanwhile, on the east coast, St Leger was loudly complaining about his treatment, and was heard by the officers of his own regiment, which were stationed, far across the country, in Travancore (another 'subsidiary force' which aimed to control the local Raja, the successor of the man who defeated Tipu). The officers decided that they would support St Leger and would not permit the order detaining him to be enforced, not that they could do much about it at that distance. At this St Leger finally understood the wider effect he was having and refused to be further involved. Instead he collected evidence for his defence, and left for London.[8]

At Masulipatam, several hundred miles north of Madras on the east coast, the regiment stationed there was ordered to go on board ships to act as marines, but refused to go, and the officers arrested the Colonel (Innes), who had issued the order and tried to insist on the embarkation. They then sent off supporting messages to the force at Secunderabad. Barlow sent Lieutenant Colonel John Malcolm, later one of the major forces in establishing British rule in India. He was to investigate the situation at Masulipatam, possibly with the intention of ending the disturbance, but Malcolm soon sympathised with the discontented officers and said so in his report, clearly misunderstanding the larger issues involved; he did, however, manage to dissuade the regiment from marching off.

Messages had been sent to other units, however, and elicited a supporting reply from Colonel T.G. Montresor at Secunderabad (one of Auchmuty's in-laws), who sent on to Barlow the demands of the commanding officers of no less than six regiments. However, the officers of these regiments were actually seriously divided over what to do, and this paralysed them – this was the lever Malcolm had used also at Masulipatam to deter their march. Neither the Secunderabad nor the Masulipatam units actually moved from their bases, and the Travancore force also stayed still, no doubt somewhat taken aback by the swift disappearance of St Leger, but also for lack of any useful target for the march.

Barlow nonetheless made serious military preparations. He sent a new officer, Colonel Barry Close, renowned as a decisive commander, to take over at Secunderabad from Montresor. The Bombay government was asked to send a British regiment round to Madras, to provide support in case one of the marches actually began, and Barlow also asked for troops to be sent up from Ceylon. A fortified camp was prepared outside Madras for the reception of these troops. All this was done publicly, obviously as a clear warning to any force marching on Madras that they would have to fight if they did so. Since no march on Madras took place, it may be that his precautions were needless; alternatively the fact that they were taken might mean that they had worked.

Barlow, having faced down, so it seemed, the near mutinous officers, having contained one particularly serious challenge from Secunderabad, and having ordered in his reinforcements, now struck a blow which was intended to remove the problem altogether. He ordered all the officers in the Madras Army to sign a document in which they asserted their loyalty. Refusal to sign the 'Test', as the Company's officers called the loyalty oath, would mean dismissal. Even those who signed – and only 150 out of 1,300 did so – disliked the procedure since they claimed that the document implied that they also had been disloyal. Such was the troubled logic of the events.

The refusers were removed from their posts, conveyed to places away from their (former) units, and were replaced by king's officers. Those who had signed were relocated to particular places – at Madras itself, and at St Thomas's Mount near the city, both places under the direct eye and control of the Madras government, at Vellore, where no doubt the consequences of losing control were still all too clear, and at the new camp near the city. But the scheme in a broader sense seemed to have failed, because of the widespread refusal to sign. At Secunderabad Colonel Close failed to impose his authority and had to leave the camp rapidly, in fear of his life, or at least of his liberty.

So far there had been no overt violence, though plenty of threats, but at Seringapatam Barlow's emissary, Colonel Henry Davis, tendered the loyalty oath, but was refused by all except Colonel John Bell, the commander of the garrison, who thus found himself isolated, and swiftly reneged. Davis was threatened with death or arrest, and then was expelled. Seringapatam of course was another connection with the former Mysore kingdom, for this had been Tipu Sultan's city, though the effect of this is difficult to gauge. It was however a fairly large garrison, and settled in a city which was still well fortified. The message from Barlow that the non-signers were to be removed from their posts brought about a dispute between the officers in the fort. The deposed officers rejected that order, and, using their sepoys, drove the British officers (that is those of the British royal army) out of the fort. These were not involved in the dispute, but they were clearly on the side of the signers, and thus of the government in Madras. A raid was then made against a nearby baggage column and a treasure was taken over; the fort was prepared for a siege.

The news of this action stimulated supporters in some places to begin marching either towards Madras or to join the rebels at either Seringapatam or Secunderabad, but none actually reached any of these destinations. Perhaps the nearest to an actual serious movement was at Jalna, in the far north of the Nizam's territory, where a march actually began, under the command of Colonel Doveton. He had taken command of the march, he explained later, in order to try to bring it to an end. And he did succeed in persuading the rebel officers to return to the garrison. Two sepoy battalions approached Seringapatam from the garrison at Chittledroog, intending to join the mutineers, presumably under the command of their own European officers, but on their march they were intercepted by loyal forces. A fight ensued, and the two battalions suffered 200 casualties, though by then they were close enough to their goal for the survivors to be able to seek refuge in the fort. Throughout the Madras Army, therefore, there were murmurings of revolt, amounting at times to direct defiance of all government authority. None, however, of the royal army units took part, and the officers of the royal army held aloof, or supported Barlow. There was apparently some sympathy for the Company officers' cause, such as it was, among the king's officers, though not a great deal, and certainly not enough to bring them out on the Company officers' side.

For two years, Lord Minto, in office as Governor-General in Calcutta from 1807, had left the solution to the problem in Barlow's hands. Whether this was because he felt it was Barlow's sphere of authority, or maybe that he felt that Barlow had stirred up the trouble and therefore had to be the one to solve it, is not clear. Probably Minto did not really want to dirty his hands with the issue. Barlow, in fact, had largely succeeded. The 'Test' was actually successful in the end, since the officers who refused had been dismissed and were sent away from their commands, lost their pay, and their pensions if they had them, and, of course, were left with no armed support. For their defiance had relied for its real strength on their command of their sepoy soldiers, and once separated from them they were largely helpless.

Certain actions were also regarded as going too far. The seizure by the officers from Seringapatam of the treasure was clearly a theft, and put off some potential supporters. Involving the sepoys in the officers' dispute was for many both unwelcome in an issue which had originated in an accusation of officers' lack of diligence, and was dangerous, even wrong. The Vellore (and other) mutinies were well remembered. It was, as the officers' supervisors explained, a quarrel between the officers and their government, or perhaps between employees and bosses – or even as an attack by the officers on the authority of one man, Barlow, who was being described, ludicrously, as a tyrant.[9] Bringing sepoys into such an argument was regarded as involving men who were not concerned in it, and should not be. The mutiny at Vellore was a warning of what sepoys who were seriously disturbed could do, so bringing them into the argument might result in further and more serious mutinies, and if they spread too far, to the overthrow of the Company's rule. The two sepoy battalions who had been roughed up on their way to Seringapatam had suffered, many felt, in a cause which was not their own.

And this, of course, was the Achilles heel of the officers: if they kept their soldiers out of the argument, they laid themselves open to the counter-attack made by Barlow in separating them from the men, and once the officers were without the command of the soldiers they were effectively helpless – as the non-signers of the Test now were. And yet using the sepoys as their blunderbuss in fighting, or even threatening, the Governor or the Governor-General would be equally counter-productive. This would open the way for their own expulsion from India, either at the hands of the outraged Company or at the hands of the royal army in India, or if the matter went really too far, at the hands of enemy Indian states (and rebellious Company sepoys) who would at least be able to mount attacks on the Company's territories and hope to conquer. It is thus no wonder that the officers located their argument on a threat to their 'honour', since this was a nebulous concept, capable of being wheeled out in any dispute. It would strike at the attitudes of the European government class as a whole, and through them at the generality of the British ruling class. But instinctively the officers also knew that resorting to violence would damage their cause irretrievably in the eyes of both their rulers in India and the Company and the political class in Britain.

Barlow clearly understood this and successfully extended an olive branch when the Secunderabad garrison changed its mind about a rising and a march on Madras. From Jalna in the far north of the Nizam's dominions, and from the Sarkars, on the east coast north of Masulipatam, some men had begun to march to join those at Secunderabad when they had the news that the latter had caved in. Had they all joined, their combined force would have been formidable, and they would no doubt have stimulated each other's resentments and bolstered their mutual determinations, so that it would have become difficult to avoid continuing their march until they were at Madras. But the news of the change of mind of the Secunderabad force – the officers signed the Test – combined with such thoughts at both Jalna and Masulipatam, punctured the movement.

Only Seringapatam was left. Here the officers had gone further in their actions than anywhere else, and found it very difficult to draw back. They were encouraged by news of other mutinies at Ellore, Vizagapatam, Cocomanda and Rajamundry, but none of these lasted very long, and all were suppressed by the operation of the Test, by the news of the ending of the mutiny at Secunderabad, and by the removal of the non-signers from their commands and regiments. The original request by Colonel Davis at Seringapatam that the officers sign the oath had failed, despite his relative politeness, though Colonel John Bell, commanding in the fort, had signed, but had then assumed the leadership of the non-signers and led the resistance to the imposition of government authority. Possibly the fact that he had reneged made him all the more determined to see the mutiny through to success, for his change of mind had damned him in the eyes of the government, and he must have felt that he had nowhere to retreat to. The attempt to bring in reinforcements from Chittledroog had resulted in open battle, and the commander of the loyalist forces who had intercepted them, Colonel Samuel Gibbs, was able to surround the fort and in effect to lay it under siege.

Gibbs was clearly unwilling to mount an assault, or perhaps it was his men who were unwilling. He commanded king's troops, and Bell's sepoys always found it difficult to face the better armed, less volatile European soldiers; maybe Gibbs' British soldiers understood that the sepoys were not really involved, and that the men thought they had been misled by their officers. The stand-off lasted for some days, but then came the news that the officers at Secunderabad had caved in and signed the oath. Maybe this news arrived after that of the similar surrenders at other places, but it was the news of the end of the Secunderabad mutiny which was decisive, here as elsewhere. All the officers in Seringapatam now signed the oath, and Bell sent out the signed forms to Davis, no doubt including his own, again. This was almost the end. It is noticeable, and has been several times commented on, that the only physical casualties in the mutiny were sepoys. So far as is known no European officer or soldier died, or was even hurt, in the mutiny.

There had to be retribution, but a moment's thought demonstrated this must be limited, not necessarily through forgiveness but because of sheer impracticality. Of the 1,300 officers of the Madras Army only 150 had demonstrated their loyalty by signing the Test when it was first presented to them. So in theory 1,150 officers had been dismissed from their posts and were liable to be court-martialled – and the most convincing charge they would face was mutiny, which carried the death penalty. They had been temporarily replaced by king's officers, but long-term replacements would require much recruitment, and would produce a lot of inexperienced officers.

That moment's thought, therefore, forced a pause for some consideration. The replacement of almost 90 per cent of the officers of any army was not something easily achieved, and certainly not quickly. Those officers were almost all British, recruited in Britain, and poorly paid – most were in debt, hence their resentment at the removal of such petty corruptions as tentage – and at the very quickest they could not be replaced in less than a year, unless king's officers already in India transferred to the Company's service – but that would require either that they be promoted at least one rank and possibly two, or the pay they received would have to rise to that of the royal army. Some replacements might be found from other armies in India, but the 1,150 dismissed men would still need to be replaced, and this would not be easy, since the British Army, which was even then involved in great expeditions in Europe (in the Peninsular and the Walcheren campaigns at the time of the mutiny) would have first call on men who were capable of being officers. King's officers might fill in the gaps for a time, but no king's officer would demean himself to join the Company's army unless he was offered serious promotion.

The only solution to the problem, as the 1,150 officers well knew, was that the vast majority of them should be re-employed. But not all. Some examples clearly needed to be made, if only to satisfy the government, and to drive home the lesson that the government had won the contest. That is, re-employment had to be on the government's terms, and some of the more egregious mutineers were singled out for court martial.

Into the situation arrived Lord Minto. He had left Barlow to do the hard work until early August in 1809, when he had set off to sail from Calcutta to Madras, fearing that the stand-off at Seringapatam, and at some other places still in mutiny, portended an enlargement of the problem and the resort to violence. But his ship took over a month to sail the relatively short distance, and he only arrived on 11 September, when it was all over. (He did not fail to claim a good deal of the credit, however.)

At least Minto's absence from the details of the conflict allowed him to play the part of a forgiving, benign Governor-General. Twenty-one officers, colonels, majors, and captains, were singled out for court martial, and the prosecutors demanded the death penalty. These were the men who had been in command of mutinous garrisons, and they included Doveton from Jalna, who had started a march and Bell from Seringapatam, the reneger. They had clearly been picked for trial simply because they were in command and therefore were responsible. Doveton, for example, had persuaded the Jalna marchers to turn back; Montresor, the instigator of the mutiny at Secunderabad, who had first threatened to march on Madras, was ignored.

The rest of the officer-mutineers were covered by a blanket amnesty and returned to their regiments at their former rank and pay.

In a court martial of the three senior men accused, Doveton was found not guilty, and the other two were found guilty but sentenced only to be cashiered. That is, the juries – eighteen fellow officers, nine from the Company's army and nine from the king's – closed ranks to avoid punishing men for whom they clearly felt a strong sympathy. It was a clear indication that the grievances which had fuelled the mutiny had not been solved, despite the defeat of the mutineers; the mutinous attitude in the Company's army obviously still existed, and the spirit of mutiny among the officers had been retained.

Of the rest who were to go to court martial, those more junior in rank than the colonels, fifteen accepted dismissal rather than go to trial, one died before he could be tried, and the other three were all involved in seizing the treasure or in committing other violent acts which were enough to ensure their condemnation – the British were, as ever, rather more outraged by theft of property than by mutiny. Those who chose dismissal were, however, soon rehired; several of them rose high in the Company's employ in later years.[10]

All this had happened before Samuel Auchmuty was appointed as the next Commander-in-Chief of the disturbed Madras Army, but he was arriving amid the still disturbed aftermath. He had been in consideration for the post since at least the beginning of 1810, when he received a letter from Robert Dundas, the President of the India Board of Control, dated 25 January, which explained that he had been proposed for the appointment by the India Board.[11] The letter was in fact at least the second stage in the process, for it was asking if Auchmuty would accept the position if it became an official offer. It therefore seems that the matter had been under discussion among the directors for some time already. Auchmuty replied in a letter dated the same day (25 January) from Exeter with a wary response, stating that he would see Dundas on 'Tuesday'.[12] He was not jumping at the chance of the job, no doubt partly because he did not need it, and partly because, as he must have known, it was, after the mutiny, likely to be difficult – and, of course, his reluctance gave him an edge in the negotiations.

The timing of the offer is important. The crisis of the mutiny at Seringapatam did not end until late in August 1809, and Lord Minto's final intervention only took place after his arrival at Madras on 11 September. It is possible that the news of the end of the mutiny had reached London by January of the next year, but it is unlikely, given the difficulties of communication between India and Britain. The normal route was, of course, by sea around the Cape of Good Hope, which would take anything up to seven or eight months, but might take only five. There was an available route for a courier by way of the Persian Gulf and Mesopotamia, or by way of the Red Sea and Egypt, but neither was secure, and both took at least three months. It seems only just possible that the news of the collapse of the last of the mutiny at Seringapatam had arrived in London by January, but the timing is too tight to be relied on. Discussions for Auchmuty's appointment were therefore very probably conducted in the months before January, and in the knowledge that the mutiny was continuing.

After a month in which the Company bureaucracy slowly operated, Auchmuty had become exasperated enough to reach the point of threatening to refuse the post. It seems that the meeting with Dundas in late January had been satisfactory, and that Auchmuty had indicated his likely acceptance of the post. On 7 February the Court of Directors was informed that at the next meeting the proposal for a new appointment would be on the agenda, and on 14 February his name was agreed unanimously. In addition 'it was resolved that Major General Sir Samuel Auchmuty be appointed Second in Council'.[13] (The removal of the Commander-in-Chief from that post, which had so annoyed General McDowell, had been, of course, cancelled several years before.) The timing indicates that all negotiations within the Company and the government had been concluded. The agreement that he be appointed 'unanimously' implies earlier discussion, and perhaps dissension, and there was certainly some difficulty in guaranteeing Auchmuty's position as Second in Council.[14]

But Auchmuty had been doing his research into the military establishment in Madras – he had served in the presidency twenty years before, so he had some background knowledge to start with – and he decided that he needed promotion if he was to operate successfully. On 27 February, he wrote to Dundas explaining the problem. He had found 'that there are senior officers to himself on the Madras staff' – that is, presumably Major-Generals who had held that rank longer than he had, and this would clearly interfere with his authority; indeed, a confusion of lines of authority and command had been one of the elements in the recent mutiny – and therefore 'either those officers must be removed … or a rank superior to the present must be enforced on him' – that is, on Auchmuty.[15]

There had clearly been discussions about this with Dundas (if not with the Directors), and by the tone of his letter Auchmuty had reached the stage that he was prepared to refuse the post unless he was promoted to the local rank of Lieutenant General. No doubt he had a good argument on his side. He had wide experience of command in India in all three Presidencies, and in all levels of command from regimental adjutant to Adjutant General. He had observed the actions of the Commander-in-Chief Abercromby and Governor-General Shore in facing down the mutiny in the 1790s, so he was speaking from knowledge of the conditions. This was also a factor in the disputes back in the 1790s over Generals Burgoyne and Stuart – and Auchmuty had been one of the officers at Burgoyne's court martial – when equality in rank had been an issue. But there was also no doubt a strong element of ambition in his ultimatum, and perhaps of a certain mercenary instinct as well. When the conditions of his employment were settled, sometime in April, he said in his letter to his nephew in Newport, Rhode Island that the position involved much expense; a rise in rank would certainly help to defray that.[16] The ultimatum was apparently successful, and on 7 March he was writing to Dundas discussing when he should be presented to the king in his new rank and position. He goes on to discuss other issues, and it now becomes clear that he has, at last, received independent information from India about what he terms, accurately, the 'insurrection'.[17]

The subject must have been discussed during his meetings with Dundas and the Directors, especially in arguments over the question of his rank. The letter he has seen, apparently anonymous, was, he claimed, inaccurate, which presupposes earlier, and detailed, knowledge of the events in India. He was clear that the 'insurrection' had been put down – he called it 'the late insurrection' – and he was in the process of suggesting what measures he would need to take, though he put these in a separate paper. A later letter discusses his requirement for patronage and for the 'disposition of the troops'. Speaking again from experience and taking account of the recent events, he points out that 'the present … system had been attended with … serious consequences and is likely to be still so very inconvenient and unpleasant', so that he wishes to make (unstated) changes. These would need to be agreed in London before he goes out to India, so that he can therefore implement them without the appeals to London which have hindered earlier attempts.[18]

There was considerable dispute within the Court of Directors in London over the conduct of Barlow in suppressing the mutiny, and on whether to restore the mutineers to their posts and ranks. This dispute was as much about feuds among the London Directors as about the conduct of affairs in India.[19] Auchmuty was, of course, caught up in these, hence in part his demand for a superior rank. He must have known, however, that he was facing a thankless task, especially in view of the divisions and arguments in the Court of Directors. It was an appointment for no more than three years, and instituting any sort of reform in such a short time in the face of the ponderous Company system was unlikely to be successful. It seems, however, from the results, that he had a notion of how to go about it; whether he told the Company what he intended in any detail is not clear. He had done his best to avoid appeals against his decisions being sent to London, and he knew perfectly well that it always took at least a year for the Directors to consider what was done in India and to decide whether to accept any changes; he could hope that what he did would be accepted simply by the lapse of time.

He made comments on earlier directorial decisions, once again on the subject of 'military patronage', and also on the issue of courts martial.[20] The latter was a serious matter in the aftermath of the mutiny, but it remained Barlow's problem, supervised from London. It does not seem that, whatever Auchmuty's views were on this, they affected matters in India at all.

He sailed for his new post on 11 May 1810, arriving at Madras on 27 September.[21] He might have started on his administrative work at once, and certainly he made it clear that as Commander-in-Chief it was his duty to support the Governor (still Barlow), presumably because he had been sounded out on this very issue by the malcontents, who presumably hoped for a reversal of the result of the mutiny. He made this clear at once in a letter written within three days of landing to the Governor-General Lord Minto: 'the disturbed state from which this presidency has been lately rescued impels me to give my support to the head of my government'.[22] But he soon found that matters between London and India did not run smoothly – not something he needed to be told, probably – at least not under so self-opinionated a Governor-General as Lord Minto.

An example of this egotistic attitude came about soon enough. A letter from Dundas, dated 14 June, followed Auchmuty on his voyage, giving him, so it seemed, the command of an expedition to capture the 'French islands', that is, Mauritius and Bourbon, and the French posts in Madagascar.[23] This letter reached Auchmuty soon after his own arrival at Madras, and he had to reply on 6 October that Dundas's instructions had been pre-empted by Minto, who had appointed Major General Sir John Abercromby, the Commander-in-Chief at Bombay, to command the expedition.[24] (This was the son of Sir Ralph, and Auchmuty will have known him in Egypt.) Minto and Abercromby had begun preparations to take the islands early in 1810, even before the decision had been reached in London to send a force, so that well before Auchmuty's arrival Abercromby had sailed. Mauritius was taken by the end of November.[25]

So whatever Auchmuty's plans for military action in India were, neither Dundas in London nor Minto in India were particularly interested in letting him get on with them. (It is not clear whether Auchmuty knew of the ambition to attack the French islands before he left London, but it seems unlikely that it was something Dundas decided on between his sailing and writing the letter. Auchmuty surely was not surprised by his appointment to the command; indeed this may have been another reason for his insistence on promotion.) Whether Auchmuty was relieved or disappointed at not commanding the expedition is not known. He did give his congratulations to Minto for 'having so fully anticipated the intention of his Majesty's ministers', which in any other man might have had the bite of sarcasm, but we do not know enough about Auchmuty's normal manner to assume anything other than sincerity.[26]

Three months later, in December, in another letter to Minto he refers to instructions from London which had just arrived and that he was available for service when required, though it is not stated what this particular service was. He did refer to 'the recent armament', which was presumably that which had been employed against the islands and would be returning to India about that time.[27] No other expeditions could have been mounted while that force was away, but it seems likely that Minto was already sounding him out about commanding the next expedition he intended to send out, that against the Dutch in Java. But the various measures which had buffeted him cannot have endeared Auchmuty to his new post.

Meanwhile Auchmuty had been considering his actual command in India and how to conduct it. In October he noted that things were quieter than he had expected, and that 'the combination of officers to control the government' was, he thought, 'forever dissolved'. And yet he still detected 'an inveterate hostility' among many of the officers, and he noted that military discipline had suffered badly.[28] The language Auchmuty used is interesting, in that he was using terms such as 'combination' which were also currently being applied in Britain to describe and decry the incipient trade unions in the industrial districts, but it was a term which also carried a strong implication of near-treason, since it had also been used to describe the corresponding societies inspired by the French Revolution, which had developed in the 1790s and were identified as insurrectionary by the government at the time. Again, as with his use of the term 'insurrection', he was one of the few who were using precise terms, rather than evasions, to describe what had happened.

By December he reported that 'the agitation continues to subside'.[29] One of the prime causes for this was undoubtedly his own determination, as he had said to Dundas in October, that he would maintain 'the utmost harmony between' himself and Barlow. 'Any difference of opinion between us, or any appearance of coolness or distrust would give hopes to his opposers, and the usual scenes of intrigue and contrast would again pervade the settlement'.[30] The discord at the top between Hay McDowell and Barlow was clearly one of the prime causes of the 'combination' and the 'insurrection', and Auchmuty's union with Barlow was one of the main reasons it 'subsided'. On the other hand, Auchmuty's language – 'subsiding' – indicates clearly enough that 'the agitation' was continuing, and that he needed to be alert, and to continue to publicly support the Governor.

Later in October he used a letter over the signature of his Military Secretary, Lieutenant Colonel Agnew, to describe what had happened as 'these late unhappy events' and 'these unfortunate transactions', modifying his bluntness for the occasion, and appealing to the addressees, who were the most senior officers in command of districts, to restore 'that mutual confidence and mutual zeal in the general cause of their country … which is essential to their honour' – thereby using the very word which the mutineers had claimed to have been insulted in.[31] Auchmuty may not have been an active politician, but he could clearly choose his words with a politician's skill.

He does not seem to have done much in the way of issuing instructions or orders during the first two months of his term of office, no doubt feeling his way in the midst of the intrigues. And then by December it had become evident that Minto was intent on 'anticipating' authority from London once again, this time to attack Java, and Auchmuty was soon busy organising the expedition. He was also clearly going to use this as a way towards reinforcing his and Minto's authority. He took some of the officers of both 'sides' in the late 'unfortunate transactions' along on the expedition, so compelling them to fight side by side. There was nothing like joining together in a fight to cement good military relationships. On the other hand, the measures he took on his return late in 1811 indicate clearly that he had by that time (and possibly earlier) identified a number of matters which he could and should attend to once the Governor-General stopped sending out expeditions.

Chapter 8

Java, 1811

Lord Minto had from the start of his term as Governor-General aimed to expand India's power and influence over a wide area. This was in part a result of the fact that he was the first of the Governors-General who could rest on a secure military base as a result of the suppression of Mysore and the defeat of the Marathas (by Wellesley in 1805); at the same time he could also deploy a commanding naval force. He was the first of the rulers of India to be in such a position, and so was capable of extending his power into the northern and eastern lands of and beyond India, but also overseas as well. His diplomacy extended into the Punjab, now united and ruled by the formidable Ranjit Singh, into Afghanistan, and into Persia, as part of the forward diplomatic defences against what was perceived as either Russian or French threats.[1] In the other direction he sent envoys into Burma in 1809, where it was feared that French intrigues were operating, only to be rebuffed by the Burmese King Bodawpaya, who required to negotiate only with another king.[2] A second diplomatic effort in 1811 got no further than Rangoon.[3] In naval terms he was able to secure the Dutch Spice Islands – the Moluccas – in August 1810, and Portuguese Macau (though the Chinese objected to his attempted takeover, and he was thus thwarted).[4] He could interfere by sea in the Persian Gulf, and now he had seized control of the French islands in the southern Indian Ocean. Beyond these factors, however, it is also necessary to acknowledge that Minto was clearly ambitious for personal renown as an imperial conqueror.

These latter islands had been rather surprisingly left largely alone by the British. There had been an active French naval force based in Mauritius all through the wars, and any British attacks had been easily driven off, usually because it was only a naval operation, and Mauritius in particular had good military defences. But the long delay had enabled Mauritius to become an active base from which French ships could intercept Company convoys, which made it necessary for those convoys to be guarded by Royal

Navy vessels; it is astonishing, and a mark of the Company's inability to comprehend the proper strategy of the war, that this had been allowed to continue for so long.[5]

And yet neither the Spice Islands nor Mauritius and Bourbon and Resolution were the real bases for French power in the Indian Ocean by 1810, but the Dutch territories in Indonesia. These now emerged, once the French islands had been taken, as the only eastern base from which French ships might be able to continue their interruptions of the Company's trade, and from a much more extensive base than a single island.

The Dutch had operated in the Indonesian archipelago for over two centuries. They had developed a system of exploitation which had ensured a regular supply of local trade goods for export to Europe, above all, spices, and by restricting production had aimed to maintain a high price in the European market.[6] They had operated the system at one remove from the home government, using, as did the British in India, a theoretically independent commercial company, the Vereenigte Oost-Indische Compagnie – the United East India Company – or VOC. This, however, had foundered into bankruptcy by the late eighteenth century, and had been forcibly nationalised back in 1795 as part of the Dutch revolution which accompanied that of the French at the same time. The Company was then dissolved in 1800 and its territories became formally Dutch colonies, and by this time many of them – Ceylon, the Cape of Good Hope, the West Indian islands – had been seized by the British.[7] The end of the Company did not, however, mean a real change in the methods of Dutch rule, other than that it had become rather less inefficient. The British naval domination of all the seas much restricted the trade of the country – indeed it was the British dominance at sea, first in 1780–4, then from 1793 onwards which effectively brought the Company to its final weakness and collapse. The surviving overseas lands were left under Dutch rule even after the imposition of Napoleon's brother Louis as king in 1806 and then the annexation of the home country into the French Empire by Napoleon in 1810, though by then the British were accustomed to refer to them as French territories.

This change of allegiance in fact presaged a very likely increase in French enterprise in the archipelago, replacing the indolent Dutch, whose local population was quite capable of ignoring events in Europe, unless they were directly affected. Two notable revolutionary Dutch generals were sent out successively as Governors-General, Herman Willem Daendels in 1808, who was then replaced by Napoleon's favourite Dutch general, Jan Willem Janssens. Janssens had already been used as governor of the Cape in 1803–6, and had faced, and lost it, in the British invasion commanded by Popham and Baird.[8] It was to be his fate to repeat that process in Java. He took over as Governor-General in May 1811, just when Auchmuty's and Minto's preparations to invade his territories were coming to fruition.

To refer to the Dutch territories as 'Indonesia' is to imply that they had secured control over the whole of the modern country of that name. In fact the territory under their direct rule was very limited, and, as in British India, substantial areas were still under local rule, in political conditions ranging from complete subordination to the Dutch to full independence. This was a condition which had obtained without much change since the mid-eighteenth century, when a war of succession in the Javanese kingdom of Mataram was ended by the division of the main kingdom into two separate kingdoms by the Treaty of Giyanti, supervised by the Dutch.[9] The arrival of Daendels as Governor-General in 1808 began a new Dutch forward movement in Java.

The Dutch had concentrated their activities in the islands in just a few areas. Java was the most important, being the most populous, wealthy, and developed island, but a good half of the island remained still under Javanese rule. Elsewhere some parts of Sumatra were subjected to Dutch influence, but scarcely to Dutch control, and many of the smaller islands east of Java could claim Dutch protection, or at least could be claimed by the Dutch to be under their protection. There were posts and areas of influence in southern Borneo and in parts of Sulawesi. The Moluccas, the original Spice Islands, between Sulawesi and New Guinea, were under direct Dutch control, though they retained their local kings, whose powers were thus limited and whose attitude as before was consistently resentful. It is evident that the Dutch had great scope for further advances, but clearly also they required considerable help from home if they were to achieve anything. The periods of isolation from the Dutch homeland, if they continued for long, might sufficiently erode Dutch power and authority to stimulate local movements to overthrow the Dutch regime.[10] It was, however, as the arrival of the new governors demonstrated, possible to remain in contact with Europe, though the capture of the French islands would make this increasingly difficult.

The British had been intermittently interested in the archipelago as long as the Dutch, but by the time of the French wars they were particularly concerned that the enmity of the Dutch and French could lay a line of hostility and interruption between the British-dominated Indian Ocean and one of the East India Company's major trading areas in southern China. More than once the China fleets of the EIC had been attacked by French or Dutch ships based in Java; on one occasion there had been a regular fleet battle between an EIC fleet from China and a French force.[11] Given that Minto was a keen imperialist and had sent an expedition against the French islands (and one to take over the Portuguese post at Macau), it was only to be expected that, with or without permission from the Court of Directors and the President of the Board of Control in London, he was going to mount an expedition against the Dutch islands – which were now, of course, technically French; success, as with the islands, would justify his impetuosity.

Daendels was an old revolutionary, and, like revolutionaries everywhere who gain power, he set about reforming institutions and in the process expanding governmental powers and authority. His major achievement was the construction of a new post road from west to east the length of Java, constructed at considerable expense and using forced Javanese labour. The constant naval activity of British ships in the seas around Java rendered communications difficult – the British operated an intermittent and inefficient blockade. Dutch communications by sea could also be interrupted completely for weeks, even months, by the monsoon winds; the new road cut the journey time through Java by land in half, to a week or less, and was much more reliable; it also made it much easier for Dutch power to reach into the interior of the island, much of which was under local rule. Daendels also began a new process of annexation, slicing off territories from several of the local states in return for, in some cases, ending a rent payment. None of this conduced to Dutch popularity in the island.[12]

Java, the most populous of the islands, was necessarily the centre of Dutch power. Most of the island had been under the rule of a local state, the Sultanate of Mataram, in the seventeenth century, and it was this which the Dutch had to control or subdue if the island was to be peaceful. They tried various methods, but by 1755 – the Treaty of Giyanti – they had settled on divide and rule. A rebellion against the Matarese Sultan had led to a division of the kingdom between the rebel leader, who became Sultan Hamengkubuwana in Jogjakarta, and the legitimate Sultan Pakubuwana III, whose court was located at Surakarta, further inland – the cities then gave their names to their kingdoms. The Surakarta Sultans were now generally referred to as the Susuhanan. In addition there were other kingdoms, at Bantam on the western end of the island which had suffered successive slices of annexation between 1774 and 1808, a kingdom centred on the island of Madura off the north-east coast, and several in the east of the island, where earlier states had crumbled into independent sections under Dutch pressure and had then come under Dutch suzerainty. The Dutch themselves controlled a substantial slice of the western part of the island, and governed from their colonial capital at Batavia; they held an enclave at Semarang on the north coast, and controlled an intermediate area between Batavia and Semarang along that north coast; one of Daendels' measures was to link these separate sections together by his annexations and by the new post road. Even so, over half of the island was still under the rule of local kings.

The rest of the archipelago was under less stringent Dutch control, though they were dominant in most areas. They maintained trading posts at several places, and political relations were maintained also with the rulers of the local states, from Acheh at the north end of Sumatra to the Moluccas near New Guinea. These were useful as a means of generating trade goods, but it was Java which was always their main concern. The Dutch system of rule had in fact developed into one very similar to that of the British in India, even to the extent of imposing 'subsidiary forces' on the local sultans and supervisory Residents – 'advisers' – at their courts. But it was a much less thoroughgoing system than that of the British, in part because imperial control had not been as necessary as the British Company in India had come to require, and in part because the Dutch had not faced serious competition for the last century, either from another European enemy or from powerful local states, as the British had in India.

The British had long had an interest in the region. The early (English) East India Company had competed vigorously in the spice trade in the early seventeenth century until driven out by the Dutch. (The Dutch did not welcome competition, and indeed deliberately restricted local production of their trade goods with the aim of keeping prices in Europe high; they also made it a policy to destroy plantations and crops which they could not otherwise control.) There had remained an EIC trading post in western

Sumatra at Bencoolen (Bengkulu), however, throughout the eighteenth century, and in 1786 the island of Penang off the western coast of Malaya was seized by the Company (having been surveyed by Captain Home Popham), to which was added part of the adjacent mainland five years later. In the 1770s William Marsden, later to be a busy Admiralty Secretary, was the Secretary at Bencoolen, and researched a book on *The History of Sumatra,* published in London in a third edition in 1811. Similarly, but even more notably, the Assistant Secretary at Penang for a time was William Stamford Raffles, who was to have a considerable influence in Java and the rest of Indonesia later. Malacca had been seized from the Dutch during the French Revolutionary War and had been returned to the Dutch in 1802 as part of the terms of the Treaty of Amiens; the town was re-occupied when war was resumed; Raffles visited the place on sick leave in 1807 and 1808, and produced a report on its usefulness; both Penang and Malacca were valued less for themselves than for their geographical position, for in the hands of a naval power they dominated the Strait of Malacca, the EIC's main route from India to China – Captain Macquarie had gone that way with his sick wife in 1794.[13]

The possibility of a successful expedition against Java had been discussed repeatedly in the times of war since 1793. So far it had been a project especially advocated by the naval commanders-in-chief. Admiral Peter Rainier in 1799 had been almost ready to sail with an expedition, but his armament had been redirected to the Red Sea to counter the French invasion of Egypt. Admiral Pellew in 1807 suggested that the Dutch naval base at 'Gressie' (Grisek) should be attacked, since it was close to the Sunda Strait, another route used by the EIC's China fleet; Gressie, with the French annexation of the Netherlands, had become a French base, and it was likely to be more active than before. Barlow as Governor-General had agreed, but then had left that office; Minto accepted the plan and Pellew carried out a raid in late 1807. In the base the only vessels he discovered were a disarmed line-of-battle ship and a disarmed frigate; he bombarded the batteries and burnt the two ships.

That is, it was clear that the Dutch alone had been no threat, and a naval blockade over the next years gradually starved them of trade and hence of income. But then Daendels' arrival reinvigorated them. The army was recruited up by enlisting new troops from among the Madurese, a notably martial people; the post road was built; coastal batteries were revived or built; the fortifications of Batavia were repaired. Dutch authority had waned in the east of the island, and Daendels campaigned to enforce it once more. A fort, or rather a large entrenched camp, was built south of Batavia at a place called Meester Cornelis, where there had been a small fortified trading post established by the original Cornelis. All this and more made Daendels deeply unpopular with both the Dutch and the Javanese, the former for upsetting their lazy ways, the latter because of increased taxation, and conscription into labouring gangs. This alienation was well understood in India through reports reaching the British at Malacca, Penang, and Bencoolen.

Pellew's successor as naval commander-in-chief, Rear Admiral Drury, was instructed by the Admiralty in 1809 to establish a blockade of Java and the Moluccas – not the first time such measures had been imposed, but it was something which was very difficult to maintain. This time the object was partly to isolate Mauritius and Java from each other while the former was attacked, but it was an unpopular measure in India. Minto urged Drury not to be too drastic in his application of the measure since this would annoy every other local power and trading interest from Burma to China, none of whom understood the purpose of the blockade, nor accepted its validity or its wider implications.[14] Drury did not like to hold back, but found that he did not have the naval strength to make his blockading efforts effective. It was at his urging that the Moluccas were occupied in 1810 – as an extension, in effect, of the blockade. With the success of the attack on Mauritius, however, Minto decided that a military invasion of Java was the answer.

It does not seem that Minto was at first inclined to use Auchmuty as his military instrument in Java. Abercromby at Bombay was perhaps his first choice as he had been for Mauritius. But Abercromby was in Mauritius for much of 1810; the Commander-in-Chief in Bengal, Sir George Nugent, was the only other alternative, but Bengal was far too large and potentially unstable to be left without a controlling military hand, and it had some threatening neighbours who might be tempted by the absence of the army. And Minto intended to go on the expedition himself, so the Commander-in-Chief in Calcutta could not.

Not only that, but Auchmuty appears to have been somewhat reluctant to command the expedition. The unsettled nature of the military in Madras was a good reason for his reluctance, even though Minto claimed to have calmed matters sufficiently; Auchmuty had also been sent out as Madras Commander-in-Chief in part to attend to the military situation in the presidency, something he could not do from Java. Further, it was necessary to convince Minto that he had to take sufficient forces to accomplish the task he was set. Minto presumably despised the Dutch military in Java, with some reason, but Auchmuty had plenty of experience of Indian armies, and of fighting in hostile territory while outnumbered. He could hardly wish to face the same difficulty as he and Whitelocke had in the River Plate.

Minto set forth his intentions to Auchmuty in a letter in mid-December.[15] His aim, he said, was to eliminate hostile European – that is, French – forces from the East. The forces sent on the Mauritius campaign were still on the island or on their way back, but once they returned to India he would send this new expedition to capture the Dutch possessions in Indonesia. Minto in effect offered Auchmuty the command, choosing him partly in compensation for his not having had the Mauritius command.

Minto had been planning a Java expedition even while the invasion of the French islands was still uncertain of success. When he wrote to Auchmuty and offered him the command he had already made widespread enquiries and had apparently come to the conclusion that the expeditionary force need be no larger than 4,000 European troops, plus an equivalent of sepoys, with artillery and pioneers. He had approached Rear Admiral Drury for his cooperation in early October, three months before approaching Auchmuty.[16]

When Auchmuty understood what was intended he and Barlow set about organising an expeditionary force. They chose not to use the Mauritius troops since they were likely to be less than fit and would be under strength after their voyages and the fighting, and they selected their force from the remainder of the Madras Army, together with others requested from the governors in Ceylon and Bombay. Drury was fully apprised of this and agreed to provide both transport and naval protection. Minto, however, was not pleased at this display of independence and made them cancel the arrangements already made and insisted that use be made of the Mauritius forces, and of some of the Bengal Army.[17]

It was not obvious how Barlow and Auchmuty chose the troops they did for the expedition, but it is a reasonable assumption that they were particularly concerned to offset the lingering adverse effects of the mutiny on the Madras Army. Employing former mutineers would both remove them from India and employ their talents in doing something useful. Whether Minto took the point is unclear, but his reaction to the measures in Madras suggests a personal annoyance rather than a longer term interest in the welfare of the Madras Army.

The Dutch forces in Java were, like the British in India, partly European and partly locally recruited – Madurese were reckoned as the best of the 'warrior peoples' in the islands. The Dutch Army in Java numbered about 17,000 men in total, though not all of these would be available at the invasion point, and a large part had been only recently recruited by Daendels. Some, for example, would be left at the courts of the Javanese rulers as what the British in India called 'subsidiary forces' (as at Hyderabad and Travancore) since it was highly likely that they might take any advantage to recover their full independence and a foreign invasion could well provide such an opportunity. Similarly Dutch garrisons would need to be stationed at several places other than Batavia – at Semarang, for example, or Gressie, or Surabaya – places in which the British had shown an interest already. The obvious ability of the invaders to concentrate their invasion force at one place while the Dutch would need to be dispersed allowed Auchmuty to command an invasion force smaller than the Dutch total force, though they could probably assemble a larger force than the British invaders at the point of attack – if they knew where that would be.[18]

Auchmuty was not happy at having to leave his Madras command. 'Situated as this army is, the control of the commander-in-chief is much required', he pointed out in his letter of acceptance to Minto on 10 January 1811.[19] Three days later the news of the surrender of Mauritius confirmed that their plans against Java would go ahead. The forces to be collected were those nominated by the Governor-General, not those intended by Auchmuty and Barlow, though there was in fact a considerable overlap between the two. Auchmuty still insisted that he needed 'a large force', and remarked that Daendels 'feels the degraded situation of his country', and might be tempted to abandon the French cause and 'lend his aid to preserve a remnant of its independence'.[20]

Here is evidence of Auchmuty putting himself into his opponent's mind. The annexation of the Netherlands to the French Empire earlier in 1810 was the effective extinction of its independence, and the nationalist in Auchmuty presumed that this was an action which would have angered Daendels, though in fact, there is no evidence that it did so, for Daendels had willingly gone out to Java already as Napoleon's appointee. At the same time Auchmuty was using his previous experience to suggest the possibility. It was a British attack in the River Plate region which had stimulated the people of Buenos Aires finally to strike for independence after years of grumbling; he clearly thought the same might happen in Java, at which point he might well face not merely the Dutch Army but also the much larger forces contributed by the local kings. And further back, his early experience of the annoyance of Americans at the exercise of the authority of the British government, though it was not an annoyance which he particularly shared, was a factor of the same type.

Auchmuty wrote to Dundas on 10 February explaining the new situation. The army in Madras was not yet settled, he said, though the officers were returning to their obedience and discipline was improving, and the 'animosities' were subsiding. He had intended to go on an inspection tour, but Minto's Java plan interrupted that. The expedition meant that they had to get away early in March to ensure favourable winds so that it could pass along the Malacca Strait. He knew that Daendels had a force said to be up to '24,000' men. Exaggerated as this was, it provided fuel for his insistence that he needed a large force for the invasion.[21]

Another potential problem developed in March when on the 11th Rear Admiral Drury died. He and Minto had not got on well – perhaps because of his support for the original planning by Auchmuty and Barlow – and his death inevitably delayed the expedition's departure. His successor was his second-in-command, Commodore William Broughton, whose position was sufficiently weak that Minto could dominate him and insist on his participation.[22] But Drury's death was to bring further repercussions later.

The eventual invasion force amounted to something over 12,000 men, an increase of perhaps a quarter on Minto's original suggestion. Of these about 1,000 were artillerymen, including three Royal Artillery companies (94 men) from Ceylon, and 6 companies from the Bengal Army (620 men), plus a troop of horse artillery and a company of gun lascars from the Madras Army (310 men). Their guns were relatively light, mainly no larger than 18-pounders, perhaps because of the anticipated difficulty of moving them, for the means of transport by land were certainly lacking.

Similarly cavalry was not likely to be of much use in the Javanese conditions, quite apart from the difficulty of transporting the horses. Only one regiment, the 22nd Light Dragoons (420 men), was taken, and even then one squadron was dismounted, though this was mainly because the ship transporting the horses was caught in a storm and 40 or more of the horses died. The commander of this regiment was Major Thomas Otto Travers, who had been with Auchmuty in South America. In addition there was a troop of the Governor-General's bodyguard (112 men); these included Lieutenant William Fielding, who compiled a useful diary of the expedition.[23]

The main force of the invading army was therefore composed of infantry. Five royal army regiments were used, and six Indian. The 5 British regiments – the 14th, 59th, 69th, 78th, and 89th (only 6 companies) – counted 4,358 men. The four battalions of Bengal Volunteers – the 3rd, 4th, 5th, and 6th – had 3,665; an Indian Light Infantry Battalion had 493 men, and one battalion made up of men from the Marines in the warships (1,463 men) completed the infantry count. There were also 6 companies of pioneers, 3 from Bengal and 3 from Madras, with 33 men from the Madras European regiment (a total of 633 men). This completed the army.[24] (The 89th had nearly been involved in the fighting in the River Plate, but it was the regiment which never arrived, its passage through the Atlantic being so slow.)

The news of the capitulation of Mauritius, and therefore that most of the expeditionary force would soon be returning to India, was known to Auchmuty and Minto in mid-January, and in March a preliminary reconnaissance of the new target was organised. Three ships, *Minden* (74), the frigate *Leda* (34), and the sloop *Procris* (18) sailed to cruise along the north coast of Java. They carried Lieutenant Colonel Colin McKenzie, a noted Company surveyor and antiquary, who was to examine the coast for possible landing places; he had with him two companies of the 89th Foot and a detachment of the 14th Foot under the command of Captain Lawrence Oakes to provide protection for landing parties who were to spy out the land, and perhaps to make contact with friendly forces.[25]

To convey all the men of the expedition, their guns and their horses, supplies and equipment, Minto had gathered 57 transport ships, which were to be escorted by 2 line-of-battle ships, *Illustrious* (74 guns) and *Lion* (64), 14 frigates, 7 sloops, and 9 small Company warships, together with a few gunboats. Commodore Hayes of the Company's Bombay Marine, organised the Madras convoys, escorting the transports with a small squadron; the Bengal convoy was organised by the Bengal Commander-in-Chief, Sir George Nugent.[26]

The main expedition left India in stages. It had been sorted into several parts, two parts sailing from Madras, the first on 18 April, the second a week later; a third section sailed from Calcutta with Minto, who sailed in the frigate *Modeste*, captained by his son Captain Hon. George Elliott. This departure was later than intended, and was into the season of bad weather – a consequence of Drury's death and the delay it caused. Not all the transports got clean away, and on 2 May a 'tremendous hurricane' struck Madras. Most of the transports survived, having got out of the storm's track just in time, but the frigate *Dover* was driven on shore, as was the transport *Kirby* and a number of other vessels. This was the point at which the dragoons' horses in one of the transports died, having been suffocated in the fastened-down hold of the ship they were in as it survived the hurricane.[27] (*Dover* had been the *Duncan*, and before that the East Indiaman *Carron*, built in the shipyard at Bombay in 1804; several of the smaller ships were Indian-built, or were former East Indiamen purchased into the Royal Navy.)

Auchmuty, travelling in the frigate *Akbar*, had two senior commanders, each of which took command of one of the Madras convoys. The first was Colonel Rollo Gillespie, he of the suppression of the Vellore mutiny, and the second was under Major General Frederick Wetherall, the second-in-command of the whole force. The voyage was long and slow, bedeviled for a while by calms and awkward winds in the Bay of Bengal. Finally on 2 May the winds came fair and, steering between the Nicobar Islands and the north end of Sumatra the fleet reached Penang, arriving in the middle of May, though various ships arrived over a period of eight days. This was the first rendezvous set for all the convoys, and the Bengal convoy came past soon afterwards, without stopping, though it was no more together than the Madras contingents. The Madras convoys replenished with water and food at Penang after their slow, long voyage. The second rendezvous was at Malacca, and the ships slowly gathered there over a period of many weeks. The convoy from Bengal had reached the rendezvous six weeks before the Madras contingents; Minto and Auchmuty met up once more in that city, perhaps for the first time during the expedition – indeed, it is not certain that they had ever met in person before Malacca.[28]

Major William Thorn, the brigade major under Gillespie, in his published account, claims that Malacca was 'the most healthy place known in India'.[29] However the fleet already had a large proportion of sick, and when it sailed it left 1,200 men – a tenth of the soldiers – at Malacca too ill to continue; Auchmuty's insistence on a larger force than Minto had planned for was thus already justified. Malacca had been taken by the British in 1795, returned to the Dutch under the Treaty of Amiens in 1802, and then the renewed war from 1803 produced a renewed British occupation. In 1808 Thomas Stamford Raffles, who had been posted originally to Penang as Assistant Secretary, went to Malacca on sick leave when it was proposed to evacuate the place and transfer the population to Penang; he argued successfully that the town should continue to be held. The prolonged process of discussion and indecision over Malacca's future which took place was a prelude to the similar argument which went on over Java during the next decade.

The preference in India for Penang was a result of viewing the East from India; for it seemed that Penang was a useful commercial station, tapping the Malayan trade and close to Acheh on the northern tip of India. But standing at Malacca the view was different. The city owed its existence and its earlier importance to being at the narrowest point of the strait named after it. Geopolitically it was a more useful site than Penang, and no doubt the sailors and the soldiers saw that quickly. It was also protected from both the north-east and the south-west monsoons by the mountains of Malaya and Sumatra. But it was important only because it commanded the strait; later, with the growth of Singapore and the activity in the region of the Royal Navy, the narrows could be controlled just as easily from there and from Penang, and Malacca did not have a sizeable port; Malacca therefore faded, but for the moment, as Raffles saw when he visited the place, it was crucial.

For once we have a description of the British Indian Army from the Malay side in the autobiography of a man who was in the town as the expedition arrived. This was Abdullah bin Kedar, and he provides a description of Auchmuty. He was 'a big man, oval face, and with a thick-set body. He was of modest height. He wore a black tunic with a medal hanging at his chest (no doubt his insignia of the Bath). Four or five his aides-de-camp accompanied him.'[30] The description fits well with the portrait of him made about this time which survives.

The expedition, Abdullah says, arrived in stages, the first in just six ships. The soldiers landed and marched through the town in a column to the sound of fifes and drums – an initial show of strength. Other sections of the convoys arrived over the next six weeks. The soldiers were generally well-behaved, he thought, but they did drink to excess; the prices of supplies rose in the city, but he thought that 'people of all races prospered greatly', so presumably not only the price of food rose. He claimed that many Hindu soldiers died, though this is not really borne out by the strength returns; perhaps their deaths were more obvious.[31]

Minto enjoyed himself in Malacca – Abdullah records that many people gathered to see him land – and stayed there for several weeks while waiting for all the convoys and ships to arrive. He imposed liberal reforms such as the abolition of torture and held a bonfire of the torture instruments he found available. He feasted the officers of the expedition on 4 June, King George III's birthday, and followed it up with a ball for 150 officers, attended by twenty or so of the local Dutch ladies (who must have been very weary at the end of the dancing).[32] Then there was a conference to discuss the way forward. So it was that it was at this ex-Portuguese, formerly Dutch city, far gone by this time in decay, that the details of the next stage of the expedition were arranged.

A good deal of information was already to hand, but the initial problem was how to get from Malacca to Java. No landing place had yet been chosen – McKenzie did not report on this until the end of July – but it was known from the intelligence reports which had been gathered assiduously by Raffles, who was employed by Minto as his secretary, that the main Dutch forces had been collected into the neighbourhood of Batavia, and since defeating the Dutch was the first necessity, a landing somewhere near there was clearly indicated.

There were several possible routes for the fleet to take to reach that part of the island. One was to cross the Malacca Strait and follow the coast of Sumatra southwards, but that would involve pushing through the Strait between the main island and the island of Bangka, which was shallow and uncharted and was liable to unpredictable silting, and so the sailors refused absolutely to consider it. The most obvious alternative was to sail directly through the island-strewn sea between Sumatra and on the seaward flank of Bangka, and some ships did take that route. But the winds which had brought the fleet from India to Malacca now prevented an easy passage onwards, and the possibility of a very slow passage and a scattering of the ships was to be avoided. For the summer monsoon blew strongly from the south-east and the south through that sea, a wind which blew directly adverse for the route needed by the ships.

Two alternatives were discussed. One was to sail east as far as the west coast of Borneo and then follow that coast southwards to the southern cape (Cape Sampur) and then sail directly through the eastern end of the Java Sea to land close to Batavia. This would make use of the land breezes in Borneo and allow the ships to use the monsoon winds as they sailed north and then south. The second alternative, surprisingly, would be to sail all the way round Borneo, taking passage through the South China Sea and then the Sulawesi Sea between Borneo and Sulawesi (Celebes). This latter alternative might have allowed the army to be landed anywhere on the north coast of Java since the winds would then favour the choice of a series of possible landing places. It was rejected only after careful consideration; the sheer length of time required was against it, even more than the distance involved.

A further factor to be taken into consideration was the prospect of the approach of the rains; this was a severe constraint. It was already mid-June, and the rains would begin in October at the latest. (Drury's death had delayed matters at least a month.) The longer voyage (round Borneo) might take so long that the expedition might not arrive until after the rains had begun, and nobody liked that idea. Also a long voyage would undoubtedly increase the number of sick; already a tenth of the army was in the hospital at Malacca, and the soldiers were left there when the expedition sailed. And, perhaps decisively, the longer Minto was away from India the more possible it was for trouble to develop there. The same applied to Auchmuty's Madras Army, only more so. The arguments against this route clearly outweighed any possible advantages.

The final decision on the approach was Auchmuty's. He had to assert his control over the expedition now that at last it was all together, though no doubt he had also to argue his main decision on the route with the Governor-General as well as the senior sailor, Commodore Broughton. Minto was clearly in favour of speed – at one point he went ahead in *Modeste* to seek out the best route – in so far as that concept could be said to operate for a seaborne expedition, subject to wind and weather. Broughton has been thought to be excessively cautious, though he had a responsibility for the whole convoy, some of whose vessels were slow. Every convoy scattered once it was at sea, hence the need for a series of rendezvous (which Minto's Bengal Army had already ignored at Penang). As it happened, just as the decision for the route along the western coast of Borneo was reached, a commercial ship, the *Minto*, returned from a reconnaissance of the coast of Borneo, and Captain Greigh reported that that route was quite feasible.[33]

Meanwhile, Auchmuty was organising the army for the coming campaign. It was only at Malacca that he could do this, for it was only there that the whole of the force was gathered in one place and he could tabulate it. The first division was put under Colonel Gillespie, and included the 89th Foot, the battalion composed of the Marines, and one formed of the grenadiers of the several regiments, and the Bengal Pioneers; the only cavalry in this division was the Governor-General's Bodyguard, but horses for Auchmuty's staff were also to be landed, as was the Royal Artillery with six of its guns, which would also need horses.

This division was called, by Auchmuty with a conscious echo of an older military terminology, the 'Advance'. It was in effect a strong brigade. There was no advantage in landing everyone at once, for this would only produce confusion at the landing site. (Auchmuty had experience of such landings, after all, at Maldonado and at Ensenada in the River Plate.) This Advance division was to seize the site of the landing, establish a defensible perimeter, and so permit the rest of the force to be put ashore without too much confusion. In modern terminology, it was to seize a bridgehead.

Major General Wetherall's division, the 'Line', as Auchmuty termed it, was divided into two brigades, each comprising two Royal Regiments of Foot and one Bengal Volunteer battalion. Colonel Gibbs – he of the siege of Seringapatam against the mutineers – commanded the 'Right Brigade', and he had the Bengal artillery added to his infantry; the 'Left Brigade' was under Lieutenant Colonel Alexander Adams of the 78th Foot, and included the Madras Pioneers and the Lascars. The third division, the 'Reserve', was commanded by Colonel George Wood of the Bengal Native Infantry.

(The employment of the antiquated terms 'Advance', 'Line', and 'Reserve' for the component parts of the army by Auchmuty strongly suggests that he had been spending time reading up on military history. Such terms are no longer in use, though they were clearly useful in the circumstances of Java.)

Captain Greigh of the *Minto* was only one of a number of agents sent out to spy out land and sea before the expedition approached Java, and were reporting back to Raffles who coordinated the information. Colonel McKenzie was another, along with the detachments of the 89th and 14th, searching along the Javanese coast for a suitable landing place for the expedition. Lord Minto had already sent envoys or agents to contact several of the local rulers. The Raja of Acheh had long been in relations with the Indian government, and hostile to the Dutch; he was anglophile of necessity since his throne was insecure. Lieutenant D. McDonald of the Company's Bombay Marine was sent to interview the Raja of Palembang. Raffles organised the sending of envoys to two rajas in Bali, and to Lombok, two islands to the east of Java; rajas in Bali had old political connections with some of the minor states in the eastern end of Java. He sent one agent also to the Sultan in Jogjakarta.[34] These rulers were warned that the expedition was heading for Java: they generally welcomed the prospect – or said they did – but since they were all in close relations with the Dutch in Java, no doubt the Dutch were well informed of what was impending. Such contacts clearly undermined the Dutch position, though if Minto and Raffles believed they were gaining friends they were deluding themselves. The sultans and rajas were certainly interested in ridding themselves of the Dutch, but not in subjecting themselves to the British. Minto had already been fed with copious information about Java and the archipelago by Raffles from his post at Malacca.

Raffles had made himself the centre of the network of intelligence, both Javanese and European. He had worked out the strength of the Dutch forces, and had the names of numerous Javanese men of importance, even of Dutchmen, who might be useful either for providing information for assisting the troops or for participation in the subsequent government. Raffles was looked on with some suspicion by others in the expedition, but Minto was an enthusiastic supporter, and had made him his Secretary back in October. The route taken by the fleet from Malacca to Borneo took the ships through the strait between the Malayan mainland and the island and town of Singapore; this was the first time Raffles will have seen the place he was later in part responsible for developing.

Minto was also much taken by Dr John Leyden, an excitable linguist and botanist, and the presence of these two odd civilians, Raffles and Leyden, cannot have endeared Minto to the soldiers and sailors, who had necessarily to be more cautious and careful than these armchair statesmen. But Raffles was already looking to become the governor, or at least having an influential administrative position, in the conquest; in this context he was also busy operating on Minto to persuade him to decide to retain those conquests.

The fleet's final rendezvous was at Cape Sampur on the south-west corner of Borneo. This was left on 26 July, and course was set for Java. Auchmuty was still uncertain as to the precise landing place, but the confirmation that most of the Dutch forces were in and about Batavia made him head for that area.

The news arrived, by way of a prize ship, that General Daendels had been replaced as Governor-General by Janssens, who had arrived in May with two French frigates, *Nymphe* and *Meduse*, which had been anchored at Surabaya.[35] Daendels had become extremely unpopular with everybody in Java due to his strict exactions of taxation and his heavy use of forced labour, and this was well understood by the British; replacing him with Janssens might well revive the Dutch government's reputation, at least temporarily. It was a matter which certainly had to be taken into consideration, though from the military point of view, Auchmuty would hardly be bothered by the arrival of the new governor, who could not have increased his military strength by any serious degree in the two or three months he had been in control.

One of the sources of the revenues of the Dutch government was revealed on 31 July, when two large Chinese ships were intercepted by two of the ships escorting the expedition, the sloops *Malabar* (20; Captain Robert Deane) and *Mornington* (20; Captain W. Maxfield). The Chinese ships were bound from Batavia to Amoy with Dutch exports which were valued at £600,000. Since Java was technically in a state of blockade, the captains at first claimed them as prize. Yet blockade was a concept nobody in the East understood and to confiscate these two rich ships would undoubtedly annoy the Chinese – already given cause for enmity by Drury's activities at Macau. At the same time the ships had been intercepted in the Strait of Gaspar, between Bangka and Billiton Islands, which suggests that they were trying to keep clear of the invasion fleet, even possibly hiding from it – which would clearly be a sensible attitude to take; it also implies that the invasion fleet was widely spread, since the two ships were wildly off the course between Cape Sampur and Batavia.

Commodore Hayes of the EIC was present on one of the two EIC ships. As the squadron commander he had long experience of the Company's ways. He pointed out to the two captains, who were claiming the Chinese ships as prize, that annoying the Chinese government would be a bad idea.

He was operating in the same vein as Minto had when he had carefully avoided prodding the Chinese into reaction by withdrawing from the seizure of Portuguese Macau. Hayes successfully dissuaded the captains and crews who thus had to forego the riches they had hoped for. No doubt Hayes will also have pointed out that the Company would be so annoyed that they would find some way of avoiding paying out any prize sums – arguing, for example, that the Company was not at war with China.[36] These encounters involving China indicate clearly where the real commercial power in the East lay.

The issue of the future of Java depended upon its preliminary conquest, of course. Colonel McKenzie and the detachment under Lieutenant Oakes joined the convoy on 2 August as it came close to Java. McKenzie reported that the most suitable landing place was at a hamlet called Chillinching (Tjilintjing), at the mouth of a small river, about 10 miles east of Batavia. The approach to the landing site from inland was impeded by the river, and by 'morasses' which were liberally strewn in the low-lying land behind the coast, so any Dutch opposition was unlikely, at least until the British were ashore.[37]

The landing began on 4 August. The Dutch made no attempt to intercept the landing forces. It was assumed by some of the British that the landing place had been undefended because it was not thought a suitable place to put an army ashore, but it is perhaps just as likely that the Dutch could not predict where the landing would take place – McKenzie's long foray along the coast was known. They therefore probably decided to let the British land where they would since the Dutch forces would not be able to concentrate in sufficient time wherever it was to be able to oppose any landing.

Careful arrangements had been made for the landing to take place in a logical sequence, but in the event the wind and the tide did not cooperate, and Auchmuty finally ordered the Advance to get ashore as and when they could and sort themselves out on shore. Colonel Gillespie was one of the first ashore and was able to send forward his battalions one by one as they were almost completed. It may therefore have been better if the Dutch had brought up forces in opposition – but they would have to have known where the landing was going to take place to do so. Some Dutch troops did find the landing as it was taking place, but this was no more than a reconnaissance party which included one of Janssens' aides-de-camp. They were greeted with some cannon fire, which must have been thoroughly convincing of the seriousness of the British arrival. (McKenzie's reconnaissance had included landings at several places, on the last of which they were attacked; the Dutch may have thought the main landing was another of McKenzie's investigations, but cannon fire would persuade them otherwise.) Gillespie efficiently sorted out his troops and took up a defensive position astride the road leading north-west towards Fort Cornelis, in front of Chillinching village. The second division, the Line, under General Wetherall, landed that same day (4 August) and took up a position astride the road leading towards Batavia.

The navies were cooperative. The frigate *Leda* (36; Captain George Sayer), which had been in the reconnaissance party, was stationed on the left of the landing area as protection against any possible Dutch ships which might have attempted to interfere, and Commodore Hayes with the Company's cruisers and gunboats was stationed on the right. The landing troops, of course, were carried to the shore by the fleet's launches and rowboats.

The third division, the Reserve, landed along with all the artillery next day. So although there was considerable confusion in the landing – not at all surprising, no matter how much preliminary planning took place – the whole force of over 10,000 men, with its impedimenta, was landed within little more than 24 hours, an impressive achievement.[38]

The confusion and effort were lightened by a couple of comedy episodes. The first man ashore was actually John Leyden, dressed as a pirate and opposed only by a flock of chickens. His performance was watched with general military and naval contempt and amusement, and no doubt ribald comments arose from the soldiery. Auchmuty and Minto went ashore more or less together but symbolically in separate boats. Minto jumped out of his boat and waded ashore through water up to his waist, no doubt enjoying himself as much as Leyden had, at least until he had to get dry. Auchmuty, who had done such landings before, organised a couple of burly sailors to carry him to land, dryshod. One of his aides, Captain Blakiston, who had been with McKenzie during his reconnaissance, observing this, only just refrained from commenting that 'that's the difference between an old soldier and an old fool'. Thus the traditional enmity of soldier and civilian was speedily exemplified and renewed.[39]

The small Dutch party had reconnoitred the landing on the 5th, and rumours arrived in the overnight camp that a much larger Dutch column had approached to within a few miles, but an investigation showed that it had just as quickly retreated. A more extensive British reconnaissance was made next day by a party headed by Gillespie, which rode to within a mile or so of Batavia as far as the Anjole River, where the bridge had been burnt. They located only a few Dutch vedettes.[40]

Auchmuty faced a choice between two targets. One was the city of Batavia, 10 miles west of the landing place, and a little way inland, though with good wharfs and warehouses along its river; its occupation would also be symbolically important. The second target was Fort Cornelis, 5 miles inland from the city. The three places, city, fort, and landing place, formed the apices of a triangle, and if the Dutch showed minimal enterprise, whichever target Auchmuty chose he might find his route back to the landing place cut. Gillespie had been surprised that in approaching Batavia through land seamed with canals and rice paddies and patches of forest and jungle that there had been no attempt to oppose him. The Dutch were clearly reserving their strength to defeat the invaders at the entrenched camp.

Given the awkwardness of the landing place at Chillinching, seizing the city would be Auchmuty's obvious priority, since this would enable him to maintain easier contact with the ships and bring ashore such stores and ammunition as he needed. This therefore became his initial target. On the 6th the Advance force moved halfway towards the city, and on the 7th a small party was passed across the Anjole River on an improvised bridge of boats to camp in the suburbs overnight. Next day two of Auchmuty's aides, Captains Tylden (his nephew) and Dickson, went into the city to summon its surrender. They brought out the 'chief magistrate' who was more concerned to get British protection against the Javanese than to maintain the honour of his government, and rapidly capitulated.[41]

It was now clear that Janssens' strategy was to concentrate his forces at Fort Cornelis and await attack. Two companies of the Advance moved into the city, and found that the Dutch residents had largely removed themselves, either voluntarily or by Janssens' order. A few soldiers remained behind to observe the new occupiers, and reported back on their numbers. An aide to Minto, Captain William Robison, was sent to Weltevreeden, the Dutch administrative centre, with a summons to Janssens to surrender the island. He was blindfolded, but he heard so much activity in the Dutch camp that when he returned with the expected refusal he could report on the likelihood of trouble approaching. During the day some looting took place in the city, and some buildings were fired by the Javanese. The British carefully made saving the warehouses stocked with trade goods and military and naval stores their priority – these would become prize – but a good deal was nevertheless wasted, and even at the end of the campaign they were still complaining that goods had been deliberately destroyed by the Dutch – clearly depriving the winners of these prize goods.

That night an attack came in, the Dutch assuming that the small British numbers had made the city's occupiers vulnerable, but Auchmuty had ordered in reinforcements after dark, and Robison's information, and the nervousness and agitation of the mayor at supper, had shown that something was expected. The troops were brought out into a defensive formation after dark, and well before the attack took place; when it did, Gillespie brought the reinforcements to strike at the Dutch column in flank. Probably as part of this attack a Javanese man (though Thorn calls him a Malay) was caught attempting to set light to the gunpowder store. He was interrupted in his task and was hanged in the morning. The mayor attempted to flee when the attack began, and was arrested.[42]

These events rather suggested that the mayor was correct in identifying British protection as something that was needed when he surrendered the city. The looting and fire raising was largely the work of the Javanese, who had no loyalty towards the Dutch. The attempt to blow up the gunpowder magazine might have been the work of either the Dutch or the Javanese, but the Dutch had had plenty of opportunity to remove the gunpowder or to destroy it before the British arrived, so it seemed more likely to have been Javanese work; to the Javanese, neither the British nor the Dutch were welcome. It was thus clear that there was a three-sided fight going on: between the Dutch, the British, and the Javanese. It was a harbinger of the much wider problem the British would face later.

Another complication arrived on 9 August in the form of Rear Admiral Hon. Robert Stopford, with three ships, *Scipion* (74) and the frigates *Phoebe* (38) and *President* (38), who had left his official command at the Cape of Good Hope on hearing both that Rear Admiral Drury was dead and that an expedition was heading for Java.[43] He was not welcome. Commodore Broughton, cautious though he was, had succeeded in conducting the expedition safely to Java but now that the main naval work had been done, he found he was superseded and reduced to second-in-command of the ships; Stopford meanwhile had put himself in the way of claiming large quantities of prize money, having done nothing so far but sail across the Indian Ocean. This was in all likelihood the real reason for his presence, though, of course, he could not say so, claiming instead that 'I have been actuated by the hopes of rendering material assistance to an important undertaking'. There is no indication that he was ever needed, but Auchmuty did make sure to use him, though keeping him away from any serious action. Unusually the Admiralty did not censure him, though other commanders who had deserted their posts had been court-martialled – Popham, for example, who had also left the Cape without authority. (Stopford had been involved in the Plate business, of course, as one of those sailors at the Cape when the decision was made to abandon the Chile expedition and concentrate all forces on Buenos Aires.)

Two frigates, *Sir Francis Drake* (38) and *Phaeton* (38), were sent from Batavia to secure the island of Madura, off the north-east coast of Java. This was the source of a large proportion of the Javanese soldiers who were serving in the Dutch Army; the capture of the island would prevent further recruiting, and might also exert some pressure on the Madurese who were already in the Dutch Army. A brisk fight at Samarap persuaded the Raja of Madura to switch sides, and the other Dutch garrisons in the island were then swiftly taken.[44]

The Dutch had established their advanced post of defence at Weltevreeden, which was about 5 miles south of Batavia, halfway between the city and Fort Cornelis. Weltevreeden was a healthier site than Batavia itself, and Daendels had been building a new governor's palace there, though Janssens had stopped work on it. In the morning Gillespie led his Advance against this position. (He and his staff had survived an apparent poisoning attempt by a French servant of Daendels; the poison was in the coffee they drank at breakfast; it was ineffective other than providing them with stomach pains, and when they administered a dose to the servant he also survived; whether it was really poison is a question, but the British were prepared to believe that anything done by a Frenchman was done underhandedly.[45])

The forces engaged in Gillespie's action were small, only 1500 or so under Gillespie, though he also had a force of horse artillery with him; supposedly 'five times' that number were on the Dutch side, though this is undoubtedly an exaggeration. The Dutch fought from within the forest and behind field fortifications. Attempts were made to outflank the position but the land was so much intersected with canals that it proved impossible to do so. However, when the Dutch artillery position was charged and seized by men of the 89th Foot, after a fight of a couple of hours, the Dutch withdrew. Thorn claims a victory of 'heroes' against odds, but in fact the Dutch withdrew more or less intact into the fortifications of Fort Cornelis, and few casualties were suffered by either side.[46]

In this campaign it is all too often that Colonel Gillespie is awarded the credit for victories. There is no doubt he was a vigorous soldier, there is also no doubt that his vigour all too easily emerged as anger, ruthlessness, and badly thought-out plans. The fight at Weltevreeden was an example: it took the defeat of his initial frontal attack over open ground against a force hidden and all-but invisible in the jungle, to convince him that the Dutch position, hidden in a forest and defended by fortifications, must be outflanked. That is, his first instinct was to charge headlong, and only when blocked did he stop to think; and in the aftermath of a fight he could lose control. The massacre at Vellore was an example of this.[47]

That is, although Gillespie was in the forefront of several fights he was always in need of higher direction. On his own he was very liable to incur needless casualties. He was what the old Norse Vikings called a 'berserker', a man who became so carried away in a fight that he was out of control. Auchmuty, by contrast, was quiet and thoughtful, one of those soldiers who planned in detail in advance, but who also was capable of adapting to circumstances and taking chances where it seemed necessary. His conduct of the siege at Montevideo is the best example, but note also his rapid adoption of improvisation at the landing, an improvisation which only worked because of his preliminary planning and organisation of the landing in three manageable divisions.

Gillespie commanded in Batavia and at Weltevreeden, but in the background Auchmuty was also consistently present close to the action. It was the general who pushed forward the reinforcements Gillespie used so effectively in the night fight in the city – for it was to Minto and Auchmuty that Captain Robison reported his suspicions that the Dutch were planning an attack, and so it was Auchmuty who sent in the reinforcements. And Auchmuty was close behind the Advance when the need came to fight at Weltevreeden. At the end of that fight Gillespie sent the 89th in pursuit of the retiring Dutch, and let them get too close to Cornelis so that they were shelled, though the troops were too sensible to get within really close range.

The fort, or rather the entrenched camp, of Fort Cornelis, had a curious structure. It was laid out between two parallel watercourses, the Slokan stream on the east, which had been canalised to flow in a series of straight sections, and the Great Batavia River on the west, which was a typical flat country river, winding and twisting in great loops and bends; these two streams were between 500 and 800m apart; the area of the fort between them was about 2,500m long. Entrance at the north and south was impeded by substantial ramparts, and the whole entrenched camp was equipped with almost 300 pieces of artillery. But the main feature of the fort was that it contained a series of redoubts, seven in all, each of which was intended to be held independently. All the crossing points over the river and the stream were guarded by one of these redoubts, and all but one of the bridges had been burnt.[48]

Auchmuty brought up his whole force. The Reserve had at first been left at the landing place at Chillinching and was now moved forward to join the Line and the Advance at the fort, leaving a relatively small garrison in the city. (The landing place at Chillinching was abandoned; Batavia provided perfectly adequate storage and landing places now that it had been secured.) The British guns were placed about 600yd from the northern rampart and protected by their own ramparts erected by the engineers and the infantry. Fielding records that for several days he and others spent the time making gabions and fascines; on the 20th they began to erect batteries, but the work went only slowly. When they were nearly finished a sortie by the Dutch put the work back, but only for a day. So there was a pause for a week while this work was done, and during that time Auchmuty worked out how to go about the assault.[49]

Attacking the northern rampart was a possibility, but two of the redoubts were positioned just beyond them, and would certainly block any further progress, and their guns and garrisons could mow down any man who climbed the rampart. The possibility of receiving heavy casualties and yet still making little progress was real. The same situation effectively blocked an assault on the southern ramparts, while getting an adequate force there would be slow and difficult, with the men having to make their way along narrow jungle paths in single file: the possibility of ambush was obvious.

Further, battering in one of these closed doors into the fort would only push the Dutch forces away, and one of Auchmuty's priorities was to capture as many of the enemy soldiers as possible. If the Dutch Army simply retreated from the fort into the interior of the island he might find himself in for a long and difficult campaign of pursuit and search.

This had been Janssens' plan at Cape Town, though he was thwarted by the unwillingness of the militia to leave their homes and families to British occupiers. But such a fighting retreat could well be possible in Java, a much bigger territory and with much better resources, and his army was overwhelmingly composed of mercenaries, who might be more amenable to a fighting retreat. Auchmuty surely knew of the Cape campaign; he had not been there himself, but he had met officers who had been – Backhouse, Vassall, Baird. He indubitably understood that Janssens might well attempt the same strategy in Java. For the present the Dutch Army had locked itself into a prison of its own making, but for a successful attack Auchmuty had now to break in to catch the men, so that he and Minto and most of the Indian soldiers could return to India as soon as possible.

A certain urgency also existed because of the damage the climate was already doing to his army. To the 1,200 men left sick at Malacca were added another 300 by the time the fleet reached Java; from the very start on the island the heat had begun to take its toll, particularly on the European soldiers. Several men died even on the first day of their landing from sunstroke and exhaustion, and the casualties would undoubtedly increase. It was with some relief that Weltevreeden had been captured, since it was a healthier place than Batavia, and the Dutch buildings provided some shelter. The Dutch had destroyed the drinking water system in the city and had clearly hoped to pen the British into that notoriously unhealthy place. These tactics had worked in the past when a British naval force had attempted a blockade, only to suffer so many sick that the ships were almost unmanageable when they finally left. It was now late August and the heat would continue for another month, and then the rains would set in, making conditions different, and even worse. It was necessary for the continued health, even existence, of the British Army in Java to defeat the Dutch forces within the next few weeks. (Again, Auchmuty, as at Montevideo, was facing a limit of time for his operation.)

An attack through the northern rampart was ruled out because of the likely cost and because the Dutch would then simply retreat behind the shelter of their redoubts. The rampart and defences at the southern end of the fort were just as strong, or stronger. The long winding course of the Great Batavia River provided a major obstacle to an assault on the western side of the fort, partly due to the size of the river and partly because the highest bank was inside the fort and overlooked any approach, and was strongly defended by batteries of artillery with a good field of fire. The eastern side of the fort, the Slokan stream, was thus the weakest. Here the waterway was narrow, and there was the one bridge which had not been destroyed. It was, however, blocked by the only redoubt which had been placed outside the fort boundary. This redoubt was also defended by a new steep ditch which cut the approach road, and by trenches and traps closer in; and inside the fort there were other redoubts placed to prevent any exploitation if the outside redoubt was taken.

Nobody in Batavia knew much about the interior of the camp, any more than did the British, and could give little information. But deserters from the Dutch Army were coming in, and one of these was a sergeant who had been stationed in that very redoubt (which the British called No. 3). Here was a stroke of luck, which helped with the plan of attack. Auchmuty had paid very little overt attention to that redoubt so far, other than making the occasional distant reconnaissance by a few officers, while looking more closely, and more obviously, at the two ramparts on north and south, and at the possibility of crossing the river on the west. This had been quite deliberate since, as the Slokan side was the weakest point of the fort, it was the obvious place for him to attack and he did not wish to alert the defenders. Now the sergeant-deserter was able to confirm that the bridge which the redoubt guarded was intact, and was able to describe the strengths and layout of the redoubt itself. This information brought Auchmuty's plans into focus.

Preparations were made for an attack on the northern rampart, and this suggested to the Dutch (and to many of the British) that the main assault would be made there; Auchmuty carefully did not disillusion the garrison. The bombarding batteries were built, and the guns were fired intermittently; infantry forces were moved about, as if preparing to attack. The 54th and 75th Foot, and the 5th Volunteer Battalion, were stationed near the batteries, and were backed up by a reserve of two of the Bengal Volunteer Battalions and some of the horse artillery. This was all under the command of General Wetherall, and for a time it seems that this had really been intended to be the main point of assault. Certainly the most obvious preparations were made at this end of the fort, and the battering train which was landed from the fleet was placed into the batteries.

The battery was hardly affected by the Dutch sortie which delayed the entrenching work, or by the bombardment from within the fort which followed its repulse. It was being built in part by the men of the various British and Indian artillery units, but also by 500 seamen from the ships commanded by Captain Sayer of the *Leda*. On 24 August the British bombardment of the northern rampart began, and was accompanied by much defensive preparation by the Dutch. It was clear to both sides that the British intended to attack there, and yet Auchmuty did not like the idea and was still actively considering alternatives. It was at this point that the sergeant-deserter's information produced the very alternative he sought.

There were in fact four attacks in his plan. At the northern rampart two detachments were prepared to be used when it seemed that an attack was feasible; a small one under Colonel Wood was to be directed at the western side of the Dutch rampart, though it was largely intended as a feint and a distraction; a second attack, consisting of the 69th Foot under Lieutenant Colonel Alexander McLeod was directed at the north-east corner of the rampart, where it seemed possible to get close to a slightly weaker section of the rampart. All this was not necessarily kept secret, since it could be assumed that it was all part of the general assault which was transparently intended on that rampart.

A third detachment, a mixture of infantry companies, horse artillery, a battalion of the Reserve, and a troop of the 22nd Dragoons under Major Yule, was sent along the narrow jungle paths beside the Great Batavia River (without being ambushed) to present a threat to the south-eastern corner of the Fort, where there was a bridge over the river. This was guarded by two redoubts placed close to the southern rampart. All these detachments were of sufficient strength to present a serious threat to the Dutch positions, and so they compelled the Dutch to maintain strong forces to face them.

But the main assault was to be on the western side of the Fort, directed at Redoubt No. 3, which guarded the intact bridge over the Slokan. This force was given to Gillespie to command – a good example of Auchmuty gauging the capabilities of his commanders accurately. For this would be a difficult fight and it needed a man of Gillespie's courage and speed and berserker inspiration to inspire his own soldiers. The redoubt had to be taken quickly, otherwise the whole assault would fail. It was not going to be an attack calling for cunning and slow preparation, but one which needed dash and fury. This was precisely what Gillespie could supply. In many ways it would be a repetition of the assault on the Vellore fort, made with speed and ferocity, with the second aim of shocking those inside the fort; exploitation at speed was also needed.

Gillespie was given a mixture of forces, light companies from four of the British regiments, four grenadier companies, two rifle companies, and so on, but no artillery or any cavalry were included; he had to move quickly and quietly, with no snorting, stamping horses, no creaking wagons, no slow, squealing artillery. The approach would be at night, and the attack was to be swift and sudden at dawn, so there was no need for anything but speed. They were guided through the jungle by the deserter-sergeant who was at times uncertain of his route, but one of the British officers who had reconnoitred the region helped out. The force had to move in a long thin column along the narrow paths, very quietly, and the rear of the column, commanded by Colonel Gibbs, became strung out and was delayed. So Gillespie, at the head of the column, arrived at the target with only part of his forces. Dawn was now near, and they were still undiscovered, but as soon as it became light they would be seen, so Gillespie could not wait for the rear of the column to catch up. True to his nature, he took forward his 'little band', as Thorn terms it (though it was a good thousand strong), to an immediate attack.

The deserter had known the Dutch password, and the attackers got past a Dutch picquet by using it; but an officer's picquet close to the redoubt was not so easily fooled, and had to be swiftly attacked and the men mainly killed. However, this could not be done silently, and so the alarm was raised. Lights and rockets flew up from the redoubt to illuminate the approaches, and the redoubt's artillery began firing from the ramparts. But the attackers were now so close to the building that the shot largely flew over their heads. Before the Dutch gunners could reload, the redoubt was stormed. Some men made sure of the redoubt, but Gillespie went straight on through to seize the bridge, where there was a stiff fight before Gillespie's impetuosity drove the Dutch away. He then pushed right on to make an attack on the nearest of the internal redoubts (No. 4), to the left of the bridge. The ferocity of the assault here cost a number of the attackers their lives, but the redoubt was quickly taken.

By this time the delayed rear of the column under Gibbs was arriving. Gillespie directed them onto a third redoubt (No. 2) to the right of the captured bridge. This was successfully stormed just as were the others, but this time two French officers blew up the magazine as the redoubt fell, killing many of the attackers, many of the defenders, and themselves.

Once the men on all sides had recovered from this explosion, the Dutch batteries inside the Fort began bombarding the area of the breach and the captured bridge. The invaders fanned out to clear the interior, attacking the batteries from behind – for most of them faced outwards. An attempted cavalry charge by a small Dutch cavalry unit was fended off. The final blow to the defence came with the capture of the original Fort Cornelis, a small star-shaped structure to the south of Gillespie's captured redoubts. When this was taken by the 59th Foot, resistance in the interior collapsed.

Gillespie's assault, however was not the only reason why the Dutch turned to flee. The assaulting parties aimed at the northern rampart, and the main force at the southern, were also busy. Major Yule's detachment found the bridge over the river in the south in flames when he arrived. His force was not strong enough to mount an assault across the river, but he was able to use his horse artillery to bombard the Dutch as they retreated. Colonel Alexander McLeod's assault in the north-east corner was directed at a narrow space between the river and the corner of the rampart; from there the assaulting force climbed into the Fort to attack Redoubt No. 1. The small force under Colonel Wood facing the northern rampart staged a mock attack when explosions indicated that Gillespie had begun his attack on the first of his ramparts. It seems that Wood's attack, making a lot of noise close to the rampart, played into Dutch expectations, and they thought that this, together with that by McLeod, was the main assault. All these subsidiary attacks successfully distracted Dutch attention from Gillespie's assault. The word soon spread, however, that the defences – on the west and on the north-east – were breached. Defensive fire slackened, so that 'all the other parties rushed in … and together joined in pursuit of the flying enemy'.

Gillespie, who had briefly fainted from his exertions, and Gibbs, presumably alerted by Auchmuty beforehand to the need to prevent the enemy from rallying, led the pursuit, along with the dragoons, the 14th Foot, and a Bengal sepoy regiment. Several times the Dutch attempted to make a stand, but Gillespie's impetuosity repeatedly bore them down. Eventually the survivors scattered, discarding uniforms and weapons on their way, but this debris only showed the pursuers where they had gone. There were 6,000 men made prisoner, including many of the senior commanders, but Janssens and his military commander General Jumel escaped, first of all to Buitenzorg, a well-sited and strong post 35 miles south of Batavia. They had little organised support left by the time they reached it, however, and they had moved away eastwards before Gibbs arrived. Janssens had also rejected another summons from Minto to surrender.[50]

The number of prisoners who had been taken amounted to about half the defending army, but this also suggested that as many had survived and got away. (The casualties in the fighting on the Dutch side seem not to have been recorded; the British forces had 143 killed and 723 wounded; the Dutch will have lost considerably more than that, in addition to the 6,000 prisoners.) Since Janssens was still at large, the fighting was clearly not yet over. It was discovered that he was heading to the eastern part of the island where there were several considerable garrisons, and from where he might be able to mount a continuing war. (There were also the French frigates at Surabaya if he wanted to get back to Europe.)

Auchmuty arranged with Stopford to send forces to attempt to intercept him and any of his forces who were with him or were following him. A sepoy battalion, carried in a squadron of frigates was landed at Cheribon, a town on the north coast at a point where the coast route was very narrow, and where the British could cut the post road. The fort surrendered instantly and this allowed the interception and capture of a small force of 750 Dutch and Javanese troops; also General Jumel arrived all unknowing and was taken captive by the new garrison. Janssens, however, had already passed through. The garrison and the refugees from the battle provided over 3,000 prisoners collected at Cheribon.[51]

At Surabaya the two French frigates, *Nymphe* and *Medusa*, which had brought out Janssens, escaped through the blockade carrying several of the senior Dutch officials (together with Janssens' account of his defeat, in which, in common with most French reports to their Emperor in this war, the numbers of troops he had commanded was understated, and that of the British exaggerated.)[52] But the fact that he did not go in the ship, and yet clearly could have done, indicated a resolve to fight on. Another landing, by a group of seamen and marines at Tagal, further east along the coast, succeeded in intercepting still more refugees. Janssens was, however, still not caught.

Auchmuty now took a hand personally. He ordered several units to make their way eastwards and to gather at a rendezvous at Zedayo, near the important centres of Gressie and Surabaya and the fortress of Fort Ludowyck. These were also close to the island of Madura which had been captured by a naval force a month earlier. He himself sailed with Stopford for the east, calling at Cheribon. There he saw some of Janssens' captured papers showing that he was probably heading for Semarang. Colonel Agnew, the Adjutant General of the expedition, and Captain Elliott (Minto's son and captain of the *Modeste*) were sent there to issue yet another summons to surrender, which was once again rejected, but they saw – and this was the main object of the journey – that Janssens really was at Semarang and that he seemed to have a considerable force with him, or that at least a camp for a sizeable force was being prepared. However, they also saw no Dutch forces moving eastwards on their journey to Cheribon and Semarang. But then a later reconnaissance discovered that the camp had been evacuated, and it was quickly occupied by Colonel Gibbs on 12 October.[53]

Janssens had in fact retired further inland to a better defensive position at Jati Ngaleh. He had received a reinforcement of 1,500 cavalry from 'Prince Prangwedon' – that is, Pakubuwana II, the Susuhanan at Surakarta, which was also known as Solo. Pakubuwana's policy was to support the colonial power in exchange for advantages, which had gained him several increases in territory in the past couple of decades, but he was hardly loyal to Dutch rule. Janssens had also gathered up a regular battalion which had been stationed at Surabaya. Auchmuty decided he would attack him.

The troops were landed from the ships he had with him, though it was by then too late to march that day. Then more arrived next day and so the march was further delayed. But most of those troops sailed right past, heading on the way to the earlier rendezvous at Zedayo, ignoring signals from the shore, so Auchmuty's march was again delayed until the 16th, and then he still had only a small force. He delayed no longer. The enemy force was approached about dawn, but the position it had occupied was so complex and appeared so formidable that some time was taken to reconnoitre it. It was a narrow pass with steep hills defending it, occupied by the Dutch and Javanese. Auchmuty had only 1,200 men with him and 6 guns, and he knew that any delay would reveal his weakness, so he decided on an immediate assault. This was not to be a Gillespie charge, rather an Auchmuty planned assault. He began with an artillery bombardment, which rather shocked the Javanese soldiers from Surakarta, and a rapid movement by the infantry to climb the hills and secure a close position to the enemy posts. The infantry then paused to catch their breath. This whole series of events and movements so shocked both the Dutch and the Javanese that there was little resistance when the final attack was put in, and as it was clearly about to begin, the enemy fled. They had not been able to make use of their strong position, or their superior numbers. The assault resulted in the capture of considerable numbers of European soldiers, but the Surakarta cavalry got away. The British force moved on to capture a brick fort at Onarang several miles further on; the garrison speedily vanished, leaving their equipment and uniforms behind.[54]

Janssens was left almost alone. Most of his aides had left the island or had already been captured. His forces had been defeated, dispersed, and mainly captured. He had retired once more from the battlefield, this time from Onarang to Salatiga, several miles southward, and now at last he owned himself beaten and asked for an armistice and for terms for a capitulation. Auchmuty was agreeable, for he still had only a small force with him and the prospect of a continuing campaign through the interior of the island was not enticing. The horsemen of the Susuhanan of Surakarta may have fled at their first encounter with the British when supporting the Dutch Governor-General, but they would undoubtedly be more resolute if the fighting extended into their homeland – and Salatiga was very close to the Surakartan territories.

So both men had powerful reasons to treat. Not that the process was easy. Janssens stood on his dignity as Governor-General and demanded to treat directly with Minto, his equal in administrative rank. Auchmuty could not accept this because of the delay it would entail – Minto was still 150 miles away at Batavia. Also Admiral Stopford was itching to launch an attack on Fort Ludowyck, between Madura and the mainland, perched on a tidal island and a menacing presence to ships using the Strait of Sunda. But the island was a tough challenge and if he began an assault it might take a long time to succeed, and concluding an armistice while the siege continued and before the fort was captured would be impossible. In that time Janssens' military strength might revive. Delay was therefore in no way in Auchmuty's interest, though Janssens' various demands and objections showed that delay and prevarication was his aim. And finally the rains were approaching. It was already the second half of September, and the monsoon could break at any time in the following fortnight.

Auchmuty therefore replied to Janssens' message with an agreed armistice for just 24 hours. In that time he produced a draft set of capitulation articles and sent them to Janssens. They were abrupt. They required the surrender of all Dutch posts in Java and elsewhere in the islands; all the soldiers were to be prisoners of war; the British were to have a free hand in organising and reforming the government. Janssens must have been expecting something very like this, for he objected only to one of the articles, a guarantee of the public debt, and played again for time by asking for a discussion on the matter, which was an issue complex and technical enough to cause much delay. Auchmuty refused any changes, and insisted on the terms as he had framed them. Since the armistice expired while this exchange was going on, he began to move his forces forwards towards Salatiga.

The bluff worked. Janssens might have simply retreated, crying foul, and spent time gathering support from wherever he could find it, though it seems unlikely he would have found much. Instead he at last gave in, contenting himself with a letter of protest. (Again, one is reminded of the campaign in South Africa, where he was brought to surrender, but only after all his forces had gone.) So Janssens for the second time as a general of France surrendered a Dutch colony to the British. And it was a bluff by Auchmuty working in other ways than on the despairing mind of General Janssens. When the word of the armistice capitulation reached Rear Admiral Stopford he had already seen to the landing of the shipborne troops for the rendezvous at Zedayo, and Major William Farquhar of the Madras Engineers had marched to capture Gressie and Surabaya. The latter had surrendered because the commander there had already heard of Janssens' capitulation. Stopford had sailed on to Fort Ludowyck, and had seen that it was much stronger than expected. He had already begun to emplace artillery for an attack when the news of the capitulation reached him. No doubt relief was felt on all sides, though Stopford and Broughton complained that they had not been consulted on the terms, which, if they were really serious in this, shows a complete lack of understanding of the time factor.[55] But, if it was any consolation, neither had Lord Minto been consulted. Auchmuty was fully capable of assuming the responsibilities of a commander-in-chief.

Back at Weltevreeden Auchmuty and Minto spent the next few days mutually congratulating each other, though it is difficult to see of what use Minto had been. They gave each other banquets and received feasts from the officers – the captured generals were included in these events as guests.[56] Reports were written both for India and for London – Auchmuty wrote directly to both Lord Liverpool and the Duke of York, bypassing Dundas. Minto then at last had some real work to do in settling the immediate future of the conquered territories. This was quickly done. For the moment at least Java had to be retained, and Minto finally realised that its ultimate retention was not his to decide. Raffles was appointed Lieutenant-Governor under Minto's ultimate authority as Governor-General, and Auchmuty put Gillespie, given the temporary and local rank of Major General, in as military commander. These appointments indicated that Java was to be seen as under the authority of the EIC in India. And yet its final disposition was, as everyone knew, to be decided in London. Both Minto and Auchmuty sailed for India early in October.[57]

Chapter 9

The East Indies after Auchmuty

Of the four men who were in command in various ways in the Java campaign in 1811, only General Auchmuty was militarily competent. Minto seems to have taken little or no part in the events of the campaign other than to send in summonses to Janssens demanding surrender, for during the whole campaign he remained at Batavia or Weltevreeden, out of reach of the fighting, or on board ship. He was in any case, and he appears to have known it, without any military expertise of any sort, and was sensible enough to leave the matter in Auchmuty's hands, both in the compilation of the expeditionary force and in its deployment and tactics. Raffles, of course, had even less military knowledge, and could be discounted as a mere courtier and intelligence gatherer until Auchmuty left the island. Gillespie certainly had military expertise of a particular sort, but he could not be trusted to plan a campaign, being all too likely to have an episode of aggressiveness and launch into a blind attack on an impregnable position, usually resulting in the deaths of many of his own soldiers. At Fort Cornelis he had wished to attack the northern rampart and its redoubts directly, just as he had originally done at Weltevreeden. It took a man with a wider view and greater military intelligence to find the enemy's weak spot, as Auchmuty did by waiting patiently for the intelligence of the weakness at Redoubt No. 3 to arrive, and meanwhile disguising from the enemy that they had that knowledge. Then he could direct Gillespie's manic energy at the right place. Note also that when it was necessary and advantageous Auchmuty was fully capable of speedy movement, as in the last campaign against Janssens, which he concluded with a clever manoeuvre; no doubt Gillespie would have charged.

But then both Minto and Auchmuty returned to India, as was their duty, leaving Raffles as Lieutenant Governor and Gillespie as his military chief. From now on, apart from later disputes over the prize money, Auchmuty had nothing to do with events in Java, but, as with his other adventures his achievement had a much larger and more lasting effect than his immediate presence in the island might have suggested. It was Auchmuty's conquest which created the situation which Raffles and Gillespie set about exploiting, and it is therefore worth a brief investigation into what they did in the next five years. Raffles had plans, concerted to some degree with Minto, for reforms to the Dutch administration, but he was hindered from the start by the limits of his authority, both legal and practical. The Directors in London had expressly forbidden Minto to annex the Dutch colonies, instead instructing him to pull out and leave the lands to the native inhabitants. Once again, Minto ignored the express orders given him and retained 'his' conquests, leaving Raffles to rule – but in whose name Raffles was operating was not altogether clear; Minto had said he had taken over on behalf of both the Company and the British government, though it was the Company which was saddled with the responsibility.

Meanwhile the fall of the Dutch regime had allowed many of the Javanese kings and princes to hope that they could reassert their political independence, a hope which had been encouraged, of course, by the earlier contacts, orchestrated by Raffles, in which the British invaders solicited the assistance, if only passive, of the Javanese in the campaign against the Dutch.

Now that Raffles was governor, of course, such implicit promises as the Javanese rulers developed in their minds were not to be realised, and whatever promises had been made to them, or they thought had been made, would not be kept. Raffles assumed the full authority which the Dutch had exercised over the several client kingdoms, as well as governing the former Dutch lands. But hopes had been raised, and the kings were unwilling to submit tamely to the new regime. It would, therefore, necessarily be tested.

The first of these tests had already happened, when the Susuhanan of Surakarta, Pakubuwana II, had loaned his cavalry to Janssens to oppose Auchmuty's forces at the last fight. They had not indulged in any fighting, and Janssens had capitulated soon after, but the apparent display of hostility by Surakarta to the British had to be investigated. Auchmuty had therefore sent Captain William Robison (who, as one of Minto's aides-de-camp, had a certain authority) to follow the withdrawing cavalry to interview the Susuhanan in Surakarta itself. This he succeeded in doing, having a private meeting, in defiance of all Javanese protocol, after which, by Robison's request, Pakubuwana had produced a letter which listed all the problems he had experienced with the Dutch administration, of which the local representative was the Resident Jacob Andries van Braam. (Listing such issues, of course, implied that the British administration would do something towards removing them.) Robison then continued on to Jogjakarta, the rival kingdom, only a day's journey away. King Hamengkubuwana II (and his rival the Crown Prince), also produced a letter listing his complaints against the Dutch. Robison then departed, assuming that both kings had shown that they were therefore amenable to British authority.[1]

It does not seem to have occurred to Robison to realise that any complaints about the Dutch would also become complaints against the British, who now claimed to have taken the place of the Dutch, and indeed Robison instructed van Braam, and his counterpart at Jogjakarta, Pieter Engelhard, to continue in their offices as Residents. This should have been, and no doubt was, a clear indication to the Javanese rulers that unless they asserted themselves, their situations would not improve.

An example of the feelings of the local rulers after two centuries of Dutch rule, influence, and – as they saw it – drunken boorishness came from Palembang. This was a substantial Sultanate in southern Sumatra, whose main palace-city lay some 50 miles or so inland along the Musi River, and whose territories included the islands of Bangka and Billiton, in which there were known to be considerable tin deposits, a metal sufficiently rare to be counted as a treasure, and which the British regarded with something approaching consuming greed.

The Sultan of Palembang had been one of those contacted by Raffles, and when the British invasion of Java began, he took advantage of the moment to turn on the Dutch Resident and the small Dutch community at his capital. Raffles had, after all, suggested to the Sultan, Badr-ud-din, that the moment was right to 'drive the Dutch out'.[2] He meant, no doubt, the elimination of Dutch influence, and the polite removal of the Dutch Resident, if there was one. But Badr-ud-din took him literally, and made his own plans. When the news arrived of the fall of Batavia to the British he arranged for his men to collect all the Dutch and their Malay and Sumatran servants, beat them up, rape at least some of the women, and put them on a ship in the river, from which they were dumped into the river to drown.[3] Eighty-six died, at least, and others escaped into the forest. The Dutch Residency was then razed.[4]

This took place in September 1811; the news did not reach Raffles until January.

Raffles had turned first to attend to Jogjakarta. Whatever agreement Robison thought he had arrived at in September, after his rapid and brief visits to the courts at Surakarta and Jogjakarta, the Sultan at the latter place was by no means prepared to be acquiescent to the new regime. He had in fact been formally deposed by the Dutch earlier in the year in favour of his son the Crown Prince, who was supposed to be acting as regent, but only the latter had accepted this decision as having any validity and he was generally ignored by the court. Soon after Robison left the court Sultan Hamengkubuwana deprived his son of all power, and then began a diplomatic correspondence with Pakubuwana II, the Susuhanan. Since the two royal houses were long at enmity – Jogjakarta was a breakaway kingdom from the ancient kingdom of Mataram, whereas Pakubuwana was of the direct royal line of that kingdom – this was a serious political development, which the British only slowly heard about and even more slowly came to appreciate its significance. Hamengkubuwana II then contrived the murder, in the palace, of the *Patih* Danureja II. This man was technically the administrator of the *kraton*, the royal compound and his dismissal was due as much for his inefficiency as for his adopting an independent position, but the British refused to accept the man chosen as his replacement.[5]

Raffles appointed a new Resident to Jogjakarta to replace Pieter Engelhard, who was ill. This was John Crawford, an Edinburgh doctor who had been with Raffles in Penang. From the beginning Crawford voiced strong objections to all that the Sultan Hamengkubuwana had done during the past few months, though there was no sign that this had any more effect than the Dutch deposition and imposition of the Crown Prince as regent.[6] Raffles himself came to the court in December and concluded a new treaty with the Sultan, which involved recognising Hamengkubuwana as Sultan once more and confirming the cession of several territories which had been taken by Daendels earlier in the year; others had been taken from Surakarta. The Sultan was not impressed. Raffles was clearly in a very weak military position, and Hamengkubuwana understood this, so Raffles' appeasement had the reverse effect of that which he had intended. It seems that Raffles was quite unable to bluff convincingly, though he was in no worse position than Auchmuty had been at Jati Ngaleh. Much of the expeditionary army had been withdrawn back to India with Minto and Auchmuty, and there were other apparently more urgent tasks for what forces remained in Java, but Raffles was not totally unarmed. The Sultan, having survived Raffles' visit, began making serious preparations for war.

One thing which the military had to deal with was a continuing uprising in an area of the north coast called Indramayu, close to Cheribon. In that territory a self-proclaimed prophet had maintained a rebellion against the Dutch and the Sultan for some years, and had convinced his followers that he was invincible; the Dutch had supposedly killed the leader several years earlier, but the uprising now revived. The 'Bagoos-Rangin', as Thorn called the new leader, had a force of 2,000 musketeers, many of whom were refugees from the former Dutch Army, the arrival of which had suddenly made the insurrection more formidable. They were attacked by a British detachment under Captain Ralph of the 59th Foot, with a mixed British and Indian force. In the fight the insurgents fired too soon, as was the local custom, the aim being to scare rather than kill; this had little effect, and they then broke and fled when the British bared their teeth and charged with the bayonet. The invincibility of 'Bagoos-Rangin' had been dented, though he survived, and the uprising collapsed, at least for a time. The continuing misery of the peasantry in the region would ensure that another rebellion would inevitably follow in a fairly short time.[7]

The apparent settlement with Jogjakarta allowed Raffles, when he heard of the events at Palembang, to send Gillespie to attend to the Sultan Badr-ud-din. He had eight companies of infantry, part of the Madras and Bengal Artillery, detachments of Indian and Amboynese forces, all of them carried in a fleet of ships and gunboats, including the frigates *Phoenix* (36) and *Cornelia* (36) and the sloop *Procris* (18), together with two EIC sloops *Mornington* (18) and *Teignmouth* (16), most of which were unable to get up the Musi River. Raffles made it clear that the prize for dealing with Palembang was to be Bangka Island, so indicating quite clearly that in fact investigating the massacre of the Dutch, and inflicting punishment for it, was a mere excuse for seizing the richest part of Palembang's territory. The expedition stopped there to construct boats, then spent several days getting some of the bigger vessels over the bar of the Musi River and upstream; a force of Bengal sepoys remained on Bangka Island when the rest moved upstream, as a sort of imperial deposit. It was the monsoon season, and the thunderstorms and heavy rain constantly upset progress upriver. All this took more than three weeks.[8]

The Sultan Badr-ud-din sent a series of messengers to enquire as to the purpose of this expedition. The second messenger pointed out that the Sultan was in fact a friend of the British, having attacked the Dutch in Palembang at the same time as the British were attacking the Dutch in Java. And, of course, from Badr-ud-din's viewpoint this was correct, for they had both been enemies of the Dutch. Gillespie ignored this and insisted that he would meet the Sultan in person in the palace to state the conditions for peace. He was deliberately vague, and the Sultan kept asking his reasons and receiving no reply. Nothing the Sultan said could deflect the monomaniac, tunnel-visioned Gillespie, nor could the Sultan convince any of the British of his sincerity or his political friendship. He clearly believed that killing and removing the Dutch had been act of friendship to the British; Raffles and Gillespie by contrast saw it as a gesture of independence – quite correctly – which, as heirs of the Dutch, they must defeat; and then, of course, there was Bangka to be seized.

A powerful position at a place called Borang was surrendered as a result of confusion among the Palembangese officials and the troops there, but resistance also began at that point, with an attempt to disrupt the advance by an attack by fire rafts. Clearly the Sultan had realised at last that words would not deter the British, and that no explanation on which to base negotiations would be forthcoming. Nor could his forces drive them away. Then information came to Gillespie from an Arab merchant whose ship had been commandeered by the Sultan but had then been captured by the British. He asked for his ship back, and at the same time reported that the Sultan had 'fled' into the forest. A Palembangese official also brought an account of this, with the further news that Palembang city was in confusion. (The disturbances followed the Sultan's departure, not the other way around, as it is often portrayed.) Gillespie forged ahead in a canoe accompanied at first by only seven grenadiers. He landed at the town and went into the confusion of the town 'with a firm step', Thorn says. He avoided a possible assassination attempt – or what was claimed as such – and got into the palace, which had been sacked by the people, but was otherwise intact. It was fortified, and he collected there a small band of soldiers and sailors, while around him much of the town went up in flames.

The arrival of further reinforcements established Gillespie in full control, but the absence of Badr-ud-din complicated his task. A narrative were swiftly concocted, perhaps by the surviving officials, but it was readily accepted by Gillespie. The Sultan's son was now assigned the blame for the murders of the Dutch, and the Sultan himself was allocated the blame for the killings and burnings in the city. Both could therefore, having 'fled' the town, be considered to have forfeited their positions, despite the fact that both were still nearby and in their kingdom. Badr-ud-din's brother, Adipati, who lived away from the town, was assigned a reputation for mildness, and was brought to the town and placed on the throne as the new Sultan Najm-ud-din, in a coronation ceremony contrived by Gillespie, replete with resounding proclamations.

Gillespie, imagining now that all was well, and that the new Sultan, having been installed with such ceremony, would therefore be obeyed, and having, so he thought, secured an ally in Najm-ud-din, embarked his forces and retired. He had extracted from the new Sultan a treaty by which the tin islands of Bangka and Billiton were ceded to the East India Company; they were already, of course, occupied by Gillespie's forces. Bangka was symbolically renamed Duke of York Island, and the camp of the new garrison became Fort Nugent (after the Commander-in-Chief of the Bengal Army, whose men formed the garrison.) Meanwhile Badr-ud-din and his son were still at large in the forest. The former had taken the palace treasure with him so that not only was Najm-ud-din seen as a puppet of the British, and guilty of handing over valuable property, but he had no protection from his protectors nor any monetary resources for acquiring any.[9] That is, whatever Gillespie felt he had accomplished, his expedition was no more than a temporary raid; conquest was a long way away.

Meanwhile in Java relations between the British and Hamengkubunara II in Jogjakarta had quickly deteriorated. The treaty Raffles had agreed with the Sultan had hardly been made in good faith on either side and, when British weakness had been appreciated, the Sultans of Surakarta and Jogjakarta had made a rival agreement, which might be considered an alliance. In March 1812, however, their mutual suspicions could not be overcome, and the contracts they had negotiated were never ratified. It was the very existence of the negotiations which alarmed Raffles when he finally heard about them in April 1812. At Jogjakarta the fortifications of the *kraton* were being strengthened, and a purge of the former Regent/Crown Prince's officials was conducted – and the Regent's life seemed to be in danger.[10]

It was as the tension between the British and Jogjakarta courts was reaching this point that Gillespie returned from Palembang with some of his troops – others had been left at Bangka, or had been taken on a lengthy voyage by way of Borneo, so that they took time to reach Batavia. He could report success of a sort, and he was at once re-employed to deal with Hamengkubuwana. After only a week at Batavia Gillespie was off to Semarang with such troops as he could collect. It was explained to him that a general alliance of the Javanese kingdoms had been formed, 'all family feuds subsided', and such danger existed that an immediate action was required – not therefore just the two sultans were involved, but other potentates as well. This was how Major Thorn understood the situation, and this was presumably what Raffles had told Gillespie, who was Thorn's commander.[11]

It was, of course, misleading in the extreme to imply the existence of a general threat. On the other hand, Raffles was clearly frightened, and a contemplation of the possible military strength which might result from the junction between the several kingdoms gave some basis for his fright. Meanwhile Raffles was using his undoubted skills of intrigue. The weak spot of the Jogjakarta regime was the Crown Prince, now justifiably angered by his father's killing of several of the officials who had been loyal to him as regent, and by the apparent threat to himself. He proved easy to subvert, and agreed that, in return for being made ruling Sultan he would agree to yet another treaty of subordination, and would pay the cost of the expedition.[12] Raffles was also using the crisis, which he greatly exaggerated, to expand British power, just as he had with Palembang.

The expedition of punishment was gathered at Semarang. Gillespie had brought up all the forces he could find, amounting to about 600 European and 1,400 Indian troops: part of the 14th Foot, two troops of the 22nd Dragoons, part of the Bengal Light Infantry, and the 3rd Volunteer Battalion; more were on the way, including men from the Palembang expedition when they arrived in Java. However, for the moment this was the main force with which he set out for Jogjakarta. Colonel Colin McKenzie reconnoitred the *kraton* on 15 June. Close by was a fort established by the Dutch as the guardian and watchtower over the *kraton*, and Gillespie with a force of dragoons arrived there two days later. He put his whole force into that fort.[13]

Gillespie met a force of Jogjakarta cavalry during his own reconnaissance. The encounter ended in violence with the dragoons having to retreat. Raffles sent in a messenger to the court next day suggesting negotiations, but this was simply a way of covering himself, for the Sultan was clearly determined to fight – and probably so was Gillespie, whose occupation of the Dutch Fort put him in a strong position. Firing broke out, with each fort bombarding the other. Major Thorn goes out of his way to emphasise the disparity of strength between the two sides, suggesting that the Sultan had 17,000 men defending the *kraton*, and a possible 100,000 'armed population' from the surrounding territory.[14] The main source of events on the Javanese side is a poem in sixty-two cantos written by the uncle of Hamemkubuwana II, Pangeron Panular, during the period of British rule. It begins at the point where the artillery duel is taking place; he remarks that the British were much more accurate and speedy in their firing than the Javanese – but then the Dutch and the British had been busy firing at people all over the world for a couple of centuries.[15]

Reinforcements arrived for Gillespie on 19 June – part of the Royal Artillery, some hussars, and some companies of infantry from the 59th Foot and the 78th Foot, with the Madras Horse Artillery. They had to fight their way through, and, despite being opposed by a large number of troops, they did so with only a few casualties.

The Sultan had adopted a policy used by the British and had sent in a messenger to ask for Gillespie's capitulation. No doubt the messenger took the opportunity to have a good look around and examine Gillespie's real strength inside the Dutch fort. The mutual bombardments had exploded powder stores on each side, but more significantly the British bombardment had set fires inside the *kraton* which spread among the wooden buildings, burning out the homes of the Sultan's troops who lived within the walls. Gillespie brought all his forces into the fort now, rested and fed them, meanwhile continuing with the bombardment. It may be that, as Thorn assumes, the Sultan thought that this was a sign that the British were about to retreat. They were in fact joined by a force of troops of Mankunegara II, the ruler of a dissident area of Surakarta.

An attack on the *kraton* went in before dawn on 20 June. One force attacked the South Gate, and a second the North. (One is reminded of Auchmuty's attack on Montevideo.) On the north side, though the men were discovered as they were about to mount their scaling ladders, they got up on to the wall and opened the way for the main party to enter; moving along the wall they drove off the defenders at the South Gate and let in the other party, which had had to disperse a large defending force. The invaders now kept together and progressively cleared the whole *kraton* of enemy troops, driving out the enemy soldiers, and finally capturing the Sultan and his family. The last focus of resistance was in a mosque near the fort, but when that was taken, about 3 hours after the attack began, resistance ceased.[16]

The palace was then looted. Crawford came in and seized a large library of manuscripts (which eventually went to the British Library) – and Raffles acquired still more. The troops grabbed what they wanted, but most of the goods went to the prize agents, and of course the new Sultan had already agreed to pay the costs of the expedition. Raffles acquired large quantities of artefacts and books, though he also complained of the way the soldiers had gone about the same task, covering himself once more. A treasure of something of the order of 800,000 Spanish dollars was supposedly obtained; how much the troops seized on their own account is not known.[17]

The political result of the fight, however, was decisive. Any possibility of a concerted attack by all the Javanese princes against the British ended with the capture of the centre of the conspiracy. Hamengkubuwana II was deposed at once, and his son, the former Regent and former Crown Prince, was installed as Habengkubuwana III, the second Indonesian ruler to owe his position to the British in three months.[18]

The former Sultan and his family were removed along with the British forces when the latter left on 3 July. Hamengkubuwana III agreed to a new political treaty, putting the British effectively in control, with Crawford as British Resident. Another principality on the south coast was created for a brother of the deposed Sultan, Natakusuma; the principality and the man took the title Pakualam (this making him the third ruler the British had installed). He had quarrelled with his brother and had just survived the various purges. These various measures reduced the Jogjakarta territory significantly, in size, in wealth, and in reputation. The Susuhanan in Surakarta took due note of all this, and when he was visited by Hugh Hope, the Commissioner for eastern Java, Pakubuwana IV succumbed at once. He also lost territory, this time to Mankunegara II, who had brought reinforcements to Gillespie in the fort. He also had to dismiss his *patih*, who had conducted the alliance negotiations with Jogjakarta.[19] It was the divisions among the Javanese rulers which opened the way for the British conquest, but the British then busily set about dividing them still further among each other, reducing the larger states and creating or enlarging the smaller. It was 'divide-and-rule' in as ruthless a way as can be found.

Raffles protested more than once that his priority was the well-being of the native Javanese, though they would surely have disagreed. He may have thought he meant it, but his actions often belied his later statements. He had revised the account of the process of the raid by Gillespie on Palembang to remove his own guilt, and he now fudged the matter of Jogjakarta. He was very good at adjusting the record so that he could claim results which occurred but had never been intended, and so to evade any blame for what had gone wrong. But he certainly intended that the administration of Java should be 'reformed'.

One of the major issues was the difficulty of getting sufficient tax revenues to maintain a proper administration. Daendels had made one change by handing over large areas of the Surakarta and Jogjakarta lands rather than pay rent for them, a transaction Raffles confirmed. But Raffles' big idea was a land survey, to find out what resources there were, and then to impose a land tax. It was Colonel McKenzie's task to carry out this survey, spurred on by a drastic shortage of money during 1812; this was also one of the reasons for the clause in the Jogjakarta treaty which made that kingdom pay for its own conquest.

In fact Raffles' reforming ideas were not usually implemented.[20] Partly this was because he found the task too great for him, partly because he tried to do too much, partly, of course, it was due to Javanese resistance to changing the way they had always done things. (It cannot have been a secret that the land survey was the preliminary to a tax, that is, that the new government was intent on extracting more money from the population than the Dutch had earlier.) The sacking of the Jogjakarta *kraton* was never something any Javanese could forget, and any goodwill arising towards the British because of their defeat of the Dutch was severely dented by the expulsion of the Sultan and his family. But more than that, the conquests of Palembang and Jogjakarta essentially failed if they were intended to cow the other kings into submission. They might submit for the moment, but never with sincerity. Raffles' policy was, as usually occurs with major changes to a well-established social and political system, mainly successful in alienating both the people and their rulers.

For the kings were not cowed by their treatment. In Palembang the supposedly deposed Sultan Badr-ud-din continued to exercise authority outside the palace and the town; it was thus seen almost from the moment that the British left that the conquest claimed by Gillespie had been merely temporary, even momentary. Raffles sent William Robison to negotiate a new settlement, not a good choice of envoy. He did so by returning Badr-ud-din to power and collecting 200,000 Spanish dollars from him. But Badr-ud-din in power was likely to be much more expensive than if he and his brother were at enmity. Robison was sent back to return the money and reverse the change, a ludicrous situation which demonstrated to all involved the general incompetence of the British government under Raffles.[21]

The settlement with Jogjakarta was no more durable. The new Sultan Hamengkubuwana III died after only two years on the throne, and his successor was a child, Hamengkubuwana IV. His Regent was Pakualam I, who was the new Sultan's uncle, and who had been given his principality by the British carved out of the Sultan's lands, but he was either inefficient or too greedy (or both) and was removed as Regent by the British in 1816. Pakubuwana IV at Surakarta was restless after being detected in his conspiracy with Jogjakarta, and continued to intrigue, developing a new conspiracy in which one of the Bengal battalions was brought to the verge of mutiny. This was discovered late in 1815 and was quickly suppressed by the arrest of twenty-six sepoys; the plot had also involved men at Weltevreeden, and included an intention to kill the British officers at Surabaya. The basic reason for the plot was that the sepoys had been in Java for five years, and when they heard that the island was to be handed over to the Dutch, they feared that they were to be handed over as well, with the prospect of the rest of their lives being served in Java. Alternatively some of the sepoys plotted to seize power in Java and declare independence. The disjunction between sepoys and officers is clear in all this, and would not have surprised Auchmuty, as will be seen in the next chapter.

The Sultan at Surakarta was peripherally involved in this, but was also subject to a plot organised by his brother and his mother against him. Raffles succeeded in removing the brother to a sort of house arrest at Surabaya, and in frightening the Sultan into submission once again, and assured him that the approaching Dutch return would not affect him, a promise he knew perfectly well he would be quite unable to keep. More precisely at Cheribon a curious dual Sultanship, which was, by Raffles' time little more than honorary, was ended, both sultans being pensioned off cheaply. The British seemed to be particularly lethal when it came to the sultans.[22]

So the effects of the conquest of the Jogjakarta *kraton* rippled outwards continually. The Sultan at Jogjakarta was clearly subject to British control, as the installation of Hamengkubuwana III and the removal of the Regent showed; the attempted conspiracy by Susuhanan Pakubuwana IV resulted in his submission being renewed at British insistence; at Cheribon the old kings were retired on 5,000 Spanish dollars a year. And meanwhile the new land rent system was gradually imposed throughout the island, in a series of experimental ways, but which ended by giving the local chiefs the duty of collection – a recipe for increased wealth for these men, to whose sticky fingers plenty of the rent revenues would adhere. It was in fact the same result which had emerged in India, where the zamindars were transformed into landlords. It was hardly a system which had the welfare of the Javanese at heart, as Raffles regularly claimed, but it was cheap to run and made for a political alliance between the government at Batavia and those local chiefs, who were perhaps more reliable than the sultans. This became one of the bases for Dutch control in the next century and a half.

Raffles' lack of military (and naval) power was made worse by his inability to pay for the forces he already had. Gillespie became angry at penny-pinching by (usually corrupt) British officials, and he and Raffles quarrelled publicly. Gillespie, promoted to substantive Major General in late 1812, left Java the next year. (He was killed in the Gurkha War in 1814, apparently assuming a personal invincibility like the prophet in Indramayu.[23]) His replacement, General Sir Miles Nightingall, a veteran of the Peninsular War, was easier to get along with, but no less willing to use violence rather than diplomacy to 'solve' minor disputes. He raided the kingdom of Bululeng in Bali when the king presumed to resume his kingdom's ancient contacts and suzerainty in East Java. Nightingall then went to Sulawesi, where the king of Bone had continued, or resumed, a traditional piracy practice. His house was burned down in reprisal, but he escaped, like Badr-ud-din, into the forest; this did not stop his piratical activities.[24]

Raffles had sent a small fleet to assert British power over the Sultan of Sambas in Borneo; the first attack was repulsed; a second attack seemed successful, but the Sultan had simply moved upriver and returned when the expedition returned to Java – rather like the Sultan of Palembang.[25] Attempts to impose British authority were generally unsuccessful, assuming too easily, like King Cnut's courtiers, that their power was real. Raffles had sponsored the deeply unpleasant Alexander Hare to settle at Banjermasin, also in Borneo, and was willing to ship people to him from Java, people whom he convicted of any sort of crime, or none; in effect he was a slave trader. At the same time Raffles deliberately campaigned to abolish slave trading and eventually slavery itself. Again, Raffles' way with words was sufficient to avoid any responsibility for Hare until historians got to work on the issues and the records.[26]

Raffles' policy was clearly imperialistic, and he was willing to use almost any method which came to hand. But he was unable to discriminate between what was possible, what was essential, what was impossible, and what was unnecessary. Nor, being profoundly unmilitary himself, did he understand the limits of military power. Expeditions to Borneo were clearly in the unnecessary category, though from the East India Company's viewpoint the suppression of piracy would seem like a good idea – if that was not simply Raffles' stated reason for the expeditions. The Dutch had tried for two centuries to gain footholds in Borneo and had finally withdrawn under Daendels in 1809; this should have made it clear that the effort was not worthwhile. Raffles also sent missions to China and Japan, neither of which succeeded in any way except to annoy those they tried to intimidate, but it seems clear he had got the expansionist fever which Minto had also suffered from.

Raffles sent an expedition – one doctor in a single ship – to Nagasaki in Japan with the intention of his taking over the Dutch factory at Deshima, the only officially sanctioned Japanese contact with Europeans. Dr Ainslie wholly failed to persuade the Dutch there to hand over their factory to Raffles' representative – they had never heard of him, and though the Japanese accepted some presents on behalf of the Emperor, they were of no assistance. This is not surprising, since a previous British ship, captained by Fleetwood Pellew, the son of Admiral Sir Edward Pellew, had turned up unexpectedly in 1809 and had behaved so boorishly that he only just escaped alive; if the Japanese realised that Ainslie was also British he would obviously be equally unwelcome.[27]

Raffles and Crawford and McKenzie are several times lauded as collectors of local plants and antiquities. Raffles in particular is notable for having investigated the archaeology of Java, and drew attention to the tremendous ninth-century Buddhist temple at Borobodur in Central Java.[28] He set about clearing the overgrowth and investigating it. But he also took away with him large quantities of remains, and both Crawford and McKenzie, who concentrated on written materials, did the same. One 4-ton inscribed stone which Raffles presented to Lord Minto has lain out in the Scottish countryside ever since, the inscription gradually wearing away. It is common to remark that by removing these materials these looters were preserving them; but that was not their purpose, of course, nor in many cases was it the result; they were really just looters, not really any better than the soldiers who sacked the *kraton* at Jogjakarta.

By 1813 the political ground Raffles was standing on was crumbling. His main supporter, Lord Minto, was recalled to Britain in that year, and died the next. Gillespie's internal demons spilled over into rage and charges of maladministration by Raffles as soon as he was in India, though his ludicrous death in 1814 somewhat reduced the impetus behind that effort. William Robison, resentfully injured by Raffles' lashing tongue over the Palembang affair, returned to Britain with similarly angered feelings, which he vented widely.

Raffles had clung to the notion that the island of Java and its dependencies could still be retained by the British when the great wars in Europe ended. So it might have been, if Napoleon had won those wars, but as one of the results of his defeat was the liberation of the Netherlands from being part of the empire of the French, as well as the liberation of all Europe from the menace of Napoleon, the return of its greatest and wealthiest colony to Dutch rule was inevitable. News of the agreement to this restitution (which followed Napoleon's defeat at Leipzig in October 1813) reached Java in August 1814, and in that same month in London, a final treaty which provided for the return of the islands to Dutch rule was agreed; the news of this arrived at Batavia early next year. The actual implementation of the treaty was then delayed by the greater problem of Napoleon's final adventure, but finally in December 1815 the handover was ordered to take place. This stuttering process was thoroughly disturbing, and Raffles was thus given hopes, repeatedly dashed, that the return would not take place, and he campaigned against it. But he did not have any real influence in Britain, and anything he said was hardly helped by the news of a near mutiny among his Indian troops in 1815. He was replaced by John Fendall, a Company man for twenty years, who would be interim governor until the new Dutch administration arrived. When Fendall arrived he faced an administrative mess; no doubt he was relieved to hand it all on to the Dutch later in 1816.[29] Raffles called at St Helena on his voyage home and talked with the exiled Bonaparte, two unsuccessful imperialists comparing failures, perhaps.

The British episode in Java, despite its brevity, had a long-lasting effect. The long business of organising the land rent was still incomplete when Raffles left Java, but it was, after some delay, taken up, adapted and retained by the Dutch, who finally realized it was a good tax producer. The humiliation of the several sultans and kings was also accepted by the Dutch, and exploited by them. The adventures and imperialism which Raffles had launched were taken up also by the Dutch with more success – though it took an expedition of 4,000 soldiers to conquer Palembang in a war which lasted several years. Sambas and Banjermasin in Borneo and Macassar in Sulawesi were similarly acquired, but it took most of the nineteenth century to expand Dutch control to what became the boundaries of Indonesia when the country became independent in the 1940s.

Raffles later returned to the region when he was appointed as agent in Bencoolen in 1817, only to find that a new Anglo-Dutch agreement exchanged that post with Malacca in 1824. By then he had taken up a brief residence in the Sultan of Johore's island of Singapore, which he promoted as an entrepôt. When he had been appointed to Bencoolen, the Governor-General in India, Lord Moira (Minto's successor) commented that this was about the right level of responsibility for his abilities – an assessment by a political enemy, but one which is nonetheless accurate.[30] (His reputation as founder of Singapore is similarly skewed – the main work was done by John Farquhar, and by the commercial abilities of the Chinese merchants who settled on the island.)

This has taken the story some distance from Samuel Auchmuty, who, like Raffles in Singapore, stayed in Java only a few months. He had been a rather reluctant commander for the expedition, which took him away from the work he had been sent to India to do, and had it been left to him it would probably have not taken place at all. Indeed the expedition looks very much like a personal whim of Minto's, and one which was thoroughly unnecessary, either in the immediate term, or in the longer term in consideration of the state of the war. Raffles clearly understood Minto's motives, and flattered him into appointing him to the Lieutenant-Governorship. The capture of Mauritius was far more important in the context of the war and of the Company's trade in India, and at least Minto had put that first; the capture of Java, even when it had come under the rule of vigorous Dutch Governors-General like Daendels and Janssens, was quite unnecessary; the island could have been isolated by sea without difficulty.

And yet the result was to shift the Dutch in Java out of their inefficient pre-Revolutionary lassitude and into a much more vigorous phase which involved the development, but also the conquest, of the whole Indonesian archipelago. This began with Raffles' expedition against Badr-ud-din in Palembang and Humengkubuwana II at Jogjakarta in 1812; the capture of these places broke the spell of the joint rule of the Dutch and sultans over the island, and significantly reduced the battered prestige of the sultans; the Dutch could now get on with the full conquest.

It was a clear sign of Dutch imperial determination when they took over the islands of Bangka and Billiton, with its tin deposits, which the British had claimed from Badr-ud-din's brother; British protests were ineffectual. Singapore, in a sense, was their reply. Raffles, flawed, incompetent, untruthful, therefore arrived, most unexpectedly, in a position where he could have a major effect on events. He is remembered in Britain mainly as the 'founder' of Singapore, but this was a mere postscript to his real work in Java, and his reputation is significantly exaggerated. The fact that the Dutch took up much of his initiatives – the land rent, Palembang, the conquests in Borneo and Sulawesi, the abolition of slavery – testifies to the effect he had, even if his efforts were clearly failing.

Whether this would have happened anyway, whether or not Raffles ruled for five years in Java, is another question. The Dutch, under French impetus, had already begun the process of reforming themselves and their empire, beginning with the abolition of the VOC, though their involvement in the great wars as French allies and subjects repeatedly interrupted those reforming efforts. It seems quite likely that they would have continued to institute such reforms even if the British had stayed at home, though perhaps their efforts would have been less brutal. On the other hand, it seems unlikely that Raffles would have found and developed Singapore if he had been left as Second Secretary in Penang rather than being taken up by Minto.

The contribution of Samuel Auchmuty to these events was in fact even more important than that of either Minto or Raffles. Neither of these was in any sense military, and the alternative commander of the expedition, Gillespie, would probably have botched it. So Auchmuty was the efficient agent in inserting the British into Java and so into South-east Asia as a whole by his military ability, by his conquest of Fort Cornelis, and his pursuit and elimination of Janssens from Semarang to Salatiga. Without his success, and the precision of his campaign, Raffles would never have been able to do his work in Java or Singapore; if the initial expedition had failed, and the army was driven into the sea at Batavia, Minto, Raffles, and the rest would have been instantly removed from India and comprehensively blamed for disobeying instructions from London. This is what would probably have happened had Gillespie been in command. To Auchmuty therefore may be attributed the initial success which allowed the British to play about with the system in Java, and give Raffles the opportunity of expanding British influence into the region and enjoy his somewhat spurious reputation.

Chapter 10

India, 1811–13

Sir Samuel Auchmuty sailed from Java on 8 October 1811, and arrived at Madras, after a slow voyage, on 16 November.[1] Even before he undertook the expedition against Janssens to Semarang and the interior of Java, and just after the initial victory at Fort Cornelis, he had been commenting on his future in India. On 2 September he wrote to Robert Dundas from Weltevreeden that although he had good health (he had earlier commented that the troops were 'sickly'), 'I must expect that my constitution will suffer from the fatigue I have been obliged to undergo' – the remark of a man clearly feeling his age (he was 55), or perhaps it was a conventional lament; it was often the practice of such men to suggest that they wished to retire or resign, so offering their superiors the opportunity to accept if they wished to; these offers were also often insincere. Auchmuty did in fact make such an offer not long afterwards. He will return in India, he says, and remain there for some time, and, though he does not give details, it is clear that he knew he had a lot of work to do there, which his participation in the Java campaign had interrupted. By 'the end of next year' – meaning the end of 1812 – he hoped, 'everything will be settled at Madras'.[2] This must mean he had a good idea what he was going to do there.

He was welcomed back by a greeting crowd at Madras, and plunged immediately into the work that had to be done to administer the army of which he was Commander-in-Chief.[3] The contrast between the Java campaign – moving masses of troops at his order, dealing with temperamental Governors-General, commanding in battles, controlling difficult subordinates, writing long reports on his successes to the statesmen in Britain and India – and the trivial items he had to deal with in India was certainly a change, but was also possibly comforting in its pettiness and detail, and certainly much less strenuous. The Indian work was in fact what he had been sent to do, and though he was a competent, if unshowy, commander of troops in the field, his real expertise, demonstrated from the time he became adjutant of the

45th Foot back at Nottingham in 1778, was military administration. At the same time the fact of his success in Java no doubt assisted him in exerting his authority in India.

He had been planning a tour of his command when he was diverted to the Java campaign, and now he undertook a wide examination of conditions. There is no itinerary of his movements surviving, but there is evidence in the administrative measures he took that he visited Seringaptam, and was at Cannanore.[4] He travelled by ship at least part of the way, which suggests that he sailed round from Madras to the west coast; this would permit visits to the several towns and garrisons all round southern India, including troubled Travancore.[5]

He also visited, in the district of Bellary, the ancient imperial capital of Vijayanagar (now the village of Hampi). It is called in the record 'the temple at Byzenuggar', and there he made a donation to the temple of the 'Veenpatatee pagoda'.[6] This is presumably the Vishnupaksha temple, one of the most notable buildings still standing on the site; such a donation – a hundred pagodas, about £40 – was not insignificant, and would no doubt be welcomed and remembered by the local priests and the inhabitants of what was by then only a village; the gift was also later approved by the Bengal government.[7] (Auchmuty was, of course, using public funds for his donation.) It was a notable gesture by a man who was a staunch and active Anglican, and may be taken as a clear statement of his attitude in the continuing dispute in British India over the activities of Christian missionaries, which had been stirring up trouble and resistance among the sepoys. The fact that it was approved at the highest government level also implies governmental dislike of the missionaries' work. As a commander-in-chief he had no doubt about the apprehensions of the Indian soldiers that they were being compelled to become Christian; it was one of the complaints of the Vellore mutineers. It is also curious that Auchmuty should apparently oppose the missionaries, for his father had been, in his own way, a missionary in New York.

Auchmuty is not recorded to have visited any other place on this tour, but if he went to the places we know about – Seringapatam in the south in Mysore, Cannanore on the Malabar coast, Vijayanagar in the border of Hyderabad, well inland – he will have visited much of the territory under his command. It may also be that he visited Jalna in the northern corner of Hyderabad, though the evidence is unspecific: he gave permission for the erection of a temporary barracks there, which would not necessarily require his personal inspection. Jalna, however, had been one of the most active of the mutinous stations, and a visit by the Commander-in-Chief would be salutary.[8] A recommendation that a prison be constructed at Bangalore in Mysore may also indicate that this town was on his route; he had of course been in this area twenty years before during his first time in India.[9]

This sort of tour was perhaps unusual for a Commander-in-Chief, at least one quite so extensive. Such a man could all too easily find himself swamped in administrative detail and so be pinned down to his headquarters. Hay McDowell, for example, confined his visits to garrisons such as Masulipatam, and only then to rant about the iniquities of Sir George Barlow and his government. But for Auchmuty, in the aftermath of the mutiny and following his absence from the command for several months on the Java campaign, such a series of visits was the best way of reminding the still disgruntled officers of the authority which he wielded. His accomplished victories in Java must also have helped. The visits also enabled him to investigate one of the recurring issues in the Indian Army, the relations between the Indian rank-and-file and the European officers, a matter he returned to later.

Auchmuty, despite his position as Commander-in-Chief with a seat on the Governor's Council, and the prestige of a victory in Java, could not always ensure that anything he wished to do would get done; the army was in essence a huge bureaucratic organisation, whose clerks were adept at delaying matters. Any matter of substance – that is, anything involving spending any money – had to be approved after investigation and discussion by the bureaucracy in Calcutta. This applied even to comparatively small items, though it is notable that a distinct generosity might apply when the Governor-General was involved. Auchmuty learned quickly how to deal with the problem, but a fair number of his proposals were rejected, and others took so long to be accepted that he had left India long before their implementation.

He had to deal with several other continuing aftermaths of the events of the mutiny. The suppression of the trouble in Travancore produced a request from Colonel St Leger to participate in the distribution of prize money.[10] This seems to have been evaded rather than directly refused – his complaints were, after all, one of the main causes of the trouble – by making a distribution of 100,000 pagodas (about £40,000) among the troops employed, out of the wealth captured in the campaign, instead of a distribution of prize money.[11] The stores captured were valued at 138,000 pagodas, so the Company clearly profited by its unusual decision.

A report on the Travancore troubles was produced about this time, though it cannot have revealed more than was already known. The detail will have put the final mark on St Leger's record, though Auchmuty attached a minute to the report insisting that discipline in the offending units needed to be restored.[12] The matter was complex, involving a mutiny against the Travancore king, which was put down by Company forces. One result was the execution of the captured leader (though the real leader had committed suicide) and twenty-two soldiers. The difference between the treatment of the Travancore mutineers and that of the Madras Army officers can be explained by the fact that the former initially fought; but it is just as likely to be a result of their being Indian.[13]

Repairs which had already been authorised for the fortifications of Seringapatam were also cancelled.[14] This was no doubt in view of the use which had been made of that fortress by the mutineers. Colonel Bell, cashiered and dismissed, was still able to claim for allowances during the time he was in command at the town, even though he was participating in the mutiny.[15] Officers dismissed as mutineers were to be given passage money to Britain; at least this would ensure that they left India.[16]

The dispatches Auchmuty and Minto had sent to London arrived in January 1812 – they must have gone by the overland route to go so quickly – and produced another vote of thanks for Auchmuty in both Houses of Parliament. The Patriotic Fund added a medal to the plate they had given him for Montevideo. The Company also presented him with a service of plate. Less tangible was an advance in the ranks of the Order of the Bath, to a supernumerary knight. He was installed by proxy on 1 June, his proxy being his nephew John Maxwell Tylden, who thus, as had Auchmuty himself back in 1803, became himself a knight. Tylden had been his aide in India and Java (and in South America), and it was he who had carried his dispatches to London. As was usual in such circumstances he was given promotion to a brevet majority. He then went on to serve in the Peninsula for the next two years.[17]

Auchmuty had to supervise the distribution of prize money. That which had been realised from the capture of Seringapatam at the close of the last

Mysore War in 1799 was still being dealt with, after more than ten years; General Harris was paid £31,000 in 1811; the Company soon after declared that distribution complete.[18] The distribution of the Java prize money was only just beginning, and went on for over twenty years, though the first payments were made in February 1812. It is not clear what amount Auchmuty received, but Gillespie collected two large payments amounting to £6,000.[19] (Gillespie's share was increased because he was left in command in Java after Auchmuty left, and he conducted several lucrative campaigns, but Auchmuty received the commanding general's share of a quarter.) Major Travers of the 22nd Light Dragoons received £2,364; captains in that regiment £286, and lieutenants £124; sergeants received £89 and the private soldiers – that is, the Europeans – received £9.[20] It would seem therefore that Auchmuty's share would be something in the region of £6,000. It is also said that Minto acquired almost ¼ million pounds as a result of his time as Governor-General.[21] This figure will have included not only his salary, and any expenses he could claim, but also his share of prize from both the Mauritius and Java campaigns, though even all this would scarcely bring him £250,000 – he must have 'acquired' more by other means. India was still the lucrative source of great fortunes, even if not quite so obviously and publicly as in the days of Robert Clive. And it may be added, since this is a biography of Auchmuty, that he had gathered one useful fortune already in India in the 1790s, another from Egypt in 1801–3, and one from South America.

As another example of the possibilities of monetary gain in the East, there is the award of 4,000 rupees (about £400) to Captain Elliott of the *Modeste* frigate for the expenses involved in conveying Auchmuty and Minto to and from Java. He would need to provide accommodation, and a more than usually rich table for his presumably fastidious passengers, and it was for the expenses involved in this that he was now claiming. The payment, it may be noted, must have been at least in part authorised by Minto himself, to his own son.[22] It also seems extremely generous.

Several items connected with the Java campaign had to be dealt with from India. General Wetherall had lost some personal kit when the storeship *Chichester* had been wrecked in the storm at Madras on 2 May; compensation was awarded.[23] A shipowner whose ship was wrecked at Masulipatam while loading stores for the expedition, presumably in the same storm, was also compensated. Auchmuty reminded regiments that native Indians who had died or who had lost dependants on the voyage should be compensated, and by this he meant not merely soldiers but their dependants and servants as well; that a reminder was necessary was surely troubling.[24]

Auchmuty also had a number of new problems which had to be dealt with in India. He entered delicately into the issue of the uniforms of the Indian soldiers, but went no further than recommending a change of colour from red to blue. This was rejected by the Company on grounds of expense, though it may also have been a nervous response in memory of the results at Vellore of Cradock's and Bentinck's disastrous last interference with soldiers' dress and adornment. Auchmuty apparently dropped the subject, though one cannot believe he had not investigated the soldiers' attitudes towards such a change before making a suggestion official. The refusal was later reversed, and the colour was changed.[25]

There was a suggestion that elephants as beasts of burden could be replaced by camels, a matter which had to be considered and investigated.[26] The government of Ceylon made a claim for the cost of equipment supplied to the Java expedition.[27] Allowances of *batta* for overseas service had to be decided; five units of Native Infantry were allowed two months' *batta*. In addition the commander of the British forces in Goa was to be granted 'superior' *batta*.[28] The Dutch prisoners of war who had been collected in India before the expedition set off, and those who had been sent there from Java, asked to be returned to Java, and, once the fighting had been ended there, and Raffles' government seemed to be more or less stable (though it was Raffles' own reports which claimed it to be so), they were allowed to return.[29] A lieutenant was sent to Baghdad as an agent for acquiring Arabian horses for the cavalry, since horses did not breed in the southern Indian climate.[30]

Allowances for equipment and clothing for the dragoon regiments had to be decided. This was exactly the sort of problem which had sparked the discontent leading to the 'White Mutiny'. It was not actually tentage in this case, but the colonels of the regiments appear to have controlled the funds, and it was difficult to get them to render believable accounts. Auchmuty remarked on the great expense which was expected to be incurred as a result of the suggested allowances which were now being claimed, and it seems that the suggestions were refused, though an allowance was certainly made for repairs to equipment. It is also clear that pointing out the expense of the change, as he did here, was almost guaranteed to bring its rejection by the Company; presumably what he was really after was the allowance for repairs; it looks very much as though Auchmuty was playing the bureaucracy at its own game in this instance. Eventually, after Auchmuty had left India, the Company decided that this amounted in some way to a double allowance, and wondered if Auchmuty's regulation on the matter should stand.[31] It was clearly just as difficult to cancel an allowance as it was to institute one – the tentage controversy was exactly that sort of problem; for a bureaucratic organisation the Company was hardly well organised or efficient. These petty details were the necessary work of the Commander-in-Chief in a bureaucratic empire such as that of the Company in India, but the bureaucratic expenses were not spared. Every detail was recorded on expensive paper, in large expansive handwriting, occupying a large space for only a few words, and bound into fat volumes of documents.

But there were also rather more soldierly activities to be undertaken. A group of *pindaris* (light horsemen from central India, regarded as bandits, at least by the Company) made raids into the Ellora district of the Marathas and had to be repelled since they threatened a Company ally.[32] Auchmuty also had to deal with a 'disturbance' at Vizagapatam in the Sarkar region. It was apparently some sort of raid from the interior, very like that of the *pindaris*.[33] These raids were no doubt stimulated by the news of the white officers' mutiny, and by the absence in Java of a large part of the Madras Army. The garrison of Dindigul had to be brought out due to sickness, and then allowed to return.[34]

A dispute developed between Auchmuty and Henry Russell, the new Resident in Hyderabad, over which of them had the authority to give orders to the Hyderabad Subsidiary Force.[35] No doubt Auchmuty was unwilling, given that Force's participation in the mutiny, to agree to any reduction in his authority. He was, no doubt, also reluctant to see a civilian given authority over a military force, not to mention maintaining the general principle that a Commander-in-Chief should exercise command over all his forces. (Colonel Montresor was still the commander at Secunderabad; his relationship to Auchmuty may well have helped smooth things over.) Russell was undoubtedly corrupt: he began his Residency with no more than £500; he had an annual salary of £3,400; he took home, after nine years, a fortune of £85,000. Keeping the Subsidiary Force out of Russell's sticky and greedy hands was clearly necessary. It took the Company nine years to understand his corrupt ways; it is probable that Auchmuty understood him much more quickly.[36]

Inevitably Auchmuty was particularly concerned with the condition of the troops of his army and their equipment. An inspection of the corps of artillery led him to conclude that it was short of both officers and men, and he recommended a reform, and he also recommended an increase in the numbers of the horse artillery. (The artillery had been conspicuously loyal in the mutinies in Bengal in Abercromby's time, and had not been at all involved in the Madras mutiny; it clearly made sense to strengthen it.) He also suggested that bullocks should be replaced by draught horses in other artillery units – bullocks, though strong, were slow, and moved at less than half the speed of the draught horses, and they also required much more fodder. In this connection he also wanted more veterinary officers to be recruited by the Company in Britain.[37] He found that there was only one Rifle Corps battalion in his region, and recommended that a second be raised. Separately, he recommended that machinery be used to produce equipment and carriages for the Indian cavalry units.[38]

He was solicitous of the well-being of the Indian soldiers, and this was shown in many details of his work. He clearly understood that they had been the main victims of the mutiny – the punishment of the Travancore mutineers took place after he had left India – and in several minor acts he showed his sympathies with them. The opposition he showed to the activities of Christian missionaries and the gift to the temple at Hampi were surely well known, as was perhaps his suggested change of uniform colour, especially as he had probably discussed the matter with the soldiers. A pension was awarded to the families of those sepoys killed at Seringapatam during the mutiny, a clear criticism of the European officers who had involved their men in affairs between officers and between officers and the government.[39] In Java he had been careful to use both Indian and European soldiers in the fighting at Cornelis, and in the pursuit of Janssens. There they had been working jointly together, and thereby no doubt he hoped to build, or rebuild, a joint *esprit de corps* and mutual regard. But he was also conscious that leaving a garrison for a long time in a single station was likely to produce lassitude, boredom, and discontent, and therefore inefficiency, and he made a very strong recommendation that there was great advantage to be had in frequently changing the postings of the various units.[40] (This would apply also, of course, to the European officers, and such moves would break up, or at least weaken, any inter-unit links such as had contributed so strongly to the mutiny.)

On a more personal and unit level he condemned the practice of the detention of pay for native officers while they were on furlough, a recommendation which was subsequently accepted.[41] It seems that it was the colonels, once again, of the regiments who held onto the money, only paying it out once the men on furlough had returned to duty. The assumption was that the men might not return, but it was also a clear example of the mistrust existing (and growing) between European officers and the native troops. Six years after the Battle of Assaye in 1805, the native troops who had taken part in that battle were to be given silver and copper badges in commemoration, while their units were also to be presented with honorary standards because of their participation, something which could have been done years before.[42]

Auchmuty also instituted the usual minor experiments in creating new units and establishing new garrisons. Any alert commander-in-chief would enjoy promoting such notions. He had already made investigations into the cavalry and the artillery. Now a 'Carnatic European Veteran Battalion' was formed out of European invalids and retired soldiers in Madras and the surrounding area. Auchmuty investigated this, and perhaps promoted it. He stressed the advantages there were in having such a unit under his hand – and in Madras, a turbulent city; he decided that the expense involved was not great enough to be a serious objection, though how far the bureaucracy agreed with this is not clear.[43] The headquarters at Fort St George had repairs authorised, and the new camp which had been begun by Barlow near Madras in the time of the mutiny continued to be developed; several building works were planned and promised.[44] Lieutenant Colonel McLeod was authorised to develop a light infantry unit recruited from the Indian regiments. This was to be called a 'corps', though it is not clear how large it was intended to be. It was to be formed out of a number of other Indian battalions, but it soon became evident that the problems of language and differing customs and food requirements were insuperable. Calling in groups of soldiers from different battalions, each of which was usually recruited from single-language populations, would mix up men with a variety of 'languages, peoples, and habits', as Auchmuty put it. This seems to have been an initiative originally of Minto's, but Auchmuty pointed to the insuperable difficulties, and the initiative thereby failed.[45] It may have been the failure of this scheme which led Auchmuty to recommend an extra Rifle battalion, which would serve much the same purpose as the light infantry battalion suggested by Minto and Colonel McLeod, but it would be staffed by European soldiers. The Company (and the later Raj) was always nervous about imparting greater skills to Indian soldiers.

It is not always clear exactly when any of these items were discussed or recommended or accepted, though the major part of this work clearly took place within the Presidency after Auchmuty's return from Java. The precise dates of any particular item do not really matter, since Auchmuty remained in India only a little over a year after his return from Java, and the processes took at least months, and in some cases years, to work through the system in each case: of recommendation, consideration, discussion, and decision – and then the decision was usually further discussed and could be reversed later. Most of Auchmuty's recommendations and suggestions were only decided one way or another after his departure. Some of the measures discussed in this chapter probably originated in the few months Auchmuty had available before he went off on the Java expedition, and the complexity and detail that he attended to in so many cases suggests strongly that he was thinking about all these details during that expedition. His work on the improvement of the Madras Army was therefore necessarily a matter of small incremental improvements and changes, rather than great reforming gestures, but it was probably all the more effective and lasting for that reason. One can see that he may well have been annoyed at being compelled to participate in the Java expedition when he had just got properly involved in the work which he had been sent to India to do.

The comment Auchmuty had made in the letter to Dundas on 2 September 1811 about feeling less energetic than before, he followed up with a letter to the Company submitting his resignation. He must have known this would take time to be acted on. The Directors considered the matter in January and February 1812 – he had written in September or October, and so almost as soon as he had returned to Java, and on 19 February they voted to appoint Lieutenant General Sir John Abercromby, the current Commander-in-Chief at Bombay, to take Auchmuty's place. But then there was also the question of the replacement of Minto and Barlow to be selected and appointed. This appears to have held up any change of the army command until all three posts were settled – and meanwhile the governor of the Bombay Presidency, Jonathan Duncan, died in the middle of the process and so he had to be replaced as well; the replacement of Auchmuty by Abercromby therefore took months to implement.

Minto was recalled, with some reluctance on his part, and his fellow Scot Lord Moira was chosen to replace him as Governor-General. It proved difficult to decide on Barlow's replacement at Madras, but eventually General Abercromby was appointed as acting Governor, so that both Barlow and Auchmuty could leave. The Directors then became enmeshed in a controversy over Barlow's replacement by Abercromby, some of them feeling that Abercromby need not be replaced in Bombay after all but that the governor should be Commander-in-Chief as well. In the end, however, Minto's younger brother, Hugh Elliot, who had some colonial administrative experience as Governor of the Leeward Islands, was chosen as a compromise.[46]

Before he left India for Britain Auchmuty spent some time writing the required reports on the condition of the Madras Army. One of these took the form of two circular letters which he produced for the information of the senior officers.[47] The first addressed the commanding officers of divisions and was concerned exclusively with drawing attention to the need for improved relations between the European officers and the Indian rank-and-file. He drew on his memories of service in his first time in India between 1783 and 1797 as a junior officer at regimental level, but also as one who had also risen steadily through the officers' ranks to commander-in-chief, all without purchasing his way up. He now had had the experience of a new period in India fifteen years later, and he was not pleased with the changes he had detected.

He stated that it was a necessity that 'feelings of mutual confidence and respect' should exist between officers and men. Without such mutuality the army could not function. (That such a point needed to be made rather suggests that such feelings did not always exist.) He pointed to the fact that the officers had to 'honour the prejudices of religion', which was a clear criticism of the attitude of superiority adopted by Christians, and aligned him on the side of those who opposed Christian evangelism in India. This indeed was one of the constant fears of the soldiers, that the Company intended to convert them forcibly to Christianity; his attitude had all the more force in that he was personally a devout Anglican. Auchmuty was blunt in pointing out the danger of a situation in which the officers too often shared a 'careless and not infrequently contemptuous' attitude to the religious feelings and practices of the men. But he went further, drawing attention to the distancing of the officers from the personal concerns of the men which had been a feature of the Indian regiments during his earlier term in India. As a particular case he instanced the old practice of enquiring of men about the condition of the families they had left at their homes, a practice which was apparently no longer common.

Several times he commented that the decay in the relationship which he was describing was likely to result in 'the most fatal consequences', '(which cannot be too often repeated)'. The mutiny at Vellore was clearly the fatal consequence being referred to, but he also had in mind the 'White Mutiny' he had come out to India to smoothe over, not to mention the Travancore mutiny. The behaviour of the officers in involving some of their men in their mutiny, on the side of the defiance of the Company government, was exactly the issue which he was identifying as crucial and damaging.

The second letter he produced drew attention to the problems inherent in the recruitment of Muslims, especially in the period following the conquest of Mysore. 'The conquest of Mysore, and the subsequent assumption of the Carnatic, threw a large body of Mussulmans, both civil and military, out of employ and the country swarmed with discontented men.' Some of these men joined the Company's army, he pointed out, but many of them 'were really the bitterest of enemies', and their enmity continued; again a danger of mutiny clearly existed among those the Company had recruited; those discontented men might be persuaded to join in any uprising. And yet the obvious alternative, recruiting Hindus, to balance or outnumber the Muslims, required 'the greatest delicacy' in selecting such men, while at the same time it was necessary to 'curb the recommendations of the young officers of companies in favour of Mussulmans', so that 'in course of time we may thus hope to see in the ranks of the native army … sufficient (Hindus) to remove the apprehension of Muhammadan intrigue'. Again he emphasised the need for the improvement 'of the European officers' deportment to the natives'.

He was here identifying the essence of the problem the Company faced in controlling a mercenary army which was composed of so many different races and religions, and who in many cases were mutually hostile. He was identifying the issue which lay at the root of the series of mutinies by Indian soldiers during the next four decades, and which culminated in the great rebellion of 1857–8. It indicates clearly enough that Auchmuty had understood the causes of the recent mutinies both at Vellore – the Muslim involvement – and among the European officers, and the problem of the requirement that the European officers were crucial to the continued control of India by the Company. The relationships of the officers with their men were at the heart of the army's success, but they were also at the heart of its problems. The officers, especially the newly recruited men from Britain, were often infused with feelings of superiority, as though the conquest of India by the Company had been accomplished by British arms, and not by an army largely composed of Indian soldiers. They must identify more closely with their men, he insisted, for unless they did so that relationship would ultimately decay, leaving the officers unable to command the men, and the men increasingly liable to disobedience and mutiny. At the same time, it was necessary that the officers and the government be united, since division between these two authorities could rot the Company's basis of control.

Auchmuty had done his best, in the two years he had held the Madras command, to remove the causes of the officers' discontent and to bring them back to unity with the government. In this he was assisted by Barlow's resolute attitude, by his victories in command in Java, and to some extent by Minto's benign if distant interventions. All this was despite what he clearly felt was the unnecessary distraction of the Java war. But he was clear that more needed to be done, and that the dangers continued to be real.

Auchmuty left India on 6 March 1813, Abercromby already being in India and able to take over at Madras. He reached England in August and found that he had become a lieutenant general in the army in June (as opposed to holding that as a local rank for the India command and the Java expedition). In January 1815 when Admiral Sir Samuel Hood's death created a vacancy, he was promoted to Knight Grand Cross in the Order of the Bath.[48] But the aftermath of the Java expedition followed him home.

Chapter 11

Britain and Ireland, 1813–22

Auchmuty returned to Britain in August 1813 to receive the honours and rewards due to a victorious soldier noted in the last chapter. He soon became involved in a controversy over the allocation of prize money from the Java expedition, and, at the same time, had to fend off criticism of his administration in Madras which had been published in a pamphlet before he arrived home.

The pamphlet had been produced by Lieutenant Colonel Agnew, who had been one of Minto's men, and who had been Adjutant General in Madras and of the Java expedition. He had also been involved rather equivocally in the mutiny of the officers in 1809, and seems to have almost immediately taken against Auchmuty because of the work he was doing to eliminate so far as possible the causes of the mutiny, and because of Auchmuty's publicly stated support for the government of Barlow. He had been sent to Britain with the dispatches from both Minto and Auchmuty (Tylden had taken other copies) when the Java expedition in its military phase had ended. He had occupied the time between his arrival and that of Auchmuty in producing his pamphlet of criticism.

As soon as he knew of the criticism Auchmuty got a copy and wrote a detailed refutation, which has ended up, curiously, in the Wellesley papers in the British Library. It is dated 23 October 1813, so that, since he only arrived home in August, he must have set to work on it within a few days of landing. Presumably his answer was convincing, since no more was heard of the matter.[1]

At least some of his recommendations to the East India Company had their effect in India House. As an example, the terms of service of the European soldiers in India had long been various and unclear, which meant that in many cases, once they were in the army, the soldiers were in effect there for life. Auchmuty recommended that after twelve years' service, a soldier should be given a bounty, and after another five years he should have the option of either being discharged or to re-enlist. Tactfully he made no recommendation as to pay, a matter which would undoubtedly raise the hackles of the commercial men among the Directors, but the notion of a bounty implies that he certainly considered the soldiers' pay to be too low. Pay also varied between the three Presidencies, and this had been one of the minor elements in the mutiny of 1809.[2]

On the question of the Java prize money the problem lay in Stopford's intervention and his subsequent claim to be a Commander-in-Chief, which Auchmuty claimed as his position; this would entitle Stopford to a much larger share than if he was simply taking part, and would significantly reduce what everyone else, including Auchmuty, received. Various attempts were made to fiddle the figures, including a comparison between the shares allocated to the Duke of Wellington in Spain and those to Auchmuty for Java. This took a good deal longer to sort out than Agnew's accusations, since it was a legal and financial matter, and involved several consultations and a good deal of politicking as well. Auchmuty may or may not have succeeded in carrying his point, but it is likely that he gained an increase in the payment which was originally assigned to him.

In the course of the correspondence and argument on the subject Auchmuty made a point which is relevant to this whole account of his life. He observed that 'in the opinion of some persons, unacquainted with a real state of fact … he [Auchmuty] has been held as the ostensible, but not the real conductor of the expedition to Java. He has been informed that the success of the expedition has been attributed by some to the presence of Lord Minto, and by others to the officers under his command' – by this he meant Gillespie at Fort Cornelis and Gibbs at the assault at Jati Ngaleh, and was probably the story being put about by Agnew and Major Thorn – and perhaps by Minto, who was good at assuming credit due to others. Auchmuty then went on to emphasise in detail that Minto had had nothing to do with any of the actual operations, and if he made a suggestion it was not accepted. (Minto had arrived in Britain before Auchmuty, and no doubt had noised it abroad that he personally had conquered Java.) Similarly Gillespie 'had proposed various plans, which Sir Samuel Auchmuty did not think prudent to adopt,' and Gibbs had opposed fighting at Jati Ngaleh. He sums up by stating, unusually emphatically for him, and using the third person, that

> Sir Samuel Auchmuty himself planned the combined movements, determined on the force to be appropriated to them, directed the movement of each separate attack, and, when the whole of the infantry had gained the works, opened the passage for the cavalry and guns without which a principal part of the enemy must have escaped. Sir Samuel Auchmuty himself followed the remnant of the enemy, again brought them to action, contrary to the opinion of an officer then next in command on the spot … and, after defeating, forced them to capitulation.[3]

It may be pointed out that a careful examination of the events in Java fully bears out Auchmuty's annoyed assertions; it may also be noted that few historians have taken note of his precise activities; indeed, none has cited the words in this published account, being enamoured of Minto, of Gillespie's violence, and of Raffles' dishonesty. That is, the false claims by Minto and Gillespie have been accepted all too readily. Auchmuty's insistence on leaving Java to pursue his real work in India, which Minto had dragged him away from, had therefore left the field open to these misrepresentations. The prize-money account with documents was published in 1816, so the dispute had dragged on for three years, and while it was being argued, Auchmuty was effectively in retirement. In 1817 he gave up Syndale House and moved to a rectory at Milton-next-Sittingbourne, which he rented from the Canterbury Cathedral Chapter, and where he lived with his nephew Sir John Maxwell Tylden – knighted after being Auchmuty's Bath proxy – who had returned intact from the last stages of the Peninsular War.[4] Auchmuty appears not to have solicited further employment – though there were, of course, few enough opportunities in the years of peace and retrenchment after 1815.

He was, however, available when required, and in 1821 he was nominated as the next Commander-in-Chief in Ireland. He was to succeed his former commander General Sir David Baird, who was no longer in good health. It would seem that Auchmuty, though by this time 64 years old, was considered both a safe pair of political hands and in good enough health to do the job for the two or three years which was the usual period of the appointment. He was appointed in June 1822 and when Baird suffered an accident in falling off his horse, and could not continue, Auchmuty took over in Dublin in August. It may well have been the case that Auchmuty was politically sound from the government's point of view, for he was a noted Anglican; but the second possible qualification – his health – was mistaken. He went riding in Phoenix Park on 19 August 1822, almost as soon as he had arrived. On the ride he had 'a fit of apoplexy' – presumably either a heart attack or a stroke – and died on the spot.

He was buried, most suitably, in Christ Church Cathedral Dublin, with a rather splendid, if wordy, monument over his tomb. (That of Sir Denis Pack, his colleague in South America, is nearby.) The length of the inscription rather suggests that it was felt necessary to say what he had done; he had not the flair for publicity, or the taste for it, which is considered necessary for some generals to succeed.

He left his moderate wealth to a variety of male relatives, with Sir John Maxwell Tylden as his executor.

The outburst in his 'Claim', insisting on his achievements in Java, and that the claims of Minto, Gillespie, and Gibbs to appropriate these achievements were false, is one of the few personal statements Auchmuty ever made. And yet his career indicates clearly that, while generating publicity did not appeal to him, and so did not enhance his public reputation, as it did with other generals and admirals, his superiors clearly appreciated his capabilities. But, apart from the inscription on his tomb, there are few notices of his achievements.

It had been, to be sure, a curious life. Driven from his home by the American rebels who were his neighbours, he joined an army which sent him to all continents except the one he came from. He kept in touch with the scattered members of his family, not only those in Kent, but those in the United States as well. Many of those in Britain included men who were involved in the fighting which continued throughout his adult life – Tylden in southern France, Captain William Howe Mulcaster in the navy in action on Lake Ontario in 1813, Commander Henry Montresor, also RN, in action at New Orleans in 1814– 15, and so on; several of his Tucker relatives served in India. In his military achievements he could count two considerable conquests, Montevideo and Java, and three successful military administrations: in Egypt, Kent, and the Madras Presidency, rather more than most generals could count.

The basis for all this was, first, his quiet religious convictions, then his education in New York, which seems to have been more effective and rigorous than anything which was available in the equivalent public schools in England. This gave him a flying start as an adjutant when he settled at Nottingham and was almost at once appointed to that position as a lieutenant in the 45th Foot. This then became the basis for several of his later appointments in military administration, by which he rose through the ranks. His abilities brought him to the notice of Lord Cornwallis, and to that of Sir Robert Abercromby in India – who became his friend – and presumably it was these senior men who recommended him to the Duke of York. Certainly the Duke knew of him while he was still in India, for he was quickly taken up by the Duke on his return for the independent expedition to Egypt which went from Britain round the Cape, with an appointment as Adjutant General in Baird's Indian expedition, a clear assertion of the priority to be assigned to British interests rather than those of the East India Company. On his return to England he was almost at once appointed to organise and command the defence of Thanet, which could have been crucial to victory if the French invasion had ever come.

But he was also clearly a generally agreeable man. Colonel Agnew may have taken against him in India, but this was clearly a political matter arising out of their disagreements over their attitudes to the Madras officers' mutiny. By contrast, there is no indication of any dispute with any other of his fellow officers. Macquarie was not pleased to miss his appointment as Adjutant-General of the Egyptian expedition, but he always over-estimated his own abilities, and an appointment by the Duke of York clearly trumped one from an Indian general or even a Governor-General. His reticence and quietness may well have assisted here, since that meant he was not competing with those others for public attention – Baird and Wellington were cases in point.

Then there was his religion. As an Anglican from birth to death, he was a member of a Church which tended to emphasise quiet devotion rather than noisy activism, and non-resistance (to political pressures) had been part of his father's attitude in politics in New York – not that it saved him. He was apparently unimpressed by the more assertive Evangelicalism which was developing in England; this was a reflection, of course, of the assertive nationalism of victorious (and Victorian) Britain in the nineteenth century. That Anglican attitude also made him politically reliable. If he was ever asked his politics, he would have claimed to be a Tory, no doubt. That there is no record of such an enquiry is, of course, part of his Anglican reticence.

This is, it seems, the rock of his basic beliefs, just as it was of the rest of his family. It is surely no accident that he was able to contact the Canterbury Chapter to rent a home, that his sister married an Anglican priest, that the members of his family were buried in an Episcopal cemetery in Newport Rhode Island, and that he himself has a substantial monument in Dublin's Anglican cathedral. The family inheritance was Anglican, all the way back to the time of the Scottish Revolution in the sixteenth century. It was bred in.

We know little or nothing about his personal life. He became fairly wealthy but not ostentatiously so, and he lived in a rented rectory at the end of his life. Whether he ever owned Syndale House, or simply rented it, is not clear. He accumulated some possessions – a sword, celebratory vase – but probably little in the way of furniture. He never married, and we have absolutely no information whatever about any of his relationships with women, other than affection for his sisters, particularly, it seems, for his youngest sister Jane. There is no indication that he had a 'bibi' to live with him in India.

So he had no posterity other than his nephews and more distant relatives. Further, on examination of his military achievements, they are seen to be curiously unproductive. He fought in North America, South America, Egypt, India, and Java; of these only his efforts during his first time in India, where he was under the command of others, remained as part of British possessions – the Third Mysore War, the Rohilla War. New York, his home, became part of the newly independent United States, and was then out of bounds for him as a serving British soldier; Montevideo was returned to Spanish rule after the defeat in Buenos Aires – for which he was not held responsible; Egypt was evacuated despite having been conquered; Java was returned to Dutch rule. Only in India, in Mysore and in the Rohilla country, was there territory which remained in British control – at one remove, of course, since it was the Company which held it – after Auchmuty had participated in their conquest. And yet later, Egypt was taken over by the British, British investments in Uruguay and Argentina were one of the bases of the prosperity of those countries, and reform in Java followed roughly the route chaotically laid out by Raffles after Auchmuty's conquest. It may well be that his most enduring accomplishment was the series of minor reforms he instituted in the Madras Army. This army was then no longer subject to mutiny, and remained loyal to the Company in the great rebellion of 1857–8. Had it joined the rebellion it is difficult to see that the British control of

India could have survived; at a considerable distance in time, Auchmuty's work may be said to have contributed to that outcome.

For a man whose military career could be claimed to be a success, the several evacuations and surrenders his work was subject to were presumably unpleasant for him to contemplate. To a man of his Anglican beliefs, and his intelligent reticence, however, they will have been quite understandable. He was a Loyalist in his homeland, and he remained a Loyalist towards Britain and its empire throughout his life, and that meant that he had to be loyal also to the decisions of his superiors and his rulers.

Notes

Introduction

1. *ODNB*, Sir Samuel Auchmuty; John D. Grainger (ed.), *The Royal Navy in the River Plate, 1806–1807* (Aldershot, 1996); John D. Grainger, *British Campaigns in the South Atlantic, 1805–1807* (Barnsley, 2015).
2. As an example, he does not appear in one of the most recent extensive discussions of the Loyalists, Maya Jasonoff's *Liberty's Exiles, the Loss of America and the Remaking of the British Empire* (London, 2011), despite the fact that his career fits precisely with her title and subtitle. Nor does he appear in any of the half-dozen books on Loyalists on my own bookshelves.

Chapter 1

1. Kenneth R. Dutton, *Auchmuty, The Life of John James Auchmuty* (Mount Nebo, Australia, 2000), 20; this is based on a manuscript written by J.J. Auchmuty, held by the family.
2. Dutton, *Auchmuty*, ch. 1.
3. The members of the family and their links to others are detailed by Annette Townshend, *The Auchmuty Family of Scotland and America* (New York, 1932), in her introduction; this source will be referred to as Townshend, *Auchmuty Family* henceforth.
4. Dutton, *Auchmuty*, 21.
5. M. Percival-Maxwell, *The Scottish Migration to Ulster in the Reign of James I* (New York, 1973).
6. John Childs, *The Williamite War in Ireland, 1688–1691* (London, 2007), 233, 330.
7. J.B. Leslie, *Armagh Clergy and Parishes* (Dundalk, 1911).
8. *Alumni Dublinenses* lists eight Auchmutys (of various spellings) at several dates in the eighteenth century; a detailed and elaborate account of the Irish family until about 1820 is in a document in the Norfolk Record Office, reference MC 34/306, 530XA.
9. There are Auchmutys still in Ireland – John James Auchmuty was one – but no longer in prominent positions; some no doubt fled from the Irish civil wars in 1919–23; as will be seen, this was no means the first of such flights.
10. V.C.P. Hodson, *Officers of the Bengal Army 1758–1834*, 4 vols (London, 1927–47).
11. *Register of Admissions to the Middle Temple*, vol. 1, 1705.
12. London Metropolitan Archive, City of London, Release of Indentures of Fine, ACC/0564/040 – 042.

13. Thomas Ely, *The Eternal Building … a sermon preached in Glass-house Street near St James's on Lord's Day, April 24, 1715 …* (London, 1715).
14. Townshend, *Auchmuty Family*, 20–1 – but Mrs Townshend has the name of his first wife as 'Clark', with no first name. She gives no information about his second wife except for her maiden name.
15. Ibid., 1–3.
16. George Arthur Wood, *William Shirley, Governor of Massachusetts 1741–1756, a History* (New York, 1920); John Shutz, *William Shirley, King's Governor in Massachusetts* (Chapel Hill NC, 1961).
17. One of the copies in the British library is attributed to a man calling himself 'Massachusettiensis'; the other copy bears Robert's name as author.
18. BL Add Mss. 32702, 320; quoted in Townshend, *Auchmuty Family*, 8–12.
19. Townshend, *Auchmuty Family*, 17–19 (for his will).
20. Ibid., 4, 12; *Dictionary of American Biography*, William Bollan; he produced several pamphlets as agent for the colony.
21. Townshend, *Auchmuty Family*, 22–3.
22. A brief biography is in Clifford K. Shipton, *New England Life in the Eighteenth Century* (Cambridge MA, 1963), 429–42; despite the all-encompassing title, this is a collection of biographies of Harvard men, and as such tends to the laudatory.
23. Townshend, *Auchmuty Family*, ch. 2.
24. For which see Fred Anderson, *Crucible of War, the Seven Years' War and the Fate of the Empire in British North America, 1754–1766* (New York, 2000).
25. Shipton, *New England Life*, 434–6.
26. Townshend, *Auchmuty Family*, 23–5; Shipton, *New England Life*; *Dictionary of American Biography*, Benjamin Pratt.
27. Robert M. Calhoun, *The Loyalists in Revolutionary America, 1760–1781* (New York, 1965), includes several essays on individual's problems, including one on 'Two Accommodating Clergyman: William Smith and Andrew Eliot' (147–58), and one on 'Colonial Anglicanism' (206–17), which unfortunately does not touch on Samuel Auchmuty (the elder).
28. Shipton, *New England Life*, 464–82 is a useful source, if rather too admiring; *Dictionary of American Biography*, Townshend, *Auchmuty Family*, ch. 3.
29. C. Ubbelohde, *The Vice-Admiralty Courts and the American Revolution* (Chapel Hill NC, 1960).
30. Oliver M. Dickerson (ed.), *Boston under Military Rule 1768–1769* (Boston MA, 1936), 58.
31. Hiller B. Zobel, *The Boston Massacre* (New York, 1970); Townshend, *Auchmuty Family*, 45–6.
32. 'A Dialogue between Sir George Cornwall, a Gentleman lately arrived from England … and Mr Flint'; see also Bernard Bailyn, *The Ordeal of Thomas Hutchinson, Loyalism and the Destruction of the First British Empire* (London, 1975), 128–30.
33. For the commissioners see gaspee.com (which is inaccurate, at least on Auchmuty); all of them were from England or in government service in

Boston; for Rhode Island, see David S. Lovejoy, *Rhode Island and the American Revolution, 1760–1776* (Providence RI, 1958), ch. 8 for the *Gaspee* incident.

34. Bailyn, *The Ordeal of Thomas Hutchinson* , 271–73.
35. *Copy of Letters sent to Great Britain …*; cf. Bailyn, *The Ordeal of Thomas Hutchinson* , 223–4.
36. Ubbelohde, *Vice-Admiralty Courts*.
37. Townshend, *Auchmuty Family*, 58, quoting the *New York Mercury* of 26 May 1766.
38. He sent regular reports on Church affairs in New York and America generally to England; these are preserved in the archives of Fulham Palace.
39. Carl Bridenbaugh, *Mitre and Sceptre, Transatlantic faiths, ideas, personalities, and politics, 1689–1775* (New York 1962), chs 9 and 10.
40. Ibid.; Arthur L. Cross, *The Anglican Episcopate and the American Colonies* (New York, 1902); the episcopate was eventually created by way of the Scottish Anglican Church, which ordained the required bishops.
41. *Dictionary of American Biography*; Montresor's Journal is in the New York Historical Society library.
42. Townshend, *Auchmuty Family*, 72, 75–8.
43. 'Dr Auchmuty's letter to Capt. Montresor …', New York, 19 April 1775, republished in the Early American Imprints, series I, no. 13818.
44. Patricia U. Bonomi, *Fraction People: Politics and Society in Colonial New York* (New York, 1971); Esmond Knight, 'The New York Loyalists, a Cross-Section of Colonial Society', in Robert A. East and Jacob Judd (eds), *The Loyalist Americans* (Tarrytown NY, 1975).

Chapter 2

1. Townshend, *Auchmuty Family*, 47, quoting the *Constitutional Gazette* (of New York), 3 July 1776.
2. Many documents he saved or generated are in TNA, AO 13/43, a file concerning Loyalist claims for compensation for losses.
3. Townshend, *Auchmuty Family*, 22–3, 82.
4. Ibid., 28–30.
5. Ibid., 54; Lorenzo Sabine, *Biographical Sketches of the Loyalists of the American Revolution*, 2 vols (Boston MA, 1864), vol. 1, 197.
6. Townshend, *Auchmuty Family*, 55; Arthur Wentworth Eaton, *The Growth of England in Nova Scotia* (New York, 1891).
7. For accounts of the experiences of the Loyalists see, apart from Sabine, *Biographical Sketches*: Claude Halstead Van Tyne, *Loyalists in the American Revolution* (Gansevoort, New York, 1902, repr. 1999; Christopher Moore, *The Loyalists, Revolution, Exile, Settlement* (Toronto, 1984); Phyllis R. Blakely and John N. Grant (eds), *Eleven Exiles, Accounts of Loyalists of the American Revolution* (Toronto, 1982) (these last concern Loyalists who moved to Canada); Simon Schama, *Rough Crossings, Britain, the Slaves, and the American Revolution* (London, 2005); and most recently, Maya Jasonoff, *Liberty's Exiles* (London, 2011).

8. The P-A Roots website on 'Robert Auchmuty M.D.', by William H. Egle, accessed 2003. Arthur Gates Auchmuty is identified as a son of Robert Auchmuty senior of Boston, but this is incorrect; the rest of the information in the article seems acceptable, however, being researched in Pennsylvania.
9. Townshend, *Auchmuty Family*, 90.
10. Ibid., 23 and ch. V.
11. For New York in the revolution see Barnett Schecter, *The Battle for New York, the City at the Heart of the American Revolution* (London, 2002) – though the subtitle ignores the fact the city was under British control almost the whole time; also Richard M. Ketchum, *Divided Loyalties, How the American Revolution came to New York* (New York, 2002).
12. This is based on the involvement of the son as a student at King's College, for Robert Nicholls had graduated in 1774; Richard and Samuel were still students in 1775.
13. Townshend, Auchmuty Family, 62–3, quoting from Wilkins Updike, James MacSparran and Daniel Goodwin, A *History of the Episcopalian Church at Narragansett Rhode Island, including a history of the other Episcopal churches in the state* (2nd edn, Boston MA, 1907), vol. 1, 167–8; allowance in all this must, of course, be made for Loyalist and Episcopalian partiality.
14. Paul David Nelson, *William Tryon and the Course of Empire, a Life in British Imperial Service* (Chapel Hill NC, 1990), ch. 8.
15. The campaign took several months, from the landing of troops in Staten Island in July to the capture of Fort Washington at the north end of Manhattan Island in November.
16. Townshend, *Auchmuty Family*, from Updike, MacSparran and Goodwin, A *History of the Episcopalian Church.*
17. Schecter, *Battle for New York*, ch. 14; the fire is variously attributed to the Loyalists or Rebels, depending on the political alignment of the authors: the British were adamant it was due to rebels, and said so as soon as the fire started.
18. 'A list of the general and staff officers … Serving in North America', 1779, in the Early American Imprints, series 1, 1639–1800.
19. *Dictionary of American Biography*, s.v. Samuel Auchmuty.
20. 'A list of the general and staff officers … serving in North America', 1779, reproduced in Early American Imprints, series 1, 1639–1800, 6; Richard Auchmuty is listed as one of twenty-seven hospital mates at the Royal Hospital. Townshend, *Auchmuty Family*, 73.
21. Robert A. East and Jacob Judd (eds), *The Loyalist Americans, a Focus on Greater New York* (Tarrytown NY, 1975), notably the essay 'The New York Loyalists, a Cross-Section of Colonial Society', by Esmond Wright, 74–94.
22. Townshend, *Auchmuty Family*, 98.
23. Schecter, *Battle for New York*, 126–203.
24. Townshend, *Auchmuty Family*, 98.
25. Ibid.; *Army List*, 1778.
26. Philip Hugh Dalbiac, *A History of the First Nottinghamshire Regiment (Sherwood Foresters)* (London, 1902).

27. John W. Jackson, *With the British Army in Philadelphia 1777–1778* (San Rafael CA, 1979); the Meschianza is in ch. 14.
28. Townshend, *Auchmuty Family*, 78–81; *ODNB*, Sir John Maxwell Tylden.
29. Townshend, *Auchmuty Family*, 78.
30. Jackson, *British Army in Philadelphia*, 54–8; Piers Mackesy, *The War for America 1775–1783* (Oxford, 1964).
31. Blake Davis, *The Campaign that Won America, the Story of Yorktown* (New York, 1970), 279–80.
32. Edward M. Riley, 'St George Tucker's Journal of the Siege of Yorktown, 1781', *William and Mary Quarterly*, 5 (1948).
33. The Tucker family's involvement in Bermuda can be followed in Wesley Craven, *An Introduction to the History of Bermuda* (Toronto, 1990). The American branch of the family is detailed in Stephen Hess, *American Political Dynasties* (Brunswick NJ, 1997), 365–92.
34. Brenton Kerr, *Bermuda and the American Revolution 1760–1783* (Princeton NJ, 1936).
35. Hess, American *Political Dynasties*, 369.
36. Ibid., 369–70.
37. *ODNB*, under these names.
38. Dalbiac, *A History of the First Nottinghamshire Regiment*, 12–13; H.L. Wylly, *The 1st and 2nd Battalions The Sherwood Foresters, 1st Nottinghamshire Regiment* (London, 1929), vol., 1, 90–4.
39. A summary is in Alan J. Guy, 'The Army of the Georges, 1714–1783', in *The Oxford History of the British Army* (Oxford, 1994), 92–111.
40. Edward E. Curtis, *The British Army in the American Revolution* (New Haven CT, 1926, repr. New York, 1998).
41. John Ellis, *The Social History of the Machine Gun* (London, 1975).
42. Wylly, *1st and 2nd Battalions The Sherwood Foresters* , vol. 1, 91.
43. Ibid.
44. Ibid., 92, quoting a letter from Lieutenant Hudson that 'the Regiment is now full'.
45. W.S. Morrison, *Historical Records of the 52nd Regiment* (London, 1860); Sir Henry Newbolt, *The Story of the Oxfordshire and Buckinghamshire Light Infantry* (London, 1915); Wikipedia, 'The Oxfordshire Light Infantry', accessed 12 July 2016.
46. WO 211/4, Harte's army list, 'Sir Samuel Auchmuty'.
47. *ODNB*, John Montresor.

Chapter 3

1. Muzaffar Alam, *The Crisis of Empire in Mughal North India, Awadd and the Punjab 1707–1748* (Oxford, 1986).
2. A useful set of documents generated in Britain over this problem is in P.J. Marshall, *Problems of Empire: Britain and India 1757–1813* (London, 1968).
3. See Herbert W. Richmond, *The Navy in India 1763–1783* (London, 1931, repr. 1993), 188–94, an example.

4. W.S. Morrison, *Historical Records of the 52nd Regiment … 1755–1858* (London, 1860).
5. A much contested issue, as is to be expected; the eventual Act was one of the first measures passed by William Pitt the Younger, the new Prime Minister, in 1784 – see Marshall, *Problems*, 120–37 and 157–71.
6. John Ehrman, *The Younger Pitt*, vol. 1 (London, 1969), 188–92; Marshall, *Problems*; T.A. Heathcote, *The Military in British India, the Development of British Land Forces in South Asia, 1600–1947* (Manchester, 1995, repr. Barnsley, 2013), is more concerned with the impact on the army in India, especially chs 2 and 3.
7. For Dundas see Michael Fry, *The Dundas Despotism* (Edinburgh, 1992).
8. For the personnel installed see Ehrman, *Younger Pitt*, vol. 1, 192–3.
9. Heathcote, *Military in British India*, 42.
10. Franklin and Mary Wickwire, *Cornwallis, the Imperial Years* (Chapel Hill NC, 1980), 8–18.
11. Townshend, *Auchmuty Family*, 101, points out that the family (in the 1930s) had letters from him, though it is not known where such letters are now; it is, therefore, only an assumption that he had any detailed news.
12. *ODNB*, Lord McCartney; it is curious that he was also employed as a diplomat; possibly he could rein in his temper on such occasions.
13. Heathcote, *Military in British India*, 39–40; Raymond Callahan, *The East India Company and Army Reform 1783–1798* (Cambridge MA, 1972), 40–2; Burgoyne was the cousin of the Burgoyne defeated at Saratoga in 1777.
14. TNA PRO 30/11/15, Auchmuty to Cornwallis; a pagoda was a gold coin current in southern India, worth about 7 shillings: 200 were thus worth 70 pounds, a substantial sum for a lieutenant.
15. Pamela Nightingale, *Trade and Empire in Western India, 1784–1806* (Cambridge, 1970), 39–42.
16. Philip MacDougall, *Naval Resistance to Britain's Growing Power in India, 1660–1800, the Saffron Banner and that Tiger of Mysore* (Woodbridge, 2014), ch. 7.
17. This is criticised as 'racist' now, though the aim was control and reform, not exclusion.
18. For Cornwallis' actions see Wickwire, *Cornwallis*, chs 3–5, Callahan, *East India Company*, 65–78, and Heathcote, *Military in British India,* 43–5.
19. Townshend, *Auchmuty Family*, 99.
20. Callahan, *East India Company*, ch. 4, on the manoeuvring in London and Calcutta to produce these regiments.
21. M.H. Ellis, *Lachlan Macquarie, His Life, Adventures and Times* (2nd edn, Sydney, 1952), 14, quotes Macquarie, an officer in the 75th recruited in Scotland, as noting that 'Major Auchmuty came on board', as soon as the ship he was on arrived at Bombay.
22. *ODNB*, Robert Abercromby; *History of Parliament 1790–1820*, accessed online 28 August 1916.
23. Denys Forrest, *Tiger of Mysore, the Life and Death of Tipu Sultan* (London 1970), 120–2; Wickwire, *Cornwallis*, 126–7.
24. Forrest, *Tiger*, 123–5; Wickwire, *Cornwallis*, 127–8.
25. Wickwire, *Cornwallis*, 126–9.

26. Ibid., 129–31.
27. Ibid., 132–4; Medows was harassed more by Cornwallis' hectoring comments on his plan and his campaign than by the enemy, at least at first.
28. Forrest, *Tiger*, 152–3.
29. Wickwire, *Cornwallis*, 138, 150; *ODNB*, Robert Abercromby.
30. Wikipedia, 'Third Anglo-Mysore war', accessed 25 June 2017.
31. Next year a French frigate, *La Resolue*, was intercepted by the *Phoenix*, Captain Sir Richard Strachan, off Mahe, when Strachan aimed to inspect two French ships for 'contraband'; Commodore Sir William Cornwallis (the Earl's brother), the overall naval commander in the region, conducted the subsequent correspondence. Apologies followed, but the affair demonstrated that the British would not permit European interference in their Mysorean war: C. Northcote Parkinson, *War in the Eastern Seas 1793–1815* (London, 1954), 57–8.
32. Wickwire, *Cornwallis*, 140–50; Forrest, *Tiger*, 151–62.
33. BL, Mss Eur B 328, Auchmuty to Byron, 4 January 1792.
34. *ODNB*, John Byron; Wikipedia, John 'Mad Jack' Byron, accessed 4 June 2017.
35. Wickwire, *Cornwallis*, 154–70; Forrest, *Tiger*, 165–84.
36. I assume that Cornwallis, as a popular and conscientious commander, will have visited the wounded at Yorktown fairly regularly, and, like Abercromby, would surely have been struck by the younger Auchmuty's unusual surname.
37. For the process in London and the details of the plan see Callahan, *East India Company*, 104–51; also Heathcote, *Military in British India*, 45–6.
38. He was promoted to major by brevet on 30 April 1794, to substantive major on 7 September 1795, and to Lieutenant Colonel by brevet on 22 September 1795.
39. These are preserved in Macquarie's Letter Book, 1794–6, accessed on microfilm (M460) in the National Library of Australia, Canberra.
40. His work is not liked now, but the critics tend to adopt a lofty view in hindsight, which is a profoundly unhistorical procedure; shifting opinions and practices in the stodgy Company was a very difficult task.
41. Callahan, *East India Company*, 127–43.
42. Wikipedia, , accessed 25 June 2017; for events at Delhi in 1788 see William Dalrymple, *The Last Mughal*, London, 2006, 37.
43. Heathcote, *Military in British India,* 36; for a convenient account of the First Rohilla War and its repercussions see Keith Feiling, *Warren Hastings*, London, 1954, ch. 10.
44. The campaign can be followed in the summaries of correspondence in BL IOR/H/577, which contains summaries of Auchmuty's regular reports.
45. Callahan, *East India Company*, 152–3 gives it a (very) brief notice, but accepts the exaggerated casualty figures and claims that 'Abercromby's fight was a bloody, inconclusive, and badly handled engagement', none of which is accurate.
46. Macquarie Letter Book, Macquarie to Auchmuty, cantonment near Calicut, 1 March 1795.
47. Callahan, *East India Company*, 152–9.
48. The following section is based on letters in Macquarie's Letter Book.
49. *Correspondence of Charles, First Marquis Cornwallis*, ed. Charles Ross, 3 vols (London, 1859), vol. 1, 225–6, Cornwallis to Duke of York, 10 March 1787.
50. BL IOR H/450.

51. Shore to Dundas, 26 August 1795, quoted in Callahan, *East India Company*, 160.
52. H.G. Keene, *Hindustan under Free Lances, 1770–1820* (London, 1907, repr. Shannon, Ireland, 1792), 55.
53. Herbert Compton (compiler), *A Particular Account of the European Military Adventurers of Hindustan from 1784 to 1803* (London, 1892), 92.
54. The measures are detailed in Callahan, *East India Company*, 171– 3; see also Compton, *A Particular Account*, 86–7.
55. Callahan, *East India Company*, 176–81; the three colonels all were soon promoted but removed: Brisco died a major general in Calcutta in 1802, Forbes retired to Scotland in that rank in 1797; Popham became a major general in 1796 and commanded the Bengal Brigade which took part in the Fourth Mysore War; he lived on until 1821.
56. Ibid., 174–5; F.G. Cardew, *A Sketch of the Services of the Bengal Army* (Calcutta, 1903), 66.
57. Cornwallis had been due to return as Governor-General, but his appointment was delayed by the government's preoccupation with first the matter of the army reform, then the naval mutinies in 1797, and then by rebellion in Ireland, which became Cornwallis' next job instead of India: Callahan, *East India Company*, 200–6.
58. It receives a single misleading paragraph in Vincent Smith, *The Oxford History of India* (3rd edn, Oxford, 1958), 550. Richard Holmes, *Sahib, the British Soldier in India* (London, 2005), 53–4, at least puts *batta* at the heart of the problem; Philip Mason, *A Matter of Honour, an Account of the Indian Army, its Officers and Men* (London, 1974), 170, allotted it half a sentence.

Chapter 4

1. *ODNB*, Sir David Baird; Theodore H. Hook, *The Life of General Rt Hon. Sir David Baird* (London, 1832. Townshend, *Auchmuty Family*, 101, assumes that Auchmuty reached England during 1797, but the length of the voyage and the regimen of the monsoon indicates a later arrival.
2. Townshend, *Auchmuty Family*, 50.
3. David Chandler, *The Campaigns of Napoleon* (London, 1966), 205–52; Tom Pocock, *A Thirst for Glory, the Life of Admiral Sir Sidney Smith* (London, 1996), 90–117; Nathan Schur, *Napoleon in the Holy Land* (London, 1999).
4. Forrest, *Tiger*, 241–3, 250–2.
5. The wider aspects of the French in Egypt are discussed by Edward Ingram in four articles under the general title 'The Geopolitics of the First British Expedition to Egypt', in *Middle Eastern Studies* 31 and 32 (1994–5).
6. Parkinson, *War in the Eastern Seas*, 139–40.
7. Piers Mackesy, *British Victory in Egypt, 1801, the End of Napoleon's Conquest* (London, 1995).
8. Parkinson, *War in the Eastern Seas*, 140–3.
9. Jac Weller, *Wellington in India* (London, 1972), ch. 4; the overall commander, General Harris, was the new owner of Belmont Park, which he had bought from the Montresors in 1787.

10. Parkinson, *War in the Eastern Seas*, 145–6.
11. An account from the French point of view of the bombardment at Cosseir in Captain Joseph-Marie Moiret, *Memoirs of Napoleon's Egyptian Expedition, 1798–1801*, trans. and ed. Rosemary Brindle (London, 2001), 119–20.
12. Ibid., 151–2.
13. Mackesy, *British Victory*, 67–77.
14. It has been the subject of detailed archaeological investigation in the past few years: Stephen E. Sidebotham, *Berenike and the Ancient Maritime Spice Route* (California, 2011) has much information on both the place and the Wadi Hammamet and other routes.
15. Dundas's conditions and plans are set out in a letter to the Admiralty, quoted in Hook, *The Life of General ... Sir David Baird*, vol. 1, 269–72.
16. Townshend, *Auchmuty Family*, 102.
17. BL IOL/H/477, 149–51.
18. Parkinson, *War in the Eastern Seas*, 175–6; Mackesy, *British Victory*, 188–90.
19. Albert Lee, *The History of the 10th Foot*, 2 vols (Aldershot, 1911).
20. Sir Robert Wilson, *History of the British Expedition to Egypt ...* (Philadelphia, 1803, repr. c. 2010).
21. Hook, *Baird*, 314–18, including Hutchinson's letter.
22. E.g., Mackesy, *British Victory*, 200–1
23. Both letters are in BL IOR/H/477.
24. Mitchell Library, Sydney, Macquarie Letterbook A790; the letters which are quoted or referred to on the next several pages are from this source; individual references will not be given.
25. Wilson, *Expedition to Egypt*, appendix, 50–2, quotes a memorandum by Colonel Montresor on the method of advance required, and detailing the stages and distances involved.
26. From Montresor's letter (see previous note) it is evident that between New Wells and Moilah (34 miles) and between 'Advanced Wells' and Legetta (38 miles), no water was available.
27. Mackesy, *British Victory*, 183.
28. Ibid., 188–98.
29. Wilson, *Expedition to Egypt*, 209–15; Mackesy, *British Victory*, 202–3.
30. Moiret, *Memoirs*, 162; Mackesy, *British Victory*, 154.
31. Wilson, *Expedition to Egypt*, 225–49; Mackesy, *British Victory*, 210–24.
32. Wilson, *Expedition to Egypt*, 249.
33. Wilson, *Expedition to Egypt*, 249–56; Mackesy, *British Victory*, 225.
34. The 10th Foot, Auchmuty's regiment, which had spent less than a year in India, was now returned to Britain: Lee, *History*.
35. Wilson, *Expedition to Egypt*, 275–7.
36. The conflict in Egypt after the British victory is illustrated by the extracts from *al-Jabarti's History of Egypt*, ed. Jane Hathaway (Princeton NJ, 2009), 206–51; for the British viewpoint John Marlowe, *Anglo Egyptian Relations 1800–1953* (London, 1954), ch. 1; see also Afaf Lutfi al-Sayyid Marsot, *Egypt in the reign of Muhammad Ali* (Cambridge, 1984), ch. 3.

37. J.D. Grainger, *The Amiens Truce, Britain and Bonaparte, 1801–1803* (Woodbridge, 2004).
38. TNA WO1/345, 385–99; Hutchinson to Lord Hobart, 16 August 1801.
39. TNA WO1/346, Lord Cavan to Lord Hobart, 5 May 1802.
40. Hathaway (ed.), a*l-Jabarti's History*, 216, 219.
41. Marsot, *Muhammad Ali*, 37.
42. TNA W01/346, Stuart to Hobart, 24 November 1802, 7 December 1802, and 29 March 1803; the withdrawal order is Hobart to Cavan, 26 November 1802.
43. Marsot, *Muhammad Ali*, 42.
44. Drovetti's reports to Paris on the situation in Egypt are a major source for events there: see Ronald T. Ridley, *Napoleon's Proconsul in Egypt, the Life and Times of Bernadino Drovetti* (London, n.d., but c. 2000).
45. Hathaway (ed.), *al-Jabarti's History*, 102–10; Marsot, *Muhammad Ali*, 21.
46. Moiret, *Memoirs*; the author romanticises events, and this may be one of his fancies; yet the fear among the Egyptian population at Mameluke behaviour is clear from other accounts; hence popular support for Muhammad Ali.
47. E. Jomard (ed.), *Description de l'Egypte*, 29 vols(Paris, 1809–29).
48. Mackesy, *British Victory*, 226; Thomas Walsh, '*Journal of the late Campaign in Egypt*', in *The Cockade in the Sand* (2014), 151–4.
49. WO1/293, 85 – 86.

Chapter 5

1. Townshend, *Auchmuty Family*, 104.
2. Syndale burnt down in 1956 (according to Pevsner's *Kent*); it is now a small hotel, with a vast imitation oast house next door used by a private medical practice.
3. All these are detailed in Townshend, *Auchmuty Family*.
4. Grainger, *The Amiens Truce*.
5. F. Nikolay, *Napoleon at the Boulogne Camp*, trans. Georgina L. Davis (London, 1907); Chandler, *Campaigns* , 319–27.
6. Even the French have doubts about the seriousness of the plans: see Harold C. Deutsch, 'Napoleonic Policy and the Project of a Descent upon England', *Journal of Modern History*, 2 (1930), 541–68; Fernand Emile Beaucour, 'Le grand projet Napoleonien d'expedition en Angleterre: Mythe ou Realite', *Proceedings of the Consortium on Revolutionary Europe* (1982), 225–45.
7. Frank McLynn, *Invasion, from Armada to Hitler (1588–1945)* (London, 2015), ch. 6, disposes most convincingly of any doubts as to Napoleon's seriousness over the invasion; he has nothing to say on British defences though, beyond Martello towers and Trafalgar.
8. J.E. Cookson, *The British Armed Nation, 1793–1815* (Oxford, 1997).
9. Sir John Moore to his mother, 20 October 1803, in J.C. Moore, *The Life of Lieutenant General Sir John Moore* (1834), 10–11, quoted in Peter Bloomfield, *Kent and the Napoleonic Wars* (Gloucester, 1987), 75–6.
10. Richard Glover, *Peninsular Preparation, the Reform of the British Army, 1795–1809* (Cambridge, 1970).

11. P.A.L. Vine, *The Royal Military Canal* (2nd edn, Stroud, 2010).
12. These are described in every guidebook on Kent, for example Caroline Hillier, *The Bulwark Shore, Thanet and the Cinque Ports* (London, 1980), but since there are none in Thanet, they will be ignored here; Michael Foley, *Martello Towers* (Stroud, 2013).
13. Broomfield, *Kent*, 23–30; Roy Ingleton, *Fortress Kent, the Guardian of England* (Barnsley, 2012) (though he has nothing on Thanet); Andrew Saunders and Victor Smith, *Kent's Defence History* (Canterbury, 2001; A.G. Hardy, 'The old Telegraph from London to the Coast of Kent', in Margaret Roche, *Essays in Kentish History* (London, 1973), 275–81.
14. C. Fussell, *A Journey round the Coast of Kent* (London, 1818).
15. The Ordnance Survey had completed its map of Kent in 1801, a copy of which was republished in 1990 by Harry Margary of Lympne Castle in association with the Kent County Library. It graphically demonstrates the intricate nature of the streams and ditches in these valleys which separate Thanet from the rest of the county. The map was surveyed by W. Mudge, and was dedicated to Earl Cornwallis, Master General of the Ordnance, another of Auchmuty's colleagues.
16. Getting out of the French harbours might have been excessively difficult; the few attempts made in exercises demonstrated that the harbour entrances were too narrow to allow the clumsy barges to get to sea more than one at a time, and they could therefore have been picked off one at a time by the Royal Navy – and widening the entrances, of course, would simply let the Royal Navy interfere all the more easily.
17. Broomfield, *Kent*, documents 16, 24, 31.
18. Kent Archives, RU/1231/023/6.
19. *A List of the Officers of the Militia, the Gentlemen and Yeomanry Cavalry, and Volunteer Infantry of the United Kingdom*, 11th edn, War Office, 14 October 1805, reprinted by Naval and Military Press, c. 2005.
20. Kent Archives, RU/1231/076.
21. Townshend, *Auchmuty Family*, 78, with references to local sources.
22. John Ehrman, *The Younger Pitt*, vol. 3 (London, 1996), 542–4.
23. Ibid., 543–44, quoted from Moore, *The Life of … Sir John Moore*, vol. II, 8; Thomas Hardy used such a scene, of course, in *The Trumpet Major*.
24. Bloomfield, *Kent*, 134–5.
25. Fussell, *Journey*; also John H. Andrew, 'The Thanet Seaports 1650–1750', in Roche, *Essays*, 119–26.
26. Kent Archives, RU/1231/047.
27. Kent Archives, KAO DO/Zl.

Chapter 6

1. Richard Glover, *Britain at Bay, Defence against Bonaparte 1803–14* (London, 1973).
2. The events dealt with in this chapter I have described in *The Royal Navy in the River Plate*, and *British Campaigns in the South Atlantic 1805–1807* (Barnsley,

2015); in addition there is Ian Fletcher, *The Waters of Oblivion* (Barnsley, 2006), and E. Costa, *The English Invasion of the River Plate* (Buenos Aires, 1937); in view of all this, and considering that this book is concerned with Auchmuty, I shall include notes only on Auchmuty's activities.

3. In fact, there was a third 'Buenos Aires'; the viceroyalty were divided into ten provinces, one of which was Intendencia of Buenos Aires, but the confusion of viceroyalty and city will be sufficient to make the point.
4. TNA ADM 50/50, Admiral Stirling's journal, 5–15 January 1807.
5. The report of events by Auchmuty is in W01/162; see also Stirling's journal.
6. G.G. Gleig (ed.), *The Hussar* (London, 1837), 192–5.
7. TNA WO1/162, 29 – 40, Auchmuty's report, 6 February 1807; Glieg (ed.), *Hussar*, 192–5; Anon., *A Narrative of the Expedition to and the Storming of Buenos Aires* ... by an officer attached to the expedition (Bath, 1807), 8.
8. TNA ADM 50/50, Stirling's Journal, 21 July 1807.
9. Ibid., 1 February 1807.
10. TNA W01/162, 15 – 29, Auchmuty's report; ADM 1/59, 7 enclosure, Stirling's report; participants' reports include: Major A. Tucker, *Narrative of the Operations of a small British force under ... Auchmuty ... at Montevideo* (London, 1807) (Tucker was probably the man who had been Auchmuty's brigade major in Kent, though the initial is different); G.N.B. Lawrence (ed.), *Autobiography of Sergeant W. Lawrence* (London, 1886), 24–5; National Army Museum 8301–102, Diary of Captain P.R. Jennings.
11. W01/162, 26–7; Grainger, *British Campaigns*, 155.
12. Sir Charles Oman, 'The Battle of Maida', in *Studies in the Napoleonic Wars* (London, 1929, repub. 1989), 37–72; this was refuted by David Chandler, 'Column Versus Line – the Case of Maida, 1806', in *On the Napoleonic Wars* (London, 1999), 130–44.
13. BL Add 37886, 38–9, Colonel Richard Bourke to William Windham, 9 February 1807.
14. Anon., *An Authentic Narrative of the Proceedings of the Expedition under the Command of Brigadier General Craufurd*, by an Officer of the Expedition (London, 1808).
15. National Army Museum 8301–102, Diary of Captain P.R. Jennings.
16. Grainger, *British Campaigns*, 160–4.
17. BL Add 37886, 39, Bourke to Windham, 9 February 1807.
18. Townshend, in *Auchmuty Family*, 106–10, quotes the resolutions of both houses, the inscription on the vase (and a photograph – it was then in the New York Historical Society collection), and Auchmuty's letters of thanks.
19. These arrivals and reconsiderations are described in the sources quoted in Grainger, *The Royal Navy in the River Plate*, 269–75, in particular Admiral Murray's letter to the Admiralty of 23 March, ADM 1/59, 37.
20. Grainger, *British Campaigns*, 175.
21. Fletcher, *Waters of Oblivion*, Appendix IV.
22. National Army Museum 6403–14, Major King's diary.
23. University College London, MS Room, Diary of Lieutenant Colonel Lancelot Holland.

24. Much detail is in the evidence produced at Whitelocke's subsequent court martial: *Trial at Large of Lieutenant-General Whitelocke ... January 28, 1808* (London, 1808); the colours carried by the British forces are still preserved in the Santo Domingo church to this day.
25. F. Whittingham, *A Memoir of the Services of Lieutenant-General Sir Samuel Ford Whittingham* (London, 1868); Whittingham became one of Wellington's more important intelligence men in the Peninsula.
26. Whittingham (previous note); [Anon.], 'Tom Plunkett', *United Services Journal* (1842), 72.
27. For example, Harry Smith: G.C. Moore Smith (ed.), *Autobiography of Sir Harry Smith* (London, 1901); Harry Smith actually married a Spanish girl in Spain, perhaps prepared by the experience at Buenos Aires; his 'autobiography' is based on an extremely scrappy diary, and the story of the advances by Spanish girls towards British soldiers was a commonplace, and may have been enlisted by the author as a romantic embellishment.
28. For this whole process in Argentina see Tulio Halperin-Donghi, *Politics, Economics and Society in Argentina in the Revolutionary Period* (Cambridge, 1975), and David Rock, *Argentina 1516–1987, from Spanish Colonisation to the Falklands War and Alfonsin* (London, 1987), chs 2 and 3; for a much wider view of the results in Spanish South America, see John Lynch, *The Spanish American Revolutions, 1808–1826* (2nd edn, New York, 1986).
29. See, as an example of the sources, M. Newitt (ed.), *War, Revolution, and Society in the Rio de la Plata, 1808–1810* (Oxford, 2010), the diary of an English observer of events; a wider discussion is in Donghi, *Politics, Economics*.
30. J. de Courcy Ireland, *The Admiral from Mayo, the Life of Almirante Brown of Foxton* (Dublin, 1995); R.A. Humphreys, *Liberation in South America 1806–1827, the Career of James Paroissien* (London, 1952).
31. Brian Vale, *A War Betwixt Englishmen, 1825–1830* (London, 2000).
32. Lynch, *Spanish American Revolutions*; Irene Nicholson, *The Liberators, a Study of the Independence Movements in Spanish America* (London, 1969) (57–95 on Miranda); Peter Dixon, *Canning, Politician and Statesman* (London, 1976), ch. 9.
33. One wonders how far the *portenos* understood that two United States merchants, Wayne and White, had been partly instrumental in provoking the British invasion.

Chapter 7

1. Quoted from the *Royal Military Calendar*, vol. 2, London 1820, 271–2 in Townshend, *Auchmuty Family*, 108–9.
2. Townshend, *Auchmuty Family*, 107, from the *Royal Military Calendar*, vol. 2, 270.
3. Townshend, *Auchmuty Family*, 111.
4. For treatments of the Company army, which do not really lay any stress on its nature as a mercenary force, see Mason, *A Matter of Honour*, which is little less than adulatory, Holmes, *Sahib*, which largely ignores the Indians and the

officers, and, for the period after Auchmuty's time, Douglas M. Peers, *Between Mars and Mammon, Colonial Armies and the Garrison State in Early Nineteenth-Century India* (London, 1995), though this is concerned more with the government in India than the army; for a curious autobiography of an Indian soldier, see Sita Ram, *From Sepoy to Subedar*, ed. James Lunt (London, 1970, originally published in England in 1873.

5. The classic account of this process is C.H. Philips, *The East India Company 1784–1834* (London, 1940), though it pays little attention to India; see also Marshall, *Problems of Empire*, a collection of documents.
6. The mutiny is discussed from different angles by John Rosselli, *Lord William Bentinck, The Making of a Liberal Imperialist, 1774–1839* (London, 1994), 50–4 and other references, by Ainslie Embree, *Charles Grant and British Rule in India* (London, 1962), 237–49, by Mason, *A Matter of Honour*, 237–42, and by W.J. Wilson, *History of the Madras Army*, 3 vols (Madras, 1882), vol. III, 163–201.
7. *ODNB*, Cradock, Bentinck; Rosselli, *Lord William Bentinck*.
8. The only account of these events which includes St Leger's actions is A.G. Cardew, *The White Mutiny* (London, 1929). Other treatments are usually much more brief: Wilson, *Madras Army*, vol. III, ch. 20, and Embree, *Grant*, 253–9 are the only ones which spend more than a page or two on the business.
9. So characterised, in an extreme sense, by Jane Hathaway, 'A Tale of Two Mutinies', csas.ed.ac.uk/mutiny/conf papers, accessed 15 May 2017.
10. Cardew, *White Mutiny*, is the best account of these events. There are full documentary sources in *Papers Relating to East Indian Affairs (Madras Army), Parliamentary Papers*, 300 and 310–20, the product of a Parliamentary inquiry in 1810. A recent account is in Ferdinand Mount, *The Tears of the Rajas* (London, 2015), which has an extensive bibliography.
11. SRO GD51, Dundas Papers, 472/1, R. Dundas to Auchmuty, 25 June 1810.
12. SRO GD51/472/2, Auchmuty to R. Dundas, 25 June 1810.
13. BL IOR/H/455a, 119.
14. Philips, *East India Company*, 172.
15. SRO GD51, Dundas Papers, 472, 3, Auchmuty to R. Dundas, 27 February 1810.
16. Townshend, *Auchmuty Family*, 111; the letter quoted is not dated by Mrs Townshend.
17. SRO GD51 Dundas Papers 472, 4, Auchmuty to R. Dundas (received 7 March 1810); it is something of a relief to find someone at last referring to the events correctly.
18. SRO GD51, 472, 5, Auchmuty to R. Dundas (received 20 March 1810).
19. Philips, *East India Company*, 172–3.
20. SRO GD51, 472, Auchmuty to R. Dundas.
21. Townshend, *Auchmuty Family*, 111.
22. SRO GD51, 472, Auchmuty to Lord Minto, 1 October 1810.
23. SRO GD51, 472, R. Dundas to Auchmuty, 14 June 1810.
24. SRO GD51, 472, Auchmuty to Minto, 6 October 1810.
25. See, most recently, and completely, Stephen Taylor, *Storm and Conquest, the Battle for the Indian Ocean, 1809* (London, 2007).

26. SRO GD51, 472, Auchmuty to Minto. 5 October 1810.
27. SRO GD51, 472, Auchmuty to Minto, 4 December 1810.
28. SRO GD51, 472, Auchmuty to R. Dundas 6 October 1810.
29. SRO GD51, 472, 12, Auchmuty to R. Dundas, Madras 10 December 1810.
30. SRO GD51, 472, 8, Auchmuty to R, Dundas, 6 October 1810.
31. SRO GD51, 472, 14, Agnew to the Officers Commanding Districts, 19 October 1810.

Chapter 8

1. Malcolm Yapp, *Strategies for British India* (Oxford, 1977); and Amita Das, *Defending British India against Napoleon*, ed. Aditya Das (Woodbridge, 2016).
2. Das, *Defending British India* 185–7.
3. C.R. Low, *The History of the Indian Navy*, vol. 1 (London, 1877, repr. 1990), 276–7.
4. Das, *Defending British India*, 189–91. For the complications of the Macau episode see Parkinson, *War in the Eastern Seas*, ch. 16.
5. For a racy account of the conquest see Taylor, *Storm and Conquest*; more sober accounts are in Das, *Defending British India*, ch. 4, Low, *Indian Navy*, 206–30, and Parkinson, *War in the Eastern Seas*, ch. 22.
6. John Keay, *The Spice Route, a History* (London, 2005), 237.
7. Simon Schama, *Patriots and Liberators, Revolution in the Netherlands, 1780–1813* (London, 1977); M.C. Ricklefs, *A History of Modern Indonesia* (London, 1981), 105–6.
8. For Janssens at the Cape see Grainger, *British Campaigns* ; Daendels features frequently in Schama, *Patriots and Liberators* (2nd edn, London, 1992).
9. Ricklefs, *Modern Indonesia*, 91–4.
10. For the political geography consult Robert Cribb, *Historical Atlas of Indonesia* (Richmond, 2000).
11. This was the Battle of Pulo Aur, 1805 – see Parkinson, *War in the Eastern Seas*, ch. 11.
12. Cribb, *Historical Atlas*, 95 and 111.
13. C.F. Wurzburg, *Raffles in the Eastern States* (London, 1954), 56–81, with extensive quotations from the report. Gerald S. Graham, *Great Britain and the Indian Ocean, 1810–1850* (Oxford, 1967), 331–5.
14. Das, *Defending British India*, 187–8; Wurzburg, *Raffles*, 83.
15. SRO GD51, 18, Minto to Auchmuty, Fort William, 17 December 1810.
16. BL IOR Factory Records, Java 16, Minto to Drury, 5 October 1810; SRO GD51, 21, Minto to Auchmuty, Fort William, 31 January 1811.
17. Das, *Defending British India*, 199, with full references.
18. John Joseph Stockdale, *Island of Java* (London, 1811, repr. Singapore, 1995), provides some information about troop numbers and fortifications, but it was out of date when he wrote.
19. SRO GD51, 18, Auchmuty to Minto, Fort St George, 10 January 1811.
20. SRO GD51, 18, Auchmuty to Minto, Madras, 13 and 20 January 1811.
21. SRO GD51, 17, Auchmuty to Robert Dundas, Madras, 10 February 1811.

22. Broughton had little experience of warfare, having spent much of his naval service in exploration in the Pacific: *ODNB*.
23. Justin Corfield and Cyril Skinner (eds), *The British Invasion of Java in 1811, the Diary of Lieutenant William Fielding HEIC* (Rosanna, Victoria, Australia, 1999).
24. William Thorn, *Memoir of the Conquest of Java* (London, 1815, repr. Singapore, 2004), 18–20. Thorn was German-born and a trained and accurate surveyor and competent artist; his book includes useful maps and illustrations of many of the Javanese places.
25. Ibid., omits this; it is described by Marcus Cunliffe, *The Royal Irish Fusiliers, 1793–1850* (Oxford, 1952), 43–4.
26. Low, *Indian Navy*, lists the ships, 236, as does Thorn, *Conquest*, 16.
27. Thorn, *Conquest*, 3.
28. Ibid., 3–6, with a map of route at plate 3; more daily details are in Corfield and Skinner (eds), *Diary of Lieutenant William Fielding HEIC*, 28–32, who sailed with the Bengal contingent.
29. Thorn, *Conquest*, 9; this is not a sentiment many would agree with.
30. The Hekayat Abdullah, *The Autobiography of Abdullah bin Kedar (1797–1854)*, trans. A.H. Hill (Singapore, 1954, repr. 1969), 88.
31. Ibid., 88–90.
32. Fielding, *Diary*, 94; Countess of Minto, *Lord Minto in India* (London, 1880), 265.
33. Thorn, *Conquest*, 10–11, on the choice of routes; Wurzburg, *Raffles*, 122, 136, 141 on the reconnaissance by Greigh.
34. Low, *Indian Navy*, 236; Wurzburg, *Raffles*, 119, 122, 136, 144; P.B.R. Carey, *The Archive of Yogyakarta*, vol. 1, *Documents Relating to Politics and Internal Court Affairs* (Oxford, 1980), appendix 5, 201–2; Das, *Defending British India*, 196.
35. Wurzburg, *Raffles*, 135–6; Das, *Defending British India*, 208.
36. Low, *Indian Navy*, 239–40, with Hayes' letter to the captains.
37. Thorn, *Conquest*, 15–14.
38. Low, *Indian Navy*, 130; Thorn, *Conquest*, 17–22; Fielding, *Diary*, 57–8.
39. Wurzburg, *Raffles*, 160; P. Carew, 'Facing the Music', *Blackwood's Magazine* (October 1949), 301–11: John Blakiston, *Twelve Years' Military Adventures* (London, 1829), vol. 2, 30–1.
40. Thorn, *Conquest*, 21–3; Fielding, *Diary*, 58.
41. Thorn, *Conquest*, 23–6; Fielding, *Diary*, 59.
42. Thorn, *Conquest*, 26–9; Fielding, *Diary*, 58.
43. His letter of justification of the Admiralty is in TNA WO1/364, 271–4, Stopford to Admiralty, Simon's Bay, 26 May 1811 – oddly it is in an army archive, not the Admiralty.
44. Das, *Defending British India*, 213.
45. Thorn, *Conquest*, 30 footnote.
46. Ibid., 30–40: the British casualties of 91 killed, wounded, and missing, included Thorn himself; Cunliffe, *Royal Irish Fusiliers*, 46–7.

47. One of the main reasons that Gillespie is given the credit for victories in Java is that Major Thorn was in his division and later wrote his biography.
48. Thorn, *Conquest*, plate XI, is clear and detailed, so long as it is recalled that north is at the bottom of the plan; there is another plan in the National Army Museum, reference 6509/34/4.
49. Fielding, *Diary*, 67–9.
50. Thorn, *Conquest*, 41–89, including the official letters from Auchmuty and Minto.
51. BL IOL, Java Factory Records 14; most of the captives were Madurese, presumably attempting to get home.
52. Thorn, *Conquest*, 90.
53. Ibid., 94–7.
54. Ibid., 98–101.
55. Ibid., 101–5.
56. Fielding, *Diary*, 89 91
57. Ibid., 93.

Chapter 9

1. T. Hannigan, *Raffles and the British Invasion of Java* (Singapore, 2014, 113–24, quoting from BL IOR 148/18 of the Raffles-Minto documents.
2. Ibid., 148. This is one of the touchstones of Raffles' reputation. Hanigan is brutal in his attribution of blame for the massacre to Raffles and his letter; Wurzburg, *Raffles*, 122–3 and 202–3, by contrast claims he was not to blame but quite naturally does not quote the letter. Blame, of course, lies with the Sultan, but Raffles' attitude and words can certainly be said to have encouraged him to act. He did send an envoy, Lieutenant McDonald, with instructions to get the Dutch out if he could.
3. The British made a particular point of elaborating the story of a Dutch woman who insisted on joining a husband in the boat, and therefore dying with him, e.g. Thorn, *Conquest*, 144–5; Hannigan, *Raffles*, 143 is predictably imaginative; Victoria Glendinning, *Raffles and the Golden Opportunity* (London, 2012), 99, is much cooler.
4. Hannigan, *Raffles*, 142–5.
5. These details are listed by Peter Carey (ed.), *The British in Java, a Javanese Account* (Oxford, 1992), 36–9.
6. Wurzburg, *Raffles*, 192–4; Carey, *The Archive of Yogyakarta*, vol. 1, 76–89.
7. Thorn, *Conquest*, 124–5.
8. Thorn, *Conquest*, 128–30; Hannigan, *Raffles*, 155–8; Low, *Indian Navy*, vol. 1, 245–6.
9. Thorn, *Conquest*, 137–56; Low, *Indian Navy*, vol. 1, 246–51.
10. Carey (ed.), *British in Java*, 38–9; Wurzburg, *Raffles*, 212–15.
11. Thorn, *Conquest*, 176–7; Ricklefs, *Indonesia*, 109.
12. Carey, *The Archive of Yogyakarta*, vol. 1, 95–6, for the treaty.
13. Thorn, *Conquest*, 197–8.
14. Ibid., 180–1.

15. The MS is BL Add 12330, 'collected' by John Crawford and published by Carey as *The British in Java*.
16. Thorn, *Conquest*, 181–9; Carey (ed.), *British in Java*; Hannigan, *Raffles*, 178–208 is a highly imaginative interpretation.
17. Glendinning, *Raffles*, 105–7; Hannigan, *Raffles*, 209–11.
18. Ricklefs, *Indonesia*, 109–10.
19. For the new geography see Cribb, *Historical Atlas*, 114.
20. Biographers – Hannigan excepted – are all too ready to admire Raffles' work; a judicious estimate is by Ricklefs, *Indonesia*, 110–11; Carey (ed.), *British in Java*, 440, note 205, for the land rent problems.
21. Glendinning, *Raffles*, 100; Hannigan, *Raffles*, 267–70.
22. Ricklefs, *Indonesia*, 110; Wurzburg, *Raffles*, 380–5; P.B.R. Carey, 'The Sepoy Conspiracy of 1815 in Java', *Bildungen tot de Taal-, Land- en Volkenkunde*, 133 (1977), 294–322.
23. Wurzburg, *Raffles*, 300–1: John Pemble, *Britain's Ghurka War, The Invasion of Nepal 1814–1816* (2nd edn, Barnsley, 2008), 149–51 for his behaviour and death.
24. Wurzburg, *Raffles*, 349–52.
25. Ibid., 266–9; Hannigan, *Raffles*, 288–94.
26. Hannigan, *Raffles*, 294–300.
27. Pellew's visit: Parkinson, *War in Eastern Seas*, 307–8; Ainslie's reports are in BL IOR L/PS/9/218.
28. Phil Grabsky, *The Lost Temple of Java* (London, 1999).
29. Glendinning, *Raffles*, 148–9; Wurzburg, *Raffles*, 387–93.
30. Quoted in Glendinning, *Raffles*, 148.

Chapter 10

1. Townshend, *Auchmuty Family*, 117.
2. SRO GD 51/472, 28, Auchmuty to Robert Dundas, Headquarters Weltevreeden, 2 September 1811.
3. BL IOR E/4/913, 261, where it is recorded that the welcoming greeting was 'allowed'.
4. Seringapatam: BL IOR E/4/916, 421; Cannanore: E/4/914, 393 and 412.
5. BL IOR E/4/914, 359.
6. The mis-spellings are those of the clerks, and presumably result from mis-pronunciation and mis-hearings; they do demonstrate a profound ignorance of Indian languages.
7. BL IOR E/4/913, 435–6.
8. BL IOR E/4/912, 427.
9. BL IOR E/4/914, 414.
10. BL IOR E/4/912, 332.
11. BL IOR E/4/912, 463.
12. BL IOR E/4/916, 495.
13. Wilson, *Madras Army*, vol. III, 350–5.
14. BL IOR E/4/916 – this was the occasion of Auchmuty's visit.

15. BL IOR E/4/914, 333.
16. BL IOR E/4/912, 425.
17. Townshend, *Auchmuty Family*, 118–21; *ODNB*, John Maxwell Tylden.
18. BL IOR E/4/914, 331 and 418.
19. TNA WO 164/218; the second payment was made in 1814, after his death.
20. Ibid.; these payments were made in instalments as the prize goods were realised into cash; some men never collected their entitlements.
21. *ODNB*, Lord Minto (Elliott).
22. BL IOR E/4/384/4781.
23. BL IOR E/4/914, 349.
24. BL IOR E/4/914, 359 and 387.
25. BL IOR E/4/920, 372; also note E/4/914, 364–6, on other clothing issues.
26. BL IOR E/4/914, 330.
27. BL IOR E/4/914, 388.
28. BL IOR E/4/914, 335, 358.
29. BL IOR E/4/914, 415.
30. BL IOR E/4/914, 337.
31. BL IOR E/4/912, 342.
32. BL IOR E/4/914, 382.
33. BL IOR E/4/914, 395.
34. BL IOR E/4/914, 360.
35. BL IOR E/4/400/10081.
36. For Russell see William Dalrymple, *The White Mughals, Love and Betrayal in Eighteenth Century India* (London, 2002), and, less highly coloured, Zubaida Yazdani, *Hyderabad during the Residency of Henry Russell, 1811–1820* (Oxford, 1976).
37. BL IOR E/4/912, 420 and E/4/916, 426 and 457.
38. BL IOR E/4/916, 426 and 494.
39. BL IOR E/4/914, 381.
40. BL IOR E/4/460/11202 and E/4/916, 479.
41. BL IOR E/4/916, 28.
42. BL IOR E/4/914, 360 and E/4/916, 49.
43. BL IOR E/4/914, 357.
44. BL IOR E/4/916, 62 and 421; E/4/914, 404–6.
45. BL IOR E/4/916, 95–8.
46. Philips, *East India Company*, 179, 195–6; Minto was promoted to Earl on his return to Britain, but died in June 1814.
47. BL IOR H/88, Military 933–70.
48. Townshend, *Auchmuty Family*, 121–3.

Chapter 11

1. BL IOR/477, Wellesley Papers, no. 21.
2. The recommendation is quoted in A.E. Mainwaring, *Crown and Company, the Records of the Second Battalion, Royal Dublin Fusiliers* (London, 1911), 214; see also Douglas Peers, 'Between Mars and Mammon: the East India Company

and Efforts to Reform the Army, 1796–1832', *Historical Journal*, 33 (1990), 385–401. (The mutiny of 1809 receives only a single paragraph in this article.)

3. This was all published in a pamphlet: *Statement of the Claim of Lieutenant-General Sir Samuel Auchmuty on the Java Prize-Money Property* (London, 1816).
4. Kent Archives, Canterbury Chapter Archives, 11 October 1817 and 30 June 1818.

Bibliography

Primary Sources
British Library:
Add Mss 37886.
BL Add Mss. 32702.

British Library, India Office Records:
Factory Records, Java.
E/4/912, 913, 914, 916, 920, Administration records.
E/4/384, 400, 460 Administration Records.
H/88, 450, 455a, 577.
H/477, Wellesley Papers.
148/18 Raffles-Minto documents.
L/PS/9/218 Ainslie in Japan.
Mss Eur B 328.

The National Archives:
ADM 1/59, South America.
ADM 50/50, Admiral Stirling's journal.
WO 1/162, 293, 345, 346, 364 South America.
WO 211/4, Harte's army list, 'Sir Samuel Auchmuty'.
AO 13/43, exiles' compensation claims.

National Army Museum, London:
6403–14, Major King's diary.
6509/34/4, Java.
8301–102, Diary of Captain P.R. Jennings, 40th Foot.

Kent Archives, Maidstone:
RU/1231/023/6, 076, 047, DO/Zl, militia records.
Canterbury Chapter Archives.

Norfolk Record Office:
MC 34/306, 530XA, Auchmuty family in Ireland.

Scottish Record Office, Edinburgh:
GD51, Dundas Papers.

University College London, MS Room:
Diary of Lieutenant Colonel Lancelot Holland.

Mitchell Library, Sydney:
Macquarie's Letter Book, 1794–6, A 790 accessed on microfilm (M460) in the National Library of Australia, Canberra.

London Metropolitan Archive, City of London:
Release of Indentures of Fine, ACC/0564/040–042.

Secondary Sources

[Anon.]. *An Authentic Narrative of the Proceedings of the Expedition under the Command of Brigadier General Craufurd*, by an Officer of the Expedition, London 1808.

[Anon.]. 'A Dialogue between Sir George Cornwall, a Gentleman lately arrived from England ... and Mr Flint', London and Boston 1769.

[Anon.]. 'Dr Auchmuty's letter to Capt. Montresor ...', New York, 19 April 1775, repub. in the Early American Imprints, series I, no. 13818.

[Anon.]. 'A List of the general and staff officers ... Serving in North America', 1779, in the Early American Imprints, series 1, 1639.

[Anon.]. *A Narrative of the Expedition to and the Storming of Buenos Aires ...* by an officer attached to the expedition, Bath, 1807.

[Anon.]. 'Tom Plunkett', *United Services Journal*, 1842, 72.

The Hekayat Abdullah, *The Autobiography of Abdullah bin Kedar (1797–1854)*, trans. A.H. Hill, Singapore, 1954, repr. 1969, 88.

Alam, Muzaffar. *The Crisis of Empire in Mughal North India, Awadd and the Punjab 1707–1748,* Oxford, 1986.

Alumni Dublinenses.

Anderson, Fred. *Crucible of War, the Seven Years' War and the Fate of the Empire in British North America, 1754–1766*, New York, 2000.

Andrew, John H. 'The Thanet Seaports 1650–1750', in Margaret Roche, *Essays in Kentish History*, London, 1973, 119–26.

Auchmuty, Robert. *The Importance of Cape Breton to the British Nation*, London, 1744.

Auchmuty, Sir Samuel. *Statement of the Claim of Lieutenant-General Sir Samuel Auchmuty on the Java Prize-Money Property*, London, 1816.

Baylin, Bernard. *The Ordeal of Thomas Hutchinson, Loyalism and the Destruction of the First British Empire*, London, 1975.

Beaucour, Fernand Emile. 'Le grand projet Napoleonien d'expedition en Angleterre: Mythe ou Realite', *Proceedings of the Consortium on Revolutionary Europe*, 1982, 225–45.

Blakely, Phyllis R. and John N. Grant (eds). *Eleven Exiles, Accounts of Loyalists of the American Revolution*, Toronto, 1982.

Blakiston, John. *Twelve Years' Military Adventures*, London, 1829.

Bloomfield, Peter. *Kent and the Napoleonic Wars*, Gloucester, 1987.

Bonomi, Patricia U. *Fraction People: Politics and Society in Colonial New York*, New York, 1971.
Bridenbaugh, Carl. *Mitre and Sceptre, Transatlantic faiths, ideas, personalities, and politics, 1689–1775*, New York, 1962.
Calhoun, Robert M. *The Loyalists in Revolutionary America, 1760–1781*, New York, 1965.
Callahan, Raymond. *The East India Company and Army Reform 1783–1798*, Cambridge MA, 1972.
Cardew, A.G. *A Sketch of the Services of the Bengal Army*, Calcutta, 1903.
Cardew, A.G. *The White Mutiny*, London, 1929.
Carey, P.B.R. 'The Sepoy Conspiracy of 1815 in Java', *Bildungen tot de Taal-, Land- en Volkenkunde*, 133, 1977, 294–322.
Carey, P.B.R. *The Archive of Yogyakarta*, vol. 1, *Documents Relating to Politics and Internal Court Affairs*, Oxford, 1980.
Carey, P.B.R. and Mason C. Hoadley (eds). *The Archive of Yogyakarta,* vol. 2, *Documents relating to Economic and Agrarian Affairs*, Oxford, 2000.
Carey, Peter (ed.). *The British in Java, a Javanese Account*, Oxford, 1992.
Carew, P. 'Facing the Music', *Blackwood's Magazine*, October 1949, 301–11.
Chandler, David. *The Campaigns of Napoleon*, London, 1966.
Chandler, David. 'Column Versus Line – the Case of Maida, 1806', in David Chandler, *On the Napoleonic Wars*, London, 1999, 130–44.
Childs, John. *The Williamite War in Ireland, 1688–1691*, London, 2007.
Compton, Herbert (compiler). *A Particular Account of the European Military Adventurers of Hindustan from 1784 to 1803*, London, 1892.
Cookson, J.E. *The British Armed Nation, 1793–1815*, Oxford, 1997.
Corfield, Justin and Cyril Skinner (eds). *The British Invasion of Java in 1811, the Diary of Lieutenant William Fielding HEIC*, Rosanna, Victoria, Australia, 1999.
Correspondence of Charles, First Marquis Cornwallis, ed. Charles Ross, 3 vols, London, 1859.
Costa, E. *The English Invasion of the River Plate*, Buenos Aires, 1937.
Craven, Wesley. *An Introduction to the History of Bermuda*, Toronto, 1990.
Cribb, Robert. *Historical Atlas of Indonesia,* Richmond, 2000.
Cross, Arthur L. *The Anglican Episcopate and the American Colonies*, New York, 1902.
Cunliffe, Marcus. *The Royal Irish Fusiliers, 1793–1850*, Oxford, 1952.
Curtis, Edward E. *The British Army in the American Revolution,* New Haven CT, 1926, repr. New York, 1998.
Dalbiac, Philip Hugh. *A History of the First Nottinghamshire Regiment (Sherwood Foresters)*, London, 1902.
Dalrymple, William. *The Last Mughal*, London, 2006.
Dalrymple, William. *The White Mughals, Love and Betrayal in Eighteenth Century India*, London, 2002.
Amita Das, *Defending British India against Napoleon,* ed. Aditya Das, Woodbridge, 2016.
Davis, Blake. *The Campaign that Won America, the Story of Yorktown*, New York, 1970.

Deutsch, Harold C. 'Napoleonic Policy and the Project of a Descent upon England', *Journal of Modern History*, 2, 1930, 541–68;
Dickerson, Oliver M. (ed.). *Boston under Military Rule 176–1769*, Boston MA, 1936.
Dictionary of American Biography.
Dixon, Peter. *Canning, Politician and Statesman*, London, 1976.
Dutton, Kenneth R. *Auchmuty, The Life of John James Auchmuty*, Mount Nebo, Australia, 2000.
Eaton, Arthur Wentworth. *The Growth of England in Nova Scotia*, New York, 1891.
Ehrman, John. *The Younger Pitt*, vol. 1, London, 1969, vol. 3, London, 1996.
Ellis, John. *The Social History of the Machine Gun*, London, 1975.
Ellis, M.H. *Lachlan Macquarie, His Life, Adventures and Times*, 2nd edn, Sydney, 1952.
Ely, Thomas. *The Eternal Building … a sermon preached in Glass-house Street near St James's on Lord's Day, April 24, 1715 …* London, 1715.
Embree, Ainslie. *Charles Grant and British Rule in India*, London, 1962.
Feiling, Keith. *Warren Hastings*, London, 1954.
Fletcher, Ian. *The Waters of Oblivion*, Barnsley, 2006.
Foley, Michael. *Martello Towers*, Stroud, 2013.
Forrest, Denys. *Tiger of Mysore, the Life and Death of Tipu Sultan*, London, 1970.
Fry, Michael. *The Dundas Despotism*, Edinburgh, 1992.
Fussell, C. *A Journey round the Coast of Kent*, London, 1818.
Gleig, G.G. (ed.). *The Hussar*, London, 1837.
Glendinning, Victoria. *Raffles and the Golden Opportunity*, London, 2012.
Glover, Richard. *Peninsular Preparation, the Reform of the British Army, 1795–1809*, Cambridge, 1970.
Glover, Richard. *Britain at Bay, Defence against Bonaparte 1803–14*, London, 1973.
Grabsky, Phil. *The Lost Temple of Java*, London, 1999.
Graham, Gerald S. *Great Britain and the Indian Ocean, 1810–1850*, Oxford, 1967.
Grainger, John D. (ed.). *The Royal Navy in the River Plate, 1806–1807*, Aldershot, 1996.
Grainger, J.D. *The Amiens Truce, Britain and Bonaparte, 1801–1803*, Woodbridge, 2004.
Grainger, John D. *British Campaigns in the South Atlantic, 1805–1807*, Barnsley, 2015.
Guy, Alan J. 'The Army of the Georges, 1714–1783', in *The Oxford History of the British Army*, Oxford, 1994, 92–111.
Halperin-Donghi, Tulio. *Politics, Economics and Society in Argentina in the Revolutionary Period*, Cambridge, 1975.
Hannigan, T. *Raffles and the British Invasion of Java,* Singapore, 2014.
Hardy, A.G. 'The old Telegraph from London to the Coast of Kent', in Margaret Roche, *Essays in Kentish History*, London, 1973, 275–81.
Heathcote, T.A. *The Military in British India, the Development of British Land Forces in South Asia, 1600–1947*, Manchester, 1995, repr. Barnsley, 2013.
Hess, Stephen. *American Political Dynasties*, Brunswick NJ, 1997.

Hillier, Caroline. *The Bulwark Shore, Thanet and the Cinque Ports*, London, 1980.
Hodson, V.C.P. *Officers of the Bengal Army 1758–1834*, 4 vols, London, 1927–47.
Holmes, Richard. *Sahib, the British Soldier in India*, London, 2005.
Hook, Theodore E. *The Life of General … Sir David Baird*, vol. 1, London, 1832.
Humphreys, R.A. *Liberation in South America 1806–1827, the Career of James Paroissien*, London, 1952.
Ingleton, Roy. *Fortress Kent, the Guardian of England*, Barnsley, 2012.
Ingram, Edward. 'The Geopolitics of the First British Expedition to Egypt', in *Middle Eastern Studies*, 31 and 32, 1994–5.
Ireland, J. de Courcy. *The Admiral from Mayo, the Life of Almirante Brown of Foxton*, Dublin, 1995.
al-Jabarti's History of Egypt, ed. Jane Hathaway, Princeton NJ, 2009.
Jackson, John W. *With the British Army in Philadelphia 1777–1778*, San Rafael CA, 1979.
Jasonoff, Maya. *Liberty's Exiles, the Loss of America and the Remaking of the British Empire*, London, 2011.
Jomard, E. (ed.). *Description de l'Egypte*, 29 vols, Paris, 1809–29.
Keay, John. *The Spice Route, a History*, London, 2005.
Keene, H.G. *Hindustan under Free Lances, 1770–1820*, London, 1907, repr. Shannon, Ireland, 1972.
Kerr, Brenton. *Bermuda and the American Revolution 1760–1783*, Princeton NJ, 1936.
Ketchum, Richard M. *Divided Loyalties, How the American Revolution came to New York*, New York, 2002.
Knight, Esmond. 'The New York Loyalists, a Cross-Section of Colonial Society', in Robert A. East and Jacob Judd (eds), *The Loyalist Americans, a Focus on Greater New York*, Tarrytown NY, 1975.
Lawrence, G.N.B. (ed.). *Autobiography of Sergeant W. Lawrence*, London, 1886, 24–5.
Lee, Albert. *The History of the 10th Foot*, 2 vols, Aldershot, 1911.
Leslie, J.B. *Armagh Clergy and Parishes*, Dundalk, 1911.
Lovejoy, David S. *Rhode Island and the American Revolution, 1760–1776*, Providence RI, 1958.
Low, C.R. *The History of the Indian Navy*, vol. 1, London 1877, repr. 1990.
Lynch, John. *The Spanish American Revolutions, 1808–1826*, 2nd edn, New York, 1986.
MacDougall, Philip. *Naval Resistance to Britain's Growing Power in India, 1660–1800, the Saffron Banner and that Tiger of Mysore,* Woodbridge, 2014,
McLynn, Frank. *Invasion, from Armada to Hitler (1588–1945)*, London, 2015.
Mackesy, Piers. *The War for America 1775–1783*, Oxford, 1964.
Mackesy, Piers. *British Victory in Egypt, 1801, the End of Napoleon's Conquest*, London, 1995.
Mainwaring, A.E. *Crown and Company, the Records of the Second Battalion, Royal Dublin Fusiliers*, London, 1911.
Marlowe, John. *Anglo Egyptian Relations 1800–1953*, London, 1954.

Marshall, P.J. *Problems of Empire: Britain and India 1757–1813*, London, 1968.
Marsot, Afaf Lutfi al-Sayyid. *Egypt in the reign of Muhammad Ali*, Cambridge, 1984.
Mason, Philip. *A Matter of Honour, an Account of the Indian Army, its Officers and Men*, London, 1974.
Minto, Countess of. *Lord Minto in India*, London, 1880.
Moiret, Captain Joseph-Marie. *Memoirs of Napoleon's Egyptian Expedition, 1798–1801*, trans. and ed. Rosemary Brindle, London, 2001.
Moore, Christopher. *The Loyalists, Revolution, Exile, Settlement*, Toronto, 1984.
Moore, J.C. *The Life of Lieutenant General Sir John Moore*, 1834.
Moore Smith, G.C. (ed.). *Autobiography of Sir Harry Smith*, London, 1901.
Morrison, W.S. *Historical Records of the 52nd Regiment*, London, 1860.
Mount, Ferdinand. *The Tears of the Rajas*, London, 2015.
Nelson, Paul David. *William Tryon and the Course of Empire, a Life in British Imperial Service*, Chapel Hill NC, 1990.
Newbolt, Sir Henry. *The Story of the Oxfordshire and Buckinghamshire Light Infantry*, London, 1915.
Newitt, M. (ed.). *War, Revolution, and Society in the Rio de la Plata, 1808–1810*, Oxford, 2010.
Nicholson, Irene. *The Liberators, a Study of the Independence Movements in Spanish America*, London, 1969.
Nightingale, Pamela. *Trade and Empire in Western India, 1784–1806*, Cambridge, 1970.
Nikolay, F. *Napoleon at the Boulogne Camp*, trans. Georgina L. Davis, London, 1907.
Oman, Sir Charles. 'The Battle of Maida', in *Studies in the Napoleonic Wars*, London, 1929, repub., 1989, 37–72.
Ordnance Survey Map of Kent, 1801, repub. 1990 Lympne Castle, Kent, 1990.
Oxford Dictionary of National Biography (ODNB).
Papers Relating to East Indian Affairs (Madras Army), Parliamentary Papers, 300 and 310–20.
Parkinson, C. Northcote. *War in the Eastern Seas 1793–1815*, London, 1954.
Peers, Douglas. 'Between Mars and Mammon: the East India Company and Efforts to Reform the Army, 1796–1832', *Historical Journal*, 33, 1990, 385–401.
Peers, Douglas M. *Between Mars and Mammon, Colonial Armies and the Garrison State in Early Nineteenth-Century India*, London, 1995.
Pemble, John. *Britain's Ghurka War, The Invasion of Nepal 1814–1816*, 2nd edn, Barnsley, 2008.
Percival-Maxwell, M. *The Scottish Migration to Ulster in the Reign of James I*, New York, 1973.
Philips, C.H. *The East India Company 1784–1834*, London, 1940.
Pocock, Tom. *A Thirst for Glory, the Life of Admiral Sir Sidney Smith*, London, 1996.
Sita Ram, *From Sepoy to Subedar*, ed. James Lunt, London, 1970, originally published in England in 1873.
Register of Admissions to the Middle Temple, vol. 1, 1705.

Richmond, Herbert W. *The Navy in India 1763–1783*, London, 1931, repr. 1993.
Ricklefs, M.C. *A History of Modern Indonesia*, London, 1981.
Ridley, Ronald T. *Napoleon's Proconsul in Egypt, the Life and Times of Bernadino Drovet*ti, London (n.d., but c. 2000).
Riley, Edward M. 'St George Tucker's Journal of the Siege of Yorktown, 1781', *William and Mary Quarterly*, 5, 1948.
Rock, David. *Argentina 1516–1987, from Spanish Colonisation to the Falklands War and Alfonsin*, London, 1987.
Rosselli, John. *Lord William Bentinck, The Making of a Liberal Imperialist, 1774–1839*, London, 1994.
Royal Military Calendar, London, 1820.
Sabine, Lorenzo. *Biographical Sketches of the Loyalists of the American Revolution*, 2 vols, Boston MA, 1864.
Saunders, Andrew and Victor Smith. *Kent's Defence History*, Canterbury, 2001.
Schama, Simon. *Patriots and Liberators, Revolution in the Netherlands, 1780–1813*, London, 1977, 2nd edn 1992.
Schama, Simon. *Rough Crossings, Britain, the Slaves, and the American Revolution*, London, 2005.
Schecter, Barnett. *The Battle for New York, the City at the Heart of the American Revolution*, London, 2002.
Schur, Nathan. *Napoleon in the Holy Land*, London, 1999.
Shipton, Clifford K. *New England Life in the Eighteenth Century*, Cambridge MA, 1963.
Shutz, John. *William Shirley, King's Governor in Massachusetts*, Chapel Hill NC, 1961.
Sidebotham, Stephen E. *Berenike and the Ancient Maritime Spice Route*, California, 2011.
Smith, Vincent. *The Oxford History of India*, 3rd edn, Oxford, 1958.
Stockdale, J.J. *Trial at Large of Lieutenant-General Whitelocke … January 28, 1808*, London, 1808.
Stockdale, John Joseph. *Island of Java*, London, 1811, repr. Singapore, 1995.
Taylor, Stephen. *Storm and Conquest, the Battle for the Indian Ocean, 1809*, London, 2007.
Thorn, William. *Memoir of the Conquest of Java*, London, 1815, repr. Singapore, 2004.
Townshend, Annette. *The Auchmuty Family of Scotland and America*, New York, 1932.
Tucker, Major A. *Narrative of the Operations of a small British force under … Auchmuty … at Montevideo*, London, 1807.
Ubbelohde, C. *The Vice-Admiralty Courts and the American Revolution*, Chapel Hill NC, 1960.
Updike, Wilkins, James MacSparran and Daniel Goodwin, A *History of the Episcopalian Church at Narragansett Rhode Island, including a history of the other Episcopal churches in the state*, 2nd edn, Boston MA, 1907.
Vale, Brian. *A War Betwixt Englishmen, 1825–1830*, London, 2000.

Van Tyne, Claude Halstead. *Loyalists in the American Revolution*, Gansevoort, New York, 1902, repr. 1999.
Vine, P.A.L. *The Royal Military Canal*, 2nd edn, Stroud, 2010.
Walsh, Thomas. '*Journal of the late Campaign in Egypt*', in *The Cockade in the Sand*, 2014.
War Office, *A List of the Officers of the Militia, the Gentlemen and Yeomanry Cavalry, and Volunteer Infantry of the United Kingdom*, 11th edn, 14 October 1805, reprinted Uckfield, c. 2005.
Weller, Jac. *Wellington in India*, London, 1972.
Whittingham, F. *A Memoir of the Services of Lieutenant-General Sir Samuel Ford Whittingham*, London, 1868.
Wickwire, Franklin and Mary. *Cornwallis, the Imperial Years*, Chapel Hill NC, 1980.
Wilson, Sir Robert. *History of the British Expedition to Egypt …* , Philadelphia, 1803, (repr. c. 2010).
Wilson, W.J. *History of the Madras Army*, 3 vols, Madras, 1882.
Wood, George Arthur. *William Shirley, Governor of Massachusetts 1741–1756, a History*, New York, 1920.
Wurzburg, C.F. *Raffles in the Eastern States*, London, 1954.
Wylly, H.L. *The 1st and 2nd Battalions The Sherwood Foresters, 1st Nottinghamshire Regiment*, London, 1929.
Yapp, Malcolm. *Strategies for British India*, Oxford, 1977.
Yazdani, Zubaida. *Hyderabad during the Residency of Henry Russell, 1811–1820*, Oxford, 1976.
Zobel, Hiller B. *The Boston Massacre*, New York, 1970.

Websites

Gaspee.com.
Jane Hathaway, 'A Tale of Two Mutinies', at csas.ed.ac.uk/mutiny/conf papers.
P-A Roots website on 'Robert Auchmuty M.D.', by William H. Egle.
Wikipedia.

Index

Abdul Ali Khan Bahadur, Nawab of Rampur, 56
Abdullah bin Kedar, 192–3
Abercromby, Gen Sir John, 177, 186, 242–3, 245
Abercromby, Gen Sir Ralph, 69, 72–3, 76–7, 83
Abercromby, Col Sir Robert, 46–7, 49–54, 59, 61–4, 66, 250
Aboukir, Egypt, 67, 72–3, 76
Acheh, Sumatra, 184, 192, 196
Acre, Palestine, 67
Adams, Lt Col Alexander, 195
Adams, John, 13–15
Aden, Yemen, 71, 75
Adipati, 221
  see also Najm ud-din
Afghanistan, 180
Africa, 98
Agnew, Lt Col, 178, 211, 246
Ahmad, Iman of Aden, 71, 75
Ahmad Pasha al-Jazzar, 67
Ainsley, Dr, 228–9
Alexandria, 67, 73, 76–7, 84, 87–8, 93, 96
Alfi Bey, 93
Algeciras, battle, 88
Ali Bey al-Kabir, 95
Allemand, Adml, 121
Alzaga, Martin de, 144
Amiens, treaty of, 99, 120, 185, 192
Amoy, China, 197
Andes, mountains, 126, 153
Anglican Church, *see* Church of England
Anjole, River, Java, 200
Arabia, 68
Arabs, in Egypt, 79–82
Arce, Brig Pedro de, 131
Arcot, India, 40, 47, 53
Argentina, 124, 128, 152–3, 155, 251
Armagh, Ireland, 3, 12, 24
Artigas, José, 128, 153
Asaf ud-Daulah, Nawab of Oudh, 54
Assaye, battle, 241
Auchmuty family,
  in Scotland, 1–2, 20–1
  in Ireland, 2–4, 21, 24
  in American war, 22–33
  in Kent, 98
Auchmuty, village, Fife, 1
Auchmuty, Arthur Gates, 4, 24, 30
Auchmuty, Deborah, née Cradock, wife of Robert, 15
Auchmuty, Elizabeth, née Clare, first wife of Robert, 4–5
Auchmuty, Henrietta (Overing), daughter of Robert, 7–8, 26
Auchmuty, Isabella (Burton), SA's sister, 18–19
Auchmuty, James Smith, son of Robert, 8, 13, 23
Auchmuty, Jane (Tylden), SA's sister, 18, 27, 29, 66, 99, 159
Auchmuty, Mary Juliana, wife of Robert, 5
Auchmuty, Mary Juliana (Mulcaster), SA's sister, 18–19, 29
Auchmuty, Mary Nicholls Tucker, SA's mother, 12–13, 19, 26–7, 29–31
Auchmuty, Richard Harrison, SA's brother, 18, 27, 30
  death, 30
Auchmuty, Robert (SA's grandfather), son of Capt John, 3–4
  lawyer, 4, 8
  marriages, 5
  to Boston, 5
  pupils, 7
  episcopalianism, 13
Auchmuty, Robert, SA's uncle,
  exile from Boston, 22
  in England, 32, 37
Auchmuty, Robert Nicholls, SA's brother, 18, 24–5, 27, 32–3
Auchmuty, Rev Samuel, SA's father, 7, 12–13, 16–20, 22, 25–6
  death, 27
Auchmuty Samuel, son of Arthur Gates Auchmuty, 24, 30–1
  death, 66
Austerlitz, battle, 136
Australia, 126, 142
Austria, 120

Backhouse, Col, 125, 127–8, 205
Badr-ud-din, Sultan of Palembang, 217, 219–21, 226, 231
Baghdad, 238
Bagoos-Rangin, 219
Baird, Gen Sir David, 66, 69, 72, 74–86, 91–3, 120–3, 125–6, 181, 205, 248
Bahamas, 18–19
Balaghat, India, 47
Bali, 195, 227
Balmerino, Fife, 1, 3

Banda Oriental (Uruguay), 128, 141, 153
Bangalore, India, 51–3, 235
Bangka island, 193, 197, 217, 219–21, 231
Banjermasin, Borneo, 228, 230
Bantam, Java, 184
Baramahal, India, 53
Barlow, Sir George, EIC Gov-Gen, 162, 185
  Gov of Madras, 163–72, 176, 178, 187–8, 235, 241, 246
Batavia, Java, 184, 188, 197–8, 200–201, 204, 206, 212, 214, 217, 222, 227, 229
Belcher, Gov of Massachusetts, 5
Bell, Col John, 168, 170–1, 236
Bellary (Hampi, Vijayanagar), 234
Belliard, Gen, 84
Bellingham, 123
Belmont House, Kent, 19, 29, 36, 98–9
Benares, India, 60, 74
Bencoolen (Bengkulu), Sumatra were, 85, 186, 230
Bengal, 39, 41, 54, 73, 161, 186, 240
Bengal, Bay of, 191
Bentinck, Lord William, Gov of Madras, 161–2, 238
Beresford, Col William Carr, 80, 97, 123–5, 127–8, 140–1, 144–5
Bermuda, 31–2
Bernard, Francis, Gov of Massachusetts, 15
Billiton Island, 217, 221, 231
Bishopthorpe, Kent, 19
Bitaura, India, battle, 56
Blakiston, Capt, 199
Blankett, Cdre John, 69–71, 73–4, 83
Bodawpaya, King of Burma, 180
Bolivia, 124
Bollan, William, 7
Bombay, 40–2, 45, 61, 78
Bombay Marine, 70, 190
Bon, Gen, 70
Bonaparte, Louis, King of Holland, 181
Bonaparte, Napoleon, 67–8, 70–1, 76, 92, 95–6, 99–100, 118, 120, 124, 153, 229–30
Bone, Sulawesi, 227
Borobodur, Java, 229
Borneo were, 94, 196, 228
Boston, Massachusetts, 5, 8–9, 18–19, 22–7
Botany Bay, Australia, 126
Boulogne, France, 100, 116, 118
Bourbon Island, 177, 180
Bourke, Col Richard, 53
Bowles, Maj, 165
Braam, Dutch resident to, 17
Braddock, Gen, 19
Brandywine, battle, 41, 47
Brazil, 126, 128, 141, 153
Brisco, Col Horton, 62
Britain,
  threatened invasion of, 99–119
  militia and volunteers, 101, 106–13
  Auchmuty in, 246–8
Broadstairs, Kent, 105, 112, 115, 118
Brogne, Benoit de, 62
Brooklyn, battle, 27
Broughton, Cdre William, 189, 194, 201, 213
Brown, Adml William, 153
Browne, Col, 143
Brunswick, New Jersey, 27
Buenos Aires, city and province, 122–8, 133, 135, 137, 139–40, 143–52, 157, 186
Buitenzorg, Java, 210
Bululeng, Bali, 227
Burgoyne, Gen Sir John, 44–5, 52, 175
Burma, 181, 186
Burton, William, SA's brother-in-law, 19, 23, 99
Byrne, Capt, 85, 88
Byron, Capt John A., 51–2, 65, 68

Cadiz, Spain, 72
Cadogan, Col, 147
Cairo, Egypt, 73, 75, 77, 84, 86–90, 93–4
Calcutta, 42, 53–4, 57, 60, 62, 66, 68, 72, 163, 169, 186, 235
Calicut, India, 50
Camden, Lord, 114
Campbell, Gen Sir Archibald, 47
Canada, 18–19, 24
Cannanore, India, 41, 50, 52, 234
Canning, George, Foreign Secretary, 154, 157
Canterbury, Kent, 105, 109, 114, 248, 251
Cape Breton, 8
Cape of Good Hope, 40, 62, 66, 69–70, 73, 76, 120–2, 135, 143, 151, 158, 162, 164, 174, 181, 201
Cape Town, 205
Cape Verde Islands, 142
Carnatic, India, 40, 49
Carrington, Lord, 114
Castle Forbes, Co Longford, battle, 2
Castlereagh, Lord, 102, 157
Cathcart, Gen Lord, 29
Cavan, Gen Lord, 89, 91, 96, 114
Ceylon, 61, 167, 181, 187, 189, 238
Charles I, 2
Charles II, 2
Chatham, Kent, 29, 33, 100, 104
Cherbourg, France, 101
Cheribon, Java, 210–11, 219, 227
Chile, 142–3, 153–5
Chillinching, Java, 198, 200, 204
China, 61, 180, 183, 186, 197–8, 228
Chittledroog, India, 168, 171
Church of England, Auchmuty family's devotion to, 11–12, 19–21, 158, 234, 250
  suggested American episcopate, 17–18
Cinque Ports, 104, 106–108
Clare, Henry, Robert's father-in-law, 4
Cleopatra's Needle, Alexandria, 96, 98
Cliffs End, Kent, 116
Clinton, Gen Henry, 30, 36
Clive, Robert, EIC Gov, 39, 62, 237
Close, Col Barry, 167–8
Cochin, India, 47–8, 61
Cocomanda, India, 170

Coimbatore, India, 49, 51
Colden, Cadwallader, 10–11, 13, 26
Colombia, 154
Colonia de Sacramento, 141
Connecticut, 17
Constantinople, 90–1, 93, 149
Coorg, India, 52
Coote, Gen Sir Eyre, 40–1, 44
Copenhagen, 149
Cork, Ireland, 121
Cornelis, Fort, 186, 199–200, 203–10, 215, 232–3, 240, 247
Cornwallis, Gen Lord, 28, 30, 90, 114, 250
  Gov Gen EIC, 43–6, 54
  and Third Mysore War, 48–53
  recommendations for army reform, 53, 58–64, 160
  and Treaty of Amiens, 99
Cosseir (Qusayr) Egypt, 71, 73, 76–80, 84–5, 88, 90
Cradock, Gen Sir John, 161–2, 238
Craufurd, Brig Robert, 126, 138, 142, 145–9, 154, 158
Crawford, John, 218, 224, 229
Crown Point, New York, 18
Culloden, battle, 56

Daendels, Herman Willem, Gov of Dutch East Indies, 182–6, 188, 197, 202, 218, 225, 231
Damanhur, Egypt, 93
Damietta, Egypt, 88
Danbury, Connecticut, 23
Danureja II, *Patih* of Jogjakarta, 218
Davie, Lt Col, 147
Davis, Col Henry, 168, 170
Deal, Kent, 101, 104, 106, 109–10, 112
Deane, Capt Robert, 197
Delaware River, 18
Denmark, 158
Deshima, Japan, 228
Dharwar, India, 50
Dickson, Capt, 200
Dilly, Mount, Malabar, 41
Dinapore, India, 62–3
Dindigul, India, 49, 52, 239
Dover, Kent, 118
Dover, Strait of, 118
Doveton, Col, 168, 172–3
Downs, the, 109
Drovetti, Bernardino, 94, 97
Drumeldrie, Fife, 1, 2
Drury, Adml, 186–7, 189, 194, 197, 201
Dublin, Ireland, 3, 248–9
Duckworth, Adml Sir John, 150
Dumpton Gate, Kent, 112, 115
Duncan, Jonathan, Gov of Bombay, 74, 78
Dundas, Gen Sir David, 109–10, 114, 118
Dundas, Henry (Lord Melville), Pres of EIC Board of Control, 42, 46, 53–4, 59–61, 69, 121
Dundas, Robert, Pres of the Board of Control, 173–5, 177–8, 214, 233, 242
Dutch,
  at the Cape, 120–1
  and Indonesia, 181–4, 228

East Anglia, 103
Eastbourne, Sussex, 104
East Cliffs, Kent, 113, 118
East India Company, 4, 16, 32, 37, 66, 172–6, 180–1, 183–4
  and Mysore, 38
  reforms in 39, 44, 58–2, 160–1, 246–7, 250
  Board of Control, 41–2
  and Rohillas, 55–8
  territories of, 39
East River, New York, 18
Egypt, 174
  and France, 67–2, 92, 95
  and Britain, 68, 72–98, 101–102, 114, 177, 185, 249
Eldon, Lord, 159
Elgin, Lord, 90
Elio, Col Javier de, 144, 155
Ellington, Maj W., 117
Elliott, Capt George, 191, 211, 237
Elliott, Hugh, 243
Ellore, India, 170, 239
Engelhard, Pieter, Dutch resident, 217–18
English Channel, 33, 66
Ensenada de Barragon, 145, 195
Eylau, battle, 136

Faizullah Khan, Nawab of Rampur, 55–6
Farquhar, John, 230
Farquhar, Maj William, 213
Fatehgarh, India, 59, 62–4
Faversham, Kent, 29, 98, 104
Fendall, John, EIC governor of Java, 230
Ferrol, Spain, 72
Fielding, Lt William, 190, 204
Fife, Scotland, 1
Firth of Forth, 1
Flanders, 105
Flodden, battle, 1
Folkestone, Kent, 102, 104
Forbes, Col John, 62
Fort Ludowyck, Java, 211–13
France, 68, 90, 106, 120, 142, 178, 249
Franklin, Benjamin, 16
Frazer, Capt Augustus, 149
Frederick, Pennsylvania, 30

Gage, Gen Thomas, 16
Gardiner, Lt Col, 35
Garrett, Capt Thomas, 108, 116, 118
Gaspar, Strait of, 197
George III, 19
Germany, 100
Gerona, Spain, 150
Ghulam Mohammed Khan Bahadur, Nawab of Rampur, 55–6
Gibbs, Col Samuel, 171, 195, 208–11, 247

Gibraltar, 72
Gillespie, Col Rollo, 162–3, 191, 195, 198, 200–203, 207–10, 214–16, 227, 229, 232, 237, 247–8
  at Palembang, 219–21
  at Jogjakarta, 222–4
Gingie, Egypt, 85–6
Giyanti, Treaty of, 182–3
Giza, Egypt, 85–7, 91
Glasgow, Earl of, 117
Goa, India, 40, 238
Godoy, Spanish minister, 136
Gower, Gen Leveson, 144–6, 150, 156
Great Batavia River, Java, 202, 206
Greigh, Capt, 191
Grenville, Lord, Prime Minister, 124, 157
Gressie (Grisek) Java, 185, 188, 211, 213
Grey, Charles, First Lord of the Admiralty, 126
Grey, Gen Sir George, Governor of the Cape, 125–6, 143

Haidar Ali, Sultan of Mysore, 38, 40
Halhall, Fife, 2
Halifax, Nova Scotia, 22–4
Hamburg, 120
Hamengkubuwa II, Sultan, 183–4, 217–18, 221–4, 231
Hamengkubuwa III, Sultan, 224, 227
Hamengkubuwa IV, Sultan to, 26
Hancock, John, 14–15
Hare, Alexander, 228
Harlem River, New York, 14–15
Harris, Gen, 99, 237
Hastings, Warren, EIC Governor-Gen, 39–40, 44–5
Haviland, Lt-Gen William, 34
Hawkesbury, Lord, 114, 157
Hayes, Cdre, 190, 197, 199
Hely-Hutchinson, Gen Sir John, 73, 77, 83–4, 86–91
Hengist and Horsa, 105
Hobart, Lord, Governor at Madras, 62
  Secretary of State, 91, 93
Hollond, John, Governor of Madras, 48–9
Holloway, Maj, 84, 86
Hope, Col Hugh, 96, 224
Howe, Gen William, 26–7, 29–30
Hutchinson, Thomas, Governor of Massachusetts, 15–16
Hyderabad, India, 40
  Nizam of, 40, 47, 50, 166, 188, 237, 239

Ibrahim Bey, 89
India, 36, 68, 76, 89, 91, 97, 125, 205
India Act, 47
Indian Ocean, 70, 72, 95, 180–1, 183, 202
Indonesia, 181
Indramayu, Java, 219, 227
Innes, Col, 166
Ionian Islands, 92
Ireland,
  Auchmuty as Commander-in-Chief, 248–9
Italy, 100

Jalna, India, 168, 170, 172, 234–5
James VI, 1
Janssens, Gen Jan Willem, 121
  governor of Dutch East Indies, 182, 197, 200, 202, 205, 210–13, 215, 231, 233, 240
Japan, 228
Jati Ngaleh, Java, battle, 211–12, 218, 247
Java, 177, 179, 182–4, 186, 188
  British invasion 185, 187–214, 237
  British rule 215–32, 233
Jay, John, 32
Jeddah, Arabia, 68, 70–1, 75, 78, 88, 94
Jefferson, Thomas, 32
Jena, battle, 136
Jennings, Cap, 139
Jervis, Adml Sir John, 67
Jogjakarta, 184, 196, 217–19, 221–6, 229
Johnstone, Cdre George, 40–1
Jumel, Gen, 210
Junumabe Adi Raja Bibi II, 41

Kanpur, India, 59, 62–3
Kartika Rana Varna, Maharaja of Travancore, 48
Keith, Adml Lord, 66, 69, 72, 97
Kenna (Qena), Egypt, 79, 82–7
Kenny, Lt, 80–1
Kent, 19, 66–7, 249
Khushraw Pasha, 93
King, Maj, 146
King's Chapel, Boston, 5, 11
King's College, New York, 17, 26, 28
Kingsgate, Kent, 112–15
Knight, Maj, 35
Kurshid Pasha, 94

Lancaster, Pennsylvania, 24, 30, 36
Landsheit, Sgt, 129
Leeds, 123
Leeward Islands, 243
Legetta (Leqeita) Egypt, 79–80, 82
Leipzig, battle, 229
Leyden, Dr John, 196, 199
Lincolnshire, 103
Liniers, Col Santiago, 126, 128, 131–5, 139–41, 148, 150–2
Liverpool, Lord, 214
  see also Lord Hawkesbury
Lloyd, Lt-Col, 75, 77, 83
Lombok, 196
London, 4–5, 12, 22, 66, 236
Longford, Co., Ireland, 2–3
Long Island, New York, 26
Long Island Sound, New York, 19
Lumley, Brig Gen, 144, 148, 158

Macartney, Lord, governor of Madras, 44–5
Macassar, Sulawesi, 230
Macau, China, 61, 180, 183, 197–8
Macquarie, Lachlan, Lt/Capt, 53–4, 57–8, 60–1, 65, 74, 78–80, 82–3, 85–6, 93, 138, 165
Madagascar, 177

Madras, 38, 40, 42, 44–5, 159–61, 167–8, 170, 174, 176, 186–8, 233, 241
Madras army,
reforms by Auchmuty, 238–45
Madura, 184–5, 188, 202
Mahe, French post in India, 47
Mahoney, Capt, 79–80
Maida, battle, 136
Malabar, India, 40
Malacca, Malaya, 61, 185–6, 191–4, 205, 230
Malacca, Strait of, 185, 189, 193
Malaya, 61, 185, 192
Malcolm, Col John, 166–7
Maldonado, 125, 127–9, 140–1, 195
Malta, 67, 89, 92, 95, 99–100, 126
Mamelukes, 67, 72, 78, 82, 84, 86–93, 95, 97
Manchester, 123
Mankunegara II, 223–4
Mangalore, India,
Mysorian naval base, 45
Mansfield, Earl of, 117
Marathas, 38, 40, 45, 50–1, 53, 56, 62, 180, 239
Mareotis, lake, Alexandria, 87, 96
Margate, Kent, 101, 105, 107, 112, 115
Marsden, William, 185
Martello towers, 103–104, 108
Massachusetts, 5, 8, 15
Masulipatam, India, 166–7, 170, 235, 237
Mataram, Javanese Sultanate, 133, 218
Mauritius, 68, 70, 231, 237
Maxfield, Capt W., 197
Maxwell, Col, 50
McDowell, Gen Hay, 164–5, 174, 178, 235
McKenzie, Col Colin, 190, 193, 195, 198–9, 222, 225, 229
McLeod, Lt-Col Alexander, 207, 209, 241–2
Mecca, Sharif of, 68, 71, 75, 78, 82
Mediterranean Sea, 67, 69, 72, 90, 95, 99
Medows, Gen Sir William, 41, 47, 49
Mendoza, Argentina, 127, 153
Menou, Gen, 84, 88
Mesopotamia, 174
Mexico, 151, 158
Middle Temple, London, 4
Mifflin, Fort, Pennsylvania, 30
Militia, 107
see also Volunteers
Millerstown, Pennsylvania, 24
Milsted, Kent, 29–30, 66
Milton-next-Sittingbourne, Kent, 248
Minorca, 89
Minto, Lord, EIC Governor-Gen, 163–4, 166, 169, 172–4, 176–7, 180, 183, 185–9, 193–6, 199, 203, 205, 211, 214–15, 229, 231, 236, 242–3, 247–8
Mocha, Yemen, 71, 75, 78
Moilah (el-Muweih), Egypt, 79–82, 84, 86
Moiret, Capt, 71, 95
Moluccas, 184, 186
see also Spice Islands
Monro, Col John, 163–5
Montevideo, 53, 127–40, 142–3, 148, 157–8, 203, 205, 236, 249
Montresor, Capt Henry, 249
Montresor, Capt John, SA's brother-in-law, 18, 27–8, 30, 36–7, 42, 98–9
Montresor, Lt-Col T.G., 73, 82–5, 167, 172, 239
Montresor, Thomas Gage, 99
Montresor's Island, New York, 18–19
Moore, Gen Sir John, 87, 89, 102, 114, 118, 162
Mornington, Lord, EIC Governor general, 62, 68–9, 78, 180
Mughal Empire, 38
Muhammad Ali, pasha of Egypt, 94–7
Muhammad Ali Khan, Nawab of Rampur, 55–6
Mulcaster, Anne, née Tucker, 109
Mulcaster, Capt William Howe, 249
Mulcaster, Frederick George, SA's brother-in-law, 19, 29
Mulcaster, Mary, née Montresor, 99
Murad Bey, 89
Murray, Lt-Col, 77–8, 82
Murray, Adml George, 142
Musi River, Sumatra, 219
Mutiny, 58, 62–4, 125, 160, 240
white officers', 161–74, 238, 244
Mysore, 52, 64, 162, 168, 180, 234, 244, 251
see also Wars

Nagasaki, Japan, 228
Najm ud-din, Sultan of Palembang, 221
Natakusuma, Pakualam, 224, 226
Nelson, Adml Lord, 67
Nether Court, Ramsgate, Kent, 108
Netherlands, 121, 229
French annexation, 185, 188
Newburn, Fife, 1, 2
New Guinea, 182
New Hampshire, 5
New Jersey, 15, 26
New Orleans, 249
Newport, Rhode Island, 22–3, 32, 159, 175, 251
New Providence, Bahamas, 18
New South Wales, 53, 138
Newtown Forbes, Co. Longford, 4
New Wells, Egypt, 79–80
New York, 1, 10–11, 15, 18, 158, 234, 249
Nicobar Islands, 191
Nightingall, Gen Sir Miles, 227
Nile, battle, 67, 68
Nile, river, 72–3, 76–9
Norfolk, England, 33–5
North Africa, 92
North, Lord, Prime Minister, 18, 55
Nottingham, 33, 99, 113, 233, 250
Nova Scotia, 22, 24
Nugent, Gen Sir George, 186, 190

Oakes, Cap Lawrence, 190, 198
Oliver, Andrew, Lt-Governor of Massachusetts, 15, 16

Oliver, David, 15
Oman, Sir Charles, 136
Onarang, Java, 212
Ontario, 24
  Lake, 249
Orkney, 108
Ospringe, Kent, 98–9, 104
Otis, James, 13
Ottoman Empire, 45, 70, 72–3, 76, 89–91, 93–4
  Grand Vizier of, 84
Oudh, India, 54–5, 62
Overing, Henrietta, née Auchmuty, 7–8, 22
Overing, Henry John, 22–3
Overing, John, 7
Oxfordshire, 34

Pacific Ocean, 142
Pack, Col Denis, 140–1, 144–5, 149–50, 249
Pakubuwana III, Sultan, 184, 211, 216–18
Pakubuwana IV, Sultan, 224, 226–7
Palembang, Sumatra, 196, 217, 219, 225–6, 229–30
Palestine, 67
Palghat, India, 49
Pangeron Panular, 223
Paraguay, 124, 144, 153
Paroissien, James, 153
Pattenden, Thomas, 116
Peake, W., 107
Pegwell Bay, Kent, 106, 116, 118
Pellew, Adml Sir Edward, 185, 228
Pellew, Capt Fleetwood, 228–9
Penang, Malaya, 185–6, 191–2, 218
Pennsylvania, 18, 24
Perim Island, 69–70, 75–6
Persia, 180
Persian Gulf, 174
Peru, 122, 153, 155
Peshwa, Maratha chief, 40
Pharos Island, Alexandria, 96
Philadelphia, 29–30
Philip II of Spain, 105
Pitt, William, Prime Minister, 42, 60, 104, 106–107, 109–10, 114, 118, 121, 157
Plymouth, Devon, 101
Point de Galle, Ceylon, 61
Poland, 120
Pompey's pillar, Alexandria, 96
Pondicherry, French post in India, 50
Poona, India, 40, 50
Poonevalle, India, 166
Popham, Capt Sir Home, 73, 75–6, 120–7, 154, 181, 185, 202
Popham, Col William, 62–3, 73
Portland, Duke of, Prime Minister, 157–8, 162
Portsmouth, 100, 125, 142
Portugal, 126, 158–9, 162
Potosi, Bolivia, 122
Pownall, Governor of Massachusettes, 9
Pratt, Benjamin, 7–11, 13–14
Pratt, Isabella, née Auchmuty, 7–8, 23
Preston Capt Thomas, trial of, 15

Prize money, 236–7, 247
Prussia, 120
Punjab, India, 68, 180

Quarrell, Lt-Col, 85
Quincy, Josiah, 15

Raffles, William Stamford, 185, 192–3, 195–6
  Lt-Governor of Java, 214–32, 238, 248
Rainier, Adml Peter, 70
Rajamundry, India, 170
Ralph, Capt, 219
Rampur, India, 55, 60, 64
Ramsay, Col, 88, 91
Ramsgate, Kent, 105, 107–108, 110, 112, 115–16, 118
Rangoon, Burma, 180
Ranjit Singh, 180
Red Sea, 68–76, 84, 98, 120–1, 174, 185
reduction, River plate, 123
Regimental County system, 34
Regiments and units,
  Bengal Volunteers, 76, 190
  Bengal pioneers, 195
  1st Bombay, 76, 79, 85, 88
  7th Bombay, 76, 79–80, 88
  Carnatic Volunteers, 241
  9th Dragoon Guards, 141–2, 146–7
  8th Light Dragoons, 76
  13th Light Dragoons, 117
  15th Light Dragoons, 110, 112, 117
  20th Light Dragoons, 129
  22nd Light Dragoons, 33, 189, 207, 222, 237
  Indian Light Infantry, 190
  Madras Europeans, 190, 206
  Madras pioneers, 195
  Royal Staff Corps, 116
  Wolseley's Horse, 3
  5th (Queens), 146, 122, 125, 135
  10th, 73, 76, 83, 85, 96
  14th, 190, 195, 209, 222
  36th, 147–8
  38th, 146–7
  40th, 137, 139, 143
  43rd, 111
  45th, 28, 33–5, 99, 113, 146–8, 150, 234
  47th, 125
  52nd, 36, 38–41, 43, 46
  54th, 206
  59th, 190, 209, 219, 223
  60th, 122, 125
  61st, 73, 76
  65th, 73
  69th, 190, 207
  71st, 140
  75th, 46, 53, 206
  78th, 190, 195, 223
  80th, 76
  86th, 73, 75–7, 83, 88, 91
  87th, 134–5, 146–7
  88th, 76, 80, 85, 146–8

89th, 190, 195, 203
95th, (Rifles) 130, 133, 137
Reis Effendi, Turkish commander, 86
Resolution Island, 181
Rhoda Island, Egypt, 88
Rhode Island, 5, 12, 27, 32–3
Ringswold, Kent, 111
Rio Chuelo, Buenos Aires, 145
River Plate, 41, 56, 123, 125–6, 154, 187, 189
Robison, Capt William, 200, 203, 216–18, 226, 229
Rochefort, France, 121
Rohillas, Rohilkhand, 55–8, 62, 74
Romney Marsh, 102, 105, 112
Rosetta, Egypt, 87–8
Rosetta Stone, 97
Roxbury, Boston, 13, 15, 22
Royal Military Canal, 102–103, 105
Ruiz Huidobro, Col Pasqual, 131, 133–4, 154
Russel, Scots pilot, 123
Russell, Henry, 239–40
Russia, 142
Rye, Sussex, 102

St Andrews, Fife, 1
St Helena, 66
St Leger, Col Arthur, 163, 165–7
Salatiga, Java, 212–13, 232
Sally Aga, 82
Saltpreston, 2
Samarap, Java, 202
Sambas, Borneo, 228, 230
Sampur, Cape, 197
Sana'a, Imam of, 75
Sandwich, Kent, 106, 111–12
San Juan, Argentina, 127
San Martin, Jose de, 153–4
Santa Teresa, Uruguay, 141
Saragossa, Spain, 150
Sarkars, India, 39, 170, 239
Sassenay, Marquis de, 153
Savandroog, India, 52
Sayer, Captain George, 190, 207
Scorf, Egypt, 85
Scotland, 1, 66
Scott, Gen Charles, 23
Seaford, Kent, 111
Sebastiani, Col Horace, 92, 95, 99
Secunderabad, India, 166–8, 170–1
Semarang, Java, 184, 188, 211, 222, 232–3
Seringapatam, India, 49–52, 66, 69, 168–73, 234, 236, 240
Sewell, Jonathan, 15
Shapter, Dr, 73
Sheerness, Kent, 100
Ships,
Customs,
Gaspee, 15–16
Merchant,
Liberty, 11
Transport,
Kingston, 38
Kirby, 191
Warships,
British,
Akbar, 191
Albatross, 70–1
Centurion, 70–1
Daedalus, 70
Dover, 191 (ex-Duncan, ex-Carron)
Fly, 142
Illustrious, 190
Leda, 190, 199
Leopard, 70
Lion, 190
Malabar, 197
Minden, 190
Minto, 195
Modeste, 191, 194, 211, 237
Mornington, 197
Orestes, 70
Phaeton, 202
Phoebe, 201
President, 201
Procris, 190, 219
Saracen, 156
Scipion, 201
Sir Francis Drake, 202
Thames, 52
French,
La Resolu, 68
Meduse, 197, 210
Nymphe, 197, 210
Shirley, William, Governor of Massachusetts, 5–7, 21–2
Shore, Sir John, EIC Governor-Gen, 53–4, 59, 61–4, 69, 175
Shorncliffe, Sussex, 102, 110–11
Shute, Samuel, Governor of Massachusetts, 5, 7–8
Sicily, 162
Sierra Leone, 24
Singapore, 196, 230–1
Sittingbourne, Kent, 29, 66
Slokan River, Java, 204, 206
Smith, Capt Sir Sidney, 67
Sobremonte Marquis de, Spanish viceroy, 127–35, 151, 154
South China Sea, 194
Southern Star/La Estrella del Sur, 143
Spain, 105, 120, 155, 162
Spice Islands, 180–2
see also Moluccas
Stirling, Scotland, 1
Stirling, Lt, 79–80
Stirling, Adml Charles, 125–7, 129, 131–2, 140, 143
Stirling, 'Lord' Alexander Turnbull, 25–6
Stirling, Reverend James, 3
Stopford, Adml Robert, 142, 201–202, 210–13, 247
Stour, River, Kent, 104, 106, 112, 116
Stuart, Gen James, 44–5, 175
Stuart, Brig Sir John, 91–3
Suez, Egypt, 70, 73–7, 83, 90
Sulawesi, 182, 191–2, 194, 227
Sumatra, 182, 217

Sunda Strait, 185, 212
Surabaya, Java, 188, 197, 210–11, 213, 226
Surakarta, Java, 184, 211–12, 216, 218, 221, 223, 225–6
Sussex, 100
Syndale House (SA's home), 98–9, 104, 109, 248, 251
Syria, 70, 73, 88, 92

Tagal, Java, 211
Tellicherry, India, 47
Temple Merchant, Co Longford, 3
Thanet, Isle of, Kent, 104, 120, 159
Thanet, Earl of, 114
The Times, 124, 141
Thorn, Maj William, 191, 203, 219–20, 222–3
Tipu, Sultan of Mysore, 40, 45, 47–53, 56, 61, 63, 67, 161, 168
  death, 68, 71
  contact with France, 68
Tobago, 23
Toulon, France, 67
Townsend, Annette, 159
Trafalgar, battle, 116–18, 120
Travancore, India, 47–8, 50, 166, 187–8, 234–6, 240
Travers, Maj Thomas, 190, 237
Trichinopoly, India, 49
Trinity Church, New York, 13, 16, 20, 25–6
Trinity Church, Newport Rhode Island, 24–5
Trinity College, Dublin, 3–4
Tryon, William, governor of New York, 26
Tucker family, in Bermuda, 13, 31–2
Tucker, Auchmuty (SA's grandnephew), 109
Tucker, Frances (Montresor), SA's step-sister, 8, 18, 27, 29
Tucker, Henry St George, 31–2
Tucker, Major John, 108–109, 117, 125
Tucker, Nathaniel, 32
Tucker, Thomas, 32
Tucuman, Argentina, 127, 153
Turin, Italy, 97
Tylden, Rev Richard, SA's brother-in-law, 29–30, 61, 98
Tylden, John Maxwell, SA's nephew, 111, 125, 159, 200, 236, 246, 248–9

Ulm, battle, 136
Umdut al-Umara, Nawab of Arcot, 44
United East India Company (Dutch VOC), 181
United States, 37, 43–4, 152, 154, 159, 249, 251
Uruguay, 124, 128, 131, 153, 154–5, 251

Valley Forge, 24
Vassall, Col, 125, 205
Vellore, India, mutiny, 125, 161–2, 163, 168–9, 181, 238
Venice, 120
Vice-Admirality Court, Boston, 14, 22
Vizagapatam, India, 170, 239
Volunteers, 106–108
  units,
    Broadstairs Artillery, 111, 115
    Cinque Ports Volunteers, 110–12, 115–17
    Deal Artillery, 111
    Deal Infantry, 111
    Dover Artillery, 111
    Dover Infantry, 111
    East Kent Militia, 114
    Isle of Thanet Cavalry, 108
    Margate Artillery, 111
    Margate Rifleman, 111, 117
    Nottingham Militia, 113, 116
    Ramsgate Artillery, 111
    Ramsgate Rifleman, 111, 117
    Renfrew Militia, 117
    Royal Perthshire Militia, 117–18
    Royal Surrey Militia, 113
    Sandwich Artillery, 116
    West Kent Militia, 114
    West Surrey Militia, 115

Wadi Hammamet, Egypt, 73, 77
Wala Jah Muhammad Ali, Nawab of Arcot, 44
Walmer Castle, Kent, 104, 106, 109–10
Wantsum, River, Kent, 104–105
Warden, Lt, 83
Wars,
  American independence, 22
  Fourth Mysore, 69
  French Revolutionary, 56, 64
  Gurkha, 227
  Napoleonic, 101
  Rohilla, 54–8, 60, 251
  Second Mysore, 38, 40, 43
  Seven Years', 8–9, 18
  Third Mysore, 47–53, 66, 251
Washington, George, 18, 26, 28
Waterloo, battle, 136
Wayne, American merchant, 122
Wellesley, Col Sir Arthur, 69, 72, 151, 158, 162
  as Duke of Wellington, 102, 136–7
Wellesley, Marquis *see* Mornington
Weltevreeden, Java, 200, 202–203, 205, 214–15, 226, 233
Western Ghats, India, 48–9, 51
West Indies, 23, 89, 127, 181
Wetherall, Gen Frederick, 191, 195, 199
White, William, 146–8
Whitelocke, Gen John, 126–7, 138, 142–52, 155, 157–8, 187
White Plains, battle, 27
Whittingham, Cap Samuel Ford, 148
Wilson, Ensign, 79
Winchester, Pennsylvania, 30
Windham, William, 138
Wood, Colonel George, 195, 207, 209

Yemen, 70–1
York, Duke of, 60, 65–6, 74, 78, 98, 114, 118, 159, 214, 250
Yorktown, 30–1, 35, 47, 52
Yule, Maj, 207, 209

Zaman Shah, Amir of Afghanistan, 68
Zedayo, Java, 211, 213